The Book of Revelation

by Jim McGuiggan

International Biblical Resources
Lubbock, Texas

ISBN 0-932397-10-7

Dedication

To my wife, Ethel.
To my three children,
Jim, Linda, and George.

7 stars = 7 angels of 7 churches
7 lampstands = 7 churches
7 Spirits of God = perfection of wisdom & knowledge
7 seven eyes = vigilance, scrutinized acceptance worship
executor of God's justice
7 lamps of fire burning before throne = 7 Spirits of God
24 elders = church
7 golden candlesticks
7 horns = perfection of power
golden bowls full of incense = prayers of saints
7 harps = praise
4 (4 winds, 4 living creatures) = universiality
world
Cherubim, chariot of God
see that holiness of God recognized
They demand punishment of transgressor
wind = activity of God, see p. 113
7 Seals = for concealing
7 trumpets warnings of judgment
hour to John carries crisis and action
critical importance
half an hour = broken hour = delay
7 angels stand before God = to stand that close to God suggests magesty. holiness honor & 7 shows completeness, fulness

mtn = kingdoms
burning mtn = destroyed by power of God
faithful people see power of God to destroy a mtn & throw it into sea Matt 21:2
like overcoming sin or anything that sets itself against a child of God
7 golden bowls of wrath of God
measuring something = (1) to stress its holiness
(2) " " " glory

Table of Contents

Foreword

Revelation has one grand thrust. Comfort in the knowledge of ultimate triumph! It has an historical setting and deals with historical events. It is Rome against the Church — it is Satan against Jesus! The principles involved in the book — the principles of good and evil — are timeless. Truth **will** triumph whether in the first centuries or in these. Evil will wage an unceasing war with truth. The record of the victory of the Church of God over Rome stands for all time as a token of its deathlessness! Of the supremacy of its Lord; the truth of its doctrines; the strength of its hope and the reality of its joys.

> You must not think, my friends, that Christianity has come down to our times without a struggle; nay, indeed, it took the nation at first by the irresistible force of its evidence. It was opposed by consolidated ranks of well-disciplined foes. Learned, cunning, bold, and powerful were its enemies. But experience taught them it was not only foolish, but hurtful to kick against the goads...
>
> The era of Christianity itself presents a very sublime spectacle: the whole world reposing under the protecting wings of the most august of all the Caesars; peace, universal peace, with her healthful arms encircling all the nations... Polytheism, with her myriads of temples and her myriads ...of priests, triumphantly seated in the affections of a superstitious people, and swaying a magic scepter from the Tiber to the ends of the earth. Legislators, magistrates, philosophers, orators, and poets all combined to plead her cause, and to protect her from insult and injury. Rivers of sacrificial blood crimsoned all the rites of pagan worship; and clouds of incense arose from every city, town and hamlet, in honor of the gods of Roman superstition... when idolatry was at its zenith in the pagan world, the Star of Bethlehem appeared...Idolatry on the throne, and the founder of a new religion and a new empire lying in a manger!
>
> ...After thirty years of obscurity, we find him surrounded ...a contemptible group...In the midst of them he uttered the most incredible oracle ever heard. I am about, says he, to found a new empire on the acknowledgement of a single truth, a truth, too, which one of you has discovered, and all the powers and malice of worlds seen and unseen shall never prevail against it...What a scene presents itself here?

> A pusillanimous, wavering, ignorant, and timid dozen of individuals, without a penny apiece, assured that to them it pleased the Ruler of the Universe to give the empire of the world...
> Such were the army of the faith. They begin their career. Under the jealous...eyes of a haughty Sanhedrin at home, and under the strict cognizance of a Roman emperor abroad...They commenced their operations. One while charged with **idolatry**; at another with **treason**. Reviled and persecuted until their chief is rewarded with a cross, and themselves with threats and imprisonment. A throne is a future world animated them, and a crown of glory after martyrdom stimulated them. On they march from conquest to conquest, till not only a multitude of the Jewish priests and people, but Caesar's household in imperial Rome, became obedient to the faith...
> The land of Judea is smitten with the sword of the Spirit. Jerusalem falls and Samaria is taken. The coasts of Asia, maritime cities, islands and provinces, vow allegiance to a crucified King. Mighty Rome is roused, and shaken, and affrighted. Sacrificies are unbought, altars moulder, and temples decay. Her pontiffs, her senate, and her emperor stand aghast. Persecution...unsheathes her sword and kindles her fires...But the scheme soon defeats itself; for ...tis found that the blood and the ashes of the martyrs are the seed of the Church. So the battle is fought till every town of note from the Tiber to the Thames, from the Euphrates to the Ganges, bows to the cross. On the one side, superstition and the sword...on the other, almighty truth alone pushes on the combat. Under these fearful odds, the truth triumphs, and shall the advocates of such a cause fear the contest now?
> Yes, my fellow-citizens, not a king nor a priest smiled upon our faith until it won the day.

Wish I'd said that! Alexander Campbell said it in the beginning of his debate with the infidel, Owen. I like the spirit of the quote. I especially like the question (challenge really): And shall the advocates of such a cause fear the contest now? The "panting huddled flock whose only crime was Christ" whipped an indignant world to a standstill. And that's what Jesus told them in Revelation they could do. That's its message for you and me today.

I think this commentary can help you. I'm not expecting you

to agree with me on every point. (To tell you the truth, I'm not sure I agree with me on every point). The text I followed was the American Standard Version (1901). I've put the questions **before** the comments because I've found in my experience (teaching and studying), that if I know what I'm looking for, I can read more profitably. Is that how it is with you? **Please** read the questions before reading the comments. Look over the analysis before you enter the section. I'm finding more and more that it's important for me to get the overall scope of things in order to understand the individual verses. I'm sure that's your experience, too. The introductions should help in this direction.

I believe the book to have been written in the later years of Vespasian, the ninth Roman emperor (see the comments on 17: 8-11). It was written to give comfort and assurance to the Church of God in the face of impending persecution. It deals with the triumph of the Church over Rome as manifested in two areas: 1) The destruction of Domitian in whose person the beast came back up "out of the abyss." 2) The ultimate and complete destruction of the whole Roman empire.

I've tried to be honest and forthright — honestly! And what is more, I've prayed daily for God to help me in my study and in the presentation of it. I hope you find this both profitable and practical.

Let me know what you think.

Love's Prayers,
Jim McGuiggan

116 Church Road,
Holywood, Co. Down,
Northern Ireland

Other Books by Jim McGuiggan

www.jimmcguiggan.com

To order the following please contact:

International Biblical Resources
Billie Paine at (877) 792-6408

The God Who Commands the Impossible
The Reign of God
The Power to See it Through
Genesis and Us
The God of the Towel
The Dragon Slayer
The Kingdom of God and The Planet Earth
The Bible, The Saint, and The Liquor Industry

Commentaries:

The Book of Isaiah
The Book of Daniel
The Book of Ezekiel
The Book of I Corinthians
The Book of Romans
The Book of Revelation

Available through Howard Publishinng
West Monroe, LA (800) 858-4109

Jesus Hero of Thy Soul
Where the Spirit of the Lord Is
Let Me Count the Ways

Available through Waterbrook Press
(A division of Random House)

Celebrating the Wrath of God

Available through Covenant Publishing
Webb City, Missouri (877) 673-1015

Life on the Ash Heap

Questions on the Section Marked "Introduction"

1. Can you say it is erroneous to claim the book of Revelation can't be understood?
2. Why do you think the average fellow would think it an overstatement to say: "To understand the book of Revelation is very simple"?
3. Is this book intended to be an "answer" to Premillennialism?
4. What is the general aim of this book?
5. Stated in a sentence, what does the author think is the main thrust of the book of Revelation?
6. Do already-fulfilled prophecies have anything to offer us today? Can you illustrate?
7. Can you say why Daniel was commanded to "**shut up the vision**" of Daniel 8?
8. Can you say why John was expressly forbidden to do so?
9. If someone gave you a revelation telling you that it deals with matters which "**must shortly come to pass**" in a period of time which is "**at hand**", would you think it dealt with matters which were soon to transpire or would you think it referred to events and a time 2000 years in the future?
10. Has God ever spoken of a period of less than 400 years and said it was a long time?
11. Do Premillennialists figurize scripture without being forced to?
12. Do you think "apocalyptic" speech was used to hide the message from hostile authorities?
13. What is the question you must constantly ask yourself when you are reading the apocalyptic speech of Revelation?
14. Can you say 1) Who thought the book of Revelation to be of little account and 2) Who refused to comment on it?

Introduction

Now don't tell me the book cannot be understood, for that would mean God had mocked us in giving it to us and in adding a blessing for those who "keep" it.

And don't tell me it is a simple book to understand, for that is clearly an overstatement. Perhaps for some of you professional students and teachers with a lot of time on your hands the book has **become** simple, but it isn't for the rest of us. And when I look at the mass of commentaries written on the book and see how they differ often and widely — I wonder if it is really simple for anyone!

Since you've picked the book up you are obviously interested in the subject. Well, let me tell you before you put it back down that the very size of the book makes it clear it can't be a definitive work, right?! So, it will raise as many questions, perhaps, as it will answer.

Here's what I'm aiming at. I'm anxious for the average reader to be able to read the book of Revelation without being overwhelmed by it. I'm anxious for the average man to have an overall grasp of the book. I want him to feel he has not been "snowed" or confused into adopting the "best thing I've ever heard." He should be able to feel within himself: This makes sense **to me**. I can understand this and see how the end is attained.

This is not written as an "answer" to Premillennialism! I will mention again and again the premillennial viewpoint. I will allude to the views of Herbert W. Armstrong and the Jehovah's Witnesses as well as Lindsey and Walvoord. But this is not a book on Premillennialism.

In a moment or two I will state my views on the book, but listen — if you are not willing to pay the price of personal study (to some degree) you will not really be helped by this or any other book. I will not be quoting a lot from writers for this often gets in the way of the reader's understanding of what the author believes.

Now, let me tell you what I think the book is all about. It deals with the struggle of the Church of our Lord against the Roman empire! All the historical events dealt with (prophesied of), in the book, have been fulfilled! However, there are truths set forth in the book which are eternal and therefore speak to us of warning and comfort today. In Genesis 15 God told Abraham he would bring his seed up out of Egypt in the fourth generation. That was fulfilled in the days of Moses but the truths set forth by the Exodus are still as applicable today as then. Right?

Before surveying the contents of the book let me make two observations in regard to its interpretation. 1) It is written, says John concerning **"things which must shortly come to pass"** and of a time which was **"at hand"** when John wrote! And, 2) it was written in "apocalyptic" speech.

Now don't argue with me. I didn't invent these things! Four times in the book John tells us what he is writing about. See for yourself. Chapter 1:1,3 and 22:6,10. Whatever you do with the book just accept John's time element. Look — suppose John came into your room right this minute with a scroll in his hand and said to you, "I have a revelation here for you about things which must shortly come to pass." What would you think? Could your mind even begin to think "40th century"? Suppose he said to you again, "This letter concerns things the time of which is at hand." How would that grab you? Would you think it was close to happening? If he said again to you, just before he was leaving, "Now remember, the letter I'm leaving with you concerns things which must shortly come to pass," would you not think he meant just what he said? And finally, suppose he said, just as he vanished, "Don't seal up that book for the time is at hand!", would you not be more than ever convinced that what he meant was "soon"? Of course you would. Now let commonsense be your guide in this matter. The contents of the book related to things close to John's day.

But what is more interesting is this: Daniel received a vision in the year 550 B.C. (8:1) which was fulfilled in 164/5 B.C. (8:13,14), and, now get this, he was told "shut up the vision; for it belongeth to many days to come" (8:26). Well? Here is a vision fulfilled in less than 400 years after it was received and God says "seal it up for its fulfillment is a long way away." John is told exactly the opposite! "Don't seal it up for the time is at hand!" Why was John told the very opposite of Daniel? Well? Come on, don't be afraid. Say it to yourself!

It is not unusual to hear "Well, **'at hand'** or **'shortly to come to pass'** may mean a short time to us but in light of 2 Peter 3:8 it might involve a long time." This would be all right except God was not speaking to himself in these passages. He was speaking to men and women like you and me. And besides, it was God himself in Daniel 8:26 who said 400 years was "many days." So we have God on record that 2000 years is not a short period and such events would not be "at hand." Re-read the previous paragraph and think about it for a while.

Now, just a word or two (only a word or two) about "apocalyptic" speech, then we'll have the survey of the book. All right?!

"Apocalyptic" speech is a phrase we moderns dug up. We use it to denote speech which is made up of symbols. In the New Testament there is only one book of "apocalyptic speech" although there are a number of examples of such speech in books written in "ordinary" speech. In the Old Testament apocalyptic speech pervades books such as Daniel, Ezekiel, Zechariah. In a number of other books (eg. Isaiah and Joel) there are many examples of apocalyptic speech.

The word itself denotes "an unveiling, or uncovering, a revealing." In light of the confusion which swirls around these books, it is hard for the average fellow to believe this. The truth is, we borrowed the word from the "**Revelation** of John" (ie. the book of Revelation) where the word was **not** used to describe the **speech** used. In Revelation 1:1 we are told God gave Jesus a "revelation" to John in symbolic speech. Paul "revealed" some things in ordinary speech but the last book in the New Testament - the last "revelation" was given in symbolic speech. Because this last book is called an "apocalypse" and it was given in symbolic speech, men then called books written in symbolic speech — apocalyptic.

Exactly what should be included in the term "apocalyptic" is hard to say. Should a metaphor ("I am the door") be said to be "apocalyptic" speech? Should we say **any** figurative expression is "apocalyptic"?

You'll draw your own conclusion since I don't think the issue can be fully resolved. I'm of the opinion that it doesn't really matter in the end. This much we can say for sure: One can go through the Bible and without much difficulty gather together the sections of scripture which remind him of the book of Revelation. These sections sound like one another. They strike the same chord in our mind — they are in a class of their own. This may be because they not only sound alike, but they have the same general import.

Apocalyptic speech is lurid in its colors and very often violent in its tone. It strikes the imagination and grabs hold of the mind. Who, having read of it, can forget the seven-headed sea beast or the scarlet prostitute on its back? Whose mind does not boggle over the falling of the stars and the rolling up of the heavens? Apocalyptic speech is vivid and easily remembered. It appeals to our imagination. It is the language of conflict and victory. It is the language used when God smites the oppressor and vindicates his people. It is the language of crisis if not of persecution.

It is the extension of the Biblically familiar. See examples of it in Isaiah 13,34; Micah 1:2ff; Zephaniah 1:2ff; Jeremiah 4:11-26. In these we read of God's attack on the world of the ungodly. A repetition of past historical events.

The earth (of the ungodly) becoming once more "without form and void;" the heavens (of the ungodly) once more coming under attack as they did in the days of Pharaoh; another Sodom and Gomorrah judgement comes on Edom; and the earth's high places tremble again at God's presence as they did at Sinai.

This is certain, though an apocalyptic book may have material in it which is to be understood literally, we must reverse the usual rule of interpretation when approaching it. Here is the usual approach to a book: Understand it literally unless forced to do otherwise. In approaching an apocalyptic **book** the rule is: Understand it figuratively unless there is good reason to do otherwise.

Whatever they may say to the contrary, the practice of Premillennialists is to figurize sections of Revelation when they are **not** forced to. Lindsey makes **fire and brimstone** equivalent to nuclear explosions; **locusts** equivalent to Cobra helicopters; **swords and shields** stand for tanks and missiles. He insists **144,000 Jews** in the text (Revelation 7) must mean just that but **fire and brimstone** must mean something else. Did it mean something else in the destruction of Sodom? If it means nuclear activity in Revelation, why does it not mean that in Genesis? Walvoord refuses to accept **10 days** in 2:10 as **10 days** but insists on **1000 years** in 20:1ff meaning **1000 years.** These are not isolated cases. So don't let anyone give you the impression Amillennialists are the only people who figurize.

There are those who affirm "apocalyptic speech" was used to hide the truth from the hostile authorities. There is no proof whatever for such a view. What's to prevent an enemy from infiltrating an assembly of believers and hearing the message explained? What's to prevent the enemy from "extorting" from a weak believer the explanation he heard? How does it come that Daniel explains a lot of the symbolic speech to the enemy? How does it come Zechariah used this type of speech in regard to matters which were not inflammatory? How come John explains some of this and that some other symbolic pictures are so thinly veiled their meaning is self-evident?

Lindsey suggests it was to make it difficult for Biblical critics to level any real criticism against the book. Perhaps so — but why wasn't the whole Bible written this way? And from the survey of the comments I've read on this book it has brought quite a bit of criticism **because** it was written in this fashion. Some said it couldn't be understood and others gave it their own strange interpretation. That interpretation proved incorrect and the book was maligned for containing false prophecies. (F.W. Farrar was fond of doing this to Daniel.)

It has also been suggested by some writers (among them Lindsey) that this speech may well have been used because the writer didn't have the words to convey the literal truth. We can hardly be expected to take this view seriously. These men believe Egypt is alluded to under the figure of one of the heads of the seven-headed beast in chapter 17. Now John knew how to say Egypt (11:8). Besides, God could have given John the vocabulary he needed had he wanted to.

Remember, then, the writer **chose** to describe the visions in the terms related. The "explanations" offered by millennialists like Lindsey and Walvoord underline the point that the book in so many areas **really is** written in non-literal speech.

Summary:

However you understand the book you must take into account that John has explicitly told us it concerns things **"which must shortly come to pass"**; things that are **"at hand."**

While there are sections of the book (eg. chapters 2-3) containing speech to be literally understood you must constantly remind yourself, "What I am reading is what he has seen but what does it mean? What is the truth behind the vision he has just related?" You must remember you are seeing a portrait and just as one does not examine every brush stroke but stands back and examines the whole so must you look for the overall import of the vision.

A Brief Survey of the Book

This epistle is written to seven literal churches in Asia Minor. **Chapter 1** is essentially an introduction in which John says hello to his readers and gives them the occasion for the epistle. He claims he saw a vision of Jesus and that Jesus told him to write the letter to the seven churches of Asia.

Chapters 2-3 are directed to the state and needs of those seven churches. Where commendation is called for, Jesus gives it. Where censure is earned he gives that also.

Chapters 4-5 begin the apocalyptic section of the book - in earnest. They are chapters loaded with comfort for people who were to see the beginning of a persecution which would stretch over two centuries. They show God to be on the throne and (in Christ) to be in love with them.

Chapter 6 introduces us to the seals. Seals (in this case) are to keep the contents of a book hidden. To tear off a seal is to reveal a certain amount of the message. The sealed book is the immediate will of God in reference to his Church amid the trials she is about to endure.

Chapter 7 is one of comfort for the people of God. It assures the saints, all the saints, that no matter the terror which is to fall on the earth, they were to be assured everything will be well with them. All the righteous receive a seal which preserves them through the tribulation and the latter half of the chapter shows that seal to be effective.

Chapters 8-9 introduce us to the seven trumpets. (The trumpets come under the heading of the **seventh** seal as subordinate points, in a speech, come under the heading of major point.) Trumpets, in the Old Testament, were to gain attention and give alarm. By trumpets the nation was assembled or warned of approaching danger. The trumpets are warning judgments on the ungodly, the oppressors of God's people. We are explicitly told they refuse to repent.

Chapters 10-12 speak of conflict and comfort. Chapter 10 assures the saints of ultimate judgment on the oppressor because he spurned the warning. Chapter 11 speaks clearly of the conflict which at times appears to be going in favor of the enemy. However, it just as clearly sets forth the ultimate triumph of the Church. Chapter 12 makes it very clear that the Devil is a three-time loser. All this comfort is needed because of what we are about to be shown.

Chapter 13 spells out clearly the three enemies of the Church. They are listed as the Dragon (Devil) and the "Sea Beast" (Rome - the civil power) and the "Earth Beast" (Rome - the religious movement). A fearsome trio indeed. Because they are so horrific the saints are warned and assured of the human and evil nature of the beasts.

Chapters 14-15 are more assurance. Chapter 13 makes that not only

desirable but needed. In spite of the nature of the enemy, the 144,000 are singing "a new song" for (as the rest of the chapter tells us) the righteous are "garnered in" and the wicked are trampled in the winepress. Then chapter 15 explicitly declares the 144,000 are victorious.

Chapter 16 introduces us to the seven bowls. (These come under the heading of the seventh trumpet, as the trumpets came under the seventh seal.) The seven bowls are the complete, outpoured wrath of God. This chapter implies **all** of the wrath of God outpoured and the **complete** victory of the saints over their enemy **even though** it leaves the details of that victory to the following three chapters. For example, the Battle of Armageddon is previewed in 16 and is described in 19. Babylon is declared destroyed in 16 but the details are left for chapters 17-18.

Chapters 17-18 speak of the fall of the city which ruled the world in John's day (17:9,18). Chapter 17 (the latter part) speaks of **how** she falls and chapter 18 gives a **description** of her fall.

Chapter 19 tells of the joy (likened to the joy at a wedding feast) of the saints at the fall of the enemy and speaks of the fall of that enemy from the divine point of view. The fall was at the hands of Jesus. Her own internal strife which was emphasized in chapter 17 is marked here as the result of Jesus' work. The enemy we are told, died in conflict with Jesus, not by accident.

Chapter 20 describes the utter defeat of Satan in the matter of using Rome against the Church. It speaks of the total and complete victory of the saints in terms of a resurrection of the martyred saints. A resurrection to thrones on which they reign a thousand years. It tells us also of the assurance given to the saints concerning the future. This is conveyed to us in the loosing of Satan - his obtaining an army colossal in size - and his utter defeat. And last, but not least, it tells us of the basic difference between the servants of God and the servants of Rome. One group, in death, rises to reign on thrones (in the vision) and the others rise only to be thrown into a lake of fire.

Chapters 21-22 are a glorious description of the victorious "new Jerusalem," the bride of the Lamb. Her glorious vindication is described much as the temple is described in the book of Ezekiel 47. That is, in respect of the river which flows from her and the trees of life which grow on either side of the river.

The book closes with the solemn warning that its message is to be taken seriously and any tampering with it (adding or taking from) would result in the individual losing his right to the tree of life and his place in the new Jerusalem.

#14 Now there you have the survey. Brief I know. The book is not really as difficult as some have said. Luther thought it of little account. Calvin refused to comment on it. Time-setters and modern prophets have brought it into disrepute in some circles. It has suffered most at the hands of its "friends." YOU **can** understand this book. Oh, perhaps not all of it. But you can begin to feel at home in, and find comfort in, its timeless and deathless principles. It is a book written expressly to comfort the Church of God. Go ahead and enjoy it!

Chp 16
implies all wrath of God poured out
& complete victory of saints
but details given in chps 17, 18, 19

details of Babylon destroyed -- Chp 17 & 18
" " Battle of Armageddon -- Chp 19

chps 17 & 18 city falls that ruled world

chp 17 latter part HOW she fell
chp 18 describes fall

Questions on the Section Marked "Romans, Jews & Christians"

1. Can you say when the Romans really entered into Judean affairs?
2. Can you say who established Herod the Great and his father in the government of Palestine?
3. Can you say who appointed Pontius Pilate to governorship in Judea?
4. Are you able to say how that emperor viewed his provincial governors?
5. Do you know who appointed Caiaphas to the high priesthood?
6. Who ruled Judea on the accession of Claudius?
7. Who mentioned riots in Rome caused by one "Chrestus"?
8. Who is said to have inadvertently caused the rise of the "Sicarii"?
9. Which governor-racketeer was said to have filled the whole province with freed jail-birds?
10. Under which scandalous governor did the exasperated Jews revolt?
11. In what two towns were a grand total of 70,000 Jews annihilated?
12. Who was sent in 67 to quell the revolt?
13. Who committed suicide in June 68?
14. Who finally took Jerusalem?
15. Which fortress stood against the Romans until the spring of 73?
16. In the end, how was it taken?
17. Was Jerusalem resettled after the 70 A.D. destruction?
18. Which emperor caused another revolt in 132 A.D.?
19. Who was the military leader?
20. Who was his religious spokesman?
21. Can you guess why the Christians had not much sympathy with the two leaders of the revolt?
22. The revolt was crushed in 135 - can you remember what Bruce had to say about that year?
23. Did "emperor worship" arise swiftly?
24. Rome had three tests for foreign worship that she would tolerate. Can you name them?
25. How come the farther east Rome went the more she headed toward emperor worship?
26. With whom did Barrow say emperor worship began?
27. Who commended the Jews for not worshiping Caligula?
28. What did Seneca think of the deification of Claudius?
29. With which emperor did the persecution of saints become prominent?
30. With which emperor did it begin **again**, in earnest?

The Romans, the Jews, and the Christians

The Romans were called into Palestinian affairs by the Maccabean boys but had no concrete contact with the Jews until Pompey defeated Jerusalem and Aristobulus II in 63 B.C. Julius Caesar in gratitude, later, made Antipater II (father of Herod the Great) governor of Judah; Herod, governor of Galilee; and John Hyrcanus II was given the priesthood in perpetuity. The nationalists hated the Herods and despised John for being their puppet. Nationalist bandits roamed the hills of Galilee troubling Herod and thus Rome. The last of the Hasmoneans, Antigonus, son of Aristobulus II, was defeated by Herod and the Roman, Sossius. Nationalism was set back but fumed and smouldered. Two strange men were born just prior to the death of Herod. One, the son of the priest Zechariah, and the other, Jesus, son of a virgin, Mary.

In A.D. 6, Archaelaus, son of Herod the Great, was deposed by Augustus and Judea came under a succession of Roman governors. Tiberius succeeded Augustus who had changed the governors in quick succession. The morose world leader appointed only two governors — Valerius Gratus and the "famous" Pontius Pilate. He knew how venal were the Roman representatives and refused to keep changing one "hungry fly" for another more hungry. This Gratus appointed Caiaphas (son-in-law of Annas), High Priest. Pontius Pilate succeeded Gratus and it is claimed he was influenced by the powerful Roman, Sejanus, to be a thorn in the side of the Jews. Philo has claimed that the Jews in Rome until the time of Caligula (Gaius) were looked upon favorably by the Roman emperors. In any case it seems Pilate went out of his way to be a troubler to the Jews. After a series of bungles relating to the Jews, Pilate attacked a Samaritan community which promptly reported him to the Syrian legate who ordered Pilate to Rome to explain and defend himself. Tiberius died while Pilate was on the way home and Gaius became emperor. The next Roman to rule over Judea was Marullus. He was followed by Herod Agrippa I on the accession of Claudius.

Herod Agrippa was a friend of Claudius (and a Hasmonean — through Mariamne I). It was due to his intercession that a full scale war didn't develop when Gaius decided to have a huge statue of himself erected in the temple at Jerusalem. Gaius, who took his divinity seriously, had become incensed at the conduct of Alexandrian Jews who denied his deity. This Herod Agrippa was made ruler of Judea by Claudius who realized the Jews would be more easily ruled by one who knew them. The Jews were pleased that now they had a Jew as their king. Agrippa served them well, killing James and laying hands on Peter because he saw this pleased the Jews. The early chapters of Acts make it plain that the Jews were firmly opposed to this new sect (at least in Palestine and in nearby areas). The treatment of Peter and John and later (though impossible to say exactly when) Stephen, at the hands of the Jews give clear testimony to this. The killing of Stephen was followed by the persecution of the area-wide Church as a whole. Agrippa died - eaten of worms.

Acts would suggest that when Paul met Priscilla and Aquila (Jews from Rome) they were aleady Christians. Suetonius (p.226) claims that Claudius drove the Jews out of Rome because of riots caused by "Chrestus" (obviously Jesus Christ). Maybe there was some unknown "Chrestus" who was causing these riots but it is certainly more probable that Suetonius heard the riots were due to the introduction and propagation of Christianity and he assumed that Christ was personally there. All this would seem clearly to suggest that the Jews were reacting to the evangelical work of the saints in Rome. This thought is set forth by F.F. Bruce (N.T. History, pp. 297-298). In Claudius' day, of course, no distinction between Jews and Jews would have been noted by the outsider (see Acts 18:14ff).

Fadius took the rule upon the death of Agrippa I. He put down many of the bandit groups which in the main, had the sympathy of the locals. He was followed in office by an apostate Jew, Tiberius Alexander. He was followed by the tactless and inconsistent Cumanus who was banished by Rome for his stupidity and tactlessness. The commoner, Felix, became governor. He was a ruthless man with money on his mind. Before him, Tertullus spoke against Paul when Paul had been attacked by the Jews while on an errand of mercy to Jerusalem with the Greek contribution for the poor saints. Felix was hated for his ruthless handling of insurgents and so the patter of Tertullus is clearly "syrup." Bruce feels it was Felix who inadvertently caused the rise of the "Sicarii" (an underground group of assassins which took the place of open revolt and battle). Felix was removed in 59 and Festus took over. He was only three days in the office when the Jews wished him to send for Paul and bring him to Jerusalem (hoping, says Luke, to kill him on the way or in the city). The young Agrippa visited Festus and Paul was paraded before him before going off to Rome. Agrippa was the king who set Annas in the office of High Priest. Between the time of the death of Festus and the arrival of Albinus, his successor, Annas convened the council and put James the Just and some other Christians to death. Albinus was a rapacious ruffian who ran a protection racket with the bandits. Annas made money hand over fist. The various high-priestly parties began to riot and murder each other in the streets and Albinus helped to keep it going. Before he was recalled, the prisons were emptied - the incorrigibles were executed and the others were permitted to obtain the money to buy their freedom. "Thus the prisons were empty, but the whole province filled with these desperate ruffians" (Milman).

Albinas left and then came the gangster, Gessius Florus, worse many times than his predecessor. A villain with influence with the Empress (herself an utter decadent). He abused, robbed, maligned and humiliated the Jews — rich and poor, noble and ignoble. He made no attempt to cover his godlessness but rather showed off his callousness and greed. He drove whole districts into flight and left villages without inhabitants and urged the Jews into open warfare that his cruelty might go uninvestigated. At last the Jews could no longer bear his pillaging and murder and, what with one thing and another, the lid blew off. Several Roman-manned fortresses were taken. The Zealots were in control and perpetrated some vile deeds. Meanwhile in Caesarea, so it is said, the Greeks arose and annihilated, to a man, every Jew in the city — 20,000. "By this act the whole nation was driven to madness" (Milman). The troubles spread to Alexandria where 50,000 were slain in their protests and revolt against the former governor of Judea, Tiberius Alexander.

Cestius Gallus marched south with insufficient man-power and was battered and humiliated by the confident Jews who destroyed almost 6,000 of their enemies. Beth-Horon, famous from the days of Judas Maccabees, and now seeming to be an omen of favor, figured in the scene of the victory. The whole world watched as a tiny little nation threw down the gauntlet to "the whole force of the civilized world." The Jews were quivering with excitement and flushed with victory. The word passing around and was being heard by everyone that this was the time when "men" from Judea were to arise and rule the world. This saying was known and reported by Josephus, Tacitus and Suetonius. These understood it of Vespasian and Titus while the Jews understood the Messiah was to arrive!

Nero sent Vespasian to put down the revolt in Judea. This was early in 67 and within a year Vespasian had slowly subdued, by bitter battle, most of the country. In June 68, Nero committed suicide and Vespasian eased operations for a year. In June 69, he left the area for Rome and left his eldest son, Titus, to take care of the only major problem left, Jerusalem! Titus paraded his men before the city for three days, doubtless hoping to intimidate the Jews into surrender — for his pains he received a "Bronx cheer" (Dimont). Jerusalem was taken after about 5 months siege. The impregnable Massada held out until the spring of 73 when the whole garrison systematically and calmly committed suicide! So ended the 66 revolt against the Roman colossus.

Bruce assures us that between 73 and 132 there was some measure of resettlement of Jerusalem on the site of the now derelict city and "to what extent sacrificial worship was resumed in the temple area is a debated subject" (page 389 of "History"). Some time later, under Hadrian (117-138 A.D.), an ardent Hellenist, another revolt broke out. Hadrian, in furthering his policy to unite the various elements within the empire, built a shrine to Jupiter on the ruins of Jerusalem and called the place "Aelia Capitolina." He forbad circumcision on pain of death. (Mutilation of the body was obnoxious to him and, in addition, such practices as would maintain the distinctivesness of the Jews were not in keeping with his overall policy.)

The Jews revolted and so did the Jewish Christians. Ben Kosheba was the new wind which was stirring the Jewish ranks. A fiery, outspoken and irreverent Roman-hater and nationalist. It is said of him that he told God not to help the Jews nor the Romans but just to stand clear and let the issue resolve itself. His "apostle and armor-bearer" was the famed Rabbi Akiba who declared Ben-Kosheba to be the promised Messiah and so he gained the name "Bar-Kokhba" ("son of the star" from Numbers 24:17). The early days of the revolt began in Alexandria but it was in Judea in 132 A.D. that the explosion took place. Bar-Kokhba organized the people, persecuted Christians "who had separated from the nation" (Tenney) and fought Rome to a standstill. Hadrian sent for one of his leading generals from Britain, Julius Severus. Severus "Shermanized" the whole of Judea exterminating everything and everyone. It was a merciless purge but Rome paid dearly. Finally, the greater numbers and better equipped army won. Dio Cassius reports that 580,000 men died in this war in additon to those who died of famine and pestilence. The rubble of Jerusalem was used to fill in some of the hollows in the Tyropean valley. The whole area was ploughed and sown with salt. Jerusalem had ceased to be Jewish and had become a Roman garrison town! Tenney has said: "Hadrian's action insured the separation of Christianity from Judaism. As long as a Jewish church existed in Jerusalem and Judea, it formed a link between Judaism and Christianity. With the dispersion of the Christians from Jerusalem, the link was permanently broken" ("Times," p. 351). Bruce has said: "The year 135 also marks the final breach between the Jewish Christians and their fellow Jews . . . From that time onward, then, the distinctively Jewish Christian communities went their own way, isolated in religion from their fellow Jews'' (''The Spreading Flame,'' p.272). The Jews were not finished, of course, and despite such horrific set backs they thrived in whatever city they settled. The Rabbinic writings inform us of the constant public debates between the Christians disturbing the synagogue services by the promoting of their views on the prophecies and of the curses in the prayer book against the ''Nazarene'' heretics. So, despite the fact of the vanished temple and ritual the Jews not only were still unconvinced of the truth of the Christians' position, in some ways they were even more ardently set for the defence of the Judaic position. **Check on ''Yohanan ben Zakkai'' and his work on the ''New Sannhedrin'' at Jamnia.**

Emperor Worship

It is not hard to see that the worship of someone or something other than God is being promulgated in the book of Revelation. Chapter 13 in particular gives us a clear picture of an ''earth beast'' who is later identified in chapter 19 as ''the false prophet.'' The ''earth beast'' has the express function of causing all the earth to worship the ''sea beast'' whose authority the earth beast possesses.

How did emperor worship arise? The process was slow but it is not hard to follow it. It began early because as MacKendrick tells us (p.59): ''Official Roman religion was inseparably bound up with politics. The **pontifex maximus**, head of a powerful board of religious advisors to the consuls, was elected . . . To be elected required political manipulation.'' The aim, according to Cicero, of religion was to ''protect ancestral institutions by retaining the old rites and ceremonies.'' Religion in Rome was rotten through and through with the usual superstitions which prevail where the word of God is not known or cared for. It wasn't helped by the slow but definite approach of Greek and particularly Eastern religions into the lives of the Romans. J.P.V.D. Balsdon tells us: To a Roman of the best days of the Republic religion represented stability in the State and in the home.'' (p.182)

With the end of the 2nd Punic war (ended 202 B.C.), foreign gods were willingly accepted into Roman thought. The Great Mother (Cybele) was brought from Phrygia to Rome and made welcome. Others followed later. Bacchus came in but was disruptive and thus had to be punished in its worshipers. R.H. Barrow informs us (p.144): The tests applied to foreign cults, therefore, were three: (1) Would they upset the dominant position of the Roman cults? (2) Were they politically unsafe? (3) Were they morally desirable? If these tests were satisified, toleration was complete.

The farther east Rome prevailed the more they heard of the generals and kings being called gods and worshiped. The line between the gods and men were not too clearly defined in eastern thought. From the idea of providence we begin to get the "divine right of kings" idea. He is the obivous representative of the gods since without the favor of the gods, he couldn't be ruler - at least so it was believed. From the idea of the representative of the gods they moved to the embodiment of the mind and desires of the gods, that is, the rulers are now the embodiment, the expression of the will of the gods. In the east, Roman governors found themselves called by titles which in Italy would have been thought absurd. Many a governor repudiated these titles - others loved and sought them. The Roman leaders in their full-dress ceremonial with their powerful, disciplined legions were more impressive than any of the kings of the east ever were and so the people used the exalted terms of them. Rome was her rulers and her generals were Rome! She became an eastern god DEA ROMA, and had her temples and altars in the eastern Mediterranean. But as Balsdon reminds us (p.187), Rome was not a goddess in Rome until the 2nd century A.D. Barrow says it was from the time of Augustus (27 B.C. to 14 A.D.) that a new form of Roman cult appeared - the worship of the emperor. MacKendrick assures us (p.61) that Augustus was never worshiped in Italy during his lifetime but that he encouraged provincial cults. Tiberius was against his own deification and Claudius wrote commending Jews in Alexandria for refusing to worship the "mad" Caligula. He thought such practice was nonsense and Seneca thought the deification of Claudius was "pumpkinification," rather than "deification." Nero, as William Barclay informs us, at no time took his divinity seriously since he wanted nothing to overshadow his own inner talent. So rather than ascribe anything to divinity he bragged on himself.

Caligula had been serious about his divinity and mercifully died before he was able to erect a statue of himself in the holy of holies at Jerusalem. With the death of Nero, the Roman world erupted. Four emperors in quick succession come on the scene. Galba, Otho, Vitellius, and then Vespasian, who brought back stability to the empire and ruled from 69-79 A.D. None of these men talked of divinity - none of them had the time or desire. Why talk of divinity when humans are on the verge of slaying you - right?! Titus, the older son of Vespasian, succeeded his father and ruled 79-81. He was not one to bother about divinity either. Following him came his brother, Domitian, who was serious about his godhood and would persecute in pursuit of it. With him began the empire policy which later grew into fierce persecution against the Church of God. Stewart Perowne in his "Caesars and Saints" said (pp. 83-84) concerning the state's view of the Church:

> First, there was the savage attack of Nero, who in the year 64 tries to divert the guilt of having burnt the city from himself to the Christians. That was a mere shift, not a settled policy. In the last decade of the century, Christians, among many others, fell as victims of the loutish brutality of Domitian. Here again, there is no evidence of any thought-out and enduring legal procedure.

Perowne goes on to discuss the reason for the slowness of the development of out and out, full scale persecution against the Church and the reasons for its inevitability. He speaks of outbursts of persecution, as for example, at Smyrna and Lyons. He speaks of the perplexity of both the saints and their rulers as to how to approach the problem of the "third race." He sums it all up in three points:
1)They worshiped a criminal (Jesus) therefore must be political offenders themselves; 2) They would pray **for** the king but would not pray **to** him; 3) They were accused of cannibalism and incest. The fire smouldered, then flickered into flame, and then devoured the saints!

The Jews were tolerated, they had no universal dominion aspirations. The saints, consisting of various nations, preached universal conquest and dominion by Jesus. Barrow's piece on "Christianity and the Roman Empire" (pp. 175ff) is obviously off the mark in many respects. The saints were called on to acknowledge the emperor as "Lord." Their refusal branded them as subversive. Persecutions followed upon persecutions but the saints came out on top. And even that which I don't think we are permitted to freely regard the Church of Christ, even that watered down Gospel with its pagan mixture was more than enough against Rome when God was through with her. Applying them where we can, the words of F.W. Farrar in his "History's Witness to Christ" (pp. 100,6,7,8) are a fitting conclusion:

> Yet unaided by any, opposed by all, Christianity won. Without one earthly weapon she faced the legionary masses, and, tearing down their adored eagles, replaced them by the sacred monogram of her victorious largarum, she made her instrument of a slave's agony a symbol more

glorious than the laticlave of consuls or the diadem of kings; without eloquence she silenced the subtle dialectics of the Academy, and without knowledge the encyclopedic ambition of the porch . . . Yes, it was of God and they could not overthrow it; the catacomb triumphed over the Grecian temples; the Cross of shame over the wine cup and the Salian banquet, the song of the siren and the wreath of the rose. These obscure sectaries, barbarians, orientals, Jews, as they were, fought against the indignant world and won. "Not by might nor by power, but by my Spirit, Saith the Lord of Hosts"; by heroic endurance, by stainless innocence, by burning zeal, by inviolable truthfulness, by boundless love. The world's seductive ideals and intoxicating joys, the world's enchanting mythologies and dissolute religions . . . all fled before a Cross of wood! Yes, my brethren, because that Cross was held by the bleeding hands of the world's true King, who perfected the strength of his followers in weakness; and having been lifted up, drew all men unto himself.

Questions on Chapter 1

1. To what events does John expressly say his book relates?
2. To what time does John expressly say his book relates?
3. What might lead you to think the **seven** churches might be intended to include all the Church?
4. When the Father reminds the saints of his eternality what would this say to first century Christians it might not (as easily) say to us?
5. What would "The Faithful Witness" remind them of?
6. And what would "Firstborn from the dead" say to them in their trials?
7. Does the mess the world is in prove Jesus does not now exercise authority over the nations?
8. Can you illustrate (Biblically) your answer?
9. Can you cite a scripture (or more than one) which expressly claims Jesus is now in control over the nations?
10. Do Premillenarians believe the millennium will be completely peaceful and without rebellion against Jesus?
11. Is the Church a "kingdom"?
12. Does this mean Christ is a "king"?
13. Does every "coming" of Christ refer to either his birth or his 2nd coming?
14. Do you know any passages which do not?
15. Was John **in** the kingdom when he wrote his letter?
16. What do you think the "Lord's day" is, in this book?
17. What is the overall impression given by the vision of Jesus?
18. What is meant by having 'the keys" of something?
19. What are the seven golden candlesticks?
20. What are the seven stars?
21. When the New Testament speaks of a "mystery" does that mean the "mystery" was utterly and absolutely unknown prior to that mention of it?

19 "Write therefore what you have seen, what is
now and what will take place later,"
20 "The mystery of the 7 stars that you saw in my right
hand and of the 7 golden lampstands is this:
The 7 stars are the angels of the 7 churches and the

Analysis of Chapter 1

7 lampstands are the 7 churches."

I. Introductory remark concerning the nature and timeliness of the book: 1-3
   - A. It is the "Revelation" given to Jesus and then to John: 1
   - B. It concerns things which are "soon to happen": 1
   - C. It concerns a time which is "near": 3
   - D. It contains a blessing for the reader and doer: 3

II. The Salutation from the Godhead: 4-8
   - A. From the Almighty Father: 4-8
   - B. From the Holy Spirit: 4
   - C. From Jesus Christ: 5-7
     1. The faithful witness
     2. The resurrected one
     3. The ruler of the kings of the earth
     4. The coming one

III. The account of John's initial vision and his commission: 9-20
   - A. The one to whom the vision came: 9
   - B. His location when the vision came: 9
   - C. His state when the vision came: 9b, 10
   - D. The voice and the vision: 11-20

9. I, John, your brother and companion in the
suffering, and k. and patient endurance
that are ours in Jesus, was on the Island of
Patmos b. the Word of God and the testimony of Jesus
10. On the Lord's Day I was in the Spirit and I heard
behind me a loud voice like a trumpet,
11. which said, "Write on a scroll what you see and send
it to the 7 churches, to Ephesus, Smyrna, Pergamum,
Thyatira, Sardis, Philadelphia, and Laodicea."
12 I turned around to see the voice that was speaking to me,
and when I turned I saw 7 golden lampstands,
13 And among the lampstands was someone like a son
of man dressed in a robe reaching down to his feet
and with a golden sash his chest.
14 His head and hair were like white wool, as white as
snow, and his eyes were like blazing fire.
15 His feet were like bronze glowing in a furnace and his
voice was like the sound of rushing waters.
16 In his right hand he held 7 stars and out of his mouth
came a sharp double-edge sword. His face was like the
sun shining in all its brilliance.

17 When I saw him I fell at his feet as though dead.
Then he placed his right hand on me and said
"Do not be afraid of me. I am the First & Last,"
18 "I am the Living One; I was dead and behold I am
alive for ever + ever. and I hold the keys of death
and Hades!"

Introduction to Chapter 1

It is an introduction to the rest of the book. But what an introduction! It is written to emphasize that what is to be read is nothing less than the express word of God. The epistle is not only the word of God but it is given just when it is needed for **"the time is at hand."**

Its three co-authors are claimed to be no less than the Father, Son, and Holy Spirit. This again underlines the divine origin of the letter. Not only so, but the attributes of these three are characteristics for which the saints will have reason to be thankful in the days ahead.

A third time (variously written) John claims the letter was the result of a direct commission from heaven. He is told explicitly by Jesus to "write in a book what you see and send it to the seven churches."

John commissioned from (Father, Son & H.S.) heaven -- specifically by Jesus to write this letter to the 7 churches -- because this letter to coauthored by Father Son & H. S.

Chapter 2 + 3 are specific instructions by Jesus to churches but he says to those who overcome I will give:

- grant to eat of the tree of life which is in the paradise of God
- Shall not be hurt by the second death
- will give some of the hidden manna and I will give him a white stone and a new name written on the stone which no one knows except he who receives it
- and he who keeps my deeds until the end I will give authority over the nations ... and I will give him the morning star
- will be clothed in white garments & I will not erase your name from the book of life & I will confess your name before My Father & before His angels
- will make you a pillar in the temple
- will grant to him to sit down w/ me on my throne

Contd
Sep 78

1-3 NASB

1 The Revelation of Jesus Christ
which God gave Him
to show to His bond-servants
the things which <u>must shortly take place</u>
and He sent and communicated it by His angel
to His Bond-servant, John
2 who bore witness
to the word of God
and to the testimony of J.C.
even to all that he saw
3 Blessed is he who <u>reads</u>
and those who <u>hear</u> the words of the prophecy
and <u>heed</u> the things which are written in it
<u>for the time is near</u>

The God Head
The Father, Son + HS

4-8 NASB

John to the seven churches that are in Asia:
4 Grace to you and peace
from Him who is, & who was & who is to come
and from the <u>seven spirits</u> (HOLY SPIRIT) who are before His throne
5 and from J.C. the faithful witness
the first born of the dead
and the ruler of the kings of the earth
To Him who loves us
and released us from our sins by His blood
6 And He has made us to be a K.
priests to His God & Father;
to Him be the glory and the dominion forever & ever
Amen AMEN
7 Behold, He is coming with the clouds
and every eye will see Him
even those who pierced Him
And all the tribes of the earth will mourn over Him
Amen
8 I am the Alpha & Omega says the Lord God
who is & who was & who is to come
the Almighty

Comments on Chapter 1

VERSES 1-3. "The Revelation of Jesus Christ" is not Jesus as a revelation but something the Father gave to him. The subjection of Jesus, even now, is implied in the passage. See I Corinthians 15:27 and Hebrews 1:3. It was Jesus' obligation then to show it unto his people. This was accomplished by getting it into the hands of John who was then to get it to the Churches of Asia.

Concerning **things which must shortly come to pass** - Despite the denials I have read I'm convinced this means just what it says! Oh, I don't think it upsets me to read of someone finding a verse here and there applying to the yet future but when chapters 4-22 are applied to the yet future that just blows my mind. All those who dismiss this phrase as an indefinite remark implicitly admit the nearness suggested by saying something like, "You must remember, something might be 'shortly' to God but be a long time in coming to us." See the introductory material on this.

John; who bare witness of the word of God - The writer is the apostle John. He bore his testimony concerning what he **knew**. He preached the word of God, testified of his faith concerning a risen Jesus and faithfully reported what he had seen in this book we are now studying.

Blessed is he that readeth - The blessing is there whether you understand or not, the nature of it. But the blessing is not just for the reader. It is for the one who "keeps" the book. How "keep" it? Are there principles in the book to be acknowledged? Do so. Are there commands to be met? The reader is urged to meet them. The book is "prophecy" not simply because it speaks of future things but because it sets forth truths in which we are to abide.

For the time is at hand - The word "eggus" means "near." When it is used of time it means "soon." We all know what it means in Mark 1:15 so why do we quibble here? Walvoord acknowledges it means "near" or "soon" but ignores it. The claim is made the early church lived believing the coming of the Lord (his "2nd" coming) was near in time. This is just not true! They may have lived aware of the possibility of his coming soon but that they believed he was coming soon is not at all established by the New Testament. And suppose they did? They were wrong - weren't they! And if Paul or any other apostle wrote the "2nd" coming is "at hand" they were wrong too - weren't they! But since these men were moved by the Spirit in their writing they couldn't have been wrong. I suggest you read right now 22:6,10 and make up your own mind.

The debate over the meaning of "**Shortly come to pass**" and "**at hand**" is one which arises because of one's overall view of the teaching of the book of Revelation, not from the words themselves. The translations are unanimous in their testimony as to the meaning of the words. Look:

The Basic English: "Things which will quickly take place." (1:1)
"The time is near." (1:3)
The New English: "What must shortly happen." (1:1)
"The hour of fulfillment is near." (1:3)
Moffatt: "What must come to pass very soon." (1:1)
"For the time is near." (1:3)
Wuest: "Things which . . . must come to pass in their entirety shortly." (1:1)
"For the . . . epochal season is imminent." (1:3)
C.K. Williams: "The things that soon must happen." (1:1)
"For the time is near." (1:3)
New American Standard: "The things which must shortly take place." (1:1)
"For the time is near." (1:3)
J.B. Phillips: "What must very soon take place." (1:1)
"For the time is near." (1:3)
Goodspeed: "What must very soon happen." (1:1)
"For the time is near." (1:3)
Spencer: "Things which must speedily happen." (1:1)
"For the time is near." (1:3)
Authentic N.T.: "What must shortly transpire." (1:1)
"For the time is at hand." (1:3)
20th Century: "What must shortly take place." (1:1)
"For the time is near." (1:3)
C.B. Williams: "What must very soon take place." (1:1)
"For the time is near." (1:3)
F. Fenton: "What must speedily happen." (1:1)
"For the time is at hand." (1:3)
W. Barclay: "Things which must soon happen." (1:1)
"For the time is near." (1:3)
N.I. Version: "What must soon take place." (1:1)
"The time is near." (1:3)
R.S.V.: "What must soon take place." (1:1)
"The time is near." (1:3)

This is, of course, in perfect agreement with the testimony of independent scholarship. Vincent, Robertson, Swete, Expositor's Greek, Thayer, and the rest!

VERSES 4-8. John to the seven churches - The letter is written to seven historical churches. Why seven? I don't know for sure but since the number seven is used so often in the book as indicative of completeness and unity (though not exclusively so), it seems safe to construe this as the Revelation's way of addressing the whole Church.

From him who is and who was and who is to come - The Father. The Eternal One. Who has seen kingdoms rise and die; seen ages come and go; heard bragging kings whose carcasses now lie mouldering in the dust and who offers **"grace and peace."** A usual salutation but one which is invested with special significance for the reader about to undergo great trials and loss of peace.

From the seven Spirits that are before his throne - The Holy Spirit. The fullness of the spirit. Jesus is spoken of as having **"Seven eyes"** which are the **"seven Spirits of God."** I know of nothing which conclusively establishes this point but the nature of the salutation seems clearly to demand this be the Holy Spirit since the salutation is from the Godhead.

From Jesus Christ who is the faithful witness - Faithful in every way! In him, claims Paul, is the **"Yea"** and the **"Amen"** of all the promises of God (2 Corinthians 1:21). **"Faithful and True"** are his names in 19:11 of this book. Had he promised the saints victory? He did't lie. Had he claimed to be in control? He spoke the truth. Would Rome's persecution indict him as a liar? No way!

The firstborn of the dead - Preeminence is in view. Colossians 1:18 specifically says he is the **"firstborn from the dead that in all things he might have the preeminence."** The firstborn was not only the first one born but also inherited the place of eminence. Jesus was not the first to rise from the dead but among all who were raised (or will be) from the dead, he is the preeminent one. Do you think this might be of interest to the saint about to die for Jesus?

Jesus was **"born again"** from the dead. This is an interesting analogy. We too must be born again. Jesus did not live a new and heavenly life until after his resurrection (or his being **"born again"**). We can't either. Until we are born again (of water and Spirit John 3:5), until we are immersed into his death and rise with him, we cannot be partakers of a heavenly life. (Romans 6:3-7)

The ruler of the kings of the earth - There are those who do not believe that Jesus is ruling. Some look at the mess the world is in and claim Jesus couldn't be ruling. This just won't do. Was the world in a mess in Nebuchadnezzar's day? Was God not ruling then? Of course it was in a mess. Nebuchadnezzar thought God was not ruling but he knew better when he was through munching and running

running with the donkeys. If world conditions proved Jesus was not ruling they would prove God never ruled, since the world has been in a mess since it started. Listen to Hal Lindsey:

> When we see the mess the world is in, it's sometimes hard for us to believe that Christ is actually the **"prince of the kings of the earth."** This is because even though Christ has the **right** to rule the earth, he isn't exercising this authority over kings and kingdoms at this time.
>
> ("There's A New World Coming," p.26)

But who says Christ is not exercising that authority now? I Peter 3:22 makes it very plain that the powers **have been** made subject to him. Paul is very clear on the matter when he says God set Jesus at his own right hand in heavenly places and that he **"put all things in subjection under his feet."** (Ephesians 1:22) Jesus claimed he had already received power over the nations (Revelation 2:27). I suppose people in the days of Nebuchadnezzar said the same thing as Lindsey is saying today. "When I look at the terrible mess this world is in I just know God isn't ruling!" What with all the flagrant, rampant idolatry; the godlessness of the government; the bewilderment of the saints and the oppression of the believer - everyone just **knew** God wasn't in control. Here is where we tell the "wishers" from the "trusters."

Two little boys were arguing over whether or not there was such a thing as a "sunrise". The first was saying there wasn't because his father told him so. The other said he **didn't** feel or see the earth turn and he **did** see the sun rise so that was good enough for him. He believed, he said, "What I see." The first said, "I believe what my father tells me!" Mister, I don't care what you see (or believe you see) - you need to believe what your Father tells you. He is either your Creator or your Savior and so his word must be right.

Besides, Premillenarians believe there will be rebellion against Jesus during and immediately after the millennium. Evil will smoulder then. There will be, we are told, some open rebellion and a lot of seething rebellion which will result in a huge host made up of nations from the four corners of the earth attacking Jerusalem. This makes it clear, on their own confession, that open and incipient rebellion is not imcompatible with the rulership of Jesus.

Reader do you **really** deny that Jesus is now ruling over the world? If Jesus isn't, who is? If Jesus isn't because the world is in such a mess - can his Father be ruling? If his Father can be ruling in spite of the mess the world's in, why cannot Jesus be ruling? If neither of the two is ruling, does this mean Satan is under no control? I think this is all so silly! Can you imagine anyone denying the plain truth of Matthew 28:18 (read it!) and then writing a commentary on Revelation?

But you say: "If Jesus is ruling, why is the world in such a mess?" Well, clearly because he wants to let it run this way until his purposes are fulfilled. You might ask the same question of the days of Nebuchadnezzar or Pharaoh. Why was God letting the world carry on as it did? It served his purposes.

Unto him that loveth us..., - Ah, but he's not just the world ruler. He doesn't just control Rome. He loves his people. He not only **did** love them, he continues to do so. The staggering historical, visible, tangible, conclusive proof of that love was the Cross! A **loosing** from sins is such a sweet deliverance. The fetters are gone from his elect. The chains are destroyed. Slavery worse than that of the body is obliterated. If he can loose from sins can he not deliver from Rome? Sins! Sins that seas cannot drown, fire cannot burn, mountains cannot hide and tears cannot wipe away! Sins of the night and sins of the day. Sins of childhood and sins of manhood. Sins of school and college; of work and play; sins of the hands and feet. Sins of the eyes, and the mouth and the imagination! So that he is not just an all-powerful ruler - he is a selfless lover.

Made us to be a kingdom, to be priests - It's not only what he did for them but what he did **to** them that makes him adorable. By tears and pleas, by conniving and treachery, by blood and fire and smoke Rome had made a kingdom. To make the nations a kingdom of servants, serfs was the aim of Rome. ("They make a desert and they call it peace." Tacitus) By his own blood did he make the saints a kingdom and **priests**! Plutarch wrote on "The Makers of Rome." John wrote on the "Creator and Redeemer of the Church." We all know which kingdom was divine and which moulders in the dust.

He cometh with the clouds..., - The "2nd" (final) coming of Jesus? Perhaps so, but before you draw your conclusion, remember 1:1,3; 22:6,7,10. Remember you're in an **apocalyptic book** and while that doesn't mean every jot and tittle is figurative it does mean you lean first in the figurative direction.

Check the word "coming" in the Bible. See for example the "comings" in the seven letters in the next two chapters. Go ahead, read the letters now. Tell me what you think of those "comings." Ask yourself about Isaiah 19:1; James 5:8 and a host of others. Don't be impatient now. Good students are thorough. And while you're looking, read Matthew 24:30,34. Note that similar language is used in verse 30 as is used in this text but that verse 34 claims it was fulfilled in the generation in which Jesus lived. This is what is known by scholars as "apocalyptic speech." (I have a little scope of "Isaiah" which touches on this sort of thing. You can order it from the same person you got this book from.)

In Acts 2:23 we learn that it was **"lawless hands"** (Roman) by which the Jews killed Jesus. They crucified Christ. Romans **and** Jews. Romans pierced him. On them he would come in judgement! He said in Revelation 22:7: **"I come quickly."** Thayer says that means "without delay." Read for yourself Zechariah 12:10 with John 19:37 and ask yourself two questions: 1) When was Zechariah 12:10 fulfilled, 2) Was it literally fulfilled. Answer those and then read this text again.

VERSES 9-20. I John your brother - The apostle wrote the book. He was with them a partaker of patience and tribulation. These they found to be in Christ. He was also partaker of the kingdom. Even if this verse did not prove it, verse 5 did. He was on the isle of Patmos **"for"** the word of God. That is, he was on the isle because he had stayed faithful to the word of God and had testified on behalf of Jesus.

I was in the Spirit on the Lord's day - The most natural sense of **"Lord's day"** is the best one. It's a day which, in some sense, is peculiarly His. **Sunday** is that day. The **"eighth day."** The **new beginning** day. The resurrection day - See Barclay's helpful little piece on this. **"In the Spirit"** means "under the influence of the Spirit." This may involve the miraculous or not. Christians are told to **"rejoice in the Spirit."** This is non-miraculous. In Matthew 22:43 David is said to have **"in the Spirit"** called the Messiah his Lord. Inspiration is involved in this and so it partakes of the nature of the miraculous. Whether John is here saying he was enjoying a spiritual period and **then** he saw the vision or whether he is saying he was in a special state in which he was enabled to see the vision, I think, is an open question.

I heard behind me a great voice - Whatever was true before he is now moved by the Spirit and experiences what he now records. The voice gave him an order: **"What you see** (are seeing, or, are continuing to see) **write in a book."** Here we have another passage which indicates that God wished us to have a book. See 2 Peter 1:15; 3:15-16.

And I turned to see the voice - The person behind the voice is meant, of course. Having turned he **"saw seven golden candlesticks."** These stand for the Churches as verse 20 tells us. The candlestick gave light in the tabernacle. The churches too are to be light-bearers to the world. There's a scripture somewhere that says something like that — isn't there?! In the midst of the candlestick was **"one like unto a son of man."** He is Jesus (verse 18). He is dressed in priestly garments. **"Clothed with a garment down to the foot, and girt about the breasts with a golden girdle."** Edersheim assures us this girdle was worn only by the priest when he was officiating on behalf of the people. (See "The Temple," p.98).

And his head and his hair were white - Here is justice, righteousness indicated. Purity **and** nobility. Spotless. This is a priest without "infirmity." His **"eyes were as a flame of fire."** The burning, piercing look of this one misses nothing. This is not stressing tenderness!

His feet like unto burnished brass - Micah 4:13 suggests destructive power under this figure. The Cherubim (the chariot of God - 1 Chronicles 28:18), the dispensers of God's wrath are said also, to have such feet. Power to trample is in view. A voice **"as the voice of many waters."** Thunderous. Like the voice at Sinai.

He had in his hand seven stars - The stars are the angels of the churches. Verse 20. **"A sharp two-edged sword"** came out of his mouth. This is the word of God. But it is not the sweetness of the Gospel. It speaks of judgmental utterances. It is the kind of speech meant when the Bible says **"Then shall he speak unto them in his wrath!"** In Isaiah 11:4 he **"smites the earth"** with **"the rod"** of his mouth. In Isaiah the speech is viewed as a rod of correction. In Revelation it is a sword or punishment. See Hebrews 4:12-13. The glory of this person is represented as showing in his face. It was like **the sun shining in its strength**. Consider the transfiguration as an illustration, in history, of what this passage is in symbol.

I fell at his feet as one dead - No wonder! So would we. Exalted power has been stressed in the vision (though somewhat mitigated by the priestly aspect). Power related to judgment. So it is not out of place for this person to say **"Fear not."** Let it ring out - Christ will reign until irreverence and rebellion are in the tombs! All will **"fall at his feet as one dead."**

I am the first and the last - He is too! He is the beginning and end of creation. He is the beginning and end of revelation. He is the beginning and end of hope. When this one speaks and tells us not to be afraid, we have good reason to be consoled!

The Living one; and I was dead - How comforting is that word **"was."** Say it with conviction. Say it with joy. Say it with self-assurance. We'll walk no road he hasn't walked. We'll meet no fear he hasn't met. We'll fight no foe he hasn't already whipped! The dying saint can know, for sure, the impotence of death. G.K. Chesterton wrote a poem in which he set forth what, to him, must have been the thoughts of one just recently resurrected. He had heard the wise men debate the resurrection and learned how such could not be. Too many wise arguments from too many learned men put it beyond possibility.

After one moment when I bowed my head
And the whole world turned over and came upright,
And I came out where the old road shone white,
I walked the ways and heard what all men said . . .
The sages have a hundred maps to give
They trace their crawling cosmos like a tree,
They rattle out reason through many a sieve
That stores the sand and lets the gold go free:
And all these things are less than dust to me
Because my name is Lazarus and I live.

I have the keys of death and of Hades - This one who is now alive forever did not just **survive** death. He conquered it! Extorted from it the keys to those massive gates. For had the keys not been turned over to him he would have ripped the gates off, posts and all as Samson did in days of old to Gaza. Behold, a greater than Samson is here.

Write therefore the things - The things which **he saw**. Start at the beginning he is told. Relate what you have already seen. Write what you **are seeing. "And then write what I'm about to show you."** Lindsey and others claim **"the things which are"** speaks of the events in the entire Church age. These are covered, we are told, in chapters 2 and 3. The **"things which thou sawest"** cannot include the whole of Chapter 1 for what John **"saw"** prior to verse 19 and following did not include this specific commission of verse 19. The **"things which are"** are the things he is at that moment seeing and hearing! Even the commission to write everything was to be included in the writing.

And besides, when the book is prefaced and concluded we are told it spoke of a time which was soon to come and events which were soon to transpire. To relegate the entire book from chapters 4-22 to a period **still** future is to mock the book. To so treat even chapters 2 and 3 as to make them apply to historical events centuries and centuries after John wrote is to miss the point entirely.

Look! You either accept John's word for it that the book was written concerning things which were to soon take place in a period of time which was near or you forfeit the right to credibility with reference to your interpretation.

The mystery of the seven stars - a "**mystery**" in the New Testament is something formerly not understood but which has now been made manifest. The idea that a "**mystery**" was not spoken of **at all** prior to a New Testament writer mentioning it is not in accord with New Testament usage. 1 Timothy 3:16 speaks of the "**mystery**" of godliness - see for yourself what was involved in it. In Ephesians 5:31-32 Paul quotes the Old Testament concerning the typical significance of Adam and Eve - claims his point to be a "**mystery**" and then says he is speaking of Christ and the Church. So Paul made manifest what the relationship of Adam and Eve taught concerning Christ and the Church. Romans 11:25 speaks of the hardening of Israel as a "**mystery**" and yet quotes Old Testament scripture concerning it in verses 9-10. So you see (check a concordance), a "**mystery**" is **not** something about which absolutely nothing has been said previously.

The seven stars are "**seven angels**" of the churches. Maybe the "**angels**" are the "**messengers**" of the churches (see 2 Corinthians 8:23). They are certainly not "the leading bishops" of the churches. Whatever may be said of that form of government it cannot be said to be reflected in the New Testament writings.

Everything in the book of Revelation has its angel. Rivers, winds, bowls, trumpets and books. I think Milligan is right. The "angel" of a given thing is that thing itself in its essential nature. It is invested with angelic personality that it may act out its part in the scheme of the book.

9-20 Chapter 1

I, John, your bro & fellow-partaker in the
tribulation and K. and perseverance
which are in Jesus was on the island
called Patmos, because of the Word of God
and the testimony of Jesus.
10 I was in the S on the Lord's Day and I
heard behind me a loud voice like
the sound of a trumpet.
11 saying "Write in a book what you see
and send it to the seven churches:
to Ephesus, etc.
12 And I turned to see the voice that
was speaking with me. And having
turned I saw seven golden lampstands
13 and in the middle of the lampstands
one like a son of man clothed in a
robe reaching to the feet and
girded across His breast w/a golden
girdle.
14 And His head and His hair was
white like white wool, like snow;
and His eyes were like a flame of fire
15 and His feet were like burnished
bronze, when it has been caused to glow
in a furnace, and His voice was like
the sound of many waters.
16. and in His right hand he held seven
stars and out of His mouth came a
sharp double-edged sword.
and His face was like the sun shining
in its strength.
17 And when I saw Him I fell at His feet as a dead man
And He laid His right hand upon me
saying Do not be afraid I am the
first and the last
18 and the living one and I was dead and
behold I am alive forevermore and I have
the keys of death and of Hades.
19 Write therefore the things which you have seen
and the things which are and the things which
shall take place after these things
20 as for the mystery of the 7 stars which you saw in
my right hand and the 7 golden lampstands: the
7 stars are 7 angels of 7 churches & lampstands are churches

Questions on Chapter 2

1. To whom is the first letter written?
2. Can you name two areas in which he commended them?
3. Can you say what their big problem was?
4. How would you number the "coming" of verse 5?
5. What does it mean to "remove a candlestick"?
6. Can you say who the Nicolaitans were?
7. What was the nature of the blessing to the "overcomer"?
8. Was he not a partaker of that blessing prior to his "overcoming"?
9. To whom was the second letter written?
10. Can you state the nature of his commendation of them?
11. Can you say in what area he condemned them?
12. Can you say who their opponents were?
13. Can you say what "10 days" of tribulation means?
14. To whom was the third letter written?
15. What is meant by "Satan's throne"?
16. Can you say in what area he commends them?
17. Can you say which individual he commends?
18. How would you number the "coming" of verse 16?
19. What is "hidden manna"?
20. What is the point of the "white stone"?
21. What is the point of a "new name"?
22. To whom was the fourth letter written?
23. Can you (speaking generally) say in what way he commended them?
24. Are you able to say what he specifically condemns?
25. What blessing is offered to the overcomer?
26. What is the "morning star" speaking of?
27. Does Christ claim in this letter to **already have** authority over the nations?

2:17 He who has an ear, let him hear what the Spirit says to the churches. To him who overcomes, to him I will give some of the hidden manna and I will give him a white stone and a new name written on the stone which no one knows but he who receives it.

Analysis of Chapter 2

I. The letter to the church at Ephesus: 1-7
- A. The author described :1
- B. The commendation:2-3,6
- C. The condemnation: 4-5
- D. The exhortation and warning: 5
- E. The consolation: 7

II. The letter to the church at Smyrna: 8-11
- A. The author described: 8
- B. The commendation and consolation: 9-11

III. The letter to the church at Pergamum: 12-17
- A. The author described: 12
- B. The commendation: 13
- C. The condemnation: 14-15
- D. The exhortation and warning: 16
- E. The consolation: 17

IV. The letter to the church at Thyatira: 18-29
- A. The author described: 18
- B. The commendation: 19,24
- C. The condemnation and the threat: 20-23
- D. The exhortation: 24-25
- E. The consolation: 26-29

2:12-17

12 And to the angel of the church in Pergamum write: The one who has the sharp two-edged sword says this:

13 I know where you dwell, where Satan's throne is; and you hold fast My name, and did not deny My faith, even in the days of Antipas, my witness, my faithful one, who was killed among you where Satan dwells

14 But I have a few things against you, because you have there some who hold the teaching of Balaam, who kept teaching Balak to put a stumbling block before the sons of Israel, to eat things sacrificed to idols & to commit acts of immorality.

15 Thus you also have some who in the same way hold the teaching of the Nicolaitans.

16 Repent therefore or else I am coming to you quickly and I will make war against them with the sword of My mouth.

2:18-29
18 And to the angel of the church in Thyatira write: The Son of God
who has eyes like a flame of fire, and His feet are like
burnished bronze says this:
19 I know your deeds, and your love & faith and service and
perseverance and that your deeds of late are greater than at first.
20 But I have this against you, that you tolerate the woman
Jezebel, who calls herself a prophetess and she teaches and

Introduction to Chapters 2 and 3

leads My bond-servants astray so that they commit acts of
immorality and eat things sacrificed to idols.

Chapters 2 and 3 contain the seven letters to the churches in Asia. They all have the same general form. Jesus, the author, describes himself and then proceeds to commend the church in the area or areas where they merit it. There then follows a declaration of the guilt of that church. That is, the specific area of trespass which he feels he must deal with.

There is no doubt in my mind that the principles dealt with in these letters are to be remembered by the Church of God of any age. In verse 23 Jesus claims that the judgment on Jezebel and her followers is to be a standing lesson to **"all the churches."** And if it be true that the Old Testament was written for our learning (Romans 15:4) it cannot be otherwise with these epistles.

The admonition to repentance or steadfastness is followed by a word of consolation. The "overcomer" is to be blessed in his/her overcoming. See the remarks in the comments concerning the identity of an "overcomer" and concerning the "when" of the blessings.

21 And I gave her time to repent and she does not want to
repent of her immorality
22 Behold I will cast her upon a bed of sickness and
those who commit adultery w/her into great tribulation
unless they repent of her deeds.
23 and I will kill her children w/pestilence; and all
the churches will know that I am He who searches
the minds and hearts, and I will give to each one
of you according to your deeds.
24 But I say to you, the rest who are in Thyatira,
who do not hold to this teaching, who have not
known the deep things of Satan, as they call them—
I place no other burden on you.
25 Nevertheless what you have hold fast until
I come
26 And he who overcomes and he who keeps My
deeds until the end, to him I will give authority
over the nations;
27 And he shall rule them with a rod of iron, as
the vessels of the potter are broken to pieces, as I
also have received authority from My Father.
28 and I will give him the morning star
29 He who has an ear, let him hear what the
Spirit says to the churches.

2:1-7, 8-11

1 To the angel of the church in Ephesus write:
The one who holds the seven stars in His right
hand, the One who walks among the seven
golden lampstands, says this:
2 I know your deeds and your toil and
perseverance, and that you cannot endure
evil men and you put to the test those
who call themselves apostles, and they
are not, and you found them to be false;
3 and you have perseverance and have endured
for my name's sake and have not grown
weary.
4 But I have this against you, that you
have left your first love.
5 Remember therefore from where you have
fallen, and repent and do the deeds
you did at first; or else I am coming to
you and will remove your lampstand
out of its place -- unless you repent.
6 Yet this you do have, that you hate the
deeds of the Nicolaitans, which I also hate.
7 He who has an ear, let him hear what
the Spirit says to the churches. To him
who overcomes, I will grant to eat of the
tree of life, which is in the Paradise of God.
8 And to the angel of the church in Smyrna write:
The first and the last, who was dead and has
come to life, says this:
9 I know your tribulation and your poverty
(but you are rich), and the blasphemy by
those who say they are Jews and are not,
but are a Synogoug of Satan.
10 Do not fear what you are about to suffer.
Behold the devil is about to cast some of you
into prison, that you may be tested and
you will have tribulation ten days. Be
faithful til death and I will give you
the crown of life.
11 He who has an ear let him hear what
the Spirit says to the churches. He who
overcomes shall not be hurt by the second
death.

Comments on Chapter 2

VERSES 1-7. To the angel of the church in Ephesus write - Here is the "2nd epistle to the Ephesians." Ephesus! The city of the "temple of Diana." "Diana" whom the "whole world worshipeth." The original temple of Diana crumbled into the dust many centuries ago. It was rebuilt and became one of the seven wonders of the world. It was to this temple Alexander came. The Macedonian wanted his name carved on one of the 127 pillars. He offered all the riches of his eastern campaign for the privilege. The city fathers turned down the offer. But **nobody** refused Alexander. The Ephesians did. They talked him into a calm acceptance by saying "If we put the name of another god on her temple it will upset her." So the mightiest mortal on earth couldn't even buy the privilege to have his name on a pillar in the temple of a god. Years later Paul wrote to a group of Ephesians telling them **they were** the temple (not of a god) but of the Almighty God.

Notice how the letter is addressed to the "angel of the church" and yet in verse 7 we hear it is addressed to the "church." This may serve to show the angel is simply the personification of the church. This is worth something, of course, only if the other reasons are worth something.

He that holdeth the seven stars in his right hand - The life or death of the churches resides within Jesus. Barclay tells us the term **"holdeth"** means to "hold all" of whatever is held. See his discussion. He has been made **"head over all things to the Church, the fullness of him that filleth all in all."** Christ is the absolute authority! Perhaps this is especially significant to the Ephesians since they are set forth as somewhat of a debating society.

I know thy works and thy toil - Their **"works" have reference to their individual good deeds. Their "toil"** has reference to their tiring labor. Not just work, but bone-wearying work! They had their equivalent to the "bus-ministry" (is there any more wearying work than that?) and they had their benevolent work. Jesus saw these and all the other fine works they performed. He had seen their stedfastness in the face of trying circumstances. (See Trench's "Synonyms" on "makrothumia" and "hupomone.") He commends all this - and means it!

Thou canst not bear evil men - These Ephesians were quick to defend the truth. They repudiated the works of the Nicolaitans. They exposed deceivers who claimed to be apostles. They were morally and doctrinally orthodox. Thank God! Wish there were more of these today!

Thou didst leave thy first love - Game ended! Without this what is there? Paul claims (do you think he had the right to speak?) without love the busiest, wisest, and most knowledgeable man is an empty churn. They were straight as a gun-barrel theologically, and spiritually just as empty. Who said that - Havner?

The "**first love**" would have reference to Jesus and/or His Church. In their striving after doctrinal purity (and let's do it!) they departed from loving Jesus and his brotherhood. You think this has no lesson for us? Have you never noticed how the development of a debating spirit seems to wither a man? Debates are right when they are carried on in the right spirit but how many have you been impressed with as far as kindness, gentleness and courtesy are concerned? (I heard recently of Johnny Ramsey debating a denominational preacher on the "**Godhead.**" The preacher denied the deity of the Son of God. Someone was telling me of Ramsey's courtesy. In fact, said he, "I think Johnny was too courteous for his own good." True or not - isn't that lovely change? Thank God for Ramsey's courtesy!)

Now don't tell me how much you love Jesus if you won't obey his commands. Don't tell me how you adore him when you refuse to submit to him. Don't tell me about your doctrinal accuracy, your theological orthodoxy or how many debates you have had when your soul is withered. When you witch-hunt. When you listen intently to every word of another with a view to deciding if he is "one of us." Away with this "**Shibboleth**" spirit.

But maybe, after having said all this, the point of leaving one's first love has not been touched on at all. Perhaps they are being accused of having lost their original fervor. Their original devotion expressed in eagerness and gratitude. See Acts 19:1-20 and note the spontaneous joy with which they received the word.

Many now go through the ritual of "church service" without enthusiasm. It is not the place here to discuss all the possible reasons for this, but let me relate what I believe to be the greatest single producer of the "ho-hum" spirit or the "I'm gonna grin and bear it anyway" attitude. It's this. The view that worship is restricted to the assembly or assembly-type activities. Read that sentence again! Read this one every morning before you begin your day. The whole of one's life can be worship. No matter what the situation or the deed. If the deeds are lawful - offer them in a lawful way to the Father and **that** is acceptable worship. Wish you could get a hold of my little thing on "Romans" and read the comments on chapter 12:1ff. **To break stones unto the Lord in work is as holy as breaking bread unto the Lord in the building!**

Remember therefore whence thou art fallen - "Remember Lot's wife!" "Remember that thou in thy lifetime receivedst thy good things." There are lots of things we need to remember. "Remember now thy Creator in the days of thy youth." To fall is not the end but there must be an acknowledgement, a recognition of that fall. **And repent**. Change your mind about it. Let that change of mind result in a change of conduct. **And do the first works!** Works motivated by love. Works with the original enthusiasm. The same works but with a different motivation.

Or else I come to thee, and will remove thy candlestick - Here is a "**coming.**" Is it the "**2nd**" coming? That can't be. This coming depends on whether or not they repent. If they repent he will not come and remove their candlestick.

What a threat. If the threefold instruction (remember, repent, and do) is not heeded obliteration comes. From what we can read from Ignatius, the church must have, for a while, heeded the warning. But now. There's no church there now; and there has not been for a long time. "Hey Joe. Like to see where the Christians used to meet?" A deserted baptistry - dry leaves fluttering around in the wind and the dust - sad scene!

Jesus visited Ephesus and removed the church (candlestick). It's gone. And who knows how many spiritless, chained-to-the-treadmill churches he will "**come to.**" The most industrious men of Jesus' day were Pharisees. They were like whited sepulchres -full of dead men's bones. Nothing is sadder than an obviously unused church library. Or mildewed song-books. Or a church building, dilapidated and unkept. These are only sad of course because of what they suggest.

But this thou hast - That's Jesus' way, isn't it? Is there something good to say? Don't forget to say it. **Thou hatest the works of the Nicolaitans which I also hate.** Ooh, what a terrible word to use. "**I hate** their works," said Jesus. One thing in your favor, he said, you hate their works. Blessed hatred. Sanctified by Jesus. In a generation which doesn't want to speak too clearly we must speak clearly. Hate the deeds. Love the people. (That's a tall order for some of us.)

The Nicolaitans are identified by Irenaeus and Hippolytus as a sect which grew out of Nicolas (Acts 6:5) who apostatised from Christ. However they originated, they were known as perverts and decadents. Loose thinking, loose living and just overall "loose" were their characteristics. The Ephesians couldn't bear them.

To him that overcometh - The overcomer is the victor whether he lives or dies in the process. The overcomer is the one who remains faithful whether it be in the face of temptation to immorality, indifference or persecution.

To him will I give to eat of the tree of life - We will discuss the **"tree of life"** when we get to chapter 22:2-3. The tree of life answers to the water of life. It is the food and the river is the drink of the saints. It is recalling the state of affairs in the garden when man had unbroken fellowship with God. So does the **"Paradise"** reference. The tree of life stands for spiritual sustenance. It is the **"food"** of the righteous.

Does the promise mean they were not already eating of the tree of life? No. Yes, I know it looks that way. In 3:5 the promise is, the overcomer is to be clothed in white garments. But in 19:8,14 we read that these garments speak of the righteous acts of the saints. It is only white-garbed ones who are allowed to fight in the army of Jesus and this is before they **"overcome."**

I'm saying each promise to the overcomer must be considered in its own light. Sometimes the promise is simply an assurance that their present blessings will continue. In 3:12 and 21 the promises there are already enjoyed by the faithful. See what I mean? So for the Christian, **"overcoming"** involves victory against the enemy and thus a continuing enjoyment of blessings. Or again, (as in, say, 2:10), the participation in new blessings. Each blessing must be looked at according to its own nature. So then, whether life or death - here or hereafter, the overcoming Christian is secure.

It is held by Lindsey and his colleagues that each of these churches represents a period of Church History. That is, one can see by the characteristics of the various churches what time period is under discussion. The Ephesian church speaks of the Church during the apostolic age. The church at Smyrna corresponds to the period 100-312 A.D., and so on.

Apart from any proof this is as good an assumption as any other. But it has the additional difficulty of depending upon similarity of circumstances to prove the point. The Smyrna church suffered, therefore it speaks of a period of suffering. The Sardis church stands for the "Reformation Period." In that period Lindsey tells us "The church was reformed but not **revived**. What church? Did the Sardis church stand for the church which was reformed and not revived? I think we'd better keep in mind that what was reformed was never the Church of Jesus Christ to begin with! How then could the Sardian church represent the church of the Reformation era?

Millennialism is enjoying a lot of attention these days because everywhere we look we hear someone saying, "You see? The events of the Middle East reflect just what Ezekiel said. The movements in Palestine are following the course laid out by the prophet Isaiah." But people have been doing this for years. Graffiti on the walls of classical Greece and republican Rome can be made to sound like today's newspaper. Anyone can search through the Bible and find events spoken of there which can be made to fit into today's scenes. (If an immediate application cannot be established clearly, then the fulfillment is said to be still in the future. If it can be shown the passage applied to a past event then you must claim, "There's a double fulfillment." You see? Anyone can do it).

I read this several mounths ago. It was in a newspaper. "Not in the lifetime of most men has there been so much grave and deep apprehension; never has the future seemed so incalculable as at this time. The domestic economic situation is in chaos. Our dollar is weak throughout the world. Prices are so high as to be utterly impossible. The potitical cauldron seethes and bubbles with uncertainty. Russia hangs, as usual, like a cloud, dark and silent, upon the horizon. It is a solemn moment. Of our troubles, no man can see the end." It was written last week - right? Wrong! It was in Harper's Weekly on October, 1857. Do I need to labor this point: Aren't you aware you can easily write a dozen newspapers for tomorrow with news and comments from newspapers over a century ago?

If you couldn't take the Bible and from "scattered pieces" put together a "picture of today," I'd be really surprised. Lindsey admits in his "Earth" that this picture is taken from "pieces" scattered "in small bits throughout the Old and New Testaments" (page 43). But he admits more than this. Having applied Ezekiel 30 to the yet future he casually adds, "For you students of the Bible, we must add that the latter part of the chapter looks at the time when Nebuchadnezzar destroyed Egypt and her allies, but its greater fulfullment is future" (page 78). Now do you see what I mean? He asserts the yet future application but knowing Nebuchadnezzar is written all over the chapter, he throws in his "double application" bit.

Now I'm not arguing against using the principles contained in these letters and in the prophets, but I'm tired of hearing this rubbish poured out. Rubbish which only serves to bring into disrespect the sacred Word of God. Want to read about wars and rumors of wars? Read Josephus, Suetonius and Tacitus. 1st century writers. Want to read of "prophecies" of the rise of Russia and the eastern powers? Go into the newspaper office and read the very old newspapers. Some of those people (and I've no wish to offend) would not know a Bible from a baseball player, and yet they spoke of the threat of Russia and the eastern powers.

VERSES 8-11. To the angel of the church in Smyrna write We all know of the wonderful Philippian church. There was a beauty in Smyrna too. Smyrna! Thirty five miles north of Ephesus. The "Glory of Asia." Proud Smyrna. Deeply religious Smyrna. Heathen Smyrna. Smyrna, the center of Caesar worship and leading city of empire worship for many years. Smyrna built a shrine to "Roma" as early as 195 B.C. As the Republic spread the worship of Rome became more widespread. In July 44 (4 months after the assassination of Julius Caesar), "an unexpected comet appeared in the sky. It was a prodigy, accepted by the populace as evidence...that Julius Caesar was now in heavan, a god, Divus Julius" (Balsdon, p. 190).

Since the spirit of the empire was reflected in the leaders it was easy enough for people to begin to believe the supreme leaders were the embodiment of the spirit of the empire. The emperors began to be viewed with awe. Barrow tells us (page 144), "From the time of Augustus a new form of Roman cult makes its appearance - the worship of the emperor." In the east, Barrow goes on to tell us, the line drawn between God and man was not too distinctly drawn. The Greeks certainly believed the distinction between gods and men was one of degree and not kind (Kitto, page 10). Farther east, religious homage was paid to rulers and kings. As Alexander and others moved east they were met with these too. Even governors of eastern provinces had such titles conferred on them. **"Soter,""Euergetes"** and the rest.

It wasn't this way in Rome. Romans were too dour for such nonsense. When Augustus accepted the name there immediately sprang up a cult around him. Herod the Great, for example, built a temple and shrine to him. No emperor, however, was consecrated to godhood until after his death. As time went by, a priesthood was formed to serve in the emperor worship and in the process of time, it became necessary that the citizen or subject show his loyalty to the state by the worship of the emperor. See Barclay's brief discussion of this in his "Revelation," Vol. 1, pp. 17-24.

Smyrna won a contest. A contest to see who would erect a shrine to the deified Tiberius. The Christians lived in a heathen town which embodied not only the eastern gods but the gods of Rome. The Roman gods were of the more dangerous kind. Their servants could bring down punishment upon the heads of the Christians for not submitting to those gods. Hard to appreciate in the

20th century but a real menace in the early centuries.

But Smyrna also has Jews. Lots of them. Hostile and vocal Jews. Jews of the sort who would take the lead in the martyrdom of Polycarp. Not faithful Jews but the sort who lived in the days of Antiochus IV Epiphanes. That kind didn't worship Jehovah, but survival. Ramsay in his "Letters to the Seven Churches" (pp.142-157), has a first rate discussion on the concentration of Jews in Asia Minor.

These things saith the first and the last, who was dead - Heavy on the word **"was."** The leading god of Smyrna was "Dionysus," the god of wine. Smyrna was famous for its vines. Each year the death and resurrection of Dionysus was acted out in public plays. The Christians there knew the difference between myth and solid, indisputable historical fact! (See Graves, "The Greek Myths," pp. 103-111).

I know thy tribulation, and thy poverty - Tribulation isn't a headache. It's not an inconvenience. It's pressure. Grinding, crushing pressure. Poverty (here) is not just being poor. It's being "poooor"! Despite the already existing pressure from the Roman worship, the slander of the Jews, and their extreme poverty, these lovely people were faithful. Quit your whining girl! Quit your moaning and murmuring mister! These faithful ones, were the "plutocrats." The "filthy" rich. Yes, we know the world smiles in amusement at this kind of talk but what does a world which rejects the loveliest man who ever lived know? What sense has a world which flagrantly spurns its Maker? Should we be intimidated by their smirks?

The blasphemy of them that say they are Jews - Heavy on the word **"Say."** They wouldn't have recognized Abraham if he had beaten their brains in. The same Jesus had spoken to an audience of Jews in John 8. He recognized their racial status but denied their relationship with Abraham. See for yourself. Paul in Romans 9:6ff makes it plain that all Israel is not Israel. Wish to God millennialists would acknowledge this today. The only "real" Jew that ever did exist was a believer. See Romans 2:28-29. In Isaiah God calls Israel **"Sodom."** In Ezekiel he says their parents were Hittite and Amorite. So proud these Jews were. So proud, I say, of their synagogues. All the while **they** were a synagogue. And the Devil dwelt in them.

Fear not the things which you are about to suffer - What? Is it possible? Can it be that God will let his people suffer? They were about to feel the pressure increasing. They were about to join the long list, the long, glorious list of those who were imprisoned for righteousness sake. Another Joseph or Daniel would join the ranks. They were to **"be tried; and ye shall have tribulation ten days."**

Lindsey and Walvoord figurize this **"ten days."** Why? Because it suits them. They claim they are committed to a policy of literal interpretation unless they are absolutley forced to figurize. So, 144,000 is literal. If 144,000 Jews are literally 144,000 Jews, why are 10 days not 10 days?

Daniel, who was thrown into the lions' den, was tried 10 days (1:12-16). Jacob was tried **"ten times"** (Genesis 31:7). Job, the persecuted, was tried **"ten times"** by his accusers. It's not hard to see then the origin of **"tried; ye shall have tribulation ten days."** It had become the expression for a period of trial by hardship.

Be thou faithful unto death - We have been reminded again and again (but not too often) that **"unto"** means "to the point of." Faithful even if it means death. Such faithfulness secures (though it does not earn) the **"crown of life."** For the Saducees and Epicureans, as well as the Buddhists, death introduces us into nothingness. It was the end. For the faithful it was the beginning. Many had served faithfully their city or country and received a victor's crown **(stephanos)**. Many had striven in the games and received a victor's crown. These crowns died because they were made of leaves and things which died. This crown lasts because it is made of life.

What the Spirit saith to the churches - Despite the fact that this letter (as are the others) written to a specific church, it applies equally to the other churches and in fact to all the churches. **"The second death."** This we'll discuss in chapter 20. It is so much better to die the first death in faithfulness to Christ than to die that second death. **"Cast into the lake which burneth with fire and brimstone."**

VERSES 12-17. To the angel of the church in Pergamum - The university of Asia Minor, with its huge and famous library. Their library was so famous (and justly so) they were regarded with some suspicion by the man who had the greatest library in the world, Ptolemy II Philadelphus. His library was in Alexandria. The king of Pergamum tried to bribe Aristophanes, the head librarian of Ptolemy II, to come to Asia Minor and work for him. Ptolemy heard of it, imprisoned Aristophanes, and stopped the supply of papyrus form Egypt (where he was king) to Pergamum. This necessitated the production of "vellum." This "vellum" (animal skins so treated as to be written upon) was called "parchment" (from Pergamum).

Pergamum. The city which forced Sir William Ramsay to say,

"A royal city!" (page 295). There it sat, like a throne, on top of a hill, surveying the valley around it. A throne indeed. Who sat on that throne? Rome did! Pergamum was the seat of state religion. It had passed the once all important (and still very important) center of Caesar worship, Smyrna. In Pergamum was the original **Augustan Temple.**

Who sat on the throne? Zeus did! One of the most famous altars in the world was there at Pergamum. Up on a ledge jutting out from the hillside — 800 feet up — sat the huge altar. Smoke ascended endlessly from the sacrifices offered there. "No one could fail to see it," since "it would look like nothing so much as a great seat or throne" (Barclay).

Who sat on that throne? Asklepios did! R.H. Charles called Pergamum (at the time of Asklepios' services), the "Lourdes of the ancient world." The I.S.B.E. draws the same picture. Thousands of the sick from near and far would visit the temple site. "Asklepios the Savior" was on the tongue of eager worshipers day after day. The Christians knew who the "Savior" was. And who was it who spoke to those who dwelled **"where Satan's throne is"**?

He that hath the sharp two-edged sword - The Romans carried a short broad-sword. The word here is, they tell me, Thracian in origin. It covers what came to be used by the Romans as distinct from a curved scimitar-type blade. No firm distinction can be maintained between "rhomphia" and "machaira." In any case, when the Romans were given governing powers, they were given power to inflict capital punishment. This was called "the right of the sword." (See Vincent on Romans 13:4). Who then had the power of life and death? Asklepios? (See Graves, "The Greek Myths," Vol.1.). Who was supposed to be able to raise the dead or slay the living? Zeus, the supreme god of the Grecian world? No! The Romans? Romans, who when Pilate asked, "Knowest thou not that I have the power to release thee, and have power to crucify thee?" he was told, "Yes, but that power comes from above." Now this Jesus, to whom all power was given, has the "Right of the sword."

Thou holdest fast my name, and didst not deny my faith - In the middle of rampant heathenism and (at times) ruthless persecution — they held on. Who was **"Antipas"**? Who knows? We know enough! We know his end. We know his faith. We know his message. We know his refusals. We can guess his sufferings. We know his influence. The faithful will one day have the eternal pleasure of fellowship with this unknown hero. He was a **"witness."** Well, well. Unless he was an apostle "bang" goes the theory of those who say the New Testament claims only apostles are "**witnesses.**" In this man's case, his "**witness**" was really **that,** his "martyrdom." We get our word "martyr" from the Greek word behind "witness" (martus).

I have a few things against thee - Those words are followed by "**but.**" What a sad word in such contexts. "**But.**" Isn't Jesus honest?! I have a "**few**" things against thee. Isn't he gentle?! He somewhere taught, when you have something against a person, go see him. He practiced what he preached, didn't he?

Some that hold the teaching of Balaam - So why should Jesus reprimand the church because "**some**" hold this teaching? Because there must have been some kind of unlawful silence by the church in regard to the matter. There must have been discipline lacking. Paul rebukes the Corinthians for not disciplining the ungodly man in their congregation.

The teaching of Balaam? The verse makes it clear which part of the teaching of Balaam is under consideration. Balaam wasn't wrong in everything. He wished to die the death of the righteous. He knew, by the word of God, what Israel would do to Moab and the rest. He knew of the "**star**" out of Jabob. He also loved gain and he urged on idolatry mingled with fornication. Oh, we know they didn't urge it on as the way to snare the church. They covered it with rights and liberties. And they were a snare to the church. They also had a problem with "**some that hold the teaching of the Nicolaitans.**" These two groups were one of a kind but they are distinguished. So hast thou "**also,**" makes that clear.

Repent therefore; or else - Does Jesus get mad? Of course he does. The "**Wrath of the Lamb**" is mentioned in the letter later. His wrath is not the wrath "of man" of course but he does get mad. It is not the final (2nd) coming of Christ. It's a coming in judgement on these ungodly sects. The implication, however, is that the church needs to make adjustments too or else they will suffer in that coming.

To him that overcometh, to him will I give of the hidden manna - This is Jesus. In John 6:31-65, he claimed to be the true (real) manna which came out of heaven. What manna was to the Israelites, Jesus was to the Christians - and more. The brothers were sustained by an invisible source - hidden manna. (See Colossians 3:1-4)

The saints were already feeding on that hidden manna of course, but the promise assures them of continued sustenance from Jesus, whatever the course of events. The Christians couldn't partake of the heathen feasts but they could feed on something better.

An idolatrous feast is no substitute for a heavenly feast.

And I will give him a white stone - "White." The color of so many good things. Standing for purity, justice, nobility, victory, and joy. There were stones which spoke of acquittal at a trial. There were stones which were rewards for heroism, faithful service, or victory and they acted as complimentary passes to the games or the theater. Then there was the white stone that friends shared with each other which guaranteed a warm reception anytime and any place they met.

All of these thoughts combine to make a "**white stone**" the symbol of something wonderful. To mention this in a religious and spiritual setting would speak volumes.

And upon the stone a new name - Only the owner of the stone would know the name written on the stone. We hear later (19:12-13) that Jesus has a name which no one but he knows. However, in verse 13 we are told what that name is and so everyone knew it. How then can it be a name which no one but he knew and yet everyone knew it? It's because of the significance of a "**name.**" In the Bible a name was very important. You can see this in the many places where the name spoke of the events surrounding the birth of a child. You can see it in the many cases where names were changed to indicate a change in circumstances of status of the one re-named.

Abram becomes Abraham. Jacob becomes Israel. Simon becomes Peter, "Desolate" and "Forsaken" (Isaiah 62:2ff) becomes "Beulah" and "Hephzibah." A new name speaks of a new status, a new relationship. You see, a name stood for the person in a much deeper sense, to them, than it does to us. "His name shall be called" (Isaiah 9:6f) means "He shall be." The name described his nature. In Luke 1:35 we are told "the holy thing which is begotten shall be called the Son of God." This was not intended to designate a name for Jesus. It was intended to declare his nature, his relationship with God.

A "new song" was a song concerning some new manifestation of God's goodness toward his people. A "**new name**" was a new relationship or status into which the child of God entered by virtue of some new experience with his Master.

But it was "**his**" name. Nobody else would know it. It was **his** trial. It was **his** experience with God. Oh, we could hear him share the trial and the joy of victory but it was still his trial and victory. We know that Jesus is the "**Word of God**" but yet that is something only he "**knows.**" No one can share that nature and status. So it is with the new name on the white stone.

VERSES 18-29. To the angel of the church in Thyatira write - Thyatira, a town long recognized as a garrison town. It was the gateway to the important areas of Asia Minor. The capital, for example. But Ramsay assures us its situation was not the least bit favorable to the town. It had no natural fortifications and consequently had to be well-built and staffed with well-trained soldiers. It was a weak town which had to be and act strong!

It was a town of trade guilds. Guilds (unions) of every kind flourished there. Lydia, the seller of purple garments lived there. Metal workers flourished there. Much later a man called Tertullian would write against all those members of the guilds who compromised principles in order that they might "live." The poet put his words together in a piece called "A Man Must Live." Having confessed Caesar as Lord or participated in some heathen ritual-dinner that they might continue to buy or sell, the compromisers would justify themselves by saying "A man must live." Tertullian would ask, "But **must** you live?" In what religion were we told a man **must** live? Imagine the soldier, the defender of freedom, walking away form the conflict saying, "A man must live." Imagine, says the poet, "A man must live," as a battle cry! And who wrote this letter to the Thyatiran saints? **The Son of God, whose eyes are like a flame of fire.**

And his feet are like unto burnished brass - Numerous coins have been found which were produced by Thyatira. On one of them is the picture of Hephaestus, the Greek smith god. Graves in his "Myths," tells us of the prevailing opinion among the ancients that "every Bronze Age tool, weapon or untensil had magical properties, and...the smith was something of a sorcerer" (page 87, Vol.1). The ugly Greek god, Hephaestus, was married to the decadent Aphrodite. She was having an affair with Ares, and Hephaestus caught and exposed them by means of a very fine bronze net.

Ramsay assures us Thyatira was very much a bronze town. The trade guilds worshiped the god who worked in bronze. Jesus is described as having feet like unto burnished brass. This speaks of destructive power. See Micah 4:13. His eyes are a **"flame of Fire."** There you have the furnace. Here you have the fire and the bronze. Isn't Jesus really speaking their language! The tracks he leaves as he tramples them into the earth are tracks of burning. Hephaestus was not "the son of god" but Jesus was the Son of God!

Thy last works are more than the first - Having commended them for specific things he acknowledges their **progress**. They were lovers. They were patient. They were benevolent and helpful (**"ministry."**). Perhaps they were too patient. They were too gently in love with people. But they "suffered" some lying woman to hurt the assembly. In John's 2nd epistle, if one reads between the lines, we have an elect lady who was so kind and gentle and loving she had to be warned against bidding the false teachers God-speed (4-11).

The woman Jezebel, who calleth herself a prophetess - There is no reason to dispute that this was a woman. Maybe her name was not Jezebel, but she was like her. Walvoord claims the name of the woman was "probably not Jezebel." Now there is nothing in the text, or out of it, to suggest this. What exegetical reason has Walvoord for doing this? He does it when it suits him. This **"Jezebel"** followed a similar line to that of the Nicolaitans and the Balaamites. Sure, what's wrong with being a part of a trade guild and attending the feasts which offered sacrifices unto the gods? It's harmless. Especially when you know that an idol is nothing. See Paul's dealings with this in 1 Corinthians 10.

I gave her time that she should repent - She obviously claimed to be one of God's people. If so, this buries the notion that she was a local fortune teller called **"Sambathe."** It wasn't her will to do so. That's her funeral. She had been lying down in bed to fornicate (literally or figuratively, and maybe even both). God swears he will cast her and her **"children"** (followers) into a bed of tribulation.

And all the churches shall know - Not just this church — but all the churches. This one with they eyes like fire — fire like a furnace — fire like in the forge used by the metal workers of Thyatira; this one with such eyes sees all. The searing look burns its way through all the veneer. It lights up the dark places. It sees down into the very heart.

But to you I say - To the saints who had not delved into wickedness. Here is his commission to the still faithful: "Hang on until I come." This must have been the word in former years to the Thyatirans. They would have to hold-off the enemy until Pergamum was ready. The city was weak but it had to make the best of it. The saints were weak but they too had to live courageously.

To him will I give authority over the nations - Walvoord holds this is a millennial promise. Fulfilled when these faithful saints share the rule of Jesus. There is not a hint of the millennium in this passage. The authority Jesus offers the overcomer is the authority that he **had already** received of his Father (v.27). Don't you think it remarkable that both Lindsey and Walvoord say absolutely nothing about **that part** of verse 27? Read it for yourself and see if

Jesus is not claiming to have already received the power from his Father. Why do you think they skipped it?

What authority is this? When is it received? It's already being enjoyed. We are fellowheirs with Christ (Romans 8:17). The world, and all things are ours (1 Corinthians 3:21-23). The prayers of the saints affect the world (Revelation 8:3-5) and cause God to send judgments on it. Don't tell me - for the argument is useless - don't tell me appearances say otherwise. Appearance would have us believe **God** is not ruling.

The very fact that Paul urges us to pray for kings and all that are in authority proves the prayers of the saints affect world leaders. Don't tell me that appearances prove otherwise!

But one day the saints will judge angels and men. That's what Paul claimed in 1 Corinthians 6:2-4. And mister, Paul wasn't a premillennialist. The church is a "royal" priesthood. They keep the world alive by being salt. They **"reign"** in life by Jesus - Romans 5:17!

He shall rule them with a rod of iron - The word **"rule"** always means "shepherd." The **"rod of iron"** is said by some to be a staff with an iron top since this was often the weapon of a shepherd. It fits well. Note that the weapon is not a sword. The smiths in Thyatira would quickly grasp the **"iron"** allusion. And the potters would grasp quickly the "shivers" or broken pieces of pottery.

As I also have received of my Father - We would have thought that this was evidence sufficient to prove that Jesus has already received authority over the nations but it isn't for the premillennialists. Matthew 28:18 isn't enough either. Have you read that passage lately? Take a look at it now. While you're at it, take a quick look a Revelation 3:7, where Jesus claims to have the authority over the house of David.

And I will give him the morning star - The morning star is Jesus. In 22:16 Jesus calls himself that very thing. He is the light-bringer. 2 Peter 1:19 gives us the same kind of picture. The day star arises in their hearts, thus flooding them with light. This promise doesn't mean they didn't already have him for they did (John 14:23). It speaks of a new appreciation of him. Paul speaks of the Galatians needing Christ to be formed in them again. Some of the Galatians had gone from Christ but many had not. It was as if they had to come to know Jesus all over again. The faithful Thyatirans had the **"morning star."** Faithfulness unto victory would see them gaining a deeper and more intimate relationship with that Savior. This would be true if they were faithful until they saw the threatening pass. This would also be true if they died in their faithfulness.

I Cor 3:21-23 So then let no one boast in men. For all things belong to you, whether Paul or Apollos or Cephas or the world or life or death or things present or things to come; all things belong to you, and you belong to Christ and Christ belongs to God.

Questions on Chapter 3

1. Who is said to have been the richest king in history? Sardis
2. How did Ramsay describe the city of Sardis? "More like" what? a robber's stronghold than an abode of civilized men
3. What did the city have (as Jesus put it)? dead
4. How did the city's historical background fit into the church's condition? promising so much but delivering nothing
5. Which Old Testament prophet speaks of the "seven eyes" of Jehovah? Zechariah
6. What is meant by the "seven Spirits of God"? seven eyes all wisdom all knowing all insight
7. To what does 2 Chronicles 16:9 relate? God strengthens those fully w/ Him — God's eyes range thru out earth to strength...
8. Why would "Be watchful" be especially significant to this church? They weren't watchful at all. They loved combat but when peace came they became lethargic and dead.
9. Who built the town of Philadelphia? Pergamene King
10. What new name did it take upon itself? Philadelfus — Neocaesarea
11. And later, what name was it known by? Flavia
12. From what did this city (among others) suffer? earthquakes
13. What does "the key of David" mean? Jesus Christ
14. Did Christ claim to have the "key of David" back when the letter was being written? yes
15. What Old Testament scripture is fulfilled in Revelation 3:7? Is 22:22
16. What is "the open door" of this letter? Jesus Christ is open door of blessings
17. Who was a "synagogue of Satan"? the Jews
18. What's the significance of the number 580,000? Jews died in war w/ Rome
19. Can one be delivered out of trials and at the same time go through them? yes
20. Why was Philadelphia known as "Little Athens"? many idols there
21. What's involved in having a name written on you? overcomer
22. Why does the "new Jerusalem" come down "out of heaven"? It is made by God — divine origin
23. Can you name two products Laodicea was famous for? eye powder, clothes
24. Why does Jesus call himself the "Amen" in the Laodicean letter? They had no such word — they were nothing
25. What is meant by the "beginning" of the creation of God? Jesus is beginning of creation
26. If God loves us, what will he sometimes do with us? chastise & reprove

3:1-6

1 And to the angel of the church in Sardis write; He who also has the 7 Spirits of God and the 7 stars says this; I know your deeds that you have a name that you are alive, and you are dead.

2 Wake up and strengthen the things that remain which were about to die for I have not found your deeds completed in the sight of My God.

3 Remember therefore what you have received and heard and keep it and repent. If therefore you will not wake up, I will come like a thief in the night and you will know at what hour I will come upon you.

4 But you have a few people in Sardis who have not soiled their garments and they will walk w/ Me in white for they are worthy.

5 He who overcomes shall thus be clothed in white garments and I will not erase his name from the book of life and I will confess his name before My Father & before His angels.

3:6 He who has an ear let him hear what the Spirit says to
the churches.
3:7-13
.7 And to the angel of the church in Philadelphia write:
He who is holy, who is true, who has the key of David
who opens and no one will shut, and who shuts and
no one opens says this

Analysis of Chapter 3

- I. The letter to the church at Sardis: 1-6
  - A. The author dsescribed: 1
  - B. The commendation: 4
  - C. The condemnation: 1-2
  - D. The exhortation and warning: 2-3
  - E. The consolation: 4-6
- II. The letter to the church at Philadelphia: 7-13
  - A. The author described: 7
  - B. The commendation and consolation: 8-13
- III. The letter to the church at Laodicea: 14-22
  - A. The author described: 14
  - B. The condemnation: 15-18
  - C. The exhortation and the appeal: 19-20
  - D. The consolation and promise: 20-22

8 I know your deeds. Behold I have put before you
an open door which no one can shut, because
you have a little power and have kept My Word
and have not denied My Name.
9 Behold I will cause those of the synagogue of
Satan who say that they are Jews and are not
but lie -- behold I will make them to come
and bow down at your feet and to know that I have
10 Because you have kept the word of My perseverance
I also will keep you from the hour of testing
that hour which is about to come upon the
whole world, to test those who dwell upon the earth.
11 I am coming quickly, hold fast what you have
in order that no one can take your crown.
12 He who overcomes I will make him a pillar
in the temple of My God and he will not
go out from it any more; and I will write
upon him the name of My God and the name
of the city of My God, the new Jerusalem,
which comes down out of heaven from My God and
13 He who has an ear let him hear what the
Spirit says to the churches.

Comments on Chapter 3

VERSES 1-6. To the angel of the church in Sardis write - Sardis. Fifteen hundred feet up in the air on a ledge of rock jutting out of the side of a mountain. Sardis, the ancient capital of Croesus, the richest king in history. The representative of the Asian kingdoms against the European powers. Steeped in glorious history and indeed, having a name. Sardis, the impregnable fortress. When Croesus crossed the river Halys and destroyed a mighty kingdom (as it worked out - his own) he ran back to Sardis. He had only lost the first round to Cyrus, and his fortress would preserve him from the pursuer until the Lydian forces gathered to crush the "mule."

But while he rested (for it must have been at night), Herodotus tells us, the Persian army entered the city and took it. You see the walls of the city were really the cliffs of the mountain. Sheer and "impossible" to scale. The truth is, carelessness made it appear that way. About 300 years later the city fell again, in the same fashion, to Antiochus III.

Ramsay describes the city as "more like a robber's stronghold than an abode of civilized men." It was a city of tremendous (past) reputation. But it was more, it was a city which spelled "failure." The city whose history was marked by the ruin of great kings and the downfall of great military strength...It was the city whose name was almost synonymous with pretension unjustified, promise unfulfilled, appearance without reality, confidence that heralded ruin. Reputed an impregnable fortress, it had repeatedly fallen short of its reputation, and ruined those who trusted in it" (Ramsay, p.376).

Its isolation made it important in times of war but when peace came, it was too far out of the way. Too difficult to get to, it became, except spasmodically, a dead city. Sardis today is a wilderness of ruins and thorns...where the only habitations are a few huts of Yuruk nomads (Ramsay).

In the earlier years of Sardis' glory the river Pactolus brought gold right to the door (Herodotus, followed by Unger). The city was noted also for its wool products and its fruit growing business. All right. What then have we said about Sardis? We said it had a glorious past but as a city it was now dead. It promised much but never delivered. It was careless and didn't watch and so was taken by night. Banks in the I.S.B.E. also tells us of its history of being an area notorious for robber bands (see on "Sardis").

He that hath the seven Spirits of God, and the seven stars - Some have suggested the "**seven Spirits of God**" are the same as the **"seven stars"** which are the seven angels (which would thus be seven spirits). This introduction makes it clear the position is untenable.

The **"seven Spirits"** are equated in 5:6 with **"seven eyes."** This would indicate clearly all-seeing power and thus imply all-wisdom. He sees and understands everything. The **"seven"** would of course indicate "fullness" or "completeness" but it may also be used to speak of the total knowledge concerning the **"seven"** churches.

In the days of Zechariah (see 3:9 and 4:10) it looked to some as though the temple (begun about 16 years previously) would never be completed. God assembles the people and has a (top) stone set before Zerubbabel (see 4:7). He swears that Zerubbabel, who started it, would finish it. On the stone (ie. either engraved on it or looking on it) are seven eyes. God's eyes. God is challenging the people in 3:9 to look at **(behold)** this top stone. What their eyes couldn't see (ie. the finishing of the job) God's could, for he was greater in knowledge and wisdom. His eyes could see all the obstacles to be removed - the things which must be taken care of, for the job to be finished. Chapter 4:6 associates this constant vigilance to the completion of the temple with the Spirit of God. **Read 2 Chronicles 16:9!**

What am I saying then? I'm saying the **"seven Spirits"** which are equivalent to the **"seven eyes"** speak of the total wisdom and insight which comes from the Spirit. You will recall that these letters are what the **"Spirit saith to the churches."**

So then, no matter what appearances say, Jesus knows everything. Someone said "Reputation is what people say we are and character is what we are." Jesus knew them as they really were. He has the **"seven angels"**. This simply strengthens what we have already said if it be conceded that the **"angels"** of the churches simply stand for the real nature and inner state of the churches.

I know thy works, that thou hast a name - This was a church which worked. They probably broke bread every first day of the week and contributed of their means. But these were only the grave clothes wrapped around a corpse (Morgan). In days gone by (and for all I know, today still), in one of the east European countries, when a man died they dressed him up in his finest, set him at the head of a table and held a feast in his honor. He was there. But he was dead. **"Thou hast a name that thou livest and thou art dead."** Promising so much, delivering so little. Wax flowers! A whited sepulchre in which death ruled supreme and was having a carnival. A snow-covered graveyard. Clean! Crisp and sharp on the surface. Hot, sweet and stinking underneath the fresh cover. A pure mantle, a delight to the innocent. A natural hypocrisy when it covers the dead who rot and fester below.

The city was "alive" during time of strife and war. It couldn't live with peace. The church in Sardis had not been at war with Rome. There is no indication in the Bible, or out of it, that she was having any trouble with the prominent group of Cybellian worshipers which lived there. No slanderous Jews attacked her. In her peace she seems to have drifted into a coma and on into death. Is the Sardian threat really gone? Are there not those among us who live to war? Is not conflict our "bag" at times? The sound of the trumpet and the rumble of chariots make the blood race and the pulse quicken. Debate gives us identity. Conflict is our life-blood. Peace leaves us bewildered, frustrated, and without identity. Sad story. (Of course the truth is, we have plenty with which to war if it is war we want. 1 Peter 2:11.)

You will have noticed that in this epistle Jesus does not follow the usual (commendation-condemnation) pattern but reverses it. He reprimands first and then commends (such as the commendation is).

Be thou watchful, and establish the things which remain - One would have thought there was nothing to establish. The rest of the verse suggests that there were "works" which could be perfected. A few in Sardis had yet remained faithful which tells us that the "death sentence" was of the church in a general way. It would be silly to attempt to press the "death" of the church too far since **"be thou watchful"** would have no significance to a wholly dead assembly. There were survivors. Their works were to be encouraged and the remnant was to have its way. **"Be watchful,"** would speak volumes in a city which twice had been humiliated because they did not watch.

I will come as a thief - Robber bands hid in the hills (says Banks) and so coming as a thief would be especially significant. This may well be so, but surely it is the unexpectedness which is being stressed. The night climb against Croesus would fit well with the language aimed at impressing the hearers.

Thou hast a few names - Names stand for people! Wish to God we could have this ever in our hearts, and especially when we flip through a phone book. The list of the damned. These few names are unknown heroes. Their garments they kept clean — their conduct and character spoke of their relationship to Jesus. These brave souls would walk with Jesus "in white." There we have it again. White, the symbol of purity and victory. They would be sustained in their purity By Him who makes us **"perfect in every good**

work, working in us that which is well pleasing in his sight." White garments (eg. fine linen, bright and pure 19:8) spoke of the righteous deeds of the saints. These would become his garment and Jesus would be proud to name his as his own. Not that anyone earns anything. **"They are worthy,"** does not mean they merited anything. It means their conduct reflected their profession.

Ramsay tells us of the "triumphs" of the Roman generals. The generals would conduct the parade dressed in a white toga - the symbol of victory. This may be John's point. Still, in chapter 7:9 we have the picture of a white-robed multitude and it certainly isn't a Roman triumph, but a picture of the Feast of the Tabernacles. This is a more likely explanation of the white-robed promise. The Feast of Tabernacles was the most joyful of all Jewish feasts. It followed the harvest of the crops and the ingathering of the grapes. It followed the Great Day of Atonement when the sins of the nation were removed. Why wouldn't it be the most joyful?!

VERSES 7-13. To the angel of the church in Philadelphia write -This city was built by a Pergamene king called Attalus Philadelphus. Its position on the trade routes easily conjures up the name of a doorway. A city devastated (as many others) by earthquakes. Earthquakes for which one would wait with held breath - fearing the arrival of the turmoil. Philadelphia produced grapes in abundance and so the god Dionysus was prominent. There were Jews there. Powerful in their influence and slanderous in their speech as well as scornful in their attitude.

Tiberius helped the town to come back to life after an earthquake during his rule. In gratitude for this they renamed the city "Neocaesarea." Unger (following Ramsay) reminds us that this was not permitted without the permission of the emperor. So the name change was tantamount to the emperor putting his name there. The new name died quickly, but later, in the reign of Vespasian, the town was called "Flavia" (his own name was "Flavius" and his wife's "Flavia").

The church in Philadelphia is praised by Jesus, not for its numerical strength, but for its faithfulness though weak. Now the "weakness" cannot have reference to their character as a group of Christians, for such weakness doesn't show in the letter. They were undoubtedly small in number and influence compared with the power of the opposition - pagan and Jewish.

These things saith he that is holy, he that is true - Christ's opposition to the Jewish enemy is written all over the epistle. The Jews claimed themselves to be a holy nation - set apart. The claim had only an appearance but no substance. Jesus was the sanctified one and his claim had substance. Check the lexicons on the word "truth" and see that the one used here means "genuine, the substantial reality." The shadow is always associated with the Jewish religion (see Colossians 2:9, 16-17; Heb. 10:1). It was not substantial truth but truth in a shadow (See too, John 1:17).

He that hath the key of David - Not, **"He that one day will have the key of David."** Jesus claimed to have it. Even Walvoord admits, whatever is involved in having the key of David, Christ already has it. Walvoord says this passage "seems" to allude to Isaiah 22:22. Read the passage for yourself and see if you have any doubt about the matter.

This claim of Christ's is an awful rebuke of the Jews - the Christless Jews. It is the Crucified One who claims to have this authority. But what authority? Over the treasury? This Walvoord concedes. But the authority here under consideration is a whole lot more than city treasurer. Read it for yourself in Isaiah 22:15-25. Shebna was treasurer **and** governor. His authority was to be taken from him, and God says, 'I will commit thy government into his hand; and he shall be a father to the inhabitants of Jerusalem, and to the house of Judah. And the key of the house of David will I lay upon his shoulder; and he shall open and none shall shut; and he shall shut and none shall open" (verses 21,22).

Is there any doubt in you mind that Revelation 3:7 alludes to Isaiah 22:22? How could there be? Why then are we told it "seems" to allude to it? To weaken the connection of course and thus to make the point which obviously flows from the connection less obvious. In the remarkable Isaiah 9:6,7 we hear of the child who is born, the son who is given. We hear "and the government shall be upon his shoulder...of the increase of his government and of peace there shall be no end, upon the throne of David. .." Now read the two passages together. Aren't you satisfied that 22:22 doesn't speak only of a treasurer? Eliakim was to be put over the **"house of David."** In Isaiah 36:3 we read of the deposed Shebna as being a scribe and Eliakim as being **"over the household."** He represented the city against the invader.

Jesus claimed to have the authority of (the key of) David. The Jew was to know assuredly that God had made this same Jesus whom they had crucified, both Lord and Christ (Acts 2:36). The Jews would exclude from any hope of Messianic blessing, the hated Gentiles. The haughty among them would exclude even those of their own countrymen who did not toe their line. "Woe unto you Scribes and Pharisees, hypocrites! Because ye shut the kingdom of heaven against men: for ye enter not in yourselves, neither suffer ye them that are entering in to enter" (Matthew 23:13).

I have set before thee a door opened, which none shall shut -Jesus in claiming to be the promised Messiah claims the right of inclusion and exclusion. He had let the Philadelphians in. He had opened the door and not all the Jews under heaven could close it. Not their slanders or mockery made any difference.

The open door is the door to blessing. Perhaps he also has in mind the **"open door"** or opportunity to preach the Gospel but there is nothing in the text which would suggest this.

But Jesus was also a shutter of doors. To enter the presence of God meant going through Jesus. There is a way into the holy of holies but it is through his flesh. There can be no entrance into the presence and blessing of God except through Jesus (John 14:6; Hebrews 10:19-23). For all their slandering, the door to blessing was closed against them. For all their pleas of descent from Abraham, the door was firmly shut. Despite their ritual, history, Law and prophets, the door was shut fast by him who had the key of the house of David.

I know thy works...that thou hast a little power - Not "a" little power but **"little"** power. They were weak in influence and had no political sway. (But then with Jesus I'm sure it didn't worry them.) Despite the littleness of their power they were powerful in their faithfulness to Christ.

Behold I give of the synagogue of Satan - How blunt. And no less true today. No one is serving the Jews' best interests who does not confront him (kindly but plainly) with his spiritual state. He is lost, undone, Christless and therefore priestless. That being true, he is hopeless. Apart from Jesus there is no hope.

They that say they are Jews, and they are not, but do lie -Well? Were they or weren't they? Is the case any different today? The real Jew is a physical descendant of Abraham through Jacob who has given his life to Christ. If he hasn't done that he is no Jew! Romans 2:28-29 and 9:6-7 are very clear on the matter.

I will make them come and worship before thy feet - I don't know of what people the Philadelphian church was constituted. If they were Gentiles then the "insult" here is of the plainest kind which must have made the Jews howl when they heard it. In Isaiah 60:14, we read, "And the sons of them that afflicted thee shall bow themselves down at the soles of thy feet; and they shall call thee the city of Jehovah, the Zion of the Holy One of Israel."

Jesus will later say he will write on them "the name of the city of my God." His favored ones will be "called" the "city of Jehovah." The Philadelphians will know the joy of having the Isaiah passage fulfilled in them. They will be called the city of God. The **"Holy One"** who is also the **"True One,"**will cause the arrogant despisers to bow down before them. And these Jewish despisers will know that God loved (in Christ) the church there.

There was in store for the Philadelphians a day of vindication. A day when the Jews would be humiliated. It was the church's assurance that in the coming hour of trial that they would be kept. **I also will keep thee from the hour of trial** - Walvoord thinks this means "If the Great Tribulation is to occur in your day, don't worry about it because you will be raptured and thus not go through it." (That's not a quote.) Whatever the hour of trial is, it isn't this "Great Tribulation" of which millennialists speak. It may not always be possible to know what a text teaches, but this doesn't mean we can't know what it **doesn't** teach.

With the rise of Domitian persecution began. Those who refused to worship the emperor became enemies of the state. The persecution which began with him intensified later. Christians came under the terrible pressure of Rome for about two and a half centuries until the Edict of Toleration under Galerius. The Jews too had their troubles with Rome, for it was Hadrian who urged the cessation of circumcision and aimed at building a shrine to Jupiter on the site of Jerusalem.

This rebellion of the Jews in 132 under Bar Kosheba was perhaps the bloodiest of the Jewish battles with Rome. Dio Cassius reports that over 580,000 died, of the Jews, in the war. In addition there were the many thousands who died of famine, pestilence and fire. In the early stages prior to the revolt, the Christians were suffering greatly at the hands of the Roman (Dimont, p.108). The Roman governor, Rufus, prior to the arrival of Severus, slew "in heaps thousands of men, women, and children" (Eusebius, p.311).

In a book, claimed by Will Durant to be "fascinating," Max Dimont tells us this third war cost the Romans more than the previous conflict. In Hadrian's reports to the Senate (including the final report when the rebels had been destroyed), Milman tells us, he did not include his customary sign-off, "I and my army are well!" So with the Christians, Jews, and Romans all taking a terrible beating in the years which followed the writing of the letter to the Philadelphians, is it unreasonable to speak of these events as fulfilling the hour of trial which came on the whole earth?

But how about **"I will keep thee from the hour"**? Does this not mean the church was not to suffer? Indeed not. If you notice, verse 11 urges them to **"hold fast."** This sounds like fortification for pressure rather than assurance of complete exemption. In Ezekiel 9:1-8 we are told the righteous would be kept from the hand of the destroyer but the **"keeping"** was not that they were saved from physical suffering or death. In Ezekiel 21:3-4 we read of the same judgment as taking away the righteous as well as the wicked. The point is they were preserved all the way through it and thus they came **"out of"** it (see 7:14). This deliverance is the kind of deliverance spoken of in **"Deliver us from temptation."** The request is not to "keep us from losing under temptation." Jesus keeping them from the hour is keeping them from what the hour could produce, ie. apostasy. He would safely see them through their time of trouble. The Jews had no such promise. Nor did anyone else.

I will make him a pillar in the temple of my God -Philadelphia was known as "Little Athens" for it was full of idols and idol temples. It would not have been the first time that the worshipers of the idols had felt the ground shake and the pillars crack and tumble. At such a time there would be only one thing to do — run! But God's temple cannot crumble whatever happens in the physical realm. The pillars in that temple are mature Christians — solid, stable and immovable. Such would be the overcomers. They'd be like Peter, James and John as related in Galatians 2:9. **"He shall go out thence no more,"** may well have reference to the fact that the saints would never have occasion to run out for fear (this would require a dropping of the figure of a pillar of course — which isn't at all unusual in Revelation). On the other hand it may be allusion to the perpetual priestly work of the saint who, as well as being a stone in the temple, is a priest (see 1 Peter 2:5-9).

Isaiah 56:3-8 is a remarkable piece of scripture which fits in so well with that we are reading here that it is well worth reading. Whether the church here is Jew or Gentile (or both) the lessons in the symbols are clearly seen . On the hypothesis the church is Gentile we have Isaiah speaking of the foreigners who have said, **"Jehovah will surely separate me from his people..."** The eunuchs (the despised group) have the same reservations believing they will not be acceptable to God. But we are told the foreigners and eunuchs are not to worry for, "Unto them will I give in my house and within my walls a memorial and a name better than of sons and of daughters...them will I bring to my holy mountain, and make them joyful in my house of prayer...for my house shall be called a house of prayer for all peoples."

Here indeed is an open door. For both Jew and Gentile. If the congregation is Gentile (or predominately so) we have the scriptural assurance for them. If the congregation is Jewish (or predominately so) we have comfort for them. So, whoever they be, the scorned, weak ones have the son of David behind them. An open door for both Jew and Gentile. "Other sheep I have which are not of this fold, them also I must bring."

V12 **The name of the city of my God, the new Jerusalem** - This and the "**new**" name of Jesus will be written on them. The Jerusalem of Judea had long since ceased to be the "**city of God.**" There God was plainly examined and cruelly rejected! There was another Zion. This Zion had as its foundation, Jesus the Christ (Isaiah 28:16; 1 Peter 2:6 et al). This was the "**new**" Jerusalem the "**stones**" of which were members of the "**new**" covenant.

Someone has suggested the old Jerusalem must still have been a contender for God's favor because "**new**" Jerusalem implies a (then) present contrasting of the **old** with the **new.** This is without foundation. Because he uses "**new**" we are not to conclude he is therefore "contrasting" it with the "**old.**" "New" York is not now used in contrast to York. "New" Amsterdam is not now used in contrast with Amsterdam. "New" England is not now being contrasted with England. Those "new" names are now well-established names for those locations. When the "new" names were first used, they were undoubtedly used in contrast to (or in memory of) those other locations.

In writing the name of God on these Christians we have a bald repudiation of the Jewish arrangement. (Not that it was a matter of doubt. It had already been done — and done decisively.) God had claimed he would put his name on the literal Jerusalem forever (2 Chronicles 7:16). "**Forever**" and "**Everlasting**" must be studied in the light of their contexts. Look in a concordance. And check Genesis 17:8,13; Exodus 21:6; 40:15; Leviticus 16:34; 24:8; Numbers 25:13; Deuteronomy 28:45-47.

Walvoord says the "**new Jerusalem**" must be a reference to the future, physical, and eternal city Jerusalem. (At least he says something about it. Lindsey, as is usual for him on passages which trouble the millennial position, says absolutely nothing about it. Lindsey says nothing about it despite the fact that he has a section dealing with the "**Promise**" to the Philadelphians. Not a word! Still, maybe Lindsey is smarter.)

On Walvoord's terms the promise to the overcomer is that he will have the name of the physical "**new**" Jerusalem written on him. (?) This literal new Jerusalem of which Walvoord speaks is described (literally, he tells us) in chapter 21.

And the **"new"** name of Jesus would be written on them. As we've said above, the idea of the name being written on them speaks of endorsement, a being identified with. Jesus would own the overcomer as his own (see Matthew 10:32). The **"new"** name of Jesus is not hard to understand or identify. It is **"Lord"** or any such synonym. Philippians 2:5-11 speaks of Christ's **"overcoming"** name - **Lord.** This, says Paul, will have to be confessed, one way or another. In Hebrews 1:4 we hear of him having inherited a name more excellent than that of angels. All other "names" (you know by now what a name stands for!) are placed under him (Ephesians 1:21). So living or dying - in peace or in war - in prosperity or poverty, the overcomers are unashamedly owned by Jesus. What a staggering rebuke to Christ-rejecting Jews - then and now. What a staggering word to a Christ-rejecting world - then and now!

That the city comes **"down out of heaven"** is significant. It shows its divine origin. This is a city, made without hands, whose builder and maker is God. While the bestial kingdoms of Daniel 7 rise out of the water or the earth - the Messianic kingdom is set forth in the Son of Man who rides in the heavens.

Let the churches of today heed what the Spirit taught about the place and authority of Jesus. He taught it to that church that all churches might pay attention.

VERSES 14-22. To the angel of the church in Laodicea write - Laodicea. Synonym for indifference through self-satisfaction. Sad to say, probably the most preached-on church of the seven. The church that made famous the startling (and almost crude in its plainness) saying of Jesus, **"I will spew thee out of my mouth!"** The town lay 43 miles southeast of Philadelphia and a million miles below the spirit of Philadelphia's saints lay the Laodicean church members.

Of the town Ramsay said, "There are no extremes, and hardly any very strongly marked features...It is the only one of the Seven Cities in which no relation is discernible between the natural features that surround it and its part and place in history" (pages 422-423).

I'm not sure I understand his last sentence but the first one is so like the description of the church one would hardly think it coincidental. The Laodiceans were a rich community. They were famous for glossy black woolen garments and for their famous eye-powder. This powder was exported all over the world in tablet form. It was then ground into powder and used to relieve eye complaints. Phrygia was one of the areas in Asia Minor where eye diseases were rampant.

These things saith the Amen - And there are few words which are more definite in their meaning than "**Amen.**" It doesn't matter what the statement was which prompts the "**amen,**" - good or bad, the word is **definite!** The Laodiceans had no such word in their vocabulary.

The faithful and true witness - There was nothing distinctive about the Laodiceans. They had no "**witness.**" They were not faithful to the testimony they had concerning Jesus. Heresy wouldn't bother them. It would just have been "a difference over words. Nothing to get excited about." They would never have promoted heresy, for that takes energy and they didn't have it. Nor did they have sufficient interest or enthusiasm to become heretics. At least heresy is a stand. Heretics "**witness**" concerning something.

The beginning of the creation of God - The word "**beginning**" doesn't mean that Jesus was the first thing created. It means he is the "Cause" or "Source" of the creation of God (Hebrews 1:2; John 1:1-3). The same word is used of the Father in chapter 1:8 and in 21:6. The rich, self-reliant Laodicean is reminded from whom all blessings flow. Pigs are expected to eat the acorns without looking up to see from where they came. People are supposed to be better than pigs!

Thou art neither cold nor hot; I would thou wert cold or hot - They were tepid (going from hot to cold - not from cold to hot). There is something about tepid water that is nauseating. The hot springs of Laodicea were not really hot but comfortably warm. Good for bathing in but lousy to drink.

Did Jesus want them to become cold? Would he **really** rather have had them cold as tepid? That's what he said. Maybe he said it that way simply to stress the horror of their position. But what was the horror of their position? They were neither hot nor cold. In their present state they couldn't claim they hadn't known; that they have never been moved. It would have been better for them never to have been moved than having been moved to become "moderate." (Isn't there a scripture somewhere about it being better never to have known the way of righteousness than having known it to turn from it?) "**I will spew thee out of my mouth,**" needs no comment.

Because thou sayest - Someone said, "Let your words be few and sweet. It's better this way when you come to eating them." How many of us open our mouths only to change feet?! The trouble with God is, he always hears what we say and he has this tremendous memory. The trouble with us is, we have such large mouths and so little worth the saying. **"I am right, and have gotten riches, and have need of nothing."** Jesus said of his apostles (and us), **"Apart from me ye can do nothing"**. This church is guilty of the "atheism of the dollar". In comes the dollar and out goes God. We can buy our way to congregational success. We'll hire the best preacher. The best youth minister. Our meetings will be held by the best visiting evangelist. We'll hire us the best song-leader and build us the fanciest or finest building. With this all accomplished the results are bound to follow — with God or without him. And no doubt, "results" follow.

Before him who said, **"The world is mine and the fullness thereof,"** they said "I am become rich." Before him who said, **"Let there be...,"** they said "I need nothing." Most of us hate to be pitied. At least when we are normal and healthy in mind. We hate rebuke and deliberate rebuff but we abhor being pitied.

Thou art the wretched one and miserable, - Tell an educated man he is woefully ignorant and only semi-literate (and if he even half believes you), he will "come unglued." Hear the embarrassed blustering of the tycoon when in a foreign or isolated place he discovers **his** money is just so much paper. Watch the blush of the ranking diplomat (the pompous ranking diplomat) when he learns his hotel reservation was never confirmed. Oh, how we hate to see ourselves levelled! "You are not rich, you are impoverished," said Jesus. The word "wretched" speaks of "affliction." "You are not blessed," he says, "You are afflicted." The word "miserable"? "An object of pity is what you are," the Lord tells them. An object of pity such as one would see lying on the straw in an attic. Almost sarcasm, isn't it?! **"And blind and naked."**

Their wonderful medicine for the eyes can't help them. Their beautiful black, shiny garments which cover the bodies of so many, even in foreign lands, can't hide their own embarrassing nakedness. "All the looms of their city could not weave cloth to cover their sins." (Kiddle)

Gold refined by fire...and white garments, - It was a banking center but its vaults didn't hold the **"gold of God."** Theirs was perishable gold (1 Peter 1:18). Their black garments covered the body — God's white garments covered the soul. His eye-salve dealt with the eyes of the real man, the inner man. And why was he saying all this?

As many as I love, I reprove and chasten, - Maybe it's trite but here it is. Chastening is needed spiritually even as it is physically.

Children who know no form of chastening are either mythical or gangsters. Hebrews 12:4-13 sets forth part of God's philosophy on chastening. Elderships, parents, and children need to bring it out of the moth-balls. If we ever survive long enough to grow enough, each of us will one day long for the chastening hand of God, which moulds and makes us. Of whom was it said, "He learned obedience through the things which he suffered?" If he did that, and for our benefit, can't we begin to want **God's** way with us?

I stand at the door an knock - The little girl was with her father at the art gallery. They both stopped to look at the portrait of Jesus knocking at the door. He looked a little weary. She wanted to know from her irreligious father who the door-knocker was. "Jesus" he said rather sharply (but not intending to be sharp). "Is he tired?" she asked. "Looks like it," he answered more patiently. "Why won't they let him in?" "How do I know, baby...now come on." Conscience is now at work. Later that day - "How come they wouldn't let Jesus in, dad?" Irritated, "I told you I don't know!" That night, on her way to bed, "Why wouldn't they let Jesus in?" A soft answer in a subdued voice, "I guess because they're bad, kitten. And foolish." After the goodnight kiss and on her way to the bedroom, "Well, we'd let him in — wouldn't we, daddy!" That night he lay wrestling with the question on his mind, "Why don't I let him in?" He did what he needed to do and let Jesus into his life. Why don't you? If you've been immersed into Jesus Christ for the remission of sins and have drifted away — come on home again. This passage is written about people such as yourself. Let him in. If you've never been a Christian — read Acts 2. All of it. See what they believed and did in order to have the remission of sins and then go and do the same.

I will give to him to sit down with me in my throne - And to whom is this promise made? "A band of obscure slaves. To the proud Roman leading his armies to victory, to the proud Jew counting his ancestors by hundreds, there must have been something almost grotesque in the claim. Here was a company of men not yet dignified with the name of humanity — the butt of the satirist, the jest of the poet, the neglect of the historian — spending their days in menial toil, passing their nights in outhouses or top garrets, leaving their bodies to a pauper's grave. And yet these men make the claim to an empire compared to which the dreams of Caesar grow pale. They aspire to a scepter higher than the Latin race had ever aimed at — above aedile, praetor, consul, senate, emperor — above every name that is named to constitute authority. To sit on the judgment throne of God..." (Matheson, p.89)

See what I've said on 2:26, 27. Lindsey says this promise speaks of ruling with Jesus on his throne through eternity. Walvoord says it has reference to entering "fully into the blessings of the Christian life." (!) Again, Lindsey has done better (I think) than his teacher.

3:14-22
14 And to the angel of the church in Laodicea
write: The Amen, the faithful and true
Witness, the Beginning of the Creation of God
says this
15 I know your deeds, that you are neither hot
nor cold; I would that you were cold or hot
16 So because you are lukewarm, and
neither hot nor cold, I will spit you
out of my mouth
17 Because you say I am rich and have
become wealthy and you have need of
nothing, and you do not know that
you are wretched and miserable and
poor and blind and naked
18 I advice you to buy from Me gold
refined by fire, that you may become
rich and white garments that you
may cloth yourself and that the
shame of your nakedness may not
be revealed and eyesalve to anoint
your eyes that you may see
19 Those whom I love I reprove and
discipline; be zealous therefore & repent
20 Behold I stand at the door & knock; if
anyone hears My voice and opens the door
I will come in to him and will dine
w/him and he w/me.
21 He who overcomes I will grant to him to
sit down w/ Me on My throne as I also
overcame and sat down w/ My Father on
His throne
22 He who has an ear let him hear
what the Spirit says to the churches.

Questions on Chapter 4

1. Why is the vision of chapter 4 placed where it is?
2. Who "dwells in heaven" even though on earth?
3. Do you know of a scripture which supports your answer?
4. What does "hereafter" in 4:1 signify to Premillennialists?
5. How is the word used in the Bible and daily speech?
6. Where, in Revelation, is the the throne of God usually situated?
7. Where does the Old Testament often say he is enthroned?
8. What is the overall appearance of the throne scene?
9. Where in the Old Testament do we find the 7 lamps were placed?
10. Is Lindsey right in saying the 7 lamps in heaven represent **the church?**
11. Is he right in saying the 7 lamps **in heaven** mean the Church is raptured?
12. Who are the 24 elders? And why 24?
13. What is the thunder and lightning usually associated with?
14. What is an "anthropomorphism"?
15. Of what does the "rainbow" speak?
16. What "forces" Lindsey and Walvoord to say the 24 elders are not 24 elders?
17. Who or what is the "royal priesthood"?
18. Do you have a scripture to support your answer?
19. What is the "sea of glass"?
20. Where might the symbol have originated?
21. Do you know what 2 Chronicles 4:2-6 speaks of?
22. Who are the 4 living creatures?
23. Why are they full of eyes?
24. Do you know what 1 Chronicles 28:18 calls them?
25. Why the multiple-creature form?
26. Why a "lion"?
27. Why an "eagle"?
28. Why a "calf/bull"?
29. Why a "man"?
30. What is the main thrust of the song sung by the 24 elders?

Analysis of Chapter 4

I. The visit to heaven: 1

II. The throne scene in heaven: 2-11
- A. The king and the throne: 2-3
- B. The 24 elders and the throne: 4
- C. The lightnings and thunders of the throne: 5
- D. The Spirit, the temple and the throne: 5-6
- E. The living creatures and the throne: 6-8
- F. The worship and the throne: 9-11

A Summary of Chapters 4 and 5:

These two chapters are the door into the central thrust of the book. The book teaches the victory of the Church over her enemy (Satan in Rome). In the course of the struggle the saints will have occasion to quake but these two chapters tell them, no matter how it looks, all is well. Scary material is to be presented in the ensuing chapters and so these two are initial assurance. The book is one of comfort and so we read of numerous deviations from the main line of thought, which are designed expressly to bring comfort in the face of terror.

Chapter 4 says, **"Believe in God,"** and chapter 5 says, **"Believe also in me!"** (Milligan). Chapter 4 speaks of the Creator and 5 of the Redeemer. Chapter 4 speaks of Power and 5 of Love and Mercy.

Chapter 4 will say the throne which rules the universe is not in Italy and chapter 5 will say the co-ruler of the universe is an all-sacrificing Lover of the saints.

The two chapters will together say that worship, glory, and honor should be given to the Father and the (once dead) Lamb and not to any arrogant and evil earthly ruler. They will say: "No matter what you hear from here you can be assured everything is under my control and to your ultimate benefit!"

Comments on Chapter 4

VERSE 1. A door opened to heaven - Thank God the door to heaven is opened. Not only can we see into heaven (thanks to the revealing work of the Lamb who has the seven Spirits of God) but we can get into it. Sometimes the word "heaven" is used in the singular but it is also used, often, in the plural. (See 12:12 and 13:6)

There are times when John uses "heaven" as simply a location. That is, heaven is where God is, as earth is where men are. But this isn't always what he means by it. This is hard to put into words, but, sometimes it means a state rather than a locality. In 12:12 and 13:6 we read of "dwellers in heaven." On the surface it would seem as if this meant people (or beings) who live in the realm beyond our world; the place outside our world. In 13:6 it is clear, however, that they who dwell in heaven are those in whom God tabernacles — his temple or church.

But this is not an unusual thought for Paul often speaks of the saints as sitting with Jesus in the "heavenlies." He speaks of our life as hid with Christ (Colossians 3:3); of our being raised to sit with Christ in heavenly places (Ephesians 2:6); and as presently having our citizenship in heaven (Philippians 3:20).

You must understand that John is relating a vision. There was no literal door open in heaven. The entrance into Heaven gives John the information he is to convey to us. No one would dare suggest that John couldn't have seen a literal door into heaven. Nor would anyone suggest he couldn't have been taken up into heaven (for Paul was). The description of his other experiences in the book are not to be understood as historical and literal (eg. seeing the seven-headed beast coming up out of the water) so we are safe in concluding he didn't actually go into heaven. His going into heaven, in vision, stresses his "first-hand" knowledge of what he is relaying. It adds vividness and point to his claim of presenting a revelation.

It's remarkable (and yet so common it shouldn't be) that Walvoord and his colleagues deny that John was taken up into heaven. In pages 101-104 Walvoord argues for a literal fulfillment of the visions of 4-22 and then assures us John was not literally taken up into heaven. He claims "a normal interpretation of this section which understands these prophecies as literal events would require that they be viewed as future" (page 101). Then he goes on to tell us "A literal interpretation of the prophecies beginning in chapter 4 is not fulfilled in any historic event and must therefore be regarded from the futuristic viewpoint if it is indeed valid prophecy" (page 102). One would almost conclude from this that all valid prophecy has to be "**fore**-telling." In addition, we would feel secure in concluding that Walvoord will accept John's literal transportation into heaven. He explicitly denies it.

Things which must come to pass hereafter - These are the same things which John said "must shortly come to pass." To claim that "hereafter" means "after the Church Age" assumes the seven letters to the Churches embraces the whole church age. Where is the proof of this? Perhaps it's so — but where is the proof that we might examine it? Each of the churches was combed for a "characteristic" and then it was assigned a "historical period." Besides the tenuous nature of such evidence we have no one's authority to give us the right to do this.

But as if this were not enough, the view runs directly contrary to John's express four-fold declaration that the time of which he would speak was "near" and the events of which he would speak were to "shortly come to pass." Now in all fairness, it must be conceded that a Bible writer's plain statement beats an uninspired assumption every time!

To make 1:19 an inspired outline is commendable. To make the "things which you sawest" refer to what John had already seen, is most reasonable. To hold "the things which are" refers to "the whole church age" is without a vestige of proof. Can we, in the face of the seven letters, deny that all the characteristics mentioned there were already present in the first century? If all those characteristics were already present in the first century, why are we required to assign them to various periods? The "things which are," if it speaks of historical conditions, must surely refer to the time when the speaker is speaking. For of a truth, in the first century, the "Reformation Period" was not one of the "things which are"!

Can you imagine Jesus saying "write the things which are" and having in mind the 20th century? He then speaks of "hereafter." The things "which are" are obviously "here" and thus he speaks of "hereafter" and "thereafter." Check the word "hereafter" in the Bible! You see, for Walvoord and company to have a case, the word "hereafter" must embrace a period about 1900 years after the writing of the book of Revelation. Do you understand that? Think about it a moment. Lindsey and Walvoord claim that when Jesus says "the things **hereafter,**" he means "the things after the Church age ends." So that the word **"hereafter"** embraces 1900 years of the future. The word knows no such use in the Bible! The word "hereafter" means in the Bible what it means everywhere else — "after the here and now." You don't need that proven to you, do you? You pick up a concordance and see this for yourself. Jesus is saying to John, "Let me show you what is to develop from **this moment** onward." Now read 1:9 again and see what comes to you: This: "Write...the things which shall come to pass after the Church age," or this: "Write...the things which shall come to pass from this time on."

VERSES 2-11. There was a throne set in heaven - The throne of God is everywhere present in the book of Revelation. It is mentioned 38 times in the book. I guess that gives us a clue about its importance — right?! In the vision John manifestly sees a "piece of furniture." But we are right in concluding this simply speaks of the kingly authority of God. What he saw was **"a throne set in heaven."** Ultimately this is where all thrones are set. There is no power but of God. No one reigns except heaven decrees it. Nebuchadnezzar learned this lesson.

That God is enthroned in heaven, the Bible everywhere declares, but in apocalyptic speech there is a combining of **"heaven"** as a locality and as the dwelling place of the righteous. See the brief remarks on verse 1 above. As we go on we will see God is enthroned amidst the living creatures. In chapter 22:1-2 we will see his throne is in the midst of the new Jerusalem, the Church of God. In Ezekiel 43:6-7 we hear of God being enthroned in the temple, his house. Over and over again we read of God as enthroned above the Cherubim. (See Psalm 80:1; 99:1; 1 Samuel 4:4; 2 Samuel 6:2; Isaiah 37:16. Note the footnote of the ASV and the modern versions).

The throne of God is the **"reign of God."** It is his sovereign power. Yes, it's true that he is in heaven (the locality) but it is also true that the **"kingdom of God"** is within (Luke 17:21). He reigns and rules in his people — the heavenly Jerusalem.

In fact, this whole temple scene has the overall appearance of the tabernacle or temple of the Old Testament. In the tabernacle (and later, in the temple) we have God enthroned above the cherubim which were placed on the ark of the covenant. The living creatures in this chapter are the cherubim. We have the seven lamps which burn before the throne in this chapter and in the tabernacle we have the seven lamps which were kept burning before the holy of holies where God was enthroned above the cherubim. (See Exodus 25:37; 40:25) We have the 24 elders in this chapter and we have the 24 orders of priesthood in the temple of the Old Testament. (See 1 Chronicles 27:7-18 and Isaiah 43:28).

The throne was set **in heaven** to suggest the sovereignty of heaven over the kingdoms of men. The world, the saints are being told, is not ruled from Rome but from heaven where God dwells and the saints live. The throne is central! And so it should be. What else would you put at the center? Money? Prestige? Military might? "Man's ultimate hour cries for ultimate power. Only God is enough!"That's what the poet said — and that's right. The throne, as we subsequently learn, is in the midst of God's people. Ah this world needs to know there is in heaven a throne — not a doddering old "father time." Not a super Santa Claus, but an indestructible King.

And he that sat was to look upon like a jasper - There is as little anthropomorphism in the "description" as is possible. Anthropomorphism takes place when a writer attributes to his non-human subject human characteristics. We read of this process often in the scriptures. We read of God's eyes, ears, hands, and nostrils. This kind of literary device is often very valuable in bringing home to us God's interest in our affairs. It is used in numerous ways. There are those who ridicule Christians for speaking of God as "he" (and using other such anthropomorphic terms). I think sometimes this critcism has helped us to examine our speech and has resulted in much good. When we examine how we talk, we often gain much with regard to accuracy and clarity. Still, these who harp on our speech still load theirs with the same kind. We hear again and again what "Nature" has given us — how "Natural Selection" has helped us. Oh well. The occupant of the throne is the Father.

There was a rainbow round the throne - The symbol of a merciful God. The symbol of a covenant-keeping God. In the vision of Ezekiel 1, we have the terrifying picture of the Almighty advancing on his chariot to judge. The only mitigating element in the whole picture is the "bow." Thank God for the mercy. Thank God for the faithfulness which continues to extend mercy even though we don't deserve it.

And round about the throne were four and twenty thrones - Here is royalty in the presence of supreme royalty. Whatever these thrones are, they **are** thrones. And on these thrones sat "24 elders." Who are they? On Walvoord's "literal-unless-forced-to be-otherwise" view, they must surely be 24 elders. In chapter 11:3 the "two witnesses" **must** be "two witnesses." In chapter 7:4-8, the 144,000 out of the 12 tribes of Israel **must** be 144,000 out of the 12 tribes. In 9:16 and 16:12, the 2 billion soldiers from the east **must** be 2 billion soldiers from the east. In this place the 24 elders, are

are what? 24 elders? No sir, they are the Church. Can you beat that? And what of Lindsey? He's in the same league. He is amazed at the lengths some will go to figurize the book of Revelation. When people tell him the 144,000 Jews cannot be literally 144,000 Jews, he says "To all this sort of speculation I say,'"Why not?"' (page 120 of "New World Coming"). He then speculates on the 24 elders and says, "I personally believe that they are representatives of the Church." I'm amazed!

The "24 elders" are royal. They are dressed in white garments which are the righteous deeds of the overcoming saints (2:4,5; 19:8). They wear the crown of overcomers (stephanoi). They are 24 in number, which is the number of the courses of the priests in the Old Testament. See 1 Chronicles 24:7-18. They are priestly in their activity in respect to harping and offering up incense (5:8). We have in these the royal priesthood. This is the church of God. See 1 Peter 2:5,9, as well as Revelation 1:6; 5:9,10; 20:4,6. You say, why this is what Walvoord and Lindsey believe — why were you objecting to it? Simply to let you know that on their canons of interpretation, they have no right to make the "24 elders" figurative. And to let you know this school drops its canon of interpretation when it is to its advantage, while they scathe others for not adopting that canon.

The 24 elders are the royal priesthood. In Zechariah 6:9-15, we have the high priest brought before the assembly and crowned with a crown. He symbolized the coming Messiah who would combine in him both the priesthood and the kingly power. This Priest-King has as his followers those who offer themselves willingly "in holy array" (Psalm 110:3), that is, priestly garments. As their Master combines in himself royalty and priestly authority, so do the followers of Jesus. His is merited — theirs is derived. Derived, but real nevertheless! See further comment on 5:10.

And out of the throne proceed lightnings - Has thunder and lightning ever been anything else but a fearful exhibition of God's power to the guilty conscience? Throughout the Bible, thunder and lightning are associated with the manifestation of God's justice and wrath. Just glance at a concordance and see that this is true. To those who trust Him the same exhibition of power is thrilling, to say the least. We will have occasion to speak later about the words of the seven thunders, so it would be as well to settle now in your mind the place of thunder in the Bible.

And there were seven lamps of fire - In the Tabernacle, they kept the seven lamps burning in the holy place before the holy of holies. These were the lightgivers. Because of these, everything was visible. The seven lamps here represent the Holy Spirit. He is the Revealer. He makes the things clear. He also sees all (the seven eyes

5:6 suggest this). But the "lamps" here are not (at least in choice of words) the same as the "lamps" in chapter 1. The word occurs again in 8:10 and Milligan thinks it speaks more of a "torch." This may mean it introduces a judgmental aspect to the picture. Maybe so. Still, it is perhaps better understood as suggesting that he who rules has all the wisdom, knowledge, and vision of the omniscient Spirit as his disposal. Lindsey's point here is ludricrous. Read it.

A sea of glass like unto crystal - Whatever is the precise origin of the symbol, we must surely conclude that separation is being stressed. Since we truly have a tabernacle or temple scene here, it is best with Milligan to find the origin of the symbol in the "sea" of Solomon's temple (2 Chronicles 4:2-6). This sea stood between the priest and the holy place where God dwelt. That was separation (holiness).

Four living creatures full of eyes - These are the cherubim. They are the defenders of God's holiness. The vindicators of his honor. They are his chariot on which he rides to judgment. 1 Chronicles 28:18 calls them just that, the chariot. Psalm 18:10 speaks of God riding on a cherub. Ezekiel, chapters 1 and 10, speaks at length of the cherubim as God's war wagon. They stand between Adam and the way to the tree of life. They are woven into the veil which stands between all men and the presence of God. They are standing over the ark of the covenant, looking down toward the Law inside. The Law which was broken every minute of every day. And they would demand immediate justice were it not for the mercy seat which covered the transgressions because of the blood which was sprinkled there. I have discussed the cherubim with a little more detail in my little book on "Ezekiel" (The "Looking Into The Bible" Series).

However exalted these beings be, they are servants to God. However awe-inspiring, they are creatures. "Eyes" speak of sight. Multiple eyes speak of all-seeing ability. These beings are represented by the king of predators, the lion. The king of the airborne predators, the eagle. The powerful and full of fury bull-calf. The shrewdest of all God's earthly creation, man. The bestial aspect of these beings speaks of their fury, power, and relentless nature. The human aspect balances the bestial so that we don't have blind savagery at work when justice is wrought. See Matthew 24:28 and Luke 17:37 on the "eagle."

These creatures are the judge of all who enter the presence of God. The high priest couldn't enter the holy of holies and offer sacrifice to God unless he "passed" the cherubim — covered by the spotless blood of an innocent victim. No praise or prayer got to God except through them. They are endlessly concerned about God's reputation and the vindication of his character. They unendingly say, **"Holy, holy, holy."** I don't know why they have **six** wings. They have only four in Ezekiel. It need hardly be said that this description is not to be understood as saying there are beings in heaven who are literally built this way!

And when the living creatures shall give glory - And that's unendlingly. And as they do it the 24 elders fall down and worship the Father. They throw their crowns before his throne and profess only he is worthy of any glory. But since the living creatures without ceasing offer glory to the King, the elders would without ceasing be throwing their crowns at the feet of him who rules. Some have supposed the throwing down of the crowns was at some particular outburst of praise. Maybe. But that is an unnecessary hypothesis. The point being stressed (by a scene which would be difficult to picture literally) is unending worship by the creatures and the elders.

Worthy art thou our Lord - Well worth singing. We praise everything else under the sun. We couldn't do worse in praising God. We exult in our business acumen. We bask in the warmth of our intellect. We gaze adoringly at our achievements. We are like pigs eating the acorns and refusing to look up.

WOW GOD — The song of the elders is essentially one to a Creator. The stress is laid on the power of God and his sovereignty. It was by his power that they began and it was because he willed it they had existence ("were") conquerors. He is surrounded by staggering power. The power of the cherubim who see all the dangers and threats of the ungodly. The King has at his disposal the limitless wisdom and knowledge of the omniscient Spirit. 30

4:1-11

1 After these things I looked and behold a door
standing open in heaven and the first voice
which I had heard like the sound of a trumpet
speaking w/ me said Come up here and I will show
you what must take place after these things.
2 Immediately I was in the Spirit and behold
a throne was standing in heaven and One
sitting on the throne.
3 And He who was sitting was like a jasper stone
and a sardius in appearance; and there was a
rainbow around the throne like an emerald in
appearance
4 And around the throne were 24 thrones and upon
the thrones I was 24 elders sitting clothed in
white garments & golden crowns on their heads.
5 And from the throne proceed flashes of lightening &
sounds and peals of thunder. And there were 7
lamps of fire burning before the throne which are
the seven Spirits of God

6 And before the throne there was as it
were a sea of glass like crystal and in
the middle and around the throne four
living creatures full of eyes in front & behind
7 And the first creature was like a lion and the
second creature like a calf, and the third
creature had a face like that of a man
and the 4th creature was like a flying eagle
8 And the 4 living creatures, each one of them
having 6 wings are full of eyes around &
within and day & night they do not
cease to say
"Holy, holy, holy is the Lord God
the Almighty who was and who is
and who is to come."
9 And when the living creatures give glory & honor
and thanks to Him who sits on the
throne to Him who lives forever & ever
10 the 24 elders will fall down before Him
who sits on the throne and will worship
Him who lives forever & ever and will
cast their crowns before the throne, saying
11 "Worthy art Thou our Lord and
our God to receive glory and
honor and power for Thou
didst create all things and
because of Thy will they existed
and were created."

Chapter 5

1 And I saw in the right hand of Him who
sat on the throne a book written inside
and on the back, sealed up w/seven seals.
2 And I saw a strong angel proclaiming
w/a loud voice, "Who is worthy to open the
book and to break its seals?"
3 And no one in heaven or on the earth or
under the earth was able to open the book
or to look into the book.
4 And I began to weep greatly because no
one was found worthy to open the book
or to look into it;
5 and one of the elders said to me, "Stop
weeping; behold the Lion that is from
the tribe of Judah, the Root of David, has
overcome so as to open the book and its seven
seals.

10. Bc Jesus overcome as a human, He is worthy to open the scroles, the seals. - he died to redeem.

11. Bc He was slain & resurrected but also bc He purchased a people out of the earth and made them a K. and priests -- a holy nation

Questions on Chapter 5

3. Written all over
1 bc full will of God

13: new in ref to a great deliverance, greater than !! from Egypt

1. The Will of God for the immediate future

2. 7 seals - show it is perfectly sealed

1. What does the "sealed book" stand for?
2. What is the significance of "seals"? And why "seven"?
3. Why is it written within and on the back?
4. Does "seven" always have symbolic significance? No
5. What is involved in "opening" the book? Some one worthy & responsible for the people + for their destiny
6. Who is "under the earth"? prophets (the place of the dead dead)
7. What O. T. scripture suggests "The Lion of the tribe of Judah"? Gen. 49:9 Jacob's son Judah
8. What O. T. prophet suggests "the Root of David"? Isiah
9. What is being stressed when Christ's Davidic descent is mentioned? Jesus' humanity, becoming a human
10. What does Jesus' overcoming here involve? bc Jesus overcame He can open the seals bc He was resurrected + became a Kingdom + priests
11. Does "as though it had been slain" suggest mere appearance of death? No he was definitely slain
12. What do "seven horns" signify? perfection of power
13. What is a "new song"? see above
14. What O. T. reference does a "kingdom and priests" remind you of? Exodus 19:5-6
15. Is Israel now God's nation? No the new covenent [illegible]
16. Would "they shall reign upon the earth" prove saints do not now reign on earth? No,
17. Do you have a scripture to support your answer? Yes Rom 5:17
18. How do people usually "prove" saints are not now ruling on earth? bc it appears God is not in control. See on next page
19. What would that same argument prove concerning the Father? That He is not reigning
20. Why does prophetic speech often confuse us?

Establishing a Kingdom & priests redempted

all power in heaven & earth belongs to this 7-horned Lamb to fight Satan & Rome.

6 And I saw between the throne (w/ the 4 living creatures) and the elders a Lamb standing as if slain, having 7 horns and 7 eyes, which are the 7 Spirits of God, sent out into all the earth.

7 And He came, and He took it out of the right hand of Him who sat on the throne.

8 And when He had taken the book, the 4 living creatures and the 24 elders fell down before the Lamb, having each one a harp and golden bowls full of incense, which are the prayers of the saints.

9 And they sang a new song saying, "Worthy art Thou to take the book and to break its seals; for Thou wast slain and did purchase for God w/ Thy blood men from every tribe and tongue and people and nation.

Romans 5:17 (answer to question 17 on page 87)
For if by the trespass of one man (Adam)
death reigned thru that one man, how much
more will those who receive God's abundant
provision of grace and of the gift of righteousness
reign in life thru the one man Jesus Christ

Analysis of Chapter 5

I. The seven-sealed book: 1

II. The search for someone to loose the seals of the book: 2, 3

III. John's response at the failure of the search: 4

IV. The opener of the book brought forward: 5-7
- A. The assurance from the elder: 5
- B. The book-opener identified: 5, 6
- C. The taking of the book from the hand of the Ruler: 7

V. The worthiness of the book-opener acknowledged: 8-14
- A. The acknowledgment of the elders and the living creatures: 8-10
- B. The acknowledgment of innumberable angels: 11, 12
- C. The acknowledgment of all creation: 13, 14

10 and Thou hast made them to be a k. and priests
to our God, and they will reign upon the earth.
11 And I looked and I heard the voice of many
angels around the throne and the living
creatures and the elders; and the number
of them was myriads of myriads, and
thousands of thousands
12 saying w/a loud voice
"Worthy was the Lamb that was slain
to receive power and riches and wisdom
and might and honor and glory and blessing."
13 And every created thing which is in
heaven and on the earth and under
the earth and on the sea and all things
in them, I heard saying,
"To Him who sits on the throne and the
Lamb be blessing praise and honor and glory
and dominion forever and ever."
14 And the 4 living creatures kept saying
"Amen" and the elders fell down & worshiped.

Comments on Chapter 5

VERSE 1. A book written within and on the back - The contents of this book are revealed in the ensuing chapters. We don't have to guess what they are. The book contains the will of God for the immediate future. In it is written the terrors which lie ahead for the saints and the ungodly. In it is written the hurt, fear, and pressure to be experienced by the children of God. In it too, is the record of complete triumph. The triumph of the Church over her vicious oppressor — Satan in Rome!

It is written all over because it is the full will of God in this matter. Ezekiel sees a similar book in 2:8,9, but it is not to be understood as answering to this book (as against Kiddle). The book which answers to Ezekiel's is found in chapter 10.

It is sealed with seven seals. Thus it is perfectly sealed. Therefore we hear it is "**close** sealed." How the number "seven" came to speak of fullness, completeness, and unity is hard to say. I don't know if anyone knows, or will know. But this doesn't stop us from plainly recognizing that "seven" does indeed carry with it this lesson or message. We must recognize of course that "seven" is not always used in a symbolic way. There are literally scores of occasions where "seven" has no symbolic significance and merely records the number of days, wives, nations, men — or whatever — under consideration. And so we are not to go searching for symbolism where there is no indication that we should. This is where writings such as Revelation are different from the rest. In this book we expect an inner meaning in numbers. And so, the number seven is used constantly in apocalyptic writings, to signify completeness and fullness.

VERSES 2, 3. Who is worthy to open the book and to loose the seals? - Who the strong angel is seems to be of little consequence. We don't have enough information on him anyway. He asks who is "worthy" (not "able") to open the book. So it is not merely a question of "strength," but of worth. We are given the definite impression from this, and what follows, that the "opening" of the scroll involves more than simply revealing its contents. There is clearly involved a determinative function, that is, whoever opens it is responsible for the controlling and developing of what is to follow. The destinies of the people involved lie in the hands of whoever dares to step forward. No wonder John weeps.

And no one in the heaven, or on the earth, or under the earth -We are being introduced to the Lamb in this vision. Notice the vivid way in which it is happening. The all-important scroll. The challenge ringing forth. The waiting and the silence. The long drawn-out delay (?) which would give John time to think there was no one worthy to do it. The delay which would give the mightiest angel the opportunity to make his claim. This is why we have a **mighty** angel issuing the challenge. Since he issues it to all others, he himself does not feel worthy. If Samson had challenged the world (inside and out) to find someone able to do a certain feat, we would be impressed by the difficulty. In regard to this book: no angel, highest of the high though he; no living servant of God, however devoted and sacrificial he be; and no prophet of former days from under the earth (the place of the dead - Ephesians 4:9; Romans 10:7); no one...not one anywhere, could open the book!

VERSE 4. And I wept much, because no one was found worthy -The shortage of the worthy things or people in life ought to make all of us weep. The thought of millions rejecting the only worthy One ought to make us weep much. But a day is coming when there will be much weeping. Yes, and gnashing of teeth, and outer darkness.

John wants to know what is in store. He wishes for the assurance of the victory of the saints, not only for himself but that he might convey it to the rest of the "panting, huddled, little flock" against whom the Roman colossus had turned in the past, and would in the immediate future, turn again.

VERSES 5-7. Weep not; behold the Lion - Is there better advice than this for you and me? To constantly look on our troubles is to look in the wrong direction, I'm not being unrealistic. I know we must look at our troubles. I know whether we want to or not, we will. I'm saying there is nothing but foolishness in continually examining the problem without looking toward Jesus. And don't tell me I don't know what I'm taking about, for I see saints every day carrying their burdens — real burdens — burdens which drive a ploughshare right across their souls. But they look up. And in looking up, they find strength and consolation. Listen, lady, Jesus is alive. And if you and I believe just half of what we sing and pray, Christ must make a difference. We are to sorrow, but not as those who have no hope. Look, mister, Jesus lived your life and the book here tells me he **overcame.** "In the world ye have tribulation: but be of good cheer; I have overcome the world." (John 16:33)

The Lion of the tribe of Judah - When Jacob was blessing his sons he spoke of Judah as "A lion's whelp; from the prey my son, thou art gone up: he stooped down, he crouched as a lion, and as a lioness; who shall rouse him up?" (Genesis 49:9). In the next verse he prophesies concerning Jesus as the Lawgiver and King. This is where the Lion that is of the tribe of Judah comes from.

The Root of David, - The allusion is clearly to Isaiah 11:1, 10.

There Jesse is named. Here, Jesse's more illustrious son, David, is named. Christ was of the tribe of Judah (Hebrews 7:14) and of the family of David (Romans 1:3). Jesus' relationship with David is mentioned again in 22:16. He claims to have the authority over the house of David in 3:7. It is the humanity of Jesus which is being stressed when we hear of his descent from David. In Romans 1:3, 4, we have his humanity and divinity stressed when we hear that he was "of the seed of David according to the flesh (his humanity), who was declared to be the Son of God with power, according to the spirit of holiness (his divinity), by the resurrection from the dead."

Hath overcome to open the book - Overcoming is here viewed as necessary to the opening of the book. In verse 9, we are told he is worthy because he died to redeem. We must therefore conclude that the "overcoming" involves the redeeming work of Jesus. Since he was resurrected for our justification (Romans 4:25) we must understand the redeeming work of Christ includes his resurrection.

This is in keeping with the context here, since we immediately hear of a slain Lamb who is alive and well. But it wasn't simply the dying and resurrection of Jesus which are embraced in his "overcoming." He also purchased a people out of the earth and made them to be a kingdom and priests - in short a holy nation. Against all the rebellion of sinful man, Jesus by dying and living again created a kingdom. (Does this not give assurance that if he overcame to create a kingdom, he could sustain the kingdom?)

And I saw in the midst of the throne - The Lamb moves in the midst of the throne and the Lamb moves in the midst of the 7 golden candlesticks. Doesn't this suggest to us once more where the throne is located? In the midst of the throne is a Lamb which was slain. Thank God for that! The central thrust of God's dominion is one careered by loving sacrifice. If the heart that broke at Calvary is the heart which rules the world, what have the saints to fear?

A Lamb standing as though it had been slain - There is no suggestion here of the **mere appearance** of having been slain. "Although" it had been slain does not mean it was only make believe or only had that appearance. Indeed not. In verse 9, we hear the positive assertion "thou wast slain." It had the appearance of having been slain because it had been slain. The NEB renders it "with the marks of slaughter upon him." Now the affirmation is being made that the Lamb had indeed been slain; but the implication clearly is — when John sees him, he is alive. We have implicit in the text, a resurrection. **"Having seven horns,"** speaks of perfection of power. We have saints about to be slain. We have a once-slain Lamb. We have saints who need to be encouraged in the conflict. We have a Lamb which came into head-on conflict with the power with which the saints must struggle. He whipped them and was raised to God's right hand far above Rome. "All power in heaven and earth" belongs to this 7-horned Lamb. And furthermore, he has the perfection of wisdom and knowledge which comes from the all-knowing Holy Spirit. Read now 2 Chronicles 16:9. Go ahead! In these seven eyes we have the thought of vigilance on God's part. Better still, let me cite the passage for you: "Because thou didst rely on Jehovah, he delivered them into thy hand. For the eyes of Jehovah run to and fro throughout the whole earth, to show himself strong in the behalf of them whose heart is perfect toward him..." (verses 8b, 9).

And when he had taken the book - Acceptable worship, scrutinized by the living creatures and offered by the elders, arises to Jesus. Whatever the living creatures are - you can rest assured they are not the saints. Though they are having something to do with the harps (praise) and bowls of incense (prayers of the saints) it is certain they are not praying the prayers. The creatures and the elders sing a "new" song.

VERSES 8-14. And they sing a new song - The last song sung (4-11) was in regard to God as Creator. This new song has reference to redemption. It might be "new" with regard to the other song, but it is more likely that it is new in regard to the song of Moses (see 15:3). When God delivered Israel through the Red Sea, Moses sang a song (Exodus 15). A song often embodied the wonderful deliverances wrought by God and the goodness he had shown to his people (see this all over the Old Testament). A "new song" was another song of a "new" expression of God's care and love. In Isaiah 42:8,9, we hear God saying, "The former things are come to pass, and new things do I declare...Sing unto Jehovah a new song ..." In 43:18,19, he orders, "Remember ye not the former things, neither consider the things of old. Behold I will do a new thing...I will even make a way in the wilderness, and rivers in the desert..."

In the Egyptian deliverance they had been brought through the terrible wilderness. True, they were sustained but it was a hard way they came. God is telling them, "The future deliverance will be even greater than that. I will make the wilderness, no longer a wilderness." He is going to out-do himself. They are to forget the former great deliverance in light of this coming new deliverance. They had occasion to praise him in song about the deliverance out of Egypt. This they had been doing for years. They would have occasion to sing a new song concerning a greater deliverance. Thus, the "new song" in Revelation seems clearly to be set in contrast to the deliverance under Moses. Be sure to read 14:3 and 15:3 together.

Thou wast slain and didst purchase unto God - The saints have been purchased "unto God." They belong to him! The blood which purchased them was "royal" blood. Let no one be so base as to despise it. It was a "brother's" blood. Let no one be so uncaring as to minimize it. It was "innocent" blood. Let no one be such a fool as to deny it. It was "substitutionary" blood. Let no one be so proud as to refuse it. It was "efficacious" blood. Let no one be so doubtful as to not rely on it. It was "sufficient" blood. Let no one be so isolated as to feel he is not included in its offer.

And madest them to be...a kingdom and priests - The allusion in the passage is clearly to Exodus 19:5,6. The Church of God is a nation unto God. Arno C. Gaebelein claims the Church is nowhere called a nation. Hard to believe isn't it?! 1 Peter 2:9. The Church of God is called a "peculiar people" (a people for God's own possession), just as was Israel. The Church of God is called a kingdom (in this passage and others), so was Israel. Israel has now no priesthood. They have now no national covenant. They are not God's nation! The kingdom was taken from the nation of Israel with whom it had been associated and was given to "a nation" constituted of believing Jews and believing Gentiles (see Matthew 21:43). Lord willing, I hope to have a little book out on "The Kingdom of God." It's really a very interesting study.

And they reign upon the earth - Depending upon which text is followed we have either (as above)) the ASV rendering or "they shall reign upon the earth." Most of the modern versions give "shall reign." This may be right. In any case we are not to deny the present reigning of the saints in Christ. See our former comments in this in regard to 2:26,27. It cannot be said too often - appearances don't prove the saints are not now reigning. Appearances don't prove Jesus isn't reigning. The same appearances "prove" to the sceptic there is no God in control of the world. The same appearances "prove" to the drowning Christian that God doesn't care. The saints are reigning now!

What if the future tense of the passage is correct? Doesn't that prove the saints are not now reigning? Of course not. In 20:6, we hear of the saints participating in the "first resurrection" and of them it is said "they shall be priests of God..." Does that mean they weren't already priests? Indeed not. It is simply John's way of assuring the Christians that their relationship with Jesus cannot be severed by death or persecution. See comments on the promises to

Hebs 1:3 He is the radiance of His glory and the exact representation of His nature and upholds all things by the Word of His power

The Message: He holds everything together by what He says — powerful words

the overcomers, which illustrate this point further. And note too the comments on 11:15,16, when we hear of God "taking" his "great power" and ruling at the fall of the great city. See the comments there.

So then, in view of the coming struggle against Rome, the word goes out that the saints "reign" (or "shall reign") on the earth. It's no secret what Rome claimed. It's no secret either what Rome in Domitian and his successors did to the brotherhood. Neverless, the saints do rule! When the conflict is over, the Church will be the only kingdom standing. In rising-up and slaying Domitian (who claimed he was God), God defeated Rome. In his ultimate removal of that kingdom, he defeated Rome. There is but one eternal kingdom, and it was bought by the blood of the Lamb, the supreme Overcomer.

And I heard the voice of many angels - The living creatures and the elders gave forth their praise and now the angelic hosts give forth. However exalted they be — they worship the Lamb, He, who for a little while was made lower than the angels, now hears the angels willingly obey the scriptural injunction "Let all the angles of God worship him!"

And every created thing - Here is universal acknowledgement. Does this passage mean that everyone in the world in that day knew Jesus? That everyone knew and acknowledged his authority and worth? Indeed not. But the whole of creation reflects the worth and power of Jesus. It is by his word that all things hold together (Hebrews 1:3). See Isaiah 26:9; 41:5; 62:11; Psalm 2:1,2 (and too many others to list) for examples of scriptures where the prophets' words suggest something to our western mind that they wouldn't suggest to us if we were more acquainted with prophetic speech. See especially Psalm 98:2,3 and Isaiah 52:10. Read Psalm 2:1,2 and Acts 4:25-28. See if just the very wording of Psalm 2:1,2 does not seem too grand for the fulfillment Peter claims. The problem lies with us — we do not read principles, we read numbers. We do not grasp moral signifiance; we harp on the literal wording. We see brush strokes when we ought to be seeing portraits.

What then do we have in chapter 5? We have the complement to chapter 4. That saints are urged to rest assured that whatever they see hereafter — all is well, for the world is under the control of the Creator (Father, in this case) and the all-powerful, all-wise Lamb. To these and these alone must worship be directed. Emperor worship is out of place in light of such revelation. Uncontrolled fear or panic is out of place in light of such power. We have in the two chapters, "Believe in God, believe also in me!"

Questions on Chapter 6

1. Why does chapter 6, in a way, sum up the bulk of the rest of the book?
2. What purpose do seals serve?
3. What then is signified by removing them?
4. How many translators agree with Lindsey in rendering "come" as "go"?
5. How many individual white horses are mentioned in the book?
6. Who rides the white horses **not** mentioned in this chapter?
7. Is the color "white" used of anything evil in the book of Revelation?
8. What then of the idea that the first seal speaks of the Antichrist?
9. Who defeated Rome at Carrhae in 53 B.C.?
10. Upon whom is the figure of the first seal modeled?
11. Why is the first seal, the "first" seal?
12. How much proof does Walvoord offer for his belief that the Antichrist is the subject of the first seal? And how much does Lindsey offer?
13. Does the rule of Jesus ever bring strife and hardship? Have you a passage?
14. Do millennialists believe there will be war during and after the millennium?
15. What is the significance of the second seal?
16. Should we maintain a hard and fast distinction between the two words for "sword" in the New Testament?
17. Does similarity of speech prove identity of subject?
18. What could we do with graffiti on the walls in ancient Greece and Rome?
19. Why do you think that is?
20. What does Lindsey confess about his "Late Great Planet Earth"?
21. What does Walvoord confess in his "Armageddon"?
22. What is the significance of the third seal?
23. How much was a "shilling" (or a "penny")?
24. Not hurting the oil and wine, speaks of what?
25. What color is the next horse?
26. Who are the rider and his companion?
27. What ills come under the heading of the fourth horse (seal)?
28. What does Walvoord say of "beasts"? What does Lindsey say?
29. Which O.T. prophet speaks of God's "four sore judgments"?

3 And when He broke the second seal, I heard
the second living creature saying, "Come."
4 And another, a red horse went out, and
to him who sat on it, it was granted to
take peace from the earth, and that men
should ~~slay one another and a great sword~~ was
given to him.

30. Since two of them come under the heading of the fourth seal, what of the other 2? second & third seals contain others
31. How many does Lindsey say are to die of famine, etc., prior to about 1988? 1/4 th of earth's population = 1 billion people
32. What is the subject of the fifth seal? slain souls for Christ
33. Are they pre-Christian era believers? NO
34. How long would it be before they were vindicated? when time ended by God & others slain for Christ & persecution dealt w/ by God
35. With what does the sixth seal deal? judgment by God
36. Whose world perished in Noah's day? ungodly
37. Lindsey says the "stars of the heaven" are Russian bombs — why can't this be so? see p 107
38. Does Walvoord go into any detail at all concerning the elements of judgement here? NONE
39. Does the Old Testament give us reason to understand this section figuratively? Yes Egyptians, Sodom & Gomorah
40. Does commonsense require that we understand it figuratively? Yes
41. If this section is figurative — what **possibility** does this open to us? God judges & handles ungodly world, vindicates Christians
42. To whom does Isaiah 13 address itself? ungodly world
43. Who in Isaiah 13:17 is said to destroy the subject of Isaiah 13? GOD
44. If that passage is still to be fulfilled — who must arise again? ungodly
45. This judgment — whose wrath does it manifest? the wrath of the Lamb
46. What question does the chapter close with? who can stand against the wrath of the Lamb

5 And when He broke the 3rd seal I heard
the 3rd living creature saying, "Come." And
I looked and behold a black horse and he
who sat on it had a pair of scales in his
hand
6 and I heard as it were a voice in the
center of the four living creatures saying
"A quart of wheat for a denarius and
three quarts of barley for a denarius; and
do not harm the oil and the wine.
7 And when He broke the 4th seal I heard the
voice of the 4th living creature saying, "Come."
8 And I looked and behold an ashen horse,
and he who sat on it had the name "Death"
and Hades was following w/ him. And
authority was given to them over a 4th
of the earth to kill w/ sword and famine
and w/ pestilence and by the wild beasts
of the earth.

9 And when He broke the 5th seal I saw underneath the altar the souls of those who had been slain because of the word of God and because of the testimony which they had maintained;

Analysis of Chapter 6

I. The first seal: 1,2
II. The second seal: 3,4
III. The third seal: 5,6
IV. The fourth seal: 7,8
V. The fifth seal: 9-11
VI. The sixth seal: 12-17

Introduction to Chapter 6

Chapter 6 is really the beginning of the end of the book. The bulk of the book is summed up in the seventh seal, which contains the seven trumpets, which in turn contain the seven bowls. You've heard the three-point outline sermons we preachers often preach, right? Under the major heading we usually have several sub-headings. That's how it is with Revelation. It looks something like this:

I. Seal One
II. Seal Two
III. Seal Three
IV. Seal Four
V. Seal Five
VI. Seal Six
VII. Seal Seven
    A. Trumpet One
    B. Trumpet Two
    C. Trumpet Three
    D. Trumpet Four
    E. Trumpet Five
    F. Trumpet Six
    G. Trumpet Seven

Warnings

        1. Bowl One
        2. Bowl Two
        3. Bowl Three
        4. Bowl Four
        5. Bowl Five
        6. Bowl Six
        7. Bowl Seven

punishment

10 and they cried out w/a loud voice saying "How long O Lord, holy and true will You refrain from judging and avenging our blood on those who dwell on the earth."

11 And there was given to each of them a white
robe and they were told that they should
rest for a little longer until the number
of their fellow-servants and their brethren
who were to be killed even as they had
been should be completed also.

There are regular deviations form the pattern in order to bring comfort and assurance, but the pattern of the book is laid out above. As you can see, the seventh seal contains the seven trumpets, and the seventh trumpet contains the seven bowls.

2

"Seals" are for keeping things closed and hidden. To rip-off a seal is to uncover and reveal. The ripping-off of the seals reveals what is to come to pass. Picture to yourself this sealed scroll. When a seal is ripped-off, a part of the scroll falls back and you can read 3
something on it. This is sort of what happens when the seals are removed. As each one is removed, more is revealed. Until finally, the whole message is disclosed. Remember, removing the seals is not **mere** disclosure. See remarks on 5:2,5. -GOD CONTROLS EVERY JESUS THE LION

He who opens seals is in control of what is revealed!

12 And I looked when He broke the 6th seal
and there was a great earthquake and
the sun became black as sackcloth
made of hair and the whole moon became
like blood;
13 and the stars of the sky fell to the
earth as a fig tree casts its unripe figs
when shaken by a great wind.
14 And the sky was split apart like a
scroll when it is rolled up; and
every mtn and island were moved
out of their places.
15 And the kings of the earth and the
great men and the commanders and
the rich and the strong and every
slave and free man hid themselves
in the caves and among the rocks of
the mountains;
16 and they said to the mtns and the
rocks, "Fall on us and hide us
from the presence of Him who sits on
the throne and from the wrath of the
Lamb;
17 for the great day of their wrath has
come and who is able to stand?"

Comments on Chapter 6

VERSES 1,2. When the Lamb opened one of the seven seals - Only the Lamb is permitted to do so, since only he is worthy. **"A voice of thunder"** is the voice of one of these executors of God's justice. "Thunder" is always associated with judgment and sober tidings. "Come" means "come," and not "go," as Lindsey suggests. No translator agrees with him on the matter.

Behold, a white horse - There is only one other white horse in the book which is singled out. It is the horse on which Jesus rides (19:11). There are other white horses, but none are singled out. Summers thinks it objectionable for the Lamb to rip-off the seal and then, as it were, change costume and become the rider on the white horse. For this reason he rejects the rider as Jesus. That is a reason? Yet he sees nothing strange in a Lamb taking a book and ripping-off seals. Does the Lamb hold the book in its feet and rip them off with his teeth? This is a book of symbols. All such difficulties are really no difficulties at all.

The rider on the white horse is Jesus. He opens the whole affair because he is in control of the whole affair. It is also written to comfort the saints. Whatever follows this rider should be of no lasting concern — the Lamb is a conqueror. That being so, we are "more than conquerors" through him that loves us (Romans 8:37).

Jesus, in this passage, wears the crown of a conqueror. Not the crown of royalty, as in 19:12. In 19:12, his character and nature are stressed, but in this passage his overcoming work is stressed. The white horse speaks of victory. The picture is plain. Here is the image of a Parthian warrior. Coins depicting Parthian victors in just this fashion are common — astride a horse, with crown and bow. Jesus is here depicted as the enemy of Rome. The Parthian image is an apt one. In the battle of Carrhae (53 B.C.) 20,000 Romans died and 10,000 were taken captive by the Parthians. Rome never forgot that the Parthian was considered a fearful opponent.

Lindsey and Walvoord think this rider is the Antichrist who is about to arise (Whom Lindsey thinks is already living somewhere in Europe). Will you believe me if I tell you that Walvoord doesn't offer a single point in proof of his position? He "proves" it couldn't be Jesus because it wouldn't fit in with his "tribulation" theory. He quotes Peake to "prove" it couldn't be Jesus because he would have to obey his own command to "come." He quotes Jennings to "prove" it couldn't be Jesus because the rule of Jesus doesn't bring famine, war, and strife in his train. He concedes he can't settle the question as to the identity of the rider, but he does firmly hold it to be the Antichrist. He doesn't, however, give a single point in proof of it! And what **argument** does Lindsey offer? Absolutely none!

What's wrong with the Antichrist view? There's nothing for it! Isn't it very strange that both these prominent leaders in this movement give us absolutely nothing in proof of this position? Linsdey asserts it and makes no attempt to prove it. Walvoord does likewise, and half apologizes for accepting the view since it can't be settled. So there's nothing for it.

Furthermore, though "white" is used outside Revelation for evil men and objects — it is not so used in Revelation. The word (from two Greek words) occurs 16 times and at no time, in the other 15, does it **not** carry with it moral overtones. The color has moral significance. **It is never used in the book of anything evil.** We have white garments of the elders and saints; a white stone belonging to the saints; a white throne on which God sits; white horses on which the saints ride; a white horse on which Jesus sits and then we have the white horse of this passage. Now, in light of how the book uses the color, what do you think of the rider on the white horse? The book does not associate white with anything or anyone such as this blasphemous scroundrel is supposed to be! Away with the notion which has no support offered for it and which is so obviously in conflict with the pattern of the book.

That Jesus is the rider we have **argued**. What has been set against it? He couldn't answer his own command (through the living creature) to "Come"! This is little short of ludicrous. Why couldn't he? Strife and famine do not follow in the train of Jesus, Jennings said. And where does the chapter say that the first rider is the **cause** of the following seals? Even Walvoord, Jennings and Lindsey believe there will be war in, and following, the millennium — would that mean Jesus was the cause of it? Besides, did Jesus promise a rose garden to his followers in Matthew 10:34ff? Does the Psalmist not say Jesus would "rule" in "the midst of" his "enemies" and "fill" the places with dead bodies" (110:2,5,6)? What nonsense this all is — Antichrist indeed!

What of the view that the four horses are one unit speaking of the forces of punishment? At least this has a semblance of reason. Four horses are a unit in Zechariah and the four winds in Revelation are a unit. I'm not sure that this can't be reconciled with the identification of the first rider with Jesus. I'd say that going forth to conquer involved some punishment somewhere along the line.

Besides, while John does make extensive use of Old Testament symbols, he doesn't always use them in the way the Old Testament does. I think too, we will have reason to see that the first rider can't symbolize "war" as we usually speak of it, since the 2nd seal evidently speaks of that. The rider on the first horse is holy! Or at least the cause is holy. I think that this is the least we can learn. The other points, for me, carry the conclusion that the rider is Jesus. He is placed where he is to show that righteousness triumphs; that he is in control; that no matter how it looks, everything is subject to him. At least this is the story of the whole book! Only one other horse is singled-out in the book (ie, a white horse) — Jesus rides it. The color white is used 16 times and 15 of them are way beyond dispute applying to something holy and pure. Jesus has declared himself already, several times, to be the conqueror and overcomer. In him we are "more than conquerors." The thrust of the whole book is that very theme — the saints conquer because Jesus rides at their head. The conclusion? Jesus is the rider of the white horse.

VERSES 3,4. And another horse came forth, a red horse - the red horse is war. To distinguish him from the first, those who have indentified the first horse as war, make the red horse represent **civil** war. I don't know anything conclusive against this, but I will make mention of it under the fourth seal.

"To take peace from the earth," clearly marks out this horse and rider as "war." This is further evidenced by the abrupt introduction of "they." That "they" (they who?) should slay one another. Manifestly these are the people on earth between whom wars take place. **"A great sword,"** speaks again of the warlike business this horseman is on. There is much made of the difference between "Rhomphia" and "Machaira" (the two words for sword); but I'm not sure that the New Testament use warrants us to make a hard and fast distinction. The latter word is said (eg. by Hendriksen) to be only the sacrificial sword; but I doubt if you will come to that conclusion if you check the use of the word as reflected in the Englishman's Greek Concordance. The Philippian jailer carried a "machaira" and Peter was told "they that take the sword (machaira) shall parish with the sword (machaira)." Jerusalem was to fall by the same sword. Check it for yourself. It looks to me that they are used interchangeably.

I need no more than say that such war as was to come would seriously affect the welfare of the people of God. Walvoord and his company parallel this seal with the words of Jesus concerning war and rumors of wars and claim **therefore**: both passages speak of the same thing, and both passages therefore speak of a future time of trouble such as the world has never seen. I must confess this is the poorest kind of exegesis possible. We can't learn it too well or too soon — similarity of speech does not prove identity of subject.

I've said it already and will say it again, a man can re-write past history in the terms of today and you wouldn't know it was ancient history. From the graffiti of ancient Greece and Rome, you could write a moral treatise of today's ills. This is not exegesis — it's playing at exegesis. Anyone can piece scriptures together.

Lindsey confesses in his "Late Great Planet Earth" (page 43), that his picture of future events is made up of prophecies "pieced together to make a coherent picture, even though the pieces are scattered in small bits throughout the Old and New Testaments." Walvoord confesses in his "Armageddon" (page 19), that the prophecies are "intricately interwoven." And what happens when the passage in the prophets is quoted as fulfilled in the New Testament? You do what Erich Sauer does, you claim that that fulfillment is a shadow of a coming fulfillment. And what if the prophetic passage can be clearly shown to have had refernce to an event long gone? You do what Lindsey does; you confess to the "Bible students" that it has a past fulfillment but its greater fulfillment is yet future — but you don't quote scripture for the future fulfillment (op. cit., page 78). What do you think of exegetes, who, without contextual reason, hold Psalm 110:1 applies to Pentecost onward but 110:2 refers to the still future; who hold that 110:4 refers to Pentecost onward, but 110:3,5-7 refers to the yet future? Walvoord, Lindsey, Ironside, Jennings, and the whole school of dispensationalists do this.

VERSES 5,6. And behold a black horse - Here is famine and economic hardship. The rider holds a balance with which to weigh food. Once you read of measuring out food, you know hardhip in regard to food is under consideration — right? Ezekiel 4:10 and 16, among a great number of others, gives us the picture.

A "shilling" was a full day's wages. The householder in Matthew 20 agreed with his laborers for that amount per day. So a man had to work all day just to buy the necessary food. **"The oil and the wine hurt thou not."** This may well mean the rich were, to some degree, insulated against this time. But I don't think that's the point. The fact that there is food to be measured and sold tells us the famine is real but not extreme, at least, not yet. The "famine-horse" is told not to do **too** much. Remember this is a "seal" and not a "bowl."

VERSES 7,8. And behold a pale horse - The rider on this horse is "Death." Running behind (I can almost see him limping and dragging one of his twisted limbs), in ghoulish fashion, is Hades (personified also, as is Death). Both of these in Revelation are regarded as defeated enemies. This being true, they would have to submit to any service the Lamb would lay on them.

A "pale" (Chloros) horse is a "yellowy-green" horse. In early grass this is fine — in a living thing, sickening. On to the stage it stomps with its rider and associate, summing up the previous terrors in itself.

Unto them was given the power to smite one-fourth of the world. Lindsey is consistent and says this means about 1 BILLION people. Since he believes the whole thing is to be wound up by the coming of Jesus around 1988 — 1 BILLION people are to die of famine and pestilence before 1988.

In Ezekiel 14:12-23, we read of God's four sore judgments. They are sword, famine, pestilence, and wild beasts. (I notice Lindsey had no "explanation" of the beasts — in fact, no comment at all. And Walvoord? Nothing, of course.) The chapter in Ezekiel is given to prove to Ezekiel that God is driven, in justice, to punish his people (see verse 21-23). He asks, in essence, what do you know if I send a famine, or an army, or pestilence, or wild beasts on a land? Ezekiel must admit, "They must have deserved it." And what, says God, "If I send my four sore judgments on it?" The answer is, "They must really have gone way too far."

The fourth horse and rider gather together the four sore judgments of God. Note: "war," "famine," "pestilence," and "wild beasts." There is no horse for "beasts of the earth." He is brought in under the fourth horse, who also stands for pestilence. So under the fourth horse we have pestilence and beasts. That leaves war and famine. The third horse is definitely the famine-hardship-horse — where then is the "war-horse"? In the second, of course. I think this helps us to differentiate between the first horse and the second. And in regard to the second horse standing for civil war: since the second horse is one of the four sore judgments, I think we should disregard civil war. I know of no passage where civil war is used as one of the four sore judgments. All such passages speak of an invading force. Do you know of one? Perhaps there is - I must confess I just don't know of it.

From Ezekiel 14 we can see that God had a standard way of punishing those who needed it. So that you could go through history and see this again and again and again. Would these be signs of the times? Ah, but we are told, 1 BILLION are to die here! — has that ever happened? Not that I know of. But are we to understand these figures as literal and lying yet in the future? God lives, I've seen nothing which makes it clear that we should so believe. The punishment of a fraction is to point out we don't have a final and complete judgment. See this in regard to the trumpets and bowls. The dispensationalists literalize when they wish and figurize when they need to. In chapter 14:20 we have a river of blood 200 miles long and about 5 feet deep. Walvoord takes a look and figurizes. Lindsey looks and measures from Elath to Armageddon and literalizes. A friend and colleague of mine worked out how many dead would be required to produce such a river of blood — over 3.6 billion. Lindsey has forgotten to remember that he has over 2 billion already slain just in famine and by the 200 million "Reds." Walvoord is not sure the 200 million is a literal figure. Lindsey thinks "clouds" in chapter 1 are people. Both of them hold "10 days" are not days (or 10) in chapter 2.

VERSES 9-11. He opened the fifth seal . . . the souls of them that had been slain - These are martyrs for truth. They had died "for the word of God, and **for the testimony which they held.**" This last phrase is worth a word or two. It's usual when speaking of Christians for John to speak of the "testimony of Jesus" as their testimony. See 1:2; 12:17; 14:12; 19:10. Here we have just "the testimony which they held." Milligan has construed this to mean these martyrs are Jewish martyrs — prior to the work of Christ. What he has to say is interesting (as is almost everything Milligan has to say), but not at all conclusive. Think about it — consult Milligan and draw your own conclusion. There is reason to believe the seals look forward, but there is none to believe they look backward, which is what Milligan requires.

This fifth seal speaks of persecution of the saints. These saints are slain for the testimony they held. I think we are compelled to think of the persecution as yet future to John. The martyrs would thus be Christians. Revelation shows no indication of believers prior to Jesus as being under discussion. Perhaps this is the one passage. The rest of the book deals with Christians — we should view these martyrs as Christians also. **"Master"** fits well with Jesus.

"The souls of them that had been slain," would be hard to envision. And yet when the disciples saw Jesus walking on the water toward them, they thought it was his spirit; so a spirit must have been conceived as having a man-like form — right?! John may well then have seen human-shaped souls around the altar. Is it unreasonable to think he may have seen pools of blood around the altar? Since it is a sacrificial picture, and since the life is in the blood, perhaps he saw blood. The Hebrew writer speaks of the blood of Jesus and Abel, speaking! But see below, on verse 11.

How long...dost thou not judge and avenge our blood...? There is a call here for retribution. Not vindictiveness, but retribution. It is not always spite which calls for the wicked to "get what they deserve." Of Alexander, the coppersmith, who had done Paul much evil, the apostle said, "The Lord reward him according to his works." Paul wanted God to settle with Alexander, but there was no spite involved. We need not apologize for these martyrs.

Rest yet for a little time - They were overcomers. They were given white robes (see 3:4; 19:8). They were told to rest a while for vindication was coming. This wasn't written for a potential martyr so much as it was written for the living saint. If martyrdom was to take place, there would still be vindication. The end is not death. Should the enemy succeed in slaying the righteous, his voice rises even beyond the veil, against his murderers. Since they are given white robes, it would seem clear that John, in vision, saw human forms. Still a change in the structure of the visions is not unusual, so he might first have seen pools of blood and then to suit the figure the form of the vision changes from blood to human forms. Walvoord thinks their receiving white robes means they must have bodies of some sort. I suppose this must mean he believes they receive literal clothing.

Until their fellow-servants...have fulfilled their course -There were others who would be martyred for Jesus. Until they had fulfilled their course (ie. faithfully fulfilled their task for the Lord) there would be no move toward vindication of the saints. The point is, God had something in mind. That scheme would have to be carried out. It involved the using of the enemy in the persecuting of the saints. When that was accomplished, God would repay the enemy. Until that was accomplished, the enemy would prosper.

The enemy, as we'll see, was given a position of power over the saints that would be held until God was through with him. In Isaiah 33:1 God speaks the same thing concerning Assyria. When you have finished destroying, He said, I will destroy you! In Daniel 11:36b,45 He speaks the same concerning the Roman empire. That king (Rome — the king of the north) would prosper until the indignation be accomplished, for "that which is determined," (by God, of course) "shall be done." Still, when it comes the time of Rome, "He shall come to his end, and none shall help him."

The servants of Jesus have a course to "fulfill." How many live for nothing?! How many a man on the battlefield has held a dying friend, a weeping, dying friend? And how many of those dying who wept, wept not because they were dying, but because they didn't know why they ever lived. Without Christ, there is no purpose. There is nothing to "fulfill." We're going nowhere. H.J. Blackham, once chairman of the British Humanist Society, confessed that the worst criticism which could be levelled against Humanism was "It's too bad to be true!" With man the measure of all things, there is no God; there is no Biblical Jesus; and there is no purpose. Life is pointless! There are two important days in a man's life, someone said. The first, the day he was born and the second, the day he learns **why** he was born. Without the Father and the Jesus of the Bible, there is no "why." Christians **have** a course to "fulfill." It's almost too good to be true!

VERSES 12-17. And when he opened the sixth seal...a great earthquake - Whatever this seal indicates, it speaks of the wrath of the Lamb (verse 16). Here is a judgment on the ungodly. It is not the end of time. It is, as Roberts has said, "a mosaic" of Old Testament scriptures. The language of judgment is ever similar. Whether the judgment be on Assyria, Egypt, Edom or Judah. There is a combining of phrases from former judgments. There is often burning fire and brimstone (as in Isaiah 34); the blacking-out of the sunlight as in the judgment on Egypt; the staggering of the earth and the mountains as on Judah, related in Jeremiah 4:23-25; the removing of the heavens as in the judgment on Edom (Isaiah 34:4-6). But this is characteristic of the prophets. Use is made of past historical judgments on people such as the Egyptians or Sodom and Gomorrah. Earthquakes are called in as elements of judgment even as God historically used them in the days of Jonathan. The manifestation of God at Sinai caused a literal trembling of the mountain and the surrounding area. This becomes the way to speak of God when he manifests himself in holiness (see Micah 1:3-6 and Amos 4:13). Look for yourself at passages such as Zephaniah 1:2-4, and see if you think these were literally fulfilled. See God's description of the fall of Babylon in Isaiah 13:6-13, 17-22, and be sure to read his description of the judgment on Edom in Isaiah 34:1-end. Well, go ahead. Judge for yourself.

Listen, when the ungodly become dominant and oppressive, the world is said to be theirs. Peter says it was the "world of the ungodly" that perished in the flood (2 Peter 2:5). Daniel claims Nebuchadnezzar not only rules the men in the world, and the property wherever men dwell, but the beasts of the field and the very birds of the heavens. When God attacks him, it is an attack on the world (see Isaiah 13:1,11). God attacks **his** world — he dismantles his skies, shakes his earth to pieces, blacks out his suns, etc. He literally attacked the world of the Egyptian. In his prophecy that he would destroy Babylon by the Medes, God uses the language mentioned above. Did he literally fulfill it? Of course not — Babylon and the Medes are long gone. Unless both are to be resurrected to literally fulfill these things — commonsense tells you this is figurative speech. So it is in the seal under consideration.

The seals have been revealing what is ahead. This seal reveals judgment ahead. Judgment, from which we will see, the saints are exempt. Judgment on those who have reason to fear the wrath of the Lamb. Lindsey attempts to literalize here. He makes "stars" into "meteorites" and then "meteorites" into Russian nuclear missiles. Don't you tire of this? The passage speaks of "the stars of the heaven," not stars falling from heaven. These "stars" are "of the heaven." They are stars. This is the same word as used over and over again in the N.T. and there is not even one case where "meteorite" can be shown to be meant. I'm not even sure if the word itself is ever applied to a "meteorite." Try moving every mountain on earth out of its place without killing millions and then add to that every island being so moved. Then remove the sky, and see how many "mighty men" are left to run looking for a cave. And all this remember, is to happen prior to 1988.

Walvoord is shrewder than Lindsey in this place. He asserts the literal understanding, but doesn't descend to dealing with any details at all. Lindsey asserts the literal and then proceeds to figurize it, claiming John's ignorance prevented him from accurately describing nuclear warfare. Walvoord quotes Bullinger who says there are no difficulties whatever in the literalizing of the passage and insuperable difficulties in understanding it symbolically.

Walvoord, as I've said, without dealing with details in the judgment, assures us that these elements are mentioned in the Old Testament in passages dealing with the yet future judgments. He then proceeds to quote from Isaiah 13, which is said to be a judgment on Babylon through the Medes (and which he couldn't accept literally anyway.) He further quotes Isaiah 34 which Isaiah explicitly says applies to the judgment on Edom (and which Walvoord couldn't take literally anyway). He then quotes Joel 2, which Peter in Acts 2 quotes, saying, "This is that . . ." So there you have the exegesis.

What have I established concerning the meaning of the passage? So far, only that the language used is common in other passages which were not (and can't be) literally fulfilled and leave life on the earth. What does this **prove**? Only that the language can reasonably, with scriptural justification, be understood figuratively. That doesn't prove it **should** be understood literally, only that it can't be literally understood and leave people still on the earth, worrying about their welfare; carrying out buying and selling business; raising armies; persecuting saints all over the world; tattooing people and building temples. Add to that this — the book was written concerning things shortly to come to pass and a time which was near to John. The result is a figurative description of a severe judgment to fall on the ungodly.

The wrath of the Lamb - A fearful expression indeed. We've heard it so often, we've become used to it. "Made white in the blood of the Lamb," is another. How can we be made white by washing in something scarlet? I'm aware it's figurative. Still, it ought to grab the mind, but we've become used to it. "The wrath of the Lamb." What a spooky thought. Thank God for the grace which led me to him, that by trusting in his finished work, I might not have to endure the wrath of the Lamb. What about you?

They search for a hiding place. This speech is borrowed from Isaiah 2:10,11,19-22. Such language is timeless. Like the "day of the Lord." It always has the same significance, but it applies to different occasions where the circumstances demand wrath or deliverance. Check it in the Bible for yourself. This is the downfall of many a commentator (we can all be guilty if we are not careful). We read similar speech in various passages and, bingo! We string them together as if this were exegesis.

Okay, what did we see in this chapter? We saw the unveiling of the future, undergirded by the primary truth of the book of Revelation — Jesus is the Overcomer, the Conqueror. We saw Him come forth, pure and victorious. We saw him come FIRST to assure the saints. We saw the four sore judgments of God being sent into the world; we saw persecution announced as ahead for the saints; and we saw their cry for vindication being answered in the description of judgment aimed at their oppressors.

Thus we saw a glad picture and a sad picture. We saw a picture having consolation, but speaking also of trouble. We saw, since the Lamb did the opening, that everything was under his control. But the chapter did end with a horrific picture of judgment, and thus leads easily into the contents of chapter 7.

15 For this reason they are before the throne of God and they serve Him day and night in His temple and He who sits on the throne shall spread His tabernacle over them.

Christians sealed

Questions on Chapter 7

Theme: Be assured, God is on His Throne, nothing will keep you or separate you from God

1. What Old Testament section would be helpful to read before looking closely at chapter 7? Ez 9
2. Is all suffering the judgment of God on an individual? NO
3. Can one be exempt from judgment and yet suffer during it? Yes
4. Can you prove your answer? Ez 21
5. What is the usual significance of the number "4" in symbolic speech? ~~God's activity~~ the world
6. Is there a second thought in it? sometime no symbolism implied like 4 can mean 4
7. What is "wind" often used to indicate? activity of God w/spirit
8. Why is this a good choice of symbol? wind used interchangeably — See Jn 3:7-8
9. What do the 4 angels represent? Personify wind & represent judgment about ready to fall on earth
10. Is the judgment here indicated to be an "accident"? NO!
11. What does the angel from the "sunrise" carry? mercy
12. How many of the righteous are sealed? Most? Few? Or All? ALL
13. What does the "seal" signify? righteous soul not to be judged
14. Why can't the seal be the Holy Spirit? they already had the H.S.
15. What does Walvoord say the "seal" is? He won't say
16. Does the sealing assure the saints of physical preservation? NO
17. What O.T. passage helps us to answer this? Ez 9
18. What is the significance of the number "12"? ever associated w/ God's people, patriarchs, tribes
19. What does the "144,000" signify? assured of God's protection — Christians
20. Does Lindsey hold the "10 days" in chapter 2 to be literal? Yes
21. Does Lindsey hold "clouds" in chapter 1:8 to be literal? Yes
22. What chapter in Revelation helps us identify the 144,000? Ch 14
23. What is the millennial difficulty in regard to the conversion of 144,000 Jews during the Tribulation? The H.S. raptured before Tribulation, so no restrainer of sin
24. Who is the "great multitude"? the 144,000, the triumph over the tribulation
25. What feast of the Jews is in view here? Feast of Tabernacles
26. Can you list 4 points which suggest the identification of the 144,000 with the "great multitude"? see p122
27. Does Walvoord hold "temple" to be literal in verse 15? NO
28. Is the great mulititude a company of martyrs? Are they pictured as being in the next life? not necessarily — they could have survived in heaven
29. How does John describe Christians in 13:6? — See Eph 6 seated w/ Jesus in heavenly realms

16 They shall hunger no more, neither thirst any more neither shall the sun beat down on them nor any heat.
17 for the Lamb in the center of the throne shall be their shepherd and shall guide them to springs of the water of life and God shall wipe every tear from their eyes.

28. The great multitude are the 144,000 — the followers of Jesus. They may be in heaven or they may be still living.

Analysis of Chapter 7

I. The four angels of judgment: 1
   A. The four corners of the earth
   B. The four winds of the earth

II. The fifth angel of mercy: 2,3
   A. Coming from the sun rising: 2
   B. The order of delay: 3
   C. The reason for delay: 3
   D. The seal:3

III. The sealing accomplished: 4-8
   A. The number of the sealed
   B. The identity of the sealed

IV. The vision of the great multitude: 9-17
   A. Their number: 9
   B. Their origin: 9
   C. Their appearance: 9
   D. Their song: 10
   E. The heavenly response to their song: 11,12
   F. Their identity and state: 13-17

Introduction to Chapter 7

Chapter 7 is one of those deviations for comfort which take place so often in the book and which could easily be viewed as the theme of the book in reverse. You've heard me keep on saying the theme of the book is the victory of the saints, in Christ Jesus, over their oppressors. This being true, these "deviations" (while they really are deviations) are scheduled so as to keep this theme constantly in mind.

Chapter 6 closes with a horrendous picture of judgment on earth. The question is asked "Who can stand" the wrath of the Father and the Son? Chapter 7 answers that question. In the first section it shows the sealing being performed (though no details are given). In the latter section, the sealing is shown to be effective.

It is important for you and me to observe that it is modeled on Ezekiel 9. This does not interpret it for us, but it does give us the guidelines by which to find our way. I suggest you read Ezekiel 9 before you enter this section. Go ahead, it'll only take you five minutes.

A second serious and all-important consideration is this: All suffering is not the judgment of God! Sometimes the innocent suffer with the guilty, but are not being **punished** with the guilty. Look, in the days of Noah it is almost certain that babies died in the flood. These babies suffered with the guilty, but God did not punish the babies. Ezekiel 18 forbids the notion that God ever punishes one man for another man's guilt. Infants were slaughtered in Jericho, but this was not a punishment of God **on them.** That righteous people are chastened and punished, I'm not denying, but we only know they are punished of God when the Bible says so. Here's my point, at this moment: Two people may well have been involved in the terror of a famine and one suffered punishment and the other just suffered! Punishment and suffering are not synonyms! In the judgment, here under consideration, the saints are **exempt.**

A third consideration: Though the righteous are exempt from a given judgment, this doesn't mean they can't suffer during it. This is why Ezekiel 9 is so important. In it we hear of a judgment about to fall on the ungodly. The executors are told to delay until the righteous are sealed. When the righteous are sealed against the judgment, the executors, in the vision, slay everyone without the mark. The marked people go untouched! It would appear from this that when the judgment actually fell, none of the righteous would be hurt, but that's not what happened. Ezekiel 21:3,4 tells us that the righteous died as well as the wicked. How do we reconcile this? How can this be, in light of the vision? The vision is only a vision teaching certain truths and it is not to be pressed for details of history. What's the central thought? God is about to judge the ungodly! That judgment will involve the righteous in suffering and it might look as if they are being punished too. **The sealing is God's way of saying, The righteous are not being judged!** You don't like that? What are you going to do with it? Do the righteous in the vision die? Absolutely not! In the literal judgment, did righteous people die? Absolutely! What then can you be sure of? That the righteous, whether they die or not, are exempt from the judgment! Picture a wife of one of the dead, righteous Jews in Nebuchadnezzar's day. Hear her weeping and complaining that the vision had failed — her righteous husband had died. How would you console her? He's as dead as the ungodly man. Offer her comfort. Go ahead! Tell her he died faithful and hear her tell you, "On the terms of the vision, he shouldn't have died at all." You get my point, don't you?! What does this all mean? It means: 1) That the sealing visions do not guarantee physical preservation to the righteous, and 2) That the sealing visions teach the righteous are exempt from the judgment about to fall.

Chapter 7

1 After this I saw four angels standing at the
four corners of the earth, holding back the 4
winds of the earth so that no wind should
blow on the earth or on the sea or on any tree
2 And I saw another angel ascending from the
rising of the sun having the seal of the living
God and he cried out w/a loud voice to the
4 angels to whom it was granted to harm
the earth and the sea,
3 saying, "Do not harm the earth or the sea or
the trees until we have sealed the bond-
servants of our God on their foreheads."
4 And I heard the number of those sealed,
144,000 sealed from every tribe of the sons
of Israel:
5-8 from the tribe of Judah 12,000 were
sealed, from the tribe of Reuben...
Gad, Asher, Naphtali, Manasseh,
Simeon, Levi Issachar, Joseph,
Benjamin, Zebulun,... (~~Gad left out~~)
NO TRIBE LEFT OUT except DAN

12,000
x 12
24000
12000
144000
Judah

9 After these things I looked and behold
a great multitude which no one could
count from every nation and all tribes
and peoples and tongues, standing before
the throne and before the Lamb, clothed in
white robes and palm branches were in their hands
10 and they cry out w/a loud voice saying
"Salvation to our God who sits on the
throne and to the Lamb."
11 And all the angels were standing around the
throne and around the elders and the four
living creatures and they fell on their faces
before the throne and worshipped God,
12 saying, "Amen, blessing and glory and
wisdom and thanksgiving and honor and
power and might be to our God forever
and ever Amen"
13 And one of the elders answered saying to me
these who are clothed in the white robes who
are they and from where have they come?
14 And I said to him, "My Lord you know."
And he said to me These are the ones who come
out of the great tribulation and they have
washed their robes and made them
white in the blood of the Lamb.

← see back for verses 15-17

Comments on Chapter 7

VERSE 1. After this I saw four angels - These are the angels of the winds. Everything (just about) in the book of Revelation has an angel. We've discussed this in chapter 1. Those who say they know, tell us the number "4" is the number of the "world" (ie. the universe) or the earth. A lot of the speculation as to how these numbers became what they have become, is useless. But it is yet clear that certain numbers do carry a significance beyond themselves and it does appear that "four" is the number always associated with the "world." The four corners of the earth, or the four winds of the heavens are associated with man and his environment. There is the thought of **universality** about the number four. The Cherubim in Ezekiel 1 could go in all four directions — their jurisdiction was universal.

The "winds" are often used to indicate the activity of God. Check this in a concordance. See in the plagues the function of the wind in bringing salvation. In drying-off the earth to make it possible for Noah to return to his normal life, God made use of a great wind. See for yourself how often God uses the wind (as for example in Isaiah 57:13 and Jeremiah 18:17) as a symbol of his actions against a people.

In Daniel 7, having told in chapter 4 that He rules the world and raises up the kingdoms, in chapter 7, God gives us the vision of the wind blowing on the sea and 4 beasts arising out of it, clearly indicating by this that it is divine activity which raises these kingdoms.

And it's not really surprising that "wind" should be used as symbolic of God's acitivity, since it is both powerful and invisible. In fact, it is not always clear whether the translators should have put "wind" or "spirit" in a number of texts. Both words come from the same Greek or Hebrew word.

Quoting Psalm 104:4, the Hebrew writer (1:7) says, "Who maketh his angels winds, And his ministers a flame of fire." Some have rendered it "spirits." God rides on the cherubim (Psalm 18:10 and elsewhere) and also walks on the wings of the wind. So (what's the point of continuing?), "wind" is constantly associated with God and the activity of God. See John 3:7,8.

These angels (who personify the winds) represent the judgment which is about to fall on the earth. They stand at the "four corners" of the earth. Isn't it so silly for men to deduce from this that the Bible writers thought the earth was square! Isaiah 11:12 speaks of the four corners of the land. Nobody I know of has dared suggest this means Isaiah thought Palestine was a square or rectangular. What do we have then? **Judgment about to fall!** Nothing accidental, mark you, but under the control of God and in the hands of divine agents.

VERSES 2,3. And I saw another angel ascend from the sunrise This is **good** news. There is mercy implied here. His errand is one of mercy; that much is clear. The sun, among other things, symbolized the attributes and goodness of God. Check for yourself. Psalm 84:11 speaks of God as a "sun and a shield." Malachi 4:2 speaks of Jesus as "the sun of righteousness" who would "arise with healing in his wings." In Revelation, the Father and the Lamb take the place of the "sun." James speaks of God as the "Father of lights." Christ calls himself "The Bright and Morning Star" (22:16). In 2 Peter 1:19 we hear Peter speak of the "day star" (fulness of light as contrasted to a lamp). Revelation 16:12 speaks of the kings from the "sunrising." (The KJV speaks of "the east," rather than the "sunrising.")

In all these passages we have something good being discussed. "Light" is a good thing. Christ is the "true Light." God is "light." He banishes darkness and dread. This angel comes from the east with good news. He is the herald of light, even as Christ calls himself the "Morning star" (that is, the herald of the dawn). The angel comes from where light originates. His message is one of cheer. See the comments on 16:12. The judgment in the previous chapter promises the blacking-out of the sun — this angel comes from the "rising of the sun," and is the bearer of a glad message for those who will go through gloom.

(Let me say a word or two here on the question of symbolism. The use of symbols is a part of the Bible's way of teaching. Whether we like it or not, it's there. Now, because many passages are symbolic, or contain symbols, we are not to suppose every passage is symbolical. This would be unwise thinking. Sometimes "horse" is used symbolically for "war" but very often it simply means a "horse." At times "four" speaks of universality, but then again, it most often speaks of simply "four." Four of whatever is under discussion. To be convinced that "beast" is symbolic does not mean that everytime you read "beast" there must be a hidden meaning. When you're in a book such as Revelation, however, you are already aware of the manner of his writing, and so you look for a significance beyond the bare word or phrase. Okay?)

Hurt not the earth...till - He calls for a delay. He calls for a delay in carrying out the judgment. The parallel between this and Ezekiel must be taken into account. There, as here, there were agents of judgment. There, as here, there is one who is interested in a delay. And there, as here, the reason for the delay is the welfare of the righteous. Don't hurt the earth, he says, until the righteous are marked. Not the most of them, but all of them. Here as in Ezekiel 9, **all** the righteous are marked or sealed. The vision is very specific: the tribulation is not to take place until the righteous are sealed.

This creates a difficulty for any dispensationalist. You see, he believes this tribulation takes place after the Rapture (ie. the ascension of the Church, which Lindsey says will occur around 1981). But "after the Rapture" is the Tribulation. This means these 144,000 will have to be sealed during the Tribulation (ie. as the millennialists see it). But the 144,000 are sealed **before** the Tribulation begins (v.3). On Millennial terms this would have to be prior to the Rapture. But if it were prior to the Rapture, the 144,000 would be members of the Church and they would be raptured! What to do? They split the "70th week of Daniel" (ie. 7 literal years) into two 3½-year periods. Hold that the sealing of the 144,000 takes place right at the beginning of the 7 years before the judgment falls. This will do.

But Walvoord is left with the difficulty that the seals would cover the entire seven years of Daniel's "70th week." This he denies is true (page 123), saying there is no explicit evidence that Revelation deals with the full seven years, and there is evidence against such being true.

Lindsey doesn't have that difficulty, for he thinks Revelation deals with the whole seven years. He does have other difficulties, however, in keeping his two periods distinct. See the comments on chapter 11.

Having the seal of the living God - What is the "seal"? Walvoord won't touch it. He gives it a meaning, but won't say what it is. Lindsey claims it is the Holy Spirit, but how could it be? Those sealed, were sealed **because** they were saints. This would mean they already had the Holy Spirit **before** they were sealed. See Romans 8:9 and Galatians 4:6.

Millennialists must make it something — it must be a mark of some kind. They talk of tattoos and "marks of the beast." Marks on the hands and foreheads of people must be literally understood. So Lindsey makes it not only the Holy Spirit, but some kind of literal mark.

But what is the "seal? It is nothing tangible. It belongs only in the vision. It is God's way of setting forth a truth. In ancient times and today as well, people put marks on their property. Kids mark their tennis shoes and preachers mark their books. This not only is to say who owns them (which is really a secondary issue), but says, "Hands off!" The sealing is not for man, but for the agents of judgment. The seal is necessary in the vision. It is a vehicle through which the truth is told: These, my people, will be protected. They are exempt. Don't touch them. And ultimately, of course, the message is not for the four angels, but for the saints who endure.

In Ezekiel's vision, the 586 B.C. judgment on Jerusalem is in view. Broadly speaking, there were two groups — the righteous and the ungodly. He saw the righteous being marked. Were they literally marked back then? Why should they be here? I'm not saying they weren't literally back then; therefore, they couldn't be literally marked here. That would be poor reasoning. I'm saying, since they were not literally marked back then — and since the two passages are **so** alike, why must we be compelled to a literal marking here? Because the passage says it? It speaks of a literal (in the vision the marking is seen) marking in Ezekiel, but the people in actuality were not marked! Can't you see that the only thing being said here is: In the face of what is about to happen, I want you saints to know, you are under my protection! So that, as in Ezekiel, the seal here is neither the Holy Spirit or a literal mark, but a token of assurance given in picture form.

Now, does this sealing assure the saints of physical preservation? Not at all! The saints, in vision, in Ezekiel 9 were sealed, but many of them died. See the introductory remarks on this chapter. Linsdey and Walvoord agree that this sealing demands the 144,000 are physically preserved through the Tribulation. Did it in Ezekiel? Then why should it here? What is the proof?

VERSES 4-8. And I heard the number of them that were sealed John doesn't describe the process. Ezekiel does. How many were sealed? ALL OF THEM. There was no part-sealing in Ezekiel, nor is there any indicated here. "The servants of our God" are sealed — not some, or most, or few of them. In Ezekiel the word is: Mark those who sigh and cry because of all the ungodliness of this city. Whoever was righteous was marked. Here, whoever was a servant of God was marked.

How many were marked? **All of them**. How are they numbered? As 144,000. The number 12 is ever associated with the people of God. The 12 patriarchs and the 12 apostles. The twelve tribes and the twelve gates. Twelve foundations are the support of the city of God's people. To raise a number to a higher power is to emphasize its inner quality. "Twelve" speaks of the completeness of God's people. All God's saints who are to undergo this period of trial are assured of God's protection. 12 x 12 x 1000 simply underscores this. 144,000 means: "All of my saints are under my care — and I do mean all!" See Amos 9:9.

Lindsey challenges all those who claim the number is symbolical. He claims it is literal and "Why not"? Walvoord isn't too sure, though he finally (on chapter 14) agrees with a literal number. Why not "10 days" in chapter 2? Why not just plain old "fire and brimstone" in 9:18? And plain old "blood" in 8:8? Why not just clouds in 1:8? Lindsey, even for millennialists, is very inconsistent. And yet he is more consistent than Walvoord.

But who are they? We've already answered that question, but it needs to be persued. They are described as "144,000" Jews. That it **says** Israelites does not settle the issue. It says "out of every tribe of Israel" but goes on to exclude Dan. If the number is not literal, then it is possible that the physical designation is not literal.

Is there any reason to believe the designation is not literal? Of course. All saints are embraced in this sealing and unless it can be shown that only Jewish saints went through the tribulation John spoke of — the designation must not be literally understood. Since John was writing of things which must (speaking from his day) "shortly come to pass," and of a time (speaking from John's day) "near" — since this is true — we **know** the number and the mark and the physical designation are not to be taken literally. I'd say that was plenty. See 22:4.

The 144,000 are spoken of again in chapter 14:1-5. They are not only said to be Israelites, but "virgins." Lindsey symbolizes this! They are indentified as those who "were purchased from among men, to be the fristfruits unto God and unto the Lamb" (14:4). Revelation 5:9,10 and James 1:18 help us to interpret that of members of the Church (see Acts 20:28). I happen to believe Lindsey is right when he says they are "virgins" in a religious sense in keeping with, say 2 Corinthians 11:2. But with Lindsey's presuppositions, he has no right to symbolize them as "spiritual" virgins. Walvoord temporizes, as is his custom.

Who then are the 144,000? They are all of the saints who are to undergo this period of pressure. They are Christians. Christians are said to be "a kind of firstfruits unto God." They are followers of the Lamb — his sheep (John 10). They have been purchased from among men (scriptures above). They are without blemish (Ephesians 1:3,4; 5:26,27).

But why would John call them Israelites? We are in a book of symbols — why wouldn't he? "Israel" is an established name of those who were God's people, and so it is easy to see how he might appropriate the name (at the Spirit's guidance, of course) of Israel. Why did he call them "virgins"? Furthermore, the original meaning of the name Israel was "he who prevailed with God." What better symbol to use of those who indeed have prevailed with God? All the saints are explicity called the "seed of Abraham" and so it should not be surprising, if in a book of symbols, we hear the name "Israel" applied to true believers. And again, since he has already made notice of groups of fleshly Jews and denied their Jewish connection because of their inner, spritual lack — what's objectionable in his making use of the name in regard to those whose inner nature accords more with the name "Israel"? I'm not here suggesting that "Israel" does not (outside the book of Revelation) speak of fleshly Israelites; I believe it does. I'm suggesting that in a highly figurative book, it shouldn't surprise us if it is used figuratively.

Before we move on to the next section of the chapter, let me here mention the difficulty the millennial school is in with regard to the conversion of the 144,000. According to Walvoord and Lindsey, the Holy Spirit is raptured with the Church, and, that as a "restrainer of sin" he is absent from the earth. This they find in 2 Thessalonians 2:6,7. This creates the difficulty of conversion apart from the Holy Spirit, as the restrainer of sin. Both gentlemen claim that the departure of the Holy Spirit renders the situation to be as it was before the Spirit came at Pentecost. But this just won't do, for the Holy Spirit (on their view) is removed as a **restrainer of sin.** If he does no longer restrain sin, then 144,000 cannot be saved! These two men are Calvinists and this compounds their difficulties, for it means the 7 years begin with no one on earth but "totally depraved" people. The Spirit as a "restrainer of sin" is removed and thus the possibility of salvation is removed. If it be said, the Holy Spirit will work as he did prior to Pentecost, we will ask, "Will he restrain sin"? If the answer be "yes," then the Spirit is not removed as a sin restrainer. If the answer is "no," then whatever else he does do, there can be no salvation for totally depraved men!

VERSES 9-17. I saw, and behold a great multitude - They were innumerable! Can we understand that literally? They were from every nation and their garments were white because they washed them in the blood of the Lamb.

Arrayed in white robes, and palms in their hands - There is no doubt whatever that we have here a scene modeled on the Feast of Tabernacles. No matter whom you read on this subject, if they deal with it at any length at all, you will read the word "joy" or "festivity" or "jubilant" in the discussion. Of all the Jewish feasts — this was **the** Feast. It was a feast of thanksgiving for the harvest. Not only were the crops of the field already gathered in; but the vine had yielded its grapes. Thus the Feast of Tabernacles was also called the "Feast of Ingathering." But the O.T. also connects it with Israel's deliverance from Egypt and their dwelling in booths. It lasted seven days, and then an eighth "great day." The people robed themselves in bright festive robes and sang, danced, and prayed to God. Sacrifices were offered each day. Water was drawn each day in a golden basin and poured (Phariseean style) around the side of the altar. This water was associated with at least two things. It spoke of the water supply gained from the rock by Moses as the people wandered. And, secondly, it was thankfulness for the rain given and was part of a petiton for God to give more rain (at that time, in the Autumn, the Jews would be eagerly looking for the "early rains"). As the priest would head for the water he would lead a jubilant multitude. On his way back they sang Psalms (the "ascent" Psalms 120-134, and others). At certain verses the multiude would shake their "lulabs" (palm branches) and shout "Hosannas." The great Hallel Psalms were sung throughout the seven days. These were called "Hallel" because they began with "Praise the Lord." It was usual to sing 113-118. The priests would lead and there would be a response by the people. In the assemblies during this week the people would extol God for his wisdom, kindness, and salvation.

(I need no more than mention the Feast of Tabernacles recorded in John 7 when Jesus, as the feast had reached its climax, "cried" that he was the real river of "living water" (the Holy Spirit). Think of the ramifications of the claim in light of the celebration and its meaning. No wonder this blew their minds).

I think you can see from this description the elements which are called on in the passage under consideration. I will mention other points of similarity as we proceed with independent verses. I'm urging you to read on this feast and see for yourself the nature of the model of this section.

Salvation unto our God - This doesn't mean they wish God to be saved. It means "Salvation is attributable to our God." That is, "if we are saved, we can thank God for it." During the week of the Feast of Tabernacles, this was cried over and over again.

Who sitteth on the throne - This is not merely to designate where he is sitting; it is an affirmation that he is acting in power on our behalf. He is ruling! Salvation is also attributable to the Lamb, who as we know from 2:26,27 and 3:21, is also on the throne.

And all the angels...worshiped God, saying - Here is an angelic response. In the Feast of Tabernacles, the priests would lead and the people would respond in affirmation. The priest would say, "Praise ye the Lord," and the people would respond, "Hallelujah." These angels respond with an "amen." (It is not clear from the ASV whether the angels **and** the elders, with the living creatures are all saying amen).

These...arrayed in white robes, who are they...? - Where did they come from and who are they, the elder asks. John is wise, he said, "I don't know." (Wish to God we'd all say we don't know when we don't know. How often we continue to "rabbit" away, taking precious time to **prove** we don't know)?

These are they that come out of the great tribulation - That's who they are! They are surviviors of and victors through the great tribulation. They are the blood-washed fraternity out of every nation. Need more be said? The word "come" (out of the great tribulation) is a present participle. It is here acting as an adjective (as participles often do). Its point is not temporal, but descriptive. Burton (page 164 et. seq.) says of this function, "It attributes the action which it denotes to the subject as a quality or characteristic, or assigns the subject to the class marked by that action." Their "coming out of" the tribulation is a description of them, not a statement of fact that they do. Remember the question is one of identity and origin. The angel is saying, "These are the kind which come through the tribulation." And what are the kind which come out of the tribulation? Beaten and despairing? Subdued and sullen? Not at all, but like those who are enjoying the Feast of Tabernacles. This was joy unbounded, for not only was it thanksgiving for numberless blessings — this feast followed four days after the Great Day of Atonement! The national guilt had been removed by the blood of innocent victims; the harvest was safely in; prayers for the early rains had been offered; the people were ecstatic with joy! Farrar says: In the evening they abandoned themselves to such rejoicing, that the Rabbis say that the man who has not seen this "joy of the drawing water" does not know what joy means. (Vol. 2, page 54). For "white robes," see comments on 3:4-5).

What "great tribulation"? I think there can be little doubt about that. In chapter 6, we hear of one coming. In the first part of chapter 7, we have the 144,000 sealed as protection during it. This clearly implies they were to go through it. And now we have a host who are the ones who "come out of the great tribulation." Manifestly it is the tribulation of chapter 6. But you say: The seal of chapter 6 dealt with judgment on the ungodly. This is true, of course, but God's people aren't lifted out from the earth during the bad times. Ezekiel 9 speaks of judgment on the ungodly, but the righteous die in masses (21:3ff). When the world is under pressure their true colors show. It is amazing how thin is the veneer of civilization. Make no mistake, the words of the Savior have never been revoked: I chose you out of the world; therefore, the world hates you. One day the saints will be convinced by the words of their Faithful Witness with the eyes like flame of fire, the world doesn't love us! Its principles are not ours. One day we will sit in judgment on a Christ-rejecting world. But, in the meantime, if God sends the sword, we'll suffer with the world. If famine strikes, we'll get hungry and so will our children. And the more frustrated the world becomes, the tougher it will be on us. Our brothers and sisters learned this back there. Tertullian said if the rains don't come, Christians are blamed. If too much rain comes and the Tiber overflows, Christians are blamed. That's how it was.

Therefore are they before the throne of God - If you have read what I've said on the 144,000, you will know that this is the same group looked at from a different direction. The reasons for this include the reasons for identifying the 144,000 as all of the saints. Since these are **manifestly** the Church, and the 144,000 are the Church — they are the same.

Furthermore, the 144,000 are sealed with a view to coming out of the great tribulation. This group is specifically identified as those who come out of the great tribulation. It would be strange indeed to have the 144,000 sealed so as to come out of the tribulation and then speak of a great multitude who came out of the tribulation without wishing to identify them.

The 144,000 are sealed in their foreheads (7:3). The mark they have on their foreheads is said to be the name of God and of the Lamb (14:1). This mark is promised to the members of the Church (3:12). Since they are marked with the same mark, it is not unreasonable to conclude it is for the same purpose. It becomes more than **reasonable** in the light of 3:10. See the comments on that. Further, in 22:4 we find all (there is no restriction indicated) the servants of God have the same mark as the 144,000.

This great multitude is said to be "before the throne" and that is where the 144,000 sing their song in 14:3. (I recognize there is need of discussion as to the identity of the singers in 14:3. We'll deal with it when I get to that passage.)

This great multitude is led by the Lamb, and they follow him, wherever he leads them. in 14:3, the 144,000 are said to "follow the Lamb whithersoever he goeth." Let me sum all of this up. **Remember what I'm proposing:** The 144,000 are to be identified with the great multitude; they are the same group viewed from different standpoints.

1. The 144,000 are sealed for preservation in the face of the tribulation. The great multitude are the ones who come out of the great tribulation.
2. The 144,000 are sealed with the name of God and the Lamb. The members of the Church bear the same mark (3:12) and for preservation in the face of great trial (3:12). The great multitude (as everyone agrees) speaks of the Church. All God's servants have the same mark as the 144,000 (22:4).
3. The 144,000 sing before the throne; the great multitude are located there.
4. The 144,000 are viewed as followers of the Lamb and redeemed from the earth; the great multitude are identified as followers of the Lamb and redeemed from the earth.
5. You must now re-read the earlier remarks on the identification of the 144,000 in light of the name "Israel," and the number "144,000."

And they serve him day and night in his temple - We are not to suppose they are in a literal temple of any kind. Walvoord recognizes that he can't hang-on to literalism here so he figurized "his temple" to mean "his presence." The word "temple" here is the one which means "inner sanctuary." There are two Greek words for temple. The first speaks of the whole structure and the second speaks of the holy place. The fact that they serve in this speaks of their priesthood, for only priests entered the holy place. At the Feast of Tabernacles **all** the priests served!!

Notice thay they are said to be before the throne and in the temple day and night. This is possible because the throne is set in the tabernacle. See the comments on 4:2. In that place you were given evidence which shows John's throne scenes have a temple or tabernacle setting. Please read it again. This multitude is like Anna (Luke 2:37) in their devotion. She wouldn't leave the temple day or night. This expression simply indicates total devotion.

He...shall spread his tabernacle over them - This is a beautiful remark in light of the Feast of Tabernacles. It was a practice at the feast to provide for the friends and visitors, what they needed. Edersheim speaks of the "poor, the stranger, the Levite, and the homeless would be welcome guests" at the meal ("Temple," page 272). Here God shares his "booth" (tabernacle) with the homeless. His tabernacle embraces them. There, in his temple or tabernacle,

God dwells with men. During the Feast of Tabernacles, it was required that the family or group live in the booths. Here, as in 21:3, we are told the "tabernacle of God is with men, and he shall dwell (tabernacle) with them." Here is the dwelling of God in his people and the dwelling of the people with God (John 17:21,23).

They shall hunger no more - Is he speaking of physical hunger? Has anything of this been physical, so far? Is their thirst, now absent because the water is provided, their physical thirst? They will not be bothered by the sun — why?

For the Lamb...shall be their shepherd, and shall guide them Why won't they be thirsty? Because the shepherd will guide them to where there is water. They won't be hungry because their shepherd causes them to lie down in green pasture. The sun won't burn them because their shepherd will provide them shade. The picture is one of a well-guided flock. This is another passage which is a "mosaic" of Old Testament scriptures. They are all woven together to make a wonderful picture of security and prosperity. Isaiah 25:8; 40:11; 49:8-10; Psalm 121:5,6 are alluded to, as well as others. They had wept a lot over this time of trial, but those days of mourning were at an end (Isaiah 60:20).

Let me now discuss a question I've been skirting, so as to leave it to the end. **Does John teach the multitude are dead and out of this life?** Are they martyrs — that is, have they been literally slain? I don't think so! Why has it been concluded that the multitude are the martyred saints? Let's examine in the evidence — Ok?!

First of all, this group has "come out of" the great tribulation. It has been concluded that this means they are martyrs. But why? Because they have been "freed" from tribulation? This surely isn't enough, since this chapter is not speaking simply of "tribulation" **in general,** but a specific period of stress. That they successfully came through it doesn't require martyrdom (though it might involve that). "Be thou faithful unto (even if it means) death." Jesus told the brethren this, but this didn't mean that every single Christian would be a martyr. Apparently, John wasn't — at least, that's the word of tradition. But without tradition, everyone knows that many Christians survived the bloody purges of Rome by going underground.

What is involved in coming "out of" the great tribulation? As we have seen in the introductory remarks to this chapter, it doesn't require physical preservation. But neither does it require martyrdom. It didn't in Ezekiel and it does not require it here. Many a man was faithful until the day he died and there were others who were "faithful unto death."

Secondly, this group is said to be **before the throne of God.** As I have already shown, this doesn't require that one be actually dwelling in heaven. John's visions are heavenly and they include scenes set in heaven, but we must not conclude that to mean the subject under discussion is necessarily literally in heaven. He saw a "star from heaven" (9:1), which implies the star was there. We are not to suppose the "star" to have been literally in heaven. In the vision, it was in heaven. He saw a "woman" in heaven (12:1), but we are not to suppose the "woman" (**whatever** she stands for) was literally in heaven. He saw (not "an") but "the ark of the covenant in heaven" (11:19). He saw an angel "flying in mid-heaven" (14:9). There is nothing literal about this, but in the vision the angel was in heaven. He sees torment in fire and brimstone in the presence of the Lamb (in heaven), 14:10, but we are not to conclude that such was going on literally in heaven. In 13:6 he speaks of the saints as those "that dwell in heaven." Were they literally in heaven? There are too many other illustrations which preclude my having to continue.

We must keep remembering that all John sees is **vision** — he is seeing pictures. Those pictures may or may not embody some literal elements. We should no more conclude, just because the vision words it that way, that the locusts of 9:1-3 come literally out of the earth than we should conclude the woman (of 12:1) or the multitude of(7:9) were literally in heaven. Let me say it once more, plainly: Because John describes an object, person or group, as being in heaven, we are **not** to automatically conclude that's where they dwell. There are reasons why certain things are seen as in, or coming from, heaven and others are seen coming out of the earth or sea, or the abyss. We'll discuss some of them as we go.

Thirdly, the description of their blessedness is said to be greater than any state known this side of heaven. But what is there in this vision which indicates this? Is it that they don't hunger or thirst? This is promised through Isaiah (49:10) to those saved by Jesus (Paul quotes 49:8 in 2 Corinthians 6:2). Is it that tears are wiped from their eyes? This is promised to Israel in Isaiah 25:8, and in Isaiah 30:18-33, we hear it again. In this last scripture, Assyria is the problem (verse 31). Israel is to be freed from her and she would "weep no more" (19).

All right — what did we see in chapter seven? We **saw** a message of comfort to the brotherhood in the face of the coming storm. We saw the believers as a numbered throng of 144,000 sealed against **punishment** and marked out to be preserved through the strom. We then saw that same group as having victoriously come through the great tribulation. In this view they are described as

joyful worshipers at a Feast of Tabernacles and then as a flock of well-shepherded sheep! Assurance is the key thought throughout the section.

God is taking care of everything
Everything works for the good for those who love God & are called according to His purpose.

Isaiah 49 The Day of Salvation
vs. 8-13
They will not be hungry or thirsty
Neither the hot sun nor the desert wind will hurt them
The God who comforts them will lead them and guide them by springs of water

2 Cor 6:2 quoting Is 49:8.
At the right time I heard your prayers
On the day of salvation I helped you
I tell you ~~that~~ the right time is now
And the day of salvation is now.

Chap 8 + 9
See p 129, 136

Chapter 8
1 And when He broke the 7th seal there was
silence in heaven for about half an hour
2 And I saw the 7 angels who stand before
God & 7 trumpets were given to them.
3 And another angel came and stood at the
altar holding a golden censer and much
incense was given to him that he might
add it to the prayers of all the saints upon
the golden altar which was before the throne.
4 And the smoke of the incense with the prayers
of the saints went up befor God out of the
angel's hand.
5 And the angel took the censer; and he filled it
w/the fire of the altar and threw it to the
earth; and there followed peals of thunder
and sounds and flashes of lightning and
an earthquake.
6 And the seven angels who had the seven trumpets
prepared themselves to sound them.
7 And the first sounded and there came hail &
fire, mixed w/blood and they were thrown
to the earth and a third of the earth was
burnt up and a third of the trees was burnt
up and all the green grass was burnt up.
8 And the second angel sounded and
something like a great mtn burning
w/fire was thrown into the sea; and
a third of the sea became blood;
9 and a third of the creatures which were
in the sea and had life died; and a
third of the ships was destroyed.
10 And the third angel sounded and a
great star fell from heaven burning
like a torch and it fell on a third of
the rivers and on the springs of waters;
11 And the name of the star is Wormwood;
and a third of the waters became "
and many men died from the waters
because they were made bitter.
12 And the 4th angel sounded, and a third of
the sun and a third of the moon and a
third of the stars were smitten so that a
third of them might be darkened and the
day might not shine for a third of it and
the night in the same way.

Questions on Chapter 8

1. Does the word "hour" occur often in John's writings?
2. What does it characteristically suggest in his writings?
3. What tricky passage does this help to explain?
4. What does a "half-hour" silence suggest to you?
5. Can you state two O.T. usages of trumpets?
6. What is the "golden altar"?
7. From which altar did the angel get the coals?
8. What's the significance of casting the coals on the earth?
9. Which O.T. passage reminds us of this action?
10. Which plagues come to your mind relative to the first trumpet?
11. And the second trumpet — which plagues?
12. Which O.T. prophet speaks of a "burning mountain"?
13. What historical event recalls a burning mountain?
14. What do you make of the burning mountain?
15. What is smitten by the third trumpet?
16. What does it remind you of?
17. The fourth trumpet — what does it remind you of?
18. Is the day shortened, or is it just not as bright?
19. Who are they who "dwell on the earth"?

Analysis of Chapter 8

I. The seventh seal and the silence: 1,2
  A. The seventh seal ripped-off: verse 1
  B. Half an hour of silence: verse 1
  C. Seven angels "armed" with trumpets: verse 2

II. The angel with the golden censer: 3,5
  A. The offering at the golden altar: verses 3, 4
  B. Fire cast on to the earth: verse 5

III. The angels and the first four trumpets: 6-13
  A. The first trumpet blast: verse 7
    1. The hail, fire, and blood
    2. One-third of earth, trees, and grass burned
  B. The second trumpet blast: 8,9
    1. A fiery mountain cast into the sea
    2. One-third of sea turned to blood
    3. One-third of ships and marine life destroyed
  C. The third trumpet blast: 10,11
    1. A star falls, polluting one-third of the drinking water
    2. Many deaths due to drinking it
  D. The fourth trumpet blast: 12
    1. Heavenly bodies smitten — one-third
    2. Darkness ensues

IV. The eagle of warning: 13
  A. The triple woe pronounced
  B. The reason given for the woes

p. 129

Introduction to Chapters 8 and 9

The seventh seal contains the seven trumpets. Seals were for concealing. Ripping them off was to reveal. Trumpets speak of warning judgments. Notice that they are judgments on only a fraction of whatever they hit. The ungodly is supposed to pay attention and repent of his wickedness.

These trumpets remind us of the plagues that God brought on Egypt, and I believe that is how we are supposed to view them. The oppressor is being punished — brought to his knees. As it was in the days of Moses, so it is in the days of the Revelation period. The ungodly is badly hurt, but as it turns out, not hurt sufficiently to turn him from iniquity.

But these chapters do clearly tell the saints of their ultimate victory. None of them, knowing anything of the O.T. history, would fail to see the parallel between the plagues and the Revelation scenes. In chapter 8:3-5 we learn the reason for the judgments, and in 9:20-22 we are clearly taught what their purpose was.

Reasons for judgments because of prayers of saints because they persecuted — 8:3-5

Purpose of judgments was to get ungodly to repent — 9:20-22

Bowls are to punish

Comments on Chapter 8

VERSES 1,2. When he opened the seventh seal. I've already pointed out that the seventh seal contains the seven trumpets. The seventh trumpet contains the seven bowls. So that, essentially, the seventh seal contains the rest of the book. Remember, ripping-off a seal means revealing things.

There followed a silence in heaven. Most everyone I've read agrees that this silence is a sort of "drum-roll" to gain attention and to signal that something of real significance is about to follow. This is almost certainly true. The delay before the jury announces its verdict is a decent illustration of just such a silence. But I think there is something more to it. In chapter 10:6 we read the angel saying that: There shall be delay no longer. This, it seems to me, implies there had been delay. The trumpets are warning judgments giving the oppressor a chance to repent. These judgments are ignored and so the full wrath of God is to be outpoured — and without delay. The silence is said to be:

About the space of half an hour. In John's writings the word "hour" occurs over and over again. Look at a concordance. To John it is not just a time measure — it carries with it the idea of crisis and action. Over and over again we hear of Jesus (in John) saying "mine hour is not yet come." Or, "Father, save me from this hour." To his brothers, "My time is not yet fulfilled." We hear that the enemies couldn't take him because "his hour was not yet come." To John, the term is one of critical importance and activity.

This helps to explain 1 John 2:18, which says: Little children, it is the last hour... He didn't have in mind the end of the world, or the end of an age. He spoke of the arrival of the antichrists — the antichrist (singular) of whom God's spokesmen had talked. The time had arrived. The crisis was now on them. And what is a broken hour? Delay! Just as a broken seven has its significance (see later on 11:2), so it seems, does this half hour. God does not relish the idea of the wicked dying in their wickedness. The Church is being told that God has a care for even the oppressor. And who among us is not grateful that he delayed until we saw the light? "Be slow to anger and slow to wrath" are not just words with God.

VERSE 2. The seven angels that stand before God. What majesty there is implied in where they stand! What honor is suggested. And what holiness must there be required for such a place? And don't we in our sphere stand before God? What honor and holiness. There are seven of them. Here again we meet the fulness, the completeness and unity involved in that number. See the comments on "seven" churches and "seven" spirits.

There were given unto them seven trumpets - Numbers 10 tells us of the making of two silver trumpets. In the first 5 verses, we are told of at least two uses of them. They were to call the assembly to attention. They were also to be used to sound alarm. It would seem that both of the uses are here involved. God told Moses: "And if they blow but one, then the princes, the heads of the thousands of Israel, shall gather themselves unto thee." However, we are told in a previous verse (3) that if they blow "them," the whole assembly is to gather themselves unto Moses at the tent of meeting — where God spoke from!

VERSES 3-5. And another angel came and stood over the altar This altar seems clearly to be the "golden altar" of incense. In the tabernacle, this altar stood right before the curtain which separated between the holy place and the holy of holies — it was right before the (place of) the throne. In the tabernacle, God was designated as sitting above the cherubim on the ark (see Exodus 25:17-22).

There was given unto him much incense - This incense which would be offered on the golden censer is associated with the prayers of the saints. This association of incense rising to the Lord and prayers rising to the Lord is known to the O.T. as Psalm 141:2 makes clear. In Luke 1:10 we read of the time of the offering of incense as the time of the people's prayers. As the prayers went up, so went up that sweet-smelling odor which made the prayers acceptable.

VERSE 4. And the smoke of the incense with the prayers - The incense and the prayers are not confounded — they ascend together. And in the vision in Revelation, it is an angel which acts the part of the priest. Up to God have now gone acceptable prayers from "saints." Such prayers have real power!

VERSE 5. And he filled it with the fire of the altar - It is not clear that this is the same altar as earlier. It may well be the altar of burnt offering (the brazen altar) from which, Smith's Bible Dictionary (Vol. 1, part 2, p. 1437) tells us, the coals were taken for the incense offering. It was from the side of the brazen altar that the judges of Israel marched in Ezekiel 9:1,2.

And cast it upon the earth — That is, the contents of the censer. We find this implied in Ezekiel 10 concerning Jerusalem. In answer to the prayers of the saints, just mentioned, we receive the word of coming judgment. We're not wrong in attaching this verse to 6:9-11. The thunders and lightnings which follow, speak of coming judgment. Check a concordance on such a use of these elements.

The word is ringing clear: Hurt my people and you'll suffer the consequences.

VERSES 6-13. The first sounded — And there followed hail mingled with fire, and there was blood. It's not hard to see we have an allusion here to the plagues on Egypt. See Exodus 7-11. Plague seven saw a terrible hail mingled with fire — a terrible electric storm (Exodus 9:24) hit Egypt. The crops were destroyed. Fire devours one-third of the trees and the **green** grass. Food is attacked. The gods of the oppressor are exposed, as was Egypt's. There is blood involved in this judgment — reminiscent of the first plague. Can this be literal? Remember that Lindsey believes we must interpret scripture literally. He believes the events of this book will be literally fulfilled beginning around 1981 — Yes, he does! See his "Late, Great Planet Earth," pages 53,54.

What does he make of this? A nuclear war! He says John's eyes were unsophisticated and that what he saw "looked like" fire and hail and blood. But John doesn't say it "looked like" those things — he said there **was** blood, fire, and hail. Maybe John didn't know about ICBMs, but he did know about blood! And fire! Moses' eyes would have been unsophisticated too, so perhaps **he** saw a nuclear war!

As we'll see later, a full outpouring of judgment will take place, but as a warning only a fraction is hit — one-third. I want you to remember this, for it really makes it difficult to see the battle of Armageddon taking place after these series of judgments.

VERSES 8,9. And the second angel sounded - Something like a great burning mountain is cast into the sea. Commerce is hit! The sea becomes blood. And Moses so struck Egypt that the venerated Nile was turned to blood. Another judgment on the oppressor of God's people. Let the saints rejoice!

As it were a great mountain burning - Only God topples mountains! To Zerubbabel we hear encouragement given in these words: Who art thou, O great mountain? Before Zerubbabel thou shalt become a plain. (Zech. 4:7) Only God sets mountains on fire. Mount Sinai, we are told, "burned with fire" when God came down upon it. God is known in Amos' time as he who "treadeth upon the high places (mountains) of the earth" (4:13). Micah echoes the same thing when he says: For, behold, Jehovah cometh forth out of his place, and will come down, and tread upon the high places of the earth. And the mountains shall be melted under him, and the valleys shall be cleft, as wax before the fire (1:3f).

What can men do with mountains but stare at them in wonder — it is for God to tread on them, melt them, burn them, divide them, remove them! And isn't the removal of a mountain to be cast into the sea an illustration of what God could do for the faithful? (See Matthew 21:21 — Also see Apendix I). To teach his disciples the power of God manifested to the faithful, Jesus illustrates how the impossible becomes the performed. This is the work of God.

Is this the God who is **for** the Christians? Then who can be against them? But from Jeremiah we hear the word which gives us the basis for the symbol here (51:25). "I am against thee, O destroying mountain, saith Jehovah, which destroyest all the earth; and I will stretch out my hand upon thee, and roll thee down from the rocks, and will make thee a burnt mountain." In this passage the defeat and destruction of Babylon is pictured by making a destroying mountain (apparently a volcano) into a "burnt-out" (NEB) mountain. The term "mountain" is used over and over again to stand for a kingdom, as for example, in Amos 4:1 and Isaiah 2:2. Check a concordance.

What do we have here then? More nuclear war, as Lindsey and company suggest? Clearly they are not literalizing as they say we should. Or should we understand the burning mountain to be God's destruction of ungodly power which affects the commerce of the world? The sea is smitten and turned to blood!

And the third part of the sea became blood - The Nile was central to the life of Egypt. Herodotus calls Egypt "The Gift of the Nile." The smiting of the Nile to blood was a fearsome thing for God to do. This power is recalled in the vision before us. Here we have commerce hit — the lifeline of so many nations is attacked by God. Remember now that Lindsey and his company hold to taking all scriptures literally. Later, I'll list the events as these premillennialists say they are to occur.

VERSE 9. And the third part of the ships was destroyed - Here we have commerce spelled out. A fraction of the sea life dies too in oceans of blood. So it was in Egypt when God smote the Nile, Exodus 7:20,21.

VERSES 10,11. And the third angel sounded - Food and commerce have been smitten and now the drinking water is hit. They are hit by **a fallen star.** Lindsey thinks this "star" is "another thermonuclear weapon." **But it doesn't say** a "thermonuclear weapon." If "Jews" must be Jews and "144,000" must be 144,000, why isn't a "star" a star?

Sometimes "stars" are used to speak of notable individuals (eg. Isaiah 14:12, where it speaks of the king of Babylon who in turn stands for the kingdom of Babylon). Sometimes "stars" speak of the people of God as in Daniel 8:10 and 12:3 with Genesis 15:5.

Sometimes the stars are just part of a picture of divine visitation as in Revelation 6:13; Matthew 24:29. So the star should be understood here — it is a mark of divine punishment! Everything serves the God of Christians. They even sing it today when they sing the 148th Psalm. Everything is at God's command. Somewhere we are told that "the stars in their courses fought against Sisera"! Men may order men, but God orders the very stars of heaven to do his will.

Two things come to mind in this trumpet blast. God has interfered with the water supply. This he did in Egypt under the first plague. And again, Israel came across bitter water in their march to freedom and God cast into it a tree which healed the waters. For the people of God, the waters are healed — for the enemy, the water is polluted. "Wormwood" was something the prophets (in the name of God) offered the rebellious Israelites (Jeremiah 23:15 et al).

VERSE 11. And many men died because of the waters - These were not just bitter — they were badly contaminated. Can you imagine this literally being fulfilled somewhere prior to 1988 or thereabouts? Lindsey is committed to this view. But no doubt, if God permits us to live long enough here, we'll receive "explanations" as to why these events didn't occur the way they were "supposed" to.

VERSE 12. And the fourth angel sounded - Now the heavenly bodies are smitten. This is customary prophetic speech. At the fall of Babylon, it is said: For the stars of heaven and the constellations thereof shall not give their light; the sun shall be darkened in its going forth, and the moon shall not cause its light to shine...I will make the heavens to tremble, and the earth shall be shaken out of its place. (Isaiah 34:4,5): "And all the host of heaven shall be destroyed, and the heavens shall be rolled together as a scroll; and all their host shall fade away...for my sword hath drunk its fill in heaven: behold, it shall come down upon Edom, and upon the people of my curse, to judgement." In Joel (2:10) God speaks against Judah, threatening, under the figure of a locust plague, the visit of a terrible army. He describes it this way: The earth quaketh before them; the heavens tremble; the sun and the moon are darkened, and the stars withdrew their shining.

None of this was literally fulfilled. None of this was intended to be literally fulfilled. It is a description of the Almighty's attack on the world of the ungodly. Because of sin, the whole creation came under a curse — that which was to be man's home and man's servant is cursed. Each time a judgment takes place, we have a repeat of the curse. And, of course, the blessings of man are taken from him in famine — fear is generated in him — his "home" becomes one huge hall of panic-producing wonders.

In the days of Moses, the ninth plague hit the sun in the Egyptian sky. The heavens were therefore under the rule of God. So it is here. Not only does God rule the earth and the sea — he rules the heavens.

And the day should not shine for the third part of it - There is no suggestion here of the strength of the light being diminished as say, in the case of air pollution (as per Lindsey). Instead of a 12-hour day, there would be an 8-hour day. Instead of the moon and stars shining 12 hours, they would shine only 8 hours, so that, both in the nighttime and in the daytime, there would be 4 hours of utter darkness. At Egypt, there was darkness for three days.

VERSE 13. And I saw and I heard an eagle - The best Greek texts have "eagle" instead of "angel." So literally understood, we have a talking eagle. This is not preposterous, but is this what we are to understand? I think not. The eagle is chosen to add "fresh terror" to the picture. See the lonely, but fierce predator, which swoops on its victims; see it solitary in the sky and hear the awe-inspiring, spine-chilling word it has to say: Woe, woe, woe!

Them that dwell on the earth - This expression occurs often in Revelation. It speaks of the ungodly! It stands opposed to those that "dwell in the heaven" (13:6). The expression occurs in 3:10; 6:10; 8:13; 11:10 (twice); 12:12; 13:8,12,14 (twice); 14:6; 17:8. In each case we can see the evil import. Check them for yourself and draw your own conclusion. The saints, even though they live on the earth, are seen as dwellers in heaven (12:12; 13:6).

There is no justification, however, to make "earth" in Revelation stand for "Palestine." Check a concordance for yourself and try substituting "Palestine" where you read "earth." It becomes absurd!

Summary

What have we seen then in this chapter? We have seen judgments falling on an ungodly world which should draw them to repentance. Their whole world is being hit. Their home is no longer a home. It is a palace of horrors! God is bringing to the mind of the saints his authority and control. The plagues are being recalled.

Chp 9

1 And the 5th angel sounded and I saw a star from heaven which had fallen to the earth and the key of the bottomless pit was given to him,
2 And he opened the bottomless pit and smoke went up out of the pit like the smoke of a great furnace

Questions on Chapter 9

1. What plague comes to mind under the fifth trumpet? *Total darkness in Egypt's plague*
2. Who is the Bright and Morning Star with the key of death and Hades?
3. Who is the "fallen star" with the key to the abyss?
4. What does Paul say the Devil is the prince of the powers of?
5. What's the significance of the smoke-filled air?
6. Who is exempt from the locust plague?
7. What scripture comes to mind on this?
8. Are these literal locusts?
9. What do Walvoord and Lindsey think?
10. What is the symbolic meaning of "the Euphrates"? *shows military might of enemy against oppressors*

Lord = Lord
11. What reason is there to believe the "angels" stand for the huge army? *they obey God's every command + so the huge army is totally under control of God of godly*
12. Are these literal horses? *no, picture of horses to scare the ungodly*
13. What do Walvoord and Lindsey think? *Russia?*

ask "How can Rome be stopped?"
14. What would the fierce impenitence of the enemy provoke in the saints? *forewarns saints the oppressors to rebellion to het-bent on rebellion*
15. What was the aim of the trumpets? *to get ungodly rebellious from repent. Response of ungodly toward warnings - ignored God to repent.*

An Analysis of Chapter 9

I. The fifth trumpet blast: 1-12
  - A. The fallen star and his authority: verses 1,2
  - B. The locust plague: verses 3-11
    1. The nature of their devastation
    2. The limit put on them
    3. Their description
    4. Their leader *Satan*

directly at men; not their environment like last 4 plagues *hurt only ungodly*

moral internal decay of a nation + a people - people worldly like Rom 1 — God gave them up *a nation that has lowered moral standards will be burned*

II. The sixth trumpet blast: 13-21
  - A. The voice from the golden altar: verses 13,14
  - B. The amazing warrior host: verses 15,16
  - C. Their description and power: verses 17-19
  - D. The incorrigible oppressor: verses 20,21

external attack from enemies outside nation

and the sun and the air were darkened by the smoke of the pit.
3 And out of the smoke came forth locusts upon the earth and power was given them, as the scorpions of the earth have power.
4 And they were told that they shld not hurt the grass of the earth, nor any green thing, nor any tree; but only the men who do not have the seal of God on their foreheads.
5 And they were not permitted to kill anyone but to torment for 5 months; and their torment was like the torment of a scorpion when it stings a man.

6 And in those days men will seek death and
will not find it, and they will long to die
and death flees from them.
7 And the appearance of the locusts was like
horses prepared for battle, and on their heads
as it were crowns like gold and their faces
were like the faces of men.
8 And they had hair like the hair of women &
their teeth were like the teeth of lions.
9. And they had breastplates like breastplates of
iron; and the sound of their wings was like
the sound of chariots of many horses rushing to battle.
10 And they have tails like scorpions and stings
and in their tails is their power to hurt men
for 5 months.
11 They have as king over them, the angel of the
abyss: his name in Hebrew is Abaddon and
in Greek he has the name Apollyon. (destroyer)
12 The 1st woe is past; behold 2 woes are still coming
after these things.
13 And the 6th angel sounded, and I heard a voice
from the 4 horns of the golden altar which is
before God
14 one saying to the 6th angel who had the trumpet
"Release the 4 angels who are bound at the
great river Euphrates."
15 And the 4 angels who had been prepared for
the hour and day and month and year,
were released so that they might kill a
3rd of mankind
16 And the number of the armies of the
horsemen are two hundred million; I
heard the number of them
17 And this is how I saw in the vision
the horses and those who sat on them:
the riders had breastplates the color of fire
and of hyacinth and of brimstone and the
heads of the horses are like the heads of lions;
and out of their mouths proceed fire and
smoke and brimstone.
18 And a third of mankind was killed by
these 3 plagues by the fire and the smoke &
the brimstone which proceeded out of their mouths
19 For the power of the horses is in their mouth
and in their tails for their tails are like serpents
and have heads and with them they do harm.
20 And the rest of mankind who were not
killed by these plagues did not repent of the
works of their hands so as not to worship
demons and the idols of gold and of silver
and of brass and of stone & of wood, which
can neither see nor hear nor walk
21 And they did not repent of their murders
nor of their sorceries nor of their
immorality nor of their thefts.

Comments on Chapter 9

VERSES 1-12. And the fifth angel sounded - The first of the three woes predicted by the eagle. It would seem the first four trumpets were **what** was hit and the two coming up are **how** the ungodly world is hit. That is, we seem here to have the elements of the judgments suggested.

A star fallen from heaven unto the earth - This star is spoken of as "he" who has authority. He will bring darkness resulting from smoke out of the abyss. The ninth plague on Egypt was darkness. None could see enough to even go out of their houses. Here too is darkness, but produced by this "star." Who is he? It's clear to me that Satan is intended.

In 22:16 we read of "the bright and morning star." This one brings light — but the fallen star brings darkness. The Bright and Morning Star has the key of death and hades (1:18) — but the fallen star has the key of the abyss. That this star represents a personality we are not left to doubt, for verse 11 tells us so. In verse 1, the star has the authority over the abyss — the infernal region — the place of the unforgiven and the wicked. He is their god (2 Corinthians 4:4) and is the king of the locusts (9:11).

VERSE 2. There went up a smoke out of the pit - This smoke, black as out of a furnace, blots out the light. This is the work of the evil angel of the abyss. This is moral decadence! This will cause them that dwell on the earth to walk in darkness. The world is afflicted with spiritual and moral blindness. The bowls and the trumpets parallel one another and it is at the fifth bowl that darkness is poured out on the throne of the beast so that his kingdom is darkened.

The Devil, said Paul, is "the prince of the powers of the air" (Ephesians 2:2). It is he that "blinds the minds of the unbelieving, that the light of the gospel of the glory of Christ...should not dawn upon them."

The noteworthy thing in all this is, that the moral blindness brought on the world by the Devil is one of the punishments which God brings on the ungodly. In Romans 1:24-28 we are told that God punished the Gentile world by "giving them up" to do wickedness. Moral blindness eats the heart out of a nation. More than once the prophets spoke of spiritual blindness causing the ruin of the nation. And isn't that what Proverbs 14:34 said? A number of writers have noted the effect of immorality on the Roman empire. People like Scullard (from the Grachii to Nero), Barrow (The Romans), Smith (Shorter History of Rome) and others. They note that the lowering of the moral standard did to Rome what the Bible says it will do to any nation — it helped to bury it!

What then is the Christian to learn in all this? That the decadence he saw around him was part of the punishment of God on the oppressor. You'll note now, that there is nothing strange in God giving a people up for their iniquity to permit them to go further into iniquity and then, when it suits him, to destroy them for their iniquity!

VERSES 3-11. And out of the smoke came forth locusts - And another plague is recalled, the eighth! The locusts are associated with the darkness. The darkness itself brings no pain, but moral decadence does just that, so the locusts are brought in as part of the fifth blast to make it clear that there is hurt connected with this trumpet.

These are not literal locusts. Anyone can see this. What do the literalists make of them? Lindsey says they are "mutant" locusts with demons in them (p. 138). It's hard to say what Walvoord believes. He does say (p. 160) they are "not natural locusts." Quite so! He goes on to say they are "a visual representation" of hordes of demons. Now, are they locusts or not? Lindsey says nothing about the smoke and suggests the possibility that the "locusts" are really Cobra helicopters. Walvoord figurizes the "smoke." So it's figurize when you want to and insist on literalism when you can!

VERSE 4. Hurt...only such men as have not the seal of God - These locusts are not to hurt grass, but men. That makes them peculiar. This plague and the next are directed against men. The previous four related directly to man's environment, which of course affected man. These are directly against men. Their affliction is torment, not death (so much for Cobra helicopters which have been killing men for quite a while). Uncertainty, fear, discomfort, superstition, and a smitten conscience (for some) — all these bring torment.

We are told that the sealed are not to be hurt! Read again Ezekiel 9 and get light on this distinction. It is interesting too, that in the case of the plagues we are told that God made a distinction between the Israelites and the Egyptians. See Exodus 8:22; 9:4,6,26; 10:23; 11:7. These trumpets are judgments on the oppressor! The picture is one of Rome smitten!!!

VERSE 5. They should be tormented five months - What does Lindsey say of the "five months?" Nothing! Walvoord takes it literally. It has been said that a locust plague lasts about five months, so this would explain the period of time.

VERSE 6. And in those days men shall seek death - Remember this is the fifth trumpet blast — they've already been through a lot. Now they are being tormented for five months on end — no wonder they want to die! External troubles and inner conflict and all of that without assurance that everything is going to be all right!

VERSE 7. Walvoord "knows" these are ordinary locusts because (!) of their description. But why do they have to be ordinary locusts? On literalist principles, they ought to be a weird type of never-before-seen locusts! To make them a visual representation of something is to forsake the literal principle.

They were horse-like locusts. They wore "as it were" crowns of gold. The face of a man on a man is all right, but the face of a man on an animal would be spooky indeed!

VERSE 8. They had hair as the hair of women - Here is a horror indeed. They combine the beauty and softness of a woman's hair with the "teeth of a lion." This surely speaks a sinister message. The destructive power with the soft appearance. The combination of innocence and yieldingness with vicious and devastating power. And isn't this so characteristic of decadence? Doesn't it offer so much, while eating and devouring? Doesn't it combine a natural healthiness (or a healthy naturalism) with a deadly eating at the inner man?

VERSES 9,10. Breastplates of iron - How powerful they are. How hard to beat or kill. Fully equipped to dispose of the enemy. Evil seems to have the right answer to every protest of conscience or reason. Think for a moment of the decadence which threatens to devour our societies — how well it defends itself. Is the issue pornography? Well, we've got to protect freedom of speech, remember. Is the issue the homosexual legislation? Bear in mind now we have to protect the freedom of the individual, because that's plainly stated in the constitution. He must be left to do as he pleases, especially if his "crime" is a victimless crime. Remember "the pursuit of happiness" and all that. Is it the issue of abortion? For **whatever** reason? Well, after all, it **is** her baby and her life! Is the issue the ravages of the liquor business? Bear in mind it is unconstitutional to say what a man can or can't put into his belly. Breastplates of iron! That's what evil wears. And it can only be pierced by the Sword of the Spirit.

Their power to hurt men - How often do the Bible writers tell us that sin is man's own destruct button? How often do we hear that God will feed them their own ways? Isn't this what Ezekiel says (22:31)? Didn't Hosea (13:9) tell Israel: It is thy destruction, O Israel, that thou art against me. Sin hurts men! Sin is a reproach to any nation. When we grieve over slums, the jobless and the hungry, we grieving over things which should distress, but these are only fruits from a root - SIN!

VERSE 11. They have over them as king the angel of the abyss -His name in both Hebrew and Greek means "destroyer." If we've been right in indentifying the "star" as Satan, then we're right in identifying the locust leader as Satan. This leader is indentified as the "angel of the abyss." The angel "of" the abyss is the angel with the power over the abyss — that's the power attributed to the "star."

VERSES 13-21. The sixth angel sounded - Here is another instrument in the hand of the Lord against the oppressor. External attack. Warfare! Moral and spiritual blindness tear a nation down and wars exhaust her altogether. It is said by some that war made Rome. That's true from one standpoint, but the Romans in general had no love for war. When Augustus closed the temple of Janus in 29 B.C., signalling the return of peace after three severe "civil" wars — the populace was ecstatic with joy. War torments all sensitive souls.

A voice from the horns of the golden altar - That's where the prayers went up from! We are reminded here that these judgments are in response to the prayers of the saints for justice — see 8:3-5. The "horns" of anything are the strong parts of it. The horns of the altar are the most efficacious part of it. Sounds strange to western ears — but it wasn't strange at all to these people.

VERSE 14. Loose the four angels...bound at the great river Euphrates - And who are these? These are they who are appointed to attack Rome. These stand for the armies upon which God can call to do his bidding. We'll see in the following verses that the horses are the destroyers, but in this verse the angels are said to be the destroyers.

They were kept bound at the "Eurphrates." This river stood for the threat of military might. It was across the Euphrates that the Assyrians and the Babylonians came against the Jews. In a number of scriptures, the river is made to stand for the military might of the enemy. In Isaiah 8:7,8, the prophet speaks in just this very way. He says: The Lord bringeth upon them the waters of the River, strong and many, even the king of Assyria and all his glory: and it shall come up over all its channels, and go over all its banks; and it shall sweep onward into Judah...In chapter 7:20, we have this same association spoken of.

In this vision, God is saying that he will use military power against the oppressor. He then uses an expression which speaks of just such a thing. That we're on the right track is seen by the elaboration of the vision. We next read of a huge army of horesmen.

Lindsey holds the "Euphrates" to be literal. So does Walvoord. They both proceed to get the "Orient" out of there, though how they do it is not clear. It is true that they tie this passage together with a passage in chapter 16 which mentions "kings from the east," but as we'll see when we get there, this is no proof whatever. And how would the Orient be bound at the Euphrates river?

Having mentioned some things he couldn't prove, Lindsey goes on to say the four angels would help mobilize "an army of 200 million soldiers from east of the Euphrates." But that is a long way east of — not "at" or "in" — the Euphrates.

VERSE 15. That had been prepared - The saints are assured that these armies are totally under the control of God. The angels stand for the armies. They move only when God says move. They have their place in the divine program. The saints need to know this! We today need to know this! The Lord IS Lord.

That they should kill the third part of men - Here again we are reminded that this is a partial judgment in order to call the world to repentance. The premillennialists have 1 billion slain during the seals — many slain by the drinking of contaminated water and now we see a third of the remainder slain by these Red Chinese (Lindsey and Walvoord). That leaves 2 billion, minus however many die of the polluted water. That's not counting the many millions who die in the Gog-Magog affair. Bear in mind that Lindsey believes all this is to take place very soon. Somewhere around 1981-1988. I'm not telling you what I think he thinks; I'm telling you what he says he thinks! Keep all these figures in mind, and all these terrible events for these people think the world is going to enter a full-scale nuclear war AFTER all the terrors fall.

VERSE 16. And the number...twice ten thousand times ten thousand - This is not the number of the angels but the number of the horsemen. That's 200 million. Why 200 million? To scare the life out of the enemy. To make the saints rejoice that their God has such an army at his disposal. To stress the staggering control possessed by God. This is what Ezekiel says to us in the Gog-Magog affair. See the comments in my "Ezekiel" on chapters 38, 39.

VERSES 17-19. And I saw the horses - It is remarkable that we hear no more about the horsemen, but yet when we read the description of the horses, it's not really remarkable that the riders are no more mentioned. Lindsey, in his "Late Great Planet Earth" makes much of the fact that the terrain between Russia and the Euphrates is suitable for cavalry — horse-riding cavalry. Horses are mentioned here, and so you see this gives his remarks an appearance of literal truth. However, one look at these horses, and we must dismiss as subterfuge all this talk of horses.

In Ezekiel 38 and 39, the Gog hosts are said to ride on "horses" and carry "bows" and "arrows." Lindsey and his group say this is Russia heading up an army in the near future. If so, they ride horses and fight with obsolete weapons. In his "Late Great," (page 176), Lindsey complains of amillennialists not taking scripture at its face value. He says:

> As it has been demonstrated many times in this book, all prophecy about past events has been fulfilled literally...the words of prophecy were demonstrated as being literal, that is, having normal meaning understood by the people of the time in which it was written...

And does Lindsey stay with his own philosophy? Of course not! What does he make of the "horses" in Revelation 9? "Some kind of mobilized ballistic missile launcher." Are the words of Ezekiel to be taken literally? Are "bows" bows? Are "arrows" arrows? Look again at the quote and ask yourself, are these people playing the game fairly with us. And what of the fire, smoke, and brimstone? He says these are the result of nuclear warfare. **What were they when Sodom was wasted?**

These horses are not literal. In the vision they are horses, of course, but the whole thing is intended to scare the life out of the oppressor. Read the description of the locusts in Joel 2:4ff. Under the figure of a locust plague God speaks of the invasion of Judah by the Babylonian. But in the vision, the locusts are not pictured as ordinary locusts — their appearance is distorted and made to appear (if possible) even worse than they are. In Habakkuk 1:5ff, the Lord speaks of the Chaldean horsemen in graphic terms never intended to be taken literally. He is trying to frighten the rebellious Judeans. Horses, fiercer than evening wolves?

VERSE 18. By these three plagues was the third part...killed - We are told again that this is a fraction-judgment. In verse 15, we were told the angels were to kill the third part, and in this verse we hear it is the power of the horses which kills the men. Now, understanding the words as John understood them (as we have just been told to do) we can't get nuclear warfare! We can't get mobile ballistic missiles.

What are we being told in all this? That God will devour the adversary. In this case he will use an army of unbelievable might and terror. Read the passages I mentioned above on the Babylonian army and you will see what I mean about a figurative representation.

VERSES 20,21. And the rest...who were not killed with these plagues - This is really scary — they repented not! There's nothing so scary as one so soaked in sin and rebellion that he can't quit rebelling. Nothing so fearful as to see men who have been blinded by God, still seeking the door to commit iniquity as did the people of Sodom. Such hardness of heart is awe-inspiring. To see a whipped opponent keep on coming back at you makes the mind waver — can he be beaten? This would forewarn the saints that their opponents were bent on evil. It would scare them that the enemy is so hard to stop.

Twice in these two verses we are told "they repented not." The clear implication of these verses is that the trumpets were intended to bring them to their senses and to repentance. But despite what happened to their colleagues, they refused to quit!

Chps 8-9
6 Trumpet blasts of warning
judgment to come!
against ungodly

Summary

What have we seen then in chapter 9? We have seen two of the instruments of punishment used by the Lord. Internal corruption and external invasion. These have been used against the oppressor — those who have not the name of the Father written on their foreheads. They were used against him to call him to repentance, but they didn't accomplish that task. How are they to be stopped? That'd be the question in the minds of the awe-stricken saints.

God is trying to scare the daylights out of the oppressor to get him to repent. see comments under verse 16 -- a 200 million army against oppressor to help saints to see power of God. and to scare the oppressor
God will devour the adversary and will use an army of unbelievable might & terror.

One third of mankind killed by this unbelievable large army & those not killed they did not repent -- that is scary. The trumpets were meant to bring them to their senses but they refused to bow to God.

Next p. 148

Chapter 10

1 And I saw another strong angel coming down
out of heaven, clothed w/a cloud and the
rainbow was upon his head and his face
was like the sun and his feet like pillars of fire.
2 and he had in his hand a little book which
was open. And he placed his right foot on
the sea and his left on the land;
3 and he cried out w/a loud voice, as
when a lion roars and when he had cried
out the seven peals of thunder uttered their
voices.
4 And when the seven peals of thunder had
spoken I was about to write and I heard
a voice from heaven saying, "Seal up the
things which the seven peals of thunder have
spoken and do not write them."
5 And the angel whom I saw standing on the
sea and on the land lifted up his right
hand to heaven
6 and swore by him who lives forever and ever
who created heaven and the things in it
and the earth and the things in it and
the sea and the things in it that there
shall be delay no longer
7 but in the days of the voice of the 7th
angel when he is about to sound, then
the mystery of God is finished [was] as He
preached to His servants the prophets
8 And the voice which I heard from heaven
I heard again speaking with me and
saying "Go take the book which is open
in the hand of the angel who stands on
the sea and the land."
9 And I went to the angel telling him to
give me the little book. And he said to
me, "Take it and eat it; and it will
make your stomach bitter but in your
mouth it will be sweet as honey."
10 And I took the little book out of the angel's
hand and ate it, and it was in my mouth
sweet as honey and when I had eaten it
my stomach was made bitter.
11 And they said to me, "You must prophesy
again concerning many people and
nations and tongues and kings."

revelation of complete judgment against oppressors of godly — 4 means complete

BettyNote: V 4 a voice from heaven — — I think this is God because in V 5 & 6 the strong angel lifts his right hand to heaven & praises God almighty

2 commands given to John I think it's God or who is it

V 8 the voice I heard from heaven I heard again speaking

Questions on Chapter 10

1. The description of the strong angel — who does it bring to mind?
2. What did he have in his hand? *an open book — a responsibility*

the ungodly will be dealt with

3. What is the significance of what he had in his hand?
4. What do you make of the 7 thunders? *its judgment book to nations — some*
5. What is the finished mystery of verse 7? *conflict of Rome & Church is being dealt w/ by God*
6. What is the significance of John eating the book?
7. Why was it sweet in his mouth? *the Word is always powerful to the end*
8. Why was it bitter in his belly? *reveals suffering in life of follower*
9. Do we ever come across anything like this in the Bible before this? *Ez, Lamentations, Jeremiah, etc. Habbakuk, etc*
10. What do you make of the commission of John?
11. Is it to be fulfilled up future? *Its coming soon — the end of Roman Empire & vindication of godly.*

to prophesy concerning of many people & nations & tongues & Kings

No more delay - God begins dismantling the Roman Empire

An Analysis of Chapter 10

I. The strong angel and the seven thunders: 1-4 the ungodly will be dealt with*
- A. The angel's appearance: verses 1-3a
- B. The angel's book: verse 2
- C. The seven thunders and their secret utterance: verses 3a,4

II. The strong angel and John: 5-11
- A. The angel's oath: verses 5-7
- B. The instructions given to John: verse 8
- C. John's response: verse 9a
- D. The angel's commission to John: 9b-11
    1. Eat the book
    2. Prophesy

Contents of little book to be revealed in chapters 12-22

Introduction to Chapters 10, 11, and 12

Chapters 8 and 9 depicted the warning judgments on the oppressor. Though they were only warnings, they were severe. The oppressor should have repented, but didn't. He only hardens his heart further and blasphemes. In this he reminds us of Pharaoh. Such steadfast wickedness is a fearful thing to witness — it produces fear in the timid. There is nothing as awe-inspiring as to see incarnate hatred and spite clawing for victory, even though it knows it's a loser. The saints need assurance in the face of this undying malice.

In chapter 13, we will better understand the reason for this horrifying strength of purpose for wickedness — the two beasts with the Dragon's authority are a fierce pair indeed. The fiery gargantuan, the Dragon, is himself, an even more horrifying sight.

So, chapters 10-12 are well placed. They are designed to comfort. They come immediately after the manifestation of ungodly brute strength and immediately before the terrible trio. Strong angels assure! A besieged city is yet protected! Witnesses in sackcloth are still the victors! A new baby wins! A woman is protected! And the rest of her seed are victorious, too!

Comments on Chapter 10

VERSES 1-4. And I saw another strong angel - The description of this angel suggests a very high-ranking authority indeed. It might even be Jesus. But it is more likely that he is a representative of Jesus himself. I know of nowhere in the Bible where a member of the Godhead is described as an angel. (The indentification of Jesus with the "angel of Jehovah," I think is utterly unproved).

Whoever he be, he is a top-ranking authority. There are various orders of angels as well as men. There are "arch-angels." Michael is called one (Jude 9) and is called "one of the chief princes" in Daniel 10:13.

VERSE 2. He had in his hand a little book open - The little book is a commission to John — it is both the message he is to relate and the responsibility to relate it. The book will be eaten by John and in this act, we have his acceptance of the responsibility. In this he is like the prophet Ezekiel (2:8; 3:3) who was also given a roll to eat. The words of the book being related by John are a "prophecy" (1:3). What he has already been saying applied to many nations. He will accept the responsibility to say more concerning many nations. There is no indication in the text that he is to personally tour various nations speaking to them.

Jeremiah (1:5) was appointed a prophet "unto the nations" but there was no "tour of duty" involved. The young man was set "over the nations and over the kingdoms" (1:10), but he did no world travelling to get the job done!

His right foot upon the sea and his left upon the earth - Here we have authority and power reflected. His size is staggering and his power (who can stand on the sea as though it were land?) unbelievable. To the Bible writers, earth and sea were the whole world — the angel has universal authority!

VERSE 3. A great voice, as a lion roareth - Everything is geared to let us know of the power of this messenger. He has seen the impenitence — he knows the fear such could generate, and has come to make it clear that the ungodly will be dealt with.

The seven thunders uttered their voices - Thunder is ever associated with judgment. The seven speaks of completeness. Their message, whatever its nature, is one of judgment. Perhaps they stand for the seven bowls which will complete the judgment upon Rome. They may embrace **all** the elements involved in that judgment. If this be true, God does not wish for them to be known at this point — maybe they are not to be revealed at all. This would mean that there are other instruments of judgment not revealed.

Deuteronomy 29:29 speaks of things which God keeps to himself.

VERSES 5-11. Lifted up his right hand to heaven - This is done when taking an oath — see Daniel 12:7. It indicates the one performing the oath is aware that he is there in full view of heaven. Undoubtedly this is where preachers got it. We see them do it often, at baptisms. It gives a solemnity to the occasion.

VERSE 6. There shall be delay no longer - There had been delay. It was to give the ungodly time to repent. They had scorned the opportunity. Their time was now come. How many silly souls have had opportunity after opportunity to turn back to the Lord and put it off, either obstinately or by neglect, and found themselves ushered into the presence of the Almighty, unprepared?

VERSE 7. In the days of the voice of the seventh angel - Why in his day? Because, you remember, the seventh trumpet contains the seven bowls, even as the seventh seal contained the seven trumpets! With the sounding of the seventh trumphet, the whole course of judgment has been covered. In the seventh trumpet are the seven bowls. From the first bowl to the last — that is the "time" covered by the seventh trumpet.

Then is finished the mystery of God - What mystery? The one he is revealing to John in this book of Revealing. The conflict of the Church with Rome, the terrors thus ahead for the Church, and her ultimate victory over Rome!

The good tidings which he declared to his servants - This gives the cheery side of the mystery. Ultimate victory is thus shown to be the key thrust of the book! This was revealed to his servants, the prophets. In 1:1, we are told that God gave this revelation "to show unto his servants." He goes on to say in that verse he is speaking of things which "must shortly come to pass." We hear the same thing in 22:6, and this confirms us in our view here.

From the time John wrote, the things of his prophecy began to transpire and this is in accordance with the scriptures we've just mentioned. To claim that chapters 4-22 have not even begun to be fulfilled, 1900 years after the book is written, is to miss the whole point and to bring the book into disrepute! No one could write a book today and say: These things must shortly come to pass, for the time is at hand — and then profess in their old age that they were still 1800 years in the future. This is what the millennial view does to the book of Revelation. John has given us a book which is said to deal with things which "must shortly come to pass" for "the time is at hand." Not a word of 4-22 has been fulfilled (say they) and they claim they're trying to honor the Word.

VERSES 8,9. Go take the book - Some one orders John to

approach the strong angel and get the book. This he does. The angel doesn't **give** it to him — he is asked to take it. We have the response of John being emphasized here. Each man of God must volunteer his commitment to God.

Take it, and eat it up - John had to take it. John had to eat it. He had to **eat it up**! There was no nibbling at it. It was to be eaten up! It was to enter the belly. Ezekiel was told the same thing and in terms just as explicit, setting forth the prophet's personal submission in the matter. There too, we read that he was to "fill thy bowels" with it. The man was to accept fully the message and the consequent responsibility of that message. We're not talking here about the mere quoting of scriptures — the preaching of sermons. We're here in the presence of men who are making the message part of them and giving themselves to the message. Is this unnecessary today? Do we all know what we're getting into? Shall we find no instruction here for us to quit dabbling in preaching?

How lightly some of us hold the commission of God to be ministers of the Word. We speak of it as though it were just another "profession." I'm not saying that other work is not holy if lawfully offered unto the Lord. I'm saying that some are called to the sacred work of ministering in the Word as evangelists and teachers, and we have not sufficiently committed ourselves to that task.

It shall make thy belly bitter...thy mouth...sweet - And why bitter? Because it has in it bad news. The Church is to suffer much. Ezekiel had the same experience. His message was one of lamentations and woe — no wonder it is said he "went in the heat and bitterness" of his spirit (3:14). Nevertheless, it was the word of God (and in John's case it had a sweet ending); therefore, for him who loves the Word, the taste is sweet. The Psalmist (19:10) said the ordinances were "sweeter also than honey and the droppings of the honeycomb." He says the same thing in 119:103.

VERSES 10,11. Thou must prophesy again over many peoples -John found the word of the angel to be true when he ate the roll — when he committed himself to the commission. He is told what the eating of the book meant in the words we've quoted above. "Over" many peoples means "concerning" many peoples. There is enough in the rest of Revelation to fulfill the requirements of this verse. See, for example, chapters 17 and 18. See on verse 2 above.

Rev 10:11 "You must prophesy again concerning
many people & nations & tongues

Summary

p 168

What have we seen in this chapter? We've seen the appearance of an angel of breath-taking power. An angel who assures the saints that the spooky impenitence of the oppressor is not to alarm them. There will be no futher delay. God will now proceed to dismantle the oppressors. The staggering power and authority of this angel adds comfort to the words spoken. John is confirmed in his commission as the revelator to the brethren.

Chapter 11
1 And there was given me a measuring rod
like a staff and someone said "Rise
and measure the temple of God
and the altar and those who worship
it
2 and leave out the court which is outside
the temple and do not measure it for
it has been given to the nations and
they will tread under foot the holy
city for 42 months.
3 And I will grant authority to my 2 witnesses
and they will prophesy for 1260 days,
clothed in sackcloth."
4 These are the 2 olive trees and the 2 lampstands
that stand before the Lord of the earth
5 And if anyone desires to harm them, fire
proceeds out of their mouth and devours
their enemies and if any one would desire
to harm them, in this manner he must
be killed.
6 These have the power to shut up the sky
in order that rain may not fall during
the days of their prophesying and they
have power over the waters to turn them
into blood and to smite the earth w/ every
plague, as often as they desire.
7 And when they have finished their testimony
the beast that comes up out of the abyss
will make war w/them and overcome them
& kill them.
word 12 see p 139
8 And their dead bodies will lie in the
street of the great city which mystically is
called Sodom & Egypt where also their Lord
was crucified,

9 And those from the peoples and tribes + tongues and nations will look at their dead bodies for 3 days and a half and will not permit their dead bodies to be laid in a tomb.

Questions on Chapter 11

church (measured part holy = protect
(unmeasured " unholy = persecute

7

1. What's the point of the measuring?
2. Is he measuring as literal temple?
3. What's the point of leaving out the outer court and the city?
4. What's the significance of "42 months?"
5. What's the thrust of the vision as a whole?
6. What does Lindsey and company think of the 42 months?
7. Who are the two witnesses?
8. What O.T. prophet helps us in determining who they are?
9. Who does Lindsey think they are?
10. What's the point of their sackcloth?
11. What's the point of the measuring? set aside from world; make holy protected by God, assurance

12. Is he measuring a literal temple? the inner sanctuary where God resides + helps + gives courage

13. What's the point of leaving out the outer court and the city?
14. What's the significance of "42 months"? a state of affairs disciples between it will not annihilate me God God is in control

15. What's the thrust of the vision as a whole? bitter protected

sackcloth? victorious but victorious

16. What does Lindsey and company think of the 42 months?
17. Who are the two witnesses?
18. What O.T. prophet helps us in determining who they are?
19. Who does Lindsey think they are?
10. What's the point of their sackcloth? denotes suffering, persecution

see pt 56
11. What's the significance of 1260 days? a state of affairs where ↑

Rome
12. In light of this, how long do they preach? until they are killed by Rome

Rome
13. Who is the beast that comes up out of the abyss? at the end of their ministry when it was completed

14. What is the city of verse 8? Rome; not Jerusalem

total victory
15. What does the ascension of the two witnesses indicate?
16. Why are they dead "3½ days"? unstable means unstable death + incomplete death so they went stone dead

17. Does verse 15 indicate God wasn't ruling prior to the event alluded to? NO WAY

God rules everything now + Jesus rules everyday
18. How does the "kingdom of the world" become the kingdom of Christ? Acts 2:38 know assured God has made them Jesus whom you crucified both + Savior Lord

19. Is the "kingdom of Christ" restricted to the Church? No vindicate the battle

20. What do you make of the judgment of verse 18? God vindicate saint -- the great battle armag... buries Rome

21. What is the point of the vision of the ark?
22. Is there a literal temple in heaven? wherever God is there is the temple so I am the temple

23. What does Lindsey think?

10 And those who dwell on the earth will rejoice over them and make merry and they will send gifts to one another because these 2 prophets tormented those who dwell on the earth.

11 And after the 3 days and a half the breath of life from God came into them and they stood on their feet and great fear fell upon those who were beholding them.

12 And they heard a loud voice from heaven saying to them "Come up here," and they went up into heaven in the clouds and their enemies beheld them.

Analysis of Chapter 11

inner sanctuary
Church
saved individual
Church

I. The temple and the city: 1,2 God & God alone separates the holy from the unholy just like he separates those whose sins are forgiven from those who aren't; and saved from lost, etc.

A. The temple measured: verse 1

B. The outer court and city excluded: verse 2

C. The outer court and city to be profaned: verse 2

II. The witnesses and the conflict: 3-13

A. Their work: verse 3 God gives them power to prophesy

B. Their indentity: verse 4 the church representatives

C. Their ability: verses 5,6 power to devour enemies power to perform plagues

D. Their success: verse 7a They will finish their testimony

E. Their "defeat": verses 7b-10 then the beast will kill them

F. Their vindication: verses 11-13 they are resurrected and God vindicates church w/ judgment on Rome's end

III. The preparation for the third woe (the 7th trumpet blast): 14-19

A. The warning: verse 14 The 2nd woe passed 3rd woe coming

B. The seventh trumpet and the response: verses 15-18 — the wrath of God includes Battle of Armageddon

C. The temple in heaven: verse 19 heavens opened

13 And in that hour there was a great earthquake and a 10th of the city fell and 7,000 people were killed in the earthquake and the rest were terrified and gave glory to the God of heaven.

Comments on Chapter 11

VERSES 1,2. And there was given me a reed - A long cane-like stick. This reminds us of Ezekiel 40:3,5 where the prophet is given a 9-foot measuring stick. John is told to arise and measure! Now what is this measuring business? Here it clearly is to make a separation between the holy and the common — that which is to be profaned and that which is to be kept apart. Ezekiel 42:20 indicates the very same thing.

Whatever we measure, we set it apart from what we don't measure. This setting apart, in Bible terms, is sanctification — this is designating it as holy! In Zechariah 2:1-5 this idea doesn't come through. It would seem that there the point being made is that Jerusalem's inhabitants will be too numerous to be walled-in, and besides that, they won't need a wall since Jehovah will be their wall. So that while there is the thought of protection there (which is implied in our present passage), it's not quite what the Revelation passage has in mind.

As I've said, the idea of protection is implied in this passage because God is regarding the measured section "holy" (ie. not to be profaned). This holiness is not the inherent quality of the building or worshipers — it is something God makes it. This we'll see in a moment.

Measure the temple of God - What temple is this? By the time this letter was written, there was only ONE temple **of God!** The Church of God — 1 Corinthians 3:16,17; Ephesians 2:19-22. There is, by the time this letter is written, only ONE holy city! The city of God — Revelation 21:1,2,9ff.

And them that worship therein - The word "temple" here is the one which indicates the inner sanctuary (naos) and not the whole building (heiron). Them that worship "therein" would have to be priests, for only the priests entered the inner sanctuary. Note that **the worshipers** are measured!

VERSE 2. And the court...without the temple...measure it not - The reason for this is given — "for it hath been given unto the nations: and the holy city shall they tread under foot forty and two months."

We have in these two verses holiness and profanity — one is kept by God and the other is left to be profaned. The making of it holy implies protection and the permitting of the other to be profaned, implies persecution. God is responsible for both. That is, it is according to his will that both take place. And what is the point of it all?

The whole structure, the inner temple, the outer court, the

holy city — all of it, is the Church of God. The Church of God is about to enter a period when she would suffer persection, but at the same time be sustained! She would endure hardship and abuse, but would be preserved through it by the Lord.

God is saying, though the city of God will undergo abuse from the profaning forces of Rome, yet they cannot get to her heart. He permits the suffering but will not permit the annihilation — the inner sanctuary is kept by him. We'll see this developed further in the next few paragraphs.

The holy city shall they tread under foot forty and two months What is this 42 months? It is the same as 1260 days! The Jew worked on a 360-day year. (He added an intercalary month — 2nd Adhar — periodically, to bring his calendar in line with solar years.) 1260 days = 42 months. Both of these are equivalent to "time, times, and half a time." This can be seen in chapter 12:6,14 where 1260 days is interchangeable with "time, times and half a time." Read them — now.

All right — now we know what the period is — what does it mean? It is **a time figure.** It is what the "1,000 years" of Revelation 20 is — a period of time, **used to speak of a state of affairs!** Later we'll talk about this 42 months. Look at the passages in which the phrase or its equivalents occur.

1. It is the period of the beast's authority - Rev. 13:5
2. It is the period of the holy city being trodden under foot - Rev. 11:2
3. It is the period during which the witnesses prophesy - Rev. 11:3
4. It is the period the Woman is nourished in the wilderness - Rev. 12:6,14
5. It is the period the "little horn" persecutes the saints - Daniel 7:25

What does the period signify? **It speaks of a state of affairs** wherein the saints are subjected to persecution but are protected; wherein they are subjected to suffering but are sustained; wherein they are victimized but are yet victorious!

The two thoughts are ever present. In Daniel 7:25 we hear the little horn has power over the saints for "time, times, and half a time. **But...**" Blessed "but!" The judgment shall be set and the little horn will get what's coming to him, says Daniel.

In the case of the Woman, she is forced to flee into the wilderness which speaks itself of hardship, for a wilderness is not a soft-cushioned palace. But, she is "nourished" **there!** There, right in the place of her hardship, she is nourished. (Is there no lesson here for us today?)

In the case of the two Witnesses, though they are in sackcloth (which indicates hardship — occasion of mourning) they cannot be stopped in their preaching for the Lord is with them to sustain them by (in the vision) miraculous abilities.

In the case of the holy city — the citadel of it is untaken despite the abuse of the outer limits. And why does it remain untaken? Because God would have it so! Why must the witnesses wear sackcloth? The woman — why must she flee? The city — why must it be trodden under? Because God would have it so! Why is the beast given authority to continue 42 months? God wants it so!

What is the origin of the figure? You'll notice that the woman is forced to flee into the wilderness but is nourished there — we have hardship but nourishment for the period of 3½ years. In the days of Elijah, the prophet was nourished during the period of hardship (1 Kings 17:1-5; Jame 5:17; Luke 4:25). There's the origin of it.

In addition — 3½ is a broken seven. Seven speaks of the completeness of a thing, its fullness, and perfection. The authority of the beast lacks all that. The hard times are transient in nature. See this discussed in my little commentary on "Daniel."

So what is the overall thrust of the vision of verses 1,2? Here it is: The City of God (ie. the Church of God) is to undergo persecution from Rome. Despite this the Church will all the while be sustained by the Lord.

What are the alternative views? **As to the temple and the city!** Milligan thinks the "temple" speaks of the real Christian and the rest of the structure and the city speaks of the hypocrites, the compromisers. This is an interesting view. Perhaps it is right. But it seems to me to have at least two problems: 1) It would mean the hypocrites are given over to the persecution by the oppressor, while in fact, the compromisers were not persecuted. 2) This persecution was to last only 42 months. (We'll say something more about Milligan's view shortly.)

Foy E. Wallace takes a middle course, combining both the spiritual (figurative) and the literal. He holds the "temple" is the Church and that the court stands for the unbelieving Jews — the city stands for the literal city of Jerusalem (pp. 212,213). Max King, for different reasons, comes to the same conclusion. The view is interesting. Maybe it's right. We'll say more shortly.

Concerning the "42 months." Milligan makes this stand for the entire Christian era. I find this unacceptable and have stated my own views already. Milligan's view on the whole then (and

Hendriksen's) is that the inner sanctuary stands for true believers; the outer court and holy city stand for the professors; the 42 months stand for (almost — Hendriksen) the whole Christian era. Hendriksen speaks of the "treading under foot" by the nations as "excommunication" (page 154). Milligan is not clear at all as to how this 42-month trampling applies to the hypocrites.

Wallace holds the 42 months to be **exactly** that. He says it over and over again. King's book professes this literal 3½-year period, over and over again. King's position has been examined and I think adequately refuted in the McGuiggan-King Debate (pp. 17ff, 143ff, 166ff). In a personal conversation (after the debate) I understood Max to say he has changed his mind about **this** matter.

Wallace "computes" to get this 3½ years to be literal. He tells us (without **specific** documentation) that Vespasian was commissioned by Nero in February 67 to go against Jerusalem. This he hasn't established! Furthermore, he speaks of "February A.D. 67 when the war against Judea was declared" (p. 271). This is demonstrably untrue! And besides, Vespasian did not trample under foot the city of Jerusalem for 3½ years. For a solid year — June 68 until June 69 — not a hand was raised against Jerusalem (due to the Roman troubles). The war against the Jews was declared long before February 67. There is no proof whatever that Vespasian worked on the Jerusalem problem for exactly 1260 days! **Vespasian did not trample Jerusalem under his feet for 3½ years!**

I'm presuming, since the same period is used of the Woman's stay in the wilderness, that Foy believes the Church stayed exactly and literally 3½ years in Pella. This too cannot be established.

Lindsey and his group think the temple here is literal. It is the temple the unbelieving Jews will soon build. They'd have to be unbelieving Jews or they wouldn't build a temple and restore a shadow system. Lindsey says absolutely nothing about the "inner sanctuary" being measured and thus declared holy. Of course he wouldn't, because that puts him in difficulty. We can't have God regarding as holy a temple built by unbelieving Jews in a covenant with the Antichrist.

Walvoord mentions the measuring of the inner sanctuary and claims it means: God will judge a man's worship and that everyone comes short of God's measurements. But he does go on to say that by measuring "God is therefore not only claiming ownership by this measurement of the Temple...but demonstrating the shortcomings of the worshipers who do not measure up to His standards" (pp. 176,177)

This is interesting because it shows God claiming the temple as

His. But how could it be his when it is built in an antichristian spirit by unbelieving Jews with the aid of the Antichrist?

Both Lindsey and Walvoord (as do all premillennialists) hold the 42 months to be the last 3½ years of the 70th week of Daniel. See this discussed in my thing on "Daniel."

VERSES 3-13. And I will give unto my two witnesses - This "and I will give" continues the idea of God's control. The outer court and the holy city are "given" unto the nations. The two witnesses, here, are **enabled** to do whatever they are to do. Who are they? They represent the Church of God! The figure changes from a temple and city to a pair of prophets. In chapter 21 we have two figures — a bride and a city, so this change is not unusual.

What reason do we have for saying the two witnesses are the Church? The prophet Zechariah helps us in the matter. In chapter 4 we have the vision of the two olive trees which supply the candlestick with oil. The two olive trees are identified for the prophet (verses 11-14) as the "two anointed ones that stand by the Lord of the whole earth." These two "anointed" ones are the civil ruler (Zerubbabel of the royal line) and the priest (Joshua, son of Jozedek). It was by these two (kings and priests were both anointed to their office, hence they were anointed ones — see Leviticus 8 and 1 Samuel 10:1ff, 16:1ff) — it was by Zerubbabel and Joshua that God led the nation. Through them the divine direction was given. These two are said to be the "two olive trees." Here in Revelation 11, our two witnesses are said to be "the two olive trees and the two candlesticks, standing before the Lord of the earth."

The Church, as you well know, is a "royal priesthood." It combines in itself what its master combines so gloriously — priesthood and royalty. They are the "candlesticks" as we know from chapter 1:12,13,20. So the two witnesses are the Church of God.

Why two? Because that is the number of confirmed and strengthened testimony. Numerous passages set this forth. Timothy is told not to accept an accusation against an elder unless there be at least two (1 Timothy 5:19). Jesus claimed that even though he would always tell the truth, that his own testimony, if it stood alone, would not be sufficient to establish his claims (John 5:31; 8:14). In Matthew 18:16, he urges at least two witnesses, that every word may be established! In Genesis 41:32, Joseph tells Pharaoh he got the dream doubled to him to assure him of its certainty. Throughout the Bible, we have God sending men in twos. Moses and Aaron: Elijah and Elisha; Zerubbabel and Joshua; and the two sent on the limited commission — Matthew 10:1ff.

Walvoord and Lindsey think they are two individuals who will be raised up later. Lindsey thinks they are Moses and Elijah. He claims Elijah never finished his ministry. He claims Moses didn't really finish either — so they are coming back for another go. I think we've said enough about the identity of these two.

They shall prophesy 1260 days - You'll recall that this is the period of time the holy city is said to be trodden under foot of the nations. This is the period the beast is said to be permitted to continue. We're being told here that the Church cannot be stopped. They wear sackcloth. This indicates that everything is not roses — but the fact yet remains, they do continue to get the job done.

VERSES 5,6. And if any man desire to hurt them - This implies the opposition but they are adequate for that opposition. They have at their disposal (in the vision) miraculous ability to punish their opposition. We are not to suppose these miracles to have been literally carried out. This is part of the vision! It is an element in the picture which gives the picture its wholeness. In the vision, the Church is seen to be "unstoppable."

The miracles they work are recalling the deeds of other loyal pairs of God's people. Moses and Aaron brought plagues on the land of Egypt. Elijah brought on a drought. He called fire down out of heaven on the messengers of the wicked Ahaziah.

VERSE 7. When they shall have finished their testimony - That is, after the three and a half years. King sees the difficulty here to his position, but can't help it. If this is a literal, historical 3½ years, the duration of the Church's ministry was 3½ years. He denies this but says no more about it.

There is difficulty here too for Wallace. He identifies this 1260 days as the same period (he calls it an "exact mathematical application") as when the nations trample Jerusalem underfoot and as when the Woman stays in Pella. The difficulty is obvious. The Witnesses are Christians who are representative of the apostles and prophets. They preach for the full period which culminates in the destruction of Jerusalem and yet, Wallace holds, they are slain in Jerusalem after they have finished their testimony. This would have these Christians preaching in the middle of Jerusalem while the war was going on, and surviving until the very day the temple falls. This is further complicated by the fact that the Woman (whom Wallace holds is the Church) fled to Pella where she spent that 3½ years.

Let's start again. The Witneses represent the Church. They are seen here as holding to their testimony even though they are under pressure from the beast — they are wearing sackcloth. Persecution can't stop them. No one can harm them so as to cause their testimony to cease. Can they be hurt? Of course. In the previous vision, the city is under the pagan heel and yet a section of the city (its very center — the inner sanctuary of the temple) is protected. In the verses we've looked at so far concerning the witnesses all we've had is the power of the witnesses and their unbeatable nature. Now we will hear the truth stressed that the Church is to undergo pressure.

The beast...shall make war with them - Why doesn't the beast make war with them and overcome them before the 1260 days are up? That would ruin the idea that the Church can't be stopped. They must (in the vision) be seen to be able to finish their task. Two truths are to be told — two sides of one coin. The persecution but the protection. The truth is, in reality, in history — the Church told its story while the beast made war. But John is not given the story in that form here. He tells both the truths in two different sequences. The first sequence is the unbeatable Church. The second sequence is the "victorious" beast. This accords well with the other two visions — the smitten city with the preserved sanctuary! The Woman in the wilderness and the nourishment she there receives!

The beast is Rome! We'll discuss that later, at length. In the vision, Rome is seen to be victorious, but you and I know despite the blood-letting, the Church is no loser. Daniel 7:25ff is a commentary on this section. The whole of life is an illustration of it.

VERSE 8. In the street of the great city - The city is called by three different names — Egypt, Sodom, and Jerusalem! It is Egypt because Rome is also the oppressor as was Egypt — the worldly power which oppressed the people of God. It is Sodom because Rome was a foul and immoral empire as was Sodom a city — worldliness! It is Jerusalem because Rome was an empire of vile and perverted religion.

These witnesses partake of the death such as their Master endured, so they die in the same city (in the vision). They died in Jerusalem as they died in Egypt. As they died in Sodom. The witnesses die in neither of these three places — literally! There is not an illustration, in or out of the New Testament, where the Romans persecuted the Church **in Jerusalem.** That Rome persecuted the Church we all know, but where is the testimony, in or out of the scriptures, that she hunted and killed Christians, literally in Jerusalem?

The great city in view here, is Rome! In this passage it is called Egypt, Sodom, and Jerusalem, but Rome is the city in question. Especially, in relationship to Wallace's view: This cannot be the literal Jerusalem if the 3½ years be the period between February 67 and August 70. When we get to chapter 17, we'll talk again about

this "great city." We'd do well to bear in mind that the sentence of death against Jesus came from Rome. It was by "lawless" hands the Jews crucified and slew our Lord. The kings of the earth (Rome too, represented by Pilate) had gathered against the Lord and his Anointed (Acts 4:25-28). So Rome slew Jesus!

VERSES 9-10. Men look upon their dead bodies - At the end of their ministry — **but only** when they've completed it — the beast is pictured as killing the witnesses. They overcome them. This is what is stated for us in 13:5-7. The beast makes war with them and overcomes them. In this passage it is **after** the 1260 days. In 13:5ff, it is **for** 1260 days. We've already seen how these two truths are set forth. John's vision could just as easily have followed the usual form and gotten the same basic lesson across, but here it differs. This form really brings out the apparent victory of the beast.

In this vision, the witnesses are seen as **dead.** But they are not just dead — they are dead 3½ days. That's long enough for them to putrify. No one will live again under those circumstances. The beast really has worked a job on the Church. In the other visions, we hear the story of the beast's success — here we **see** it imaged. Of course, not only does the 3½ days carry with it the "well dead" notion — it also has that broken seven notion. That should warn us that they won't stay dead — death's hold on them is somehow not stable or complete.

And suffer not their dead bodies to be laid in a tomb - This looks clearly like an expression of malice. Wallace thinks it means that the sympathizers with the saints will not permit their views to perish. Interesting. It seems hard to me for Wallace to get all this to come together while holding this literal 3½-year-period view. Lindsey thinks this is literally to be fulfilled soon and that everyone will be watching it on Telstar television. At the end of the study, we'll be having a chronological layout of the premillennial view and I'll show you the difficulties that this section raises for them.

And they shall send gifts one to another - They have their own little "tabernacles feast celebration." In Nehemiah 8:9-12, when the people had something to be ecstatic over, they began to weep and mourn. Nehemiah urges them not to do that but to send portions one to another and rejoice. These who hated the Church were having their own little celebration because the Church was under the heel of the over-lords.

VERSES 11-13. And after the three days and a half - What an ominous phrase. We know already what is coming, don't we! It really is so good to be on God's side, for nothing of this sort can have any lasting gloom attached to it. This is 3½ days after what

Lindsey and Walvoord hold that this is the 70th week of Daniel! These people hold that the 70th week of Daniel is the end of Gentile dominion and the time for the 2nd coming of Jesus to set up his nationalistic kingdom. On their terms, He is already 3½ days late. Then, on their terms, all the events of chapter 15, 16 and 19 are to take place **before** the Messiah comes to set up that kingdom. That really blows their chronological arrangement.

They stood upon their feet - The Lord, says the text, had raised them from the dead! Here is a resurrection which sets forth the triumph of the Church over her enemy. We ought to have this burned in our memory. Come what may — it only lasts 3½ days and then comes the standing on our feet! Come what may — Pharaoh's army was drowned! Come what may — the three youths came out of the fire! Come what may — the lions' mouths were shut! Come what may — the tomb was empty just as He said!

VERSE 12. Come up hither. And they went up into heaven - In the vision they ascended just like their Master. Elijah did something like that, didn't he! This speaks of the vindication of the Church. For those who love the Lord it cannot be otherwise!

And their enemies beheld them - This is said to make it clear that the enemies should have understood. Men have been saying for years that one of the very strong points evidencing the resurrection of Jesus Christ from the dead is the survival of the Church. If an enemy will only look — if he will only examine the record of the Faith and see how it has conquered over everything, and then ask himself: What enabled them to do it? The only reasonable conclusion is the one given in the New Testament — a living Lord sustained it.

VERSE 13. There was a great earthquake - Another manifestation of the judgment of God. It accompanies the ascension of the witnesses and acts as an omen of things to come. A tenth part speaks, it would seem, as all fractions do, of part payment, the rest comes later.

And the rest gave glory to the God of heaven - They were not converted — just scared. See this again and again in Nebuchadnezzar and others — the God of heaven in contradistinction to the many other gods of heathenism.

Let me summarize as far as we've gone in this chapter. John is being told the Church is about to undergo hard times, but at the same time he is being assured everything is all right with them. In this chapter, he is told this in two different ways. A vision of a city trodden under the heel of the enemy while the inner sanctuary is well-protected and thus, invulnerable.

The second vision is one of two witnesses. They have a task to perform, namely, prophesy for 1260 days. They have opposition, but they have more than enough ability to take care of that opposition. They finish their task! But there's that other side of the picture to portray — the gloom. That is hinted at in their wearing sackcloth, but it is spelled out in their death at the hands of the beast. Their defeat is seen to be only apparent since they are resurrected and glorified.

The same truth is taught in chapter 12:6,14 and in 13:5ff. In the first, the woman is forced to flee into the wilderness. That speaks of hardship. But in the wilderness there is a place prepared for her to be nourished — that's protection and sustenance. In 13:5ff the beast is the successful oppressor of the saints, but it is specifically stated that his authority is "given" to him and it is circumscribed by the "42 months" phrase we talked about.

In the vision of the city and temple, the two truths are brought out as occurring in the same period. In the vision of the woman the two truths are brought out as occurring in the same period. In the vision of the two witnesses, the beast is shown to have power until after the 1260 days. I've given you the reasons why this route was taken here — still, the message, as we've seen is no different.

VERSES 14-19. The second woe is past: Behold, the third. . . cometh quickly - This is leading up to the seventh trumpet. The sixth trumpet blew back in 9:13 and we've been on a comfort-the-brethren deviation since. But that is how the book is geared — comfort and assurance is the keynote of it. When the seventh blows, we will have another deviation for illumination and comfort!

VERSE 15. And the seventh angel sounded - With this the book really ends as far as the dealing with Rome is concerned. Remember what we said about the seventh seal containing the seven trumpets and the seventh trumpet containing the seven bowls? As far as the thrust of the book is concerned, at the blowing of the seventh trumpet, the seven bowls are poured out, and that is the full and destructive wrath of God. That's the end. That's why the cry immediately goes up: The kingdom of the world is become the kingdom of our Lord and of his Christ! The cry goes up as if the job is done. This is what the angel said in 10:7, you remember?

Is become the kingdom of our Lord - Some have been foolish enough to so understand this as to say the kingdom didn't already belong to the Lord and his Christ. This won't bear looking at. In this very letter (1:9), John professes to be a member of that very kingdom which belongs to Christ. In Colossians 1:13 Paul assures the Colossians that they were translated into it. In Ephesians 5:5 we are told that the New Testament kingdom is the kingdom of God and Christ (as in this very passage).

There is no suggestion here at all that Jesus did not already have and exercise that authority over the nations, for he himself said he had **already received** (2:26,27) it from his father. This makes it very clear he already had it! And since it was given him of his Father, that means his Father had the authority to give him that dominion, which means that the Father himself already had the power.

The New Testament is full of the story that Jesus was made Lord already — long prior to the story laid out in Revelation. Isn't that what Peter told the Jews they could be assured of (Acts 2:36)? Didn't Peter say it as clearly as words could say that the principalities, powers, and angels **had been** made subject to Jesus (1 Peter 3:22)? Must we quote texts to prove that the kingdom of God had come when Jesus began to participate in the Lord's Supper with his disciples? See then Luke 22:18 and 1 Corinthians 10:16ff.

It is clear from the scriptures that there has always been a kingdom of God and cannot be a time when there will be none. This kingdom (sovereignty) of God is universal and eternal. The Psalmist (10:16) said: Jehovah is King for ever and ever. He further said (29:10): Jehovah sat as King at the flood; yea, Jehovah sitteth as King forever. Moses (Exodus 15:18) said: Jehovah shall reign for ever and ever. David said (1 Chronicles 29:11): Thine, O Jehovah, is the greatness, and the power, and the glory, and the victory, and the majesty: for all that is in the heavens and in the earth is thine; thine is the kingdom, O Jehovah, and thou art exalted as head above all...and you rule over all.

And even when foreigners ruled his people, the kingdom still belonged to the Lord. Nebuchadnezzar needed a lesson concerning this matter. God had made it very clear to him (Daniel 2:36-38) that He had given "the kingdom" unto the pagan. The Babylonian wasn't convinced and so God said he would eat with the wild animals long enough for him to have learned the lesson that: The most High ruleth in the kingdom of men, and giveth it to whomsoever he will, and setteth up over it the lowest of men. (4:17)

And who was it that raised up the Persians to waste the Babylonians? Who gave the kingdom to Cyrus? Was it not the Lord (Daniel and Isaiah 45:1ff)? And who raised up the Greeks to replace the Persians and the Romans to take the place of the Greeks? Who gave the kingdom to the Romans? And who in a public display (as in the thought of the passage now under consideration) showed that the kingdom was really his? In all of these cases, we have a public vindication of an already-existing truth. In his whipping of the Roman power (which slew Jesus), at the resurrection of Jesus, the Father set Jesus at his own right hand in heavenly places, far above **every** principality and power, and **every** name that is named. That takes in the Romans and the Jews. Jesus was made Lord — Peter said the house of Israel could know that assuredly! And so can we! That was years before this passage was written! (I'm planning a little paperback study of the "Kingdom of God in the Bible" very soon, God willing.)

What I'm claiming here is, this is not the beginning of the kingdom of God and Christ. This speaks of a public vindication of what is already true! He who thinks that Jesus was not already King of kings and Lord of lords **before** John wrote the letter needs to take another look. John claimed that Jesus was "ruler of the kings of the earth." Not "will be" ruler of the kings of the earth. In 1:5 he claims that the same Jesus who is the Faithful Witness and the Firstborn from the dead is (IS) the ruler of the kings of the earth! (This Jesus claimed to be already in possession of the key of the house of David 3:7). We've said enough.

It's worthy of note that the "kingdom" of our Lord and his Christ speaks of more than the Church here. It embraces all the sovereignties of the world. Let's quit giving premillennialists the impression that the only authority Jesus has is over believers. The kingdom of Jesus embraces the whole universe. He is King of kings and Lord of lords. Whatever he is king of, is in his kingdom! He is King of kings therefore they are in his kingdom. Most of the time in the New Testament when the kingdom is mentioned, the Church (and only the Church) is meant, but the kingdom concept is much wider than the Church.

Our text here teaches us that Jesus, who became king at his resurrection and glorification publicly manifests that power in his outpouring of wrath on the Roman power which is oppressing his people. That is the sense in which "the kingdom of the world is become the kingdom of our Lord and of his Christ."

And he shall reign for ever and ever - The present kingdom of God is another manifestation of that eternal rule of God which always has been and always must be. Jesus right now is ruling with an authority delegated to him by the Father. One day he will bring this task and work to a close and offer the kingdom unto the Father. At that point, he will begin to share the rule with the Father by virtue of his own inherent nature. It will no longer be a **delegated** authority.

VERSE 17. Thou hast taken thy great power and didst reign - Here we have the same thing as above stated from a different angle. Here it is said, if possible, even more clearly. God had always been reigning. What these are thankful for is a public demonstration of it. A fresh expression of it. C.K. Barrett (p. 243) rightly observed that in apocalyptic speech: "It becomes very clear that the 'coming of the Kingdom' is a way of expressing God's royal authority, now at length put into action." There is no thought in the minds of the 24 elders that God has not been reigning. See this for yourself in chapter 4 and 5:13f.

VERSE 18. And thy wrath came, and the time of the dead to be judged - Remember now, the blowing of the seventh trumpet contains the outpouring of the seven bowls. In the days of the seventh trumpet the full outpouring of the wrath of God is conceived as having taken place. This wrath is that wrath — the seven bowls of wrath which include the great battle of Armageddon (see chapter 16:12ff and 19:11-21.

And what dead are these? Those who will be slain in the wrath of the bowls as well as those who have already died in opposition to the Lord (eg. 11:13 and 8:11; 9:13ff). And what judgment is this? The one to be dealt with in chapter 20:11-15. See the comments there. Remember what I say — although we haven't seen the unfolding yet of the results of the seventh trumpet blast, the wrath of God is fully finished in his days. (Read again 10:6,7 and the comments there. It's important that you grasp this issue).

To give their reward to thy servants - This has reference to the joys of knowing who is victorious. We find it in Daniel 7:17-22, 25-27. See my comments on those passages in the "Daniel" commentary. The kingdom belongs to the saints, but who is exercising the power? The enemy appears to be in control for he is definitely beating-up on the saints. But the kingdom **does** belong to the saints and God makes that very clear by judging the oppressor. His powerlessness is exposed and the saints are comforted. The rule of God is manifested and the saints are assured. The world is seen to the theirs. Judgment is excerised on the destroyer of the earth.

VERSE 19. There was opened the temple of God in Heaven - Lindsey thinks there is a literal temple in heaven. This man has more temples floating around. He believes too, that there will be a 1500 square-mile city of Jerusalem floating around the sky awaiting the end of the millennium, at which time it will drop down and sit on the new earth where the old one sat on the old earth.

This is to let them see the ark of the covenant and it tells them the reason for their success. God is a faithful colleague when it comes to a covenant made. Not, I'd ask you to note, "the ark of

18 And the nations were enraged and Thy wrath came and the time came for the dead to be judged and the time to give their reward to Thy bond servants the prophets and to the saints and to those who fear Thy name, the small and the great, and to destroy those who destroy earth."

the covenant" but the ark of "his" covenant. The ark was always in the presence of God. It was never away from him, thus there was no occasion for him to forget his promises. This is why the saints can be sure of victory. God is faithful. And in his faithfulness, he will often pour out judgment upon the oppressors. This is the reason for the thunders, etc. of which the passage speaks. God's faithfulness expresses itself in mercy toward his people, but that same mercy will punish those who hurt the people to whom God will show his mercy.

Extremely encouraging 22 21

powerful encouragement

See p171 top

Summary

extremely encouraging

A chapter of real comfort in view of the fierce impenitence they have seen in the enemy and in view of what is ahead for them. The Church (city and witness) is to have hard times, but is to rest assured that they will be protected at the same time. "This too shall pass!" God is faithful and will avenge.

19 And the temple of God which is in heaven was opened; and the ark of His covenant appeared in His temple, and there were flashes of lightening and sounds and peals of thunder and an earthquake and a great hailstorm.

Chapter 12

1 And a great sign appeared in heaven; a woman clothed w/the sun and the moon under her feet and on her head a crown of 12 stars;

2 and she was w/child and she cried out being in labor and in pain to give birth.

3 And another sign appeared in heaven and behold a great red dragon having 7 heads and 10 horns and on his heads were 7 diadems.

4 And his tail swept away a 3rd of the stars of heaven and threw them to the earth. And the dragon stood before the woman who was about to give birth so that when she gave birth he might devour her child.

5 And she gave birth to a son, a male child who is to rule all the nations w/a rod of iron; and her child was caught up to God and to His throne.

6 And the woman fled into the wilderness where
she had a place prepared by God so that there
she might be nourished for 1260 days.

#8 Despite Satan's persecution of woman (God's people) she
is provided for by God, and God's people revealed as triumphant

Questions on Chapter 12

In Chp 10 John ate the book that is now being revealed in Chps 12-22

1. What chapter in the Bible is the setting for this chapter?
2. Who is the woman? [the believers of God both O.T. & N.T.]
3. What is the significance of the number 12? [God's people: tribes, apostles etc]
4. Who is the child? [the Messiah, Jesus, promised savior]
5. In what sense are saints responsible for the birth of Jesus?
6. What is the significance of "caught up"? [Jesus died yet ascended into heaven]
7. Is the throne of God Christ's throne? [Yes]
8. What is the significance of 1260 days? [period of time woman nourished] garden praying in Him 3 times
9. What's the significance of "eagles wings"? [p183]
10. What does Lindsey think this might mean?
11. Do verses 7ff speak of an actual-literal battle between Michael and Satan? [No! Jesus defeated Satan on earth & now we see the church in heaven & once again Satan defeated]
in bible middle of Great Tribulation and after resurrection of Jesus see p 175 & 176
12. Where do Lindsey and company chronologically place this battle? [after Jesus ascends back into heaven which would show Jesus death burial & resurrection didn't defeat Satan]
13. Why is the phrase "now is come" (v.10) a difficulty for pre-millennialists? [It puts them saying kingdom comes in middle of G. Tribulation]
14. To what passage is verse 10 parallel? [Acts 2:36 + now]
15. Does verse 10 teach the Devil doesn't accuse the brethren anymore? [NO Devil 3 time loser and accusing but he's totally defeated] the saints, but he doesn't have the RIGHT to accuse them
16. Can you list the three-point success plan for victory over Satan?
17. Who are the "dwellers in heaven"? [people of God]
18. What do you make of this "short time"? [Satan has short time to persecute]
19. What's the significance of the Devil using water to destroy the woman? [he loses -- God's in control 3 time loser]
20. What do you make of the earth helping the woman? [God's in control]
21. Who is the "rest of her seed"? [believers]

7 And there was war in heaven, Michael and his
angels waging war w/the dragon. And the
dragon and his angels waged war
8 and they were not strong enough and
there was no longer a place found for them
in heaven
9 And the great dragon was thrown down, the
serpent of old who is called the devil &
Satan, who deceives the whole world,
he was thrown down to earth and his
angels were thrown down w/him.
10 And I heard a loud voice in heaven
saying Now the salvation and the power
and the kingdom of our God and the authority
of His Christ have come, for the accuser of
our brethren has been thrown down, who
accuses them before our God day and night

11 And they overcame him because of the blood of the Lamb and because of the word of their testimony and they did not love their life even to death.

Analysis of Chapter 12

Chapter 12-22 reveals contents of little book John ate

universal church

I. The woman, the dragon and the child: 1-6

A. The woman described: verses 1,2

1. Her appearance 12 stars, victory wreath for a crown

painful struggle — must have baby messiah — 2. Her condition — pregnant w/ male child who will rule

B. The dragon described: verses 3,4

1. His appearance brutal & powerful

2. His position and purpose stands before woman to devour her

C. The child: verse 5

Satan tried to destroy Jesus in these 3 stages but loser & total defeat (birth, rule in ministry, resurrec)

1. His birth

2. His status ruler like shepherd

3. His ascension

D. The flight of the woman: verse 6 church

1. To a wilderness fled to place prepared BY GOD

2. To a prepared place nourished 1260 days

II. The war in heaven and its result: 7-12

Jesus works so powerful a strong angel can overpower him in spiritual battle. Satan weakend by Jesus' works. Jesus works cannot be overthrown p175-176

Heb 2 (never gave in to temp) perfect Jesus works brings kingdom + plan of salvation + success — overcome sin by blood, testimony & self-denial

A. The opponents: verse 7

B. The result: verses 8,9 — Satan

C. The response: verses 10-12

III. The dragon, the woman, and the rest of her seed: 13-17

church

Satan can't defeat the church so he goes after individuals

A. The persecution and flight of the woman: verses 13,14

B. The dragon's flood attempt: verse 15

C. The flood endeavor thwarted: verse 16

D. The dragon turns on the rest of her seed: verse 17

12 For this reason rejoice, O heavens & you who dwell in them. Woe to the earth and the sea because the devil has come down to you, having great wrath, knowing that he has only a short time.

vs. 8-9 and 10-12

II C. Jesus perfect works (Heb 2 never gave in to Satan's tempting) therefore salvation & kingdom comes w/ total defeat of Satan & total victory of Christ & my response is make Jesus Lord & fight for right because I have ① overcome by blood of lamb ② by my testimony to truth ③ decision to deny self. Therefore rejoice Rom 8:28

So when persecution & threats come don't give in to fear — have faith. Realize Satan is working harder because he knows his time is limited & for him it's all out thrust & attack because the end is near. V. 13 when Satan thrown down persecutes woman

Mt 16:18

V13-17 and the rest of her offspring

15 individual Christians because can't annihilate the universal church

Comments on Chapter 12

VERSES 1-6. And a great sign was seen in heaven: a woman -Everything worth seeing is seen when a man lifts his eyes to heaven. Ezekiel (1:1ff) was among the captives in Babylon and still he saw remarkable things. But if he had kept his eyes on the suffering and the despairing sights — if he had not lifted his eyes to God — he wouldn't have seen the "heavens open." Lift up your eyes!

He saw "a woman." She is a pure, light-hearted woman. And isn't that a great sight? Isn't that kind of vision only produced by heaven? Thank God for godly women. This woman is special. She (and a lot of things associated with her) is drawn from Genesis 3. In this chapter we have a serpent, a woman, a man-child, and the (rest of the) seed of the woman. As in Genesis 3, it is the woman who is to produce the man-child, the seed which would defeat the Serpent. It is her seed that would bruise the head of the serpent. (Paul applies Genesis 3:15 to more than Jesus when he uses it in Romans 16:20).

Who is this woman? She is the people of God! She wears the two heavenly bodies which give light to earth (Genesis 1:17,18). She is the bearer of light in the dark world. She is neither the Church of God exclusively nor the Old Testament believers exclusively. She will be used as the Church of God in the text later, but at this point she simply stands for the elect! God's people.

She wears 12 stars worked into a wreath of victory — the victory crown, the "stephanos." The number 12, as all Bible students recognize, is the number of God's people. The 12 tribes or the 12 apostles, being in mind. She is the people of God as a **corporate whole**, one body. But she is the people of God viewed as victorious — thus the wreath.

She can't be simply Old Testament believers for we read of her being persecuted by the Dragon after she has brought forth the Messiah. And the "rest of her seed" (the individual believers) hold the "testimony of Jesus" (therefore they are Christians). Nor yet can we hold her to be simply Christians (at least from the evidence in this chapter) because she is given existence prior to the birth and glorification of the Messiah.

The use of the figure of a "woman" to speak of a nation is so common that you need only to consult a concordance. See Isaiah 50:1; 54:1ff; Micah 4:9ff. In this latter passage of Isaiah we have both the "woman" and the "seed" used. Making it clear that one is the corporate concept and the other the individual. The woman then, is the people of God viewed as one triumphant body!

In what respect did the woman (if she be the people of God as a whole) bring forth the Messiah? It would be true in two senses. One, it would be literally true that Jesus descended through the Jewish line which contained in it believers. It's also true that we, as sinners, required or made necessary the birth of Jesus Christ. The woman in Genesis 3 was promised a redeemer — **the** Redeemer. He was needed. He had to be born because she and we desperately needed him.

Although the Woman is mentioned first and is mentioned again in the test in which she plays a prominent role — she is not the central figure. The central figure is the Child. The other major figure is the Dragon.

VERSE 2. And she was with child; and she crieth out - Despite the glorious description, you'll notice she is in pain. She must have this baby! Her whole destiny depends on it. The history of God's people is marked by periods of struggle, of one kind or another.

VERSE 3. Another sign in heaven: a great red dragon - This is a vision. We are not to conclude the dragon was actually in heaven. He is great because of his power. He is red because he is bloodthirsty and brutal.

Having seven heads and ten horns - This speaks of the fact that he is fully equipped with strength to do whatever he has in mind to do. But there is more to it than that. Satan is manifested in John's day, in the Roman beast, and the Roman beast is seven-headed and ten-horned (13:1; 17:7). We'll talk about the significance of this in relation to Rome when we get to chapter 13. He wears on his heads seven tokens of royalty — diadems. But then, even a defeated king can still wear his diadem. Only a victor can wear a victor's crown.

VERSE 4. The third part of the stars of heaven - Stars are often used to speak of the people of God. Genesis 15:5; Daniel 8:10f; 12:3; Matthew 13:43. So the allusion here may be that the Devil has been able to cast down (persecute, kill, and perhaps even cause to apostatize) some of God's people. But as we've already noted, sometime stars are not so used. In this case, the tearing down of the stars may simply be to convey the staggering power of the Dragon, rather than to have some independent meaning in itself.

The dragon standeth before the woman - He wants to devour her child as soon as it is born. The allusion seems clearly related to incidents such as the Pharaoh of the oppression instigated (see Exodus 1:15-19) when he told the midwives to be there at the birth and as soon as the baby boys were delivered, they were to kill them. The case of Herod and the slaughter of the innocents would be another good illustration of the principle being set forth here. In Jeremiah 51:34, the prophet speaks of the "monster" Babylon that "hath devoured me, he hath crushed me, he hath made me an empty vessel, he hath, like a monster, swallowed me up, he hath filled his maw (mouth) with my delicacies." This is enlightening too for that whole context is called on by John in chapter 18, and as we know, the Dragon's work in Revelation is done by a nation known as "Babylon." In addition, as we'll later see, Pharaoh is also alluded to numerous times in scripture as a "dragon." Remember 11:8?

VERSE 5. She was delivered of a son, a man-child - This is Jesus. We are told he is the one who is to rule the nations with a rod of iron. See Psalm 2:1-9; Revelation 2:26-28; 19:15. The saints share in this, but the Ruler is Jesus.

With a rod of iron - He is to "rule" them with a rod of iron. The word "rule" here (as in the other passages mentioned) comes from a word which means to "shepherd." Shepherds didn't rule with a rod of iron, did they? Well, not literally, but Hugh J. Schonefield renders this passage (as the others) "with an iron shod staff." He maintains that many of the shepherds had their staffs shod with iron to help deal with wild animals and such. This will certainly fit the need. This would mean Jesus would be protecting his own flock while acting as a protecting shepherd relative to the nations. On the other hand (as Morris holds) it may just be a way of saying he would shepherd with a firm hand.

Her child was caught up unto God - The child is the central figure in this chapter. The section is to give comfort in the face of the trials ahead and the success or failure of the people of God lies in the fortunes of the Lord. Here we would undoubtedly have the ascension. That is, if we hold that various stages of the experience of Jesus are being singled out. I see no alternative but to so hold. The dragon fails to destroy the child while the son is so vulnerable. Here is strong consolation to the believer. Throughout the career of Jesus, from his birth through his passion and burial, he was a victor. If ever the Devil was to win it should have been then. He was a loser. In the earthly ministry of Jesus, we hear Him saying, "I beheld Satan, fallen (not falling), as a star from heaven." He speaks of having bound the strong man and spoiling his goods. In our vision, this is what we're seeing!

And unto his throne - This is the throne of David! The throne of God is known as the throne of David. By the time Jesus appeared on the earth, the throne of David was well-known to be the throne of God. See 1 Chronicles 28:5; 29:23; 2 Chronicles 1:1; 9:8; 13:8; Luke 1:32; Mark 11:10; Psalm 2:7ff; Revelation 2:27f; 3:7,21; Zechariah 6:9-12; Hebrews 1:3; 8:1; 10:12. There is only one throne — that's God's throne and that's the one David sat in and Jesus is sitting in! Compare 1 Kings 2:12 with 1 Chronicles 29:23. Then read Acts 2:29-36.

VERSE 6. That there they may nourish her - We've already discussed the probable origin of the figure to be the case of Elijah and the 3½-year drought and his being provided for in the trial period. It's distinctly possible however that this does not exhaust the historical allusions. As I've already mentioned, the Pharaohs were alluded to as "dragons" in many places in the Old Teatament. Check a concordance. See Psalm 74:13; Isaiah 51:9; Ezekiel 29:3. See the LXX. And when Israel fled from the "dragon" in the Old Teastament, she entered into a wilderness and it was there that the Lord sustained her with manna. See the earlier discussion for the significance of the 1260 days.

VERSES 7-12. And there was war in heaven - We are not supposed to see a historical war literally take place in heaven. These are visions which embody truths. The central truth is — the Devil is a three-time loser. Where would we place this war chronologically? Would it be prior to the cross and resurrection? If so, the Devil was whipped prior to the work of Jesus. After the ascension? If so, the Devil wasn't defeated by the death, burial, and resurrection of Jesus. Does the battle really take place between Michael and Satan? If so, it wasn't the work of Jesus which destroyed the Devil's power, but the might of Michael, **after** Jesus had done all he could do. No. We're not supposed to understand this as a literal battle after the ascension.

You are supposed to see the great truth being set before you. The man-child is the Conqueror. Picture, if you will, the Dragon racing up to heaven after the man-child. Having been defeated in his earthly career, he would seek to defeat him in heaven. Heaven, where all the battles for the righteous are (as it were) fought and won. Heaven, where the man-child is now at the right hand of God and interceding for his oppressed saints. The thing which the saints must remember is that the Devil couldn't defeat their Master here on earth and he surely can't beat him now! The Mediator is Lord. The Devil has already been whipped on earth. In this case, he will be whipped in heaven. At the end of the chapter he will be again, on earth. In these first two cases the whipping is in reference to the Master, and in the latter end of the chapter it will relate to the servants of that Master.

Michael and his angels - Why Michael and not Jesus? For two reasons. One, Michael stands for Jesus! As in chapter 10, we have a strong angel who represents Jesus, so in this text, Michael stands as his representative. This is the case in Daniel 12:1, where Michael represents God in conflict on behalf of the saints. He is peculiarly the "prince" of God's people. See Daniel 12:1. His name suits him — "Who is like God?" But furthermore, although he is the representative of Jesus, he is yet a messenger of Jesus. And if the Devil can't beat the "message-boy" of the Lord, how would he fare with the Lord? That Michael here stands as the representative of Jesus, I think the terms of the victory of the saints will show.

VERSES 8,9. Neither was their place found any more in heaven - This speaks of the decisiveness of the defeat. There is nothing implied in the text (nor in the rest of the Bible) that the Devil and his angels "had a place" in heaven until this vision. The vision speaks of an assualt on heaven. He (in the vision) left the earth (apparently) to attack the man-child and was defeated. We read of the Devil appearing before God, in the book of Job, but the indications there are that he was called to give account of himself — not that he lived or "had a place" there.

There may be something to the talk that the Devil, before the finished work of Jesus, had some right (?) to accuse the faithful before the Lord, but for the life of me, I can't get that from scripture.

Supposing there to be some truth in it, we have here the declaration that he has no more right to so accuse, for their is now one in heaven, who by virtue of his blood and suffering, has silenced all cavil and protest. There stands a Mediator to intercede for the suffering saints. One whose work cannot be overthrown.

Whether or not it is true that he never had **the right** to accuse the faithful, he did it (and I don't doubt, still does) and that is why he is called the Devil and the Adversary. There is no doubt that there is much in the very best of God's people from the very beginning which could justly be spoken against, but the Devil had no real grounds for doing so. Since the finished work of Jesus and his destroying of the power of Satan, the saints have overcome the Devil by the blood of that Savior. That's what we're supposed to hold on to here. The decisive defeat of Satan.

The death of Jesus (and his subsequent glorification) was not a partial defeat of Satan — it was full victory. To this end came the Son of God into this world — that he might destroy the works of the Devil. Jesus said, the Prince of this world is judged! He told his disciples to be of good cheer because he had overcome the world. Paul told the Ephesians that in the Cross, Jesus had triumphed over the principalities and powers and made an open spectacle of them. The Spirit, Jesus said, would convict the world of judgment because the prince of the world was judged! He took upon him flesh and blood, says the Hebrew writer, to destroy him that had the power of death, the Devil.

Here is the central thought in this chapter. It deals with the destiny of the Church. John is saying, the Master has defeated the power behind the Roman empire. No matter how it looks, it's all right! Are the impenitent sinners of chapter 9 fear-inspiring? Are the two beasts of chapter 13 horrifying? Don't worry — the power behind them has been totally defeated and you cannot lose.

Lindsey and his colleagues place this battle in the middle of the Great Tribulation coming up (they say). For Lindsey, that's around 1984-5. The reasons against making this battle literal and historical, and post-resurrection, have been stated above.

VERSES 10,11. Now is come...the kingdom of our God - "Now" is come! Not, "Soon will come." If this is a historical battle in the middle of the Great Tribulation, then the kingdom comes in the **middle** of the Great Tribulation and not at the end of it. That would blow their theory on the seventy weeks of Daniel.

The time of the kingdom's coming in this passage is the time of salvation's coming. We've already seen in chapter 11:15f that such expressions do not preclude the possibility of the kingdom having already come. See the comments there. If you don't know from the New Testament that the kingdom had already come before the writing of the Revelation, I wouldn't know how to help you. That the sovereignty (kingdom) of Christ has been vindicated since its establishment, we know to be true. Luke 21:31 and Revelation 11:15 are two examples of this.

In this passage we have the coming of the kingdom associated with the coming of salvation; with the saints overcoming Satan by the blood of the Lamb and their attitude toward their service to Jesus.

And the authority of his Christ - "Let all the house of Israel therefore know assuredly, that God hath made that same Jesus whom ye crucified, both Lord and Christ." It wasn't that he "would" make him Lord, but that the Jews could know assuredly that he had done it already! There is no sense in a man or woman denying these very plain scriptures. If you can get around these, there are none which cannot be set aside. He himself said: These things saith he that hath (HATH) the key of David (3:7). That being so, it is just plainly silly to argue against Christ having the authority here mentioned until some date future to the verse under consideration.

VERSE 11. They overcame him because of the blood of the Lamb -I fervently wish that the Christians would take this to heart. The

The Devil has been whipped. Our sins **are** forgiven. "My sin, O the bliss of this glorious thought — My sin, not in part, but the whole; Is nailed to his Cross and I bear it no more; Praise the Lord, Praise the Lord — O, my soul! Romans 4:8 teaches that sins are not imputed to the faithful. Do you know that? Read it for yourself. Did you know that if you walk in the light that Jesus continues to cleanse your sin? Why must we constantly speak and act as though Jesus hasn't borne our sins? I read somewhere of an old Irish lady who was carrying a sack of potatoes down the road. The preacher came along in his horse and buggy. He offered her a ride. She accepted and he helped her into the seat. He started off and noticed she was still carrying the potatoes. "Drop them in the back," he said. "Oh," she said, "I don't want to impose on you." Poor old woman. How silly we think. We'd never do such a thing, would we? Well, how does it happen that we go around carrying our burdens of sins when Jesus has already taken that burden? Do we feel we don't want to impose on him? Come on sister, let them go and enjoy Jesus. Maybe then our neighbors will take us seriously when we say Christ gives joy. Can we know we're saved? Well, can we know we're lost? You can just as easily know you're saved as you can know you're lost. Read the Bible. Read 1 John 5:13 every morning and night and see if that doesn't help you.

The word of their testimony - This is not only **what** they said but their **saying** it. It was the message they proclaimed and trusted in. Of all the stories the Devil hates, he hates the Gospel. Of all the talk that drives him wild, the talk about Jesus drives him wildest. We have a story to tell and we need to tell it, for it is not only for the salvation of others, but in doing this we'll save both ourselves and them that hear us. Have no fear that it is irrelevant. We are told right here that it was the difference between life and death — between victory and terrible loss. Of course, it's relevant. Have no fear about its relevancy, for it deals with man's basic needs. Sometimes we might be led to wonder by the pace this world is running at, if the time won't come when the Bible is no longer needed. This will never be the case — that the Bible won't be needed. Henry Ward Beecher said:

> The Word of God is the book of the common people; it is the workingman's book; it is the child's book; it is the slave's book; it is the book of every creature that is downtrodden; it is the book that carries with it the leaven of God's soul...and do you suppose it is going to be lost out of the world? When the Bible is lost out of the world; it will be because there are no men in it who are in trouble,

and need succouring; no men who are oppressed and need release; no men who are in darkness and need light; no men who are hungry and need food; no men who are sinning and need mercy; no men who are lost and need the salvation of God.

W.H. Fitchett quoted that on page 228 of his "The Beliefs of Unbelief." Isn't that right? Doesn't that piece just demand quoting? Should I not then be anxious to state my case? Shouldn't I rest assured about the Message which has been given to me to tell? Let's quit talking about talking about it and talk about it!

They loved not their life even unto death - This is what Paul said: Neither count I my life as dear unto myself so that I may accomplish my course (Acts 20:24). The Master set forth that principle many times. In reference to his own work — but undoubtedly true of ours too — he said: Except a grain of wheat fall into the earth and die, it abideth by itself alone; but if it die, it bareth much fruit. Isn't it by being prodigal with our lives at his instruction that we win? How hard it is for us to speak of personal crucifixion — we are so soft. Aren't we? The toughest of us are soft. We take it easy on ourselves. We pray for God to have his way with us and our families and then we tie his hands by fervently praying that he keep all of us from harm. We sing of "mould me and make me" and "Thou art the potter and I am the clay" and we protest like crazy when the pressure is on. We pray for growth but want a crossless sanctification. When Jesus "from that time forth" (Matthew 16:21ff) began to show to his disciples that he must suffer and die, Peter took him and began to rebuke him saying: Be it far from thee Lord, this shall not be to thee. He wanted success for Jesus — but a painless, crossless success. Jesus bluntly tells him: Thou art an offence unto me! Peter stood there as Satan, savoring the things which were of men and not of God.

Jesus goes on to say that discipleship, real discipleship, to which he calls those already Christians (for Peter was already regarded as one of his own), is that kind of discipleship which demands "self-denial." We all know what Peter's Christ-denial was: I know not the man. This too must be involved in self-denial! We must learn to say of ourselves: I know not the man! We must learn to say it with vigor and deep conviction. At first it won't come easy, but God assures us that he will enable us, through Christ, to do anything He wants us to do.

Let's quit praying for a painless growth. Let's begin to give God permission to do with us exactly as he wishes. We don't have to like it. We only have to want it. Jesus prayed, tearfully, "Nevertheless." That implies an inner struggle but a complete victory. Let's not examine the cup before we drink it, but simply trust that He'd put nothing in there which would not be for our total well-being. Let's give him permission to do as he wishes. But do we have to give him permission? Yes! "He **that would** be my disciple, **let him deny himself,** and (let him) **take up** his cross, and (let him) follow me." There is here the personal commitment. There must be co-operation with God. God will neither **force** men to become Christians nor to remain Christians. Don't make the commitment too quickly — Jesus urged a man to count the cost: Which of you intending to build a tower sitteth not down first and counteth the cost whether he have sufficient to finish it? This question was asked when he saw many people coming after him (Luke 14:25ff).

The cost must be counted. The Master went on to say (in Luke) that we must renounce all that we have — yes, even our own lives — in order to be his disciple in this deeper sense. There is no suggesting here of **self-discipline.** That is called for as part of the Christian's life, but that's not what is in view here. This is not self-discipline, it is self-denial! There's a world of difference. We are not to subject ourselves to numerous punishments or deprivations — we are to give **God** the permission to deal out to us what HE **knows** we need! We don't know ourselves sufficiently well to know what we need. Give God permission to lay on you whatever he decides. I know of a friend who did something seriously wrong. He was penitent, of course, and so the Lord forgave him. But nothing earth-shattering happened to him. God did not lower on him some great punishment whereby the man would **feel** that his sins had been atoned for. Time passed and he began to take it upon himself to punish himself. He knew he deserved it, and if God wouldn't do it, the man himself would do it. So he began to spread the word among those who respected him — the word about his great sin. The aim was to cause himself to lose respect in their eyes. Surely this would be punishment sufficient. But this was self-punishment. The man had no right to take the place of the Judge. He had no right to determine and administer the punishment. That was God's prerogative. If God had wanted him exposed, He'd have exposed him. I suggested to my friend that he was taking upon himself too much authority, and unintentionally attributing to himself too much wisdom. Was what he was doing, what he needed? How could he know? I suggested he go to God and tell Him: I'm going to leave it with you. Bring to pass what you will. I'll drink the cup and bless your name. And should you decide that I don't need punishment, I'll graciously accept that too.

It's not for us to insist on being martyred. Let God decide our destiny. Note that we must give the heart. Here is what makes the rest easy. To count the cost and then to say to God: I freely and consciously give you the permission to do with me and mine as you see best to do — to do that is to prepare yourself for just whatever comes to pass. It's also a scary thing. What if he decides to shame us? What if illness or business failure comes our way? What if he pulls away all our props and makes us to depend nakedly on him? What if our reputation is shot? What if our children crumble? What if our marriage is permitted (by Him) to fall apart? (Remember Hosea?) BE SURE YOU COUNT THE COST BEFORE YOU MAKE THE COMMITMENT, FOR GOD WILL TAKE SUCH A COMMITMENT SERIOUSLY!

Ah, but what security will then be ours. Having committed our way to Him, totally and without reservation, we know that whatever comes to pass, we have God's clear promise that it's for our good. We'll fret not about how things might turn out, for they can't be otherwise than the road up.

I'd have you notice that our text does not say the saints loved martyrdom. It says they loved "not their lives." This is not a discussion of how they viewed death, but how they viewed their lives! If the one is taken care of, the other takes care of itself. The Master spoke in the same fashion: Whosoever would save his life shall lose it and whosoever would lose his life for my sake, shall find it. The whole thing is a question of, first, inner attitude and inner commitment. The deeper discipleship is not exhausted by outer activities. In fact, outer activities may not even touch dicipleship. You know how industrious were the Pharisees and Jesus had a word for them. Hypocrites. It's distinctly possible to be committed to a cause and not to the Cross. We can knock all the doors, give all the money, pray all the nice prayers, attend all the world-evangelism forums without having embraced the Cross. But remember, he who will not welcome the Cross does not welcome God and his Son. Somebody said: "We suffer so much, but so seldom with Christ; we have done so much, and so little will remain." And another has said: "Your trouble may be that you have been devoted to a cause instead of having the Cross as your sole inspiration, your one and only attraction. You have been ambitious to build your work. **Shamefully you have made use of Jesus Christ.**"

Paul speaks of being "crucified with Christ" and no longer living. Here's where it all begins. Give him the heart — take up the cross and let the Lord then strip you of whatever he needs to remove. Now bear in mind — Jesus did not complete the will of

God by carrying the cross — he DIED ON IT! Who knows the power that's hidden in this holy desperation? Who knows what might be unleashed on the world if our assemblies took up their crosses with Christ? Is it not true that most of our assemblies are like huge granaries full of unplanted wheat which has "become musty and mouldy, and befouled by the rats of jealousy and envy"? What do you say? How about you and me (in solitariness, secretly) giving God the "go ahead?" Such commitments ought to be made in secret.

VERSE 12. Therefore rejoice ye heavens, and ye that dwell in them - With all the spiritual, the heavens are in tune. So heaven as the home of those who are God's is called on to rejoice just as in many passages in the Old Testament, the earth and the trees are called on to rejoice and clap their hands. Those who dwell in the heavens are the people of God. This we are plainly told in 13:6. They are the tabernacle of God. He dwells in them and they in him. The saints are said to be raised with Christ and sit in heavenly places (Colossians 3:1ff). Paul claims in Philippians 3:20 that our citizenship is in heaven. Ours is a heavenly country.

Woe for the earth and the sea — This is the world, as distinct from the heavens. It's not "Palestine" (earth) and the Roman provinces ("sea") as King or Wallace would suggest. To see that the **earth** cannot be a substitute for Palestine check a concordance and try substituting them one for another. Besides, King holds that Satan is here defeated in the Palestine conflict and turns his attention to the Roman provinces, but the text says, he was cast down to the earth (which on King's terms would be Palestine again). Those who don't "dwell in the heavens" but "dwell in the earth and sea" have cause to worry for the Devil will use them for his own ends and hasn't a care about their welfare.

He hath but a short time — This is not to be construed as equivalent to the Christian age, as Milligan and Hendriksen would have it. It is not the last 3½ years of the 70th week of Daniel, as Lindsey and company would have it. It's not a special thrust of wickedness near the end of the present dispensation, as others would have it. It simply stands for an opportunity for Satan to manifest his fury against believers. The 3½ days in 11:9 spoke not of time but of apparent victory. The 10 days in 2:10 spoke of limited pressure on the saints. The 1260 days spoke of a state of affairs in which the saints suffer but are sustained. The 1000 years (as we'll see) speaks of complete victory. None of these speaks of time as such. This "short-time" stands for the (controlled) opportunity of Satan to assault his enemies.

Paul will speak of our troubles as being "for a moment" (2 Corinthians 4:17). Peter will speak of the saints undergoing trial "for a little while" (1 Peter 1:6). The issue is not time, but the nature of the suffering. It is the same in this passage. In chapter 20:3,7ff, we read of the Devil being let loose for a little season. This little season has the same point as this "short time." They apply themselves differently. The "day of the Lord" in every passage carries the same thought with it (ie. God's manifestation of wrath on the ungodly and the salvation of his people) but it applies to different events and circumstances, depending on the context. The "day of the Lord" in Nahum is the Lord's vengeance on Nineveh. In Joel, the "day of the Lord" is his vengeance on the Jews.

The Devil is given "a short time." That is, he is permitted to manifest his hatred and use the ungodly (to their own detriment) to fulfill his will. In chapter 20, he is given a "little season" to have another go at defeating the people of God. See the comments there as to its immediate application.

VERSES 13-17. When the dragon saw he was cast down...he persecuted the woman - The central battle has been fought. The Devil is the loser. Not — he **will** be loser. Not — he fought only a draw. He has been whipped, and whipped completely. That he can persecute the woman is nothing proving the contrary. Will someone dare to suggest that at the Cross God **wasn't** in control? Isn't it true that Isaiah 10:5ff makes it abundantly clear that Assyria was merely the instrument in the hand of God to punish rebellious Israel? And doesn't the prophet say: Howbeit he meaneth not so! We've got to quit implying that God is less than in complete control! Lindsey (on Revelation 1:5) says that the mess the world's in proves Jesus is not now exercising his power of control. See the comments there. This is outrageous. It permits feeble men to render their judgment on the moral governing of the world.

Walvoord is in trouble here. To him the "woman" speaks of the nation of Israel. The rest of her seed is a godly remnant of Israel. His difficulty is to get the nation protected and nourished and yet have only a remnant enter the millennium. He holds this section to teach that during the last 3½ years of history immediately prior to the 2nd coming of Jesus, the Antichrist turns on the Jewish nation and destroys two-thirds of it. Of the remaining third, he holds only a portion of that enters the millennium. This is hardly a "national" fulfillment. He strongly opposes the idea of a remnant fulfillment, but is left with it. If the "woman" is Israel the nation, then the nation is preserved in the wilderness, not just a remnant. See his "The Millennial Kingdom," pages 183-193, 302, 316f. But if the nation is preserved in the wilderness, then the talk of a remnant is unacceptable. That Walvoord feels the pressure, we know, for on page 188, he makes the "woman" speak of the "godly remnant of Israel standing true to God in the time of the great tribulation" and yet on page 196 he carefully distinguishes between the woman as the nation and the "rest of her seed" as the godly remnant. **See the McGuiggan-Jordan slide presentation on "An Examination of Millennialism."**

VERSE 14. There were given to the woman the two wings of the great eagle - Whoever this woman is, she is preserved by God. Lindsey says he thinks the "eagle" may well stand for the U.S. military, since the eagle is America's national symbol. He thinks Israel may well be airlifted by the men of the U.S. 6th Fleet in the Mediterranean. (!) Now here's real Bible exegesis! Since we're to have a revived Roman empire, and the eagle was Rome's insignia — why can't it be that Rome will airlift Israel?

Over and over again in scripture the figure of eagle's wings is used of God's protecting work. He said of Israel that he bare her out of Egypt on eagle's wings (Exodus 19:4 — a Babylonian airlift?). In Deuteronomy 32:11; Psalm 36:7; Isaiah 40:31 we have an allusion to eagle's wings, one way or another. We need to look no further for the meaning of the symbol.

It is clear from this chapter that the woman is God's people. It is one of the bad features of millennialism that it insists on teaching that the nation Israel is still the people of God. The nation Israel is not the nation of God under the Mosaic legislation, for that commonwealth no longer exists. It was laid to rest over 1900 years ago, even as Psalm 110 and other passages prophesied it would. They are not a nation under God by virtue of their relationship to Jesus for they stand to this day branded as rebels against the Lord Jesus Christ. For 1900 years they have flagrantly opposed the work of the Cross of Jesus which was to make of the two (Jew and Gentile), one new man! Their independent existence today, as a religious and social community based on the Mosaic law, is strong testimony to their repudiation of Jesus. They are not related to God by the old covenant and they are not related to Him on the basis of the new covenant. They have been declared to be Jews only in name and flesh, both by Jesus (John 8:32-44) and the Revelation letter (2:9; 3:9). They were repudiated as real children of Abraham, despite their physical kinship, by no less a one as (The Holy Spirit by) Paul! He made it very clear that "they are not all Israel which are of Israel. Neither because they are Abraham's seed, are they all children." See Romans 9:6ff. Let's have it clearly stated — today — there is no real Jew but a believing Jew! A relationship with God never has and never will depend simply upon fleshly kinship with anyone!

VERSES 15,16. And the serpent cast out of his mouth...water as a river - Out of the mouth of the Lord comes a sword with which to smite the nations (1:16; 19:15 and Isaiah 11:4). With his lips and the breath of his lips he slays the wicked (Isaiah 11:4 and 2 Thessalonians 2:8). The Devil tries to ape the Lord. As in the beast, he apes the death, burial, and resurrection of Jesus (13:3,12; 17:8,11) so he tries here to imitate him in destructive power. But what have we already been told? He's been whipped! God is able to use a flood to destroy the wicked world. He has used flood waters to drown the armies of the dragon (the Red Sea), but Satan is not God! As God used the dry land to whip the dragon before (Exodus 14:21-31), so he does here. Now get the picture — there is a dragon in pursuit of his people and they are fleeing toward a prepared place; water is a threat to them and the Lord handles it for them. When Israel, in the Old Testament, was fleeing from the dragon (Egypt — see the scriptures given), there was water that was a threat to them. On the other side lay safety, a wilderness in which God would sustain them. David, speaking of the occasion, said: "He rebuked the Red Sea also, and it was dried up: so he led them through the depths, as through a wilderness (Psalm 106:9).

Literally understood, the passage would demand a flood of water. Lindsey makes it a "flood of pursuers," but this is figurizing the passage. So you see, he figurizes when he wants to.

And the earth helped the woman — Now everyone knows that the earth does nothing of itself. The plain meaning is, God made the earth to help the woman. We are being told here that even on earth, the Devil is a loser. He has been cast down to the earth, but can't even win against the people of God on earth. Woe to the earth and sea, we were warned. But earth and water are at God's command. He rebukes the water when it would be against his people, and yet uses it to destroy the enemy. The dry land becomes a servant to God when his people are in need of it. What have we learned in all this? That heaven and earth and all that is in them are under the control of God — Satan is a whipped enemy! Psalm 148 makes it very clear that all things everywhere are the servants of God. WHY IN GOD'S NAME WON'T WE BELIEVE THIS? AND LIVE IN BELIEVING IT?

VERSE 17. And went away to make war with the rest of her seed - You notice that she is pictured as the mother of the man-child and these others. The Devil has been whipped in regard to the man-child

15 And the serpent poured water like a river
out of his mouth after the woman so that
he might cause her to be swept away w/the flood.

(which is, as we know, the decisive defeat). The people of God, viewed as a corporate whole, are beyond his power (eg. Matthew 21
16:18f) to hurt, and so he turns to Christians as individuals. Because of their Redeemer, the people of God can't be defeated, but the individual saints can be "got at." Nevertheless, as will be developed, he can do nothing against them either. You'll remember we've already discussed the issue of the Christian's success, whether he lives or dies.

See p 189

Summary

What have we seen in this chapter? We've seen only one story. Victory! We've seen not just victory, but victory for the saints. But we've seen more on this theme. We've seen the two real opponents in all this. It's not just the seed of the woman (believers) against the unbelievers. It is **the** Seed of the woman against the Dragon. These are the real forces behind the whole struggle. If it were merely men against men, the outcome might be doubtful. If it were merely men against Satan, the outcome would surely be in favor of the Dragon. But since it is Jesus against the Dragon, the future is secure — the present is victory!

The victory wrought for the saints has already been worked in heaven, and the manifestations of that victory work themselves out in history, on earth. The corporate body, the Lord's nation, can't be whipped, so the attention is drawn to the Devil's frustration being worked out against the individual saints. But the victory note has been sounded. The story has been told. The demonstration has been given, so chapter 13 holds no lasting menace!

16 And the earth helped the woman and
the earth opened its mouth and drank up
the river which the dragon poured out
of his mouth.
17 And the dragon was enraged w/the woman
and went off to make war w/the rest of
her offspring who keep the commandments
of God and hold to the testimony of Jesus.

Chapter 13
1 And he stood on the sand of the seashore.
And I saw a beast coming up out of the sea
having 10 horns and 7 heads and on his
horns were 10 diadems and on his head
were blasphemous names.
2 And the beast which I saw was like a
leopard and his feet were like those of
a bear and his mouth like the mouth of
a lion. And the dragon gave him his power
and his thrown and great authority.
3 And I saw one of his heads as if it had
been slain and his fatal wound was healed.
And the whole earth was amazed & followed after the
beast
4 And they worshiped the dragon because he
gave his authority to the beast and they
worshiped the beast saying, "Who is like
the beast, and who is able to wage war w/ him.
5 And there was given to him a mouth
speaking arrogant words & blasphemies &
authority to act for 4 2 months was given to him
6 And he opened his mouth in blasphemies
against God to blaspheme His name and
His tabernacle that is those who dwell in heaven.
7 And it was given to him to make war w/ the
saints and to overcome them; and authority
over every tribe and people and tongue &
nation was given to him.
8 And all who dwell on the earth will worship
him every one whose name has not been
written from the foundation of the world in
the book of life of the lamb who has been slain
9 If anyone has an ear let him hear.
10 If anyone is destined for captivity, to captivity
he goes; if anyone kills w/ the sword, w/ the
sword he must be killed. Here is the
perseverance and the faith of the saints.

11

Questions on Chapter 13

1. In apocalyptic speech, what does the "sea" stand for?
2. What do Milligan and Hendriksen think of the sea beast?
3. What do Lindsey and the premillennialists think of the sea beast?
4. What view does this book hold to?
5. King thinks it's the Roman empire manifested under which emperor?
6. Why are the dragon and the sea beast similar in appearance?
7. What does Milligan make of the seven heads?
8. Can you list them?
9. What does this book make of the seven heads?
10. Can you list them?
11. What else do the seven heads stand for?
12. From what O.T. book is this vision essentially taken?
13. Are heads and horns interchangeable in apocalyptic speech?
14. Is there an eighth head to this sea beast?
15. How many horns does Daniel 7 have on the fourth beast — to begin with?
16. How many does he end up with?
17. In chapter 17:10 which are the five kings that have fallen?
18. Who is the one that "is"?
19. Who is the "other" that is not yet come but must continue a little while?
20. Who is the eighth?
21. Why may John have ignored three emperors?
22. How can John say the beast "is not" when there is a king ruling?
23. Does chapter 17 teach the eighth head grew out of the seventh head?
24. Who was regarded as Nero's "successor" and a "limb" of the bloody Nero?
25. What three phases of the beast does John speak about?
26. What is the symbolic import of the number "8"?
27. In what way is the eighth head "of the seven"?
28. What do you make of the ten horns?
29. What two chapters in Daniel help us with this problem?
30. Which head is smitten unto death?
31. Why is the sea beast a composite?
32. In whom does the beast "resurrect"?
33. What two opposite views has Lindsey promoted concerning the seven heads?
34. What does the "name" of the beast mean?

35. What does **the number** of his name mean?
36. What two lessons are the saints receiving in this name and number matter?
37. What head does Lindsey equate with the Antichrist?
38. Who does he think is smitten (and **almost** killed)?
39. How does all this conflict with the text of chapter 13?
40. Having read Lindsey's two quotes, say:
    A. Whether a modern statesman is smitten or an ancient kingdom:
    B. Whether a modern statesman or the Antichrist is smitten:
    C. Whether (in light of 13:3) the eighth head or one of the first seven is smitten to death.
41. What does King make of the "earth" in apocalyptic speech?
42. Why can't this be right?
43. What does Milligan get from it?
44. Why can't that be right?
45. What's the point of its rise "from the earth"?
46. Who or what is the earth beast?
47. In what way is the hypocrisy of the earth beast set forth?
48. What do you make of the "miracles" he wrought?

An Analysis of Chapter 13

I. The beast from the sea: 1-10
   A. Its origin and appearance: verses 1,2
   B. Its wound and recovery: verses 3,4
   C. Its nature and dominion: verses 5-8,18
   D. Its destiny: verses 9,10

II. The beast from the earth: 11-17
   A. Its origin and function: verses 11,12
   B. Its miraculous abilities: verses 13-15
   C. Its demands: verses 16,17

Chp 13 The Great Tribulation

Chp 13 shows why the oppressor bent on their purpose for wickedness & their horrifying strength in 2 beasts & dragon

Introduction to Chapter 13

In chapter 12, we've seen the two main actors in the whole scheme of the Revelation. The Lord and the Dragon. We saw the battle between the two leaders and the victory went to the Lord. This is comfort. That battle in its essential details was spiritual and invisible (that's an overstatement). The Church stood by and watched that battle. They saw the Dragon defeated again and again. He then turned on the woman and the rest of her seed and persecuted them. The chapter does not tell us in what way. Chapter 13 will show the instruments of his persecution. Chapter 12 was well placed (as is chapter 14), for chapter 13 has fierce, horrifying news to tell. The dragon has as his henchmen, a horrible pair. The saints are to receive much tribulation at their hands. Comfort and victory are notes that must be sounded over and over again. You know what I mean. In the face of the trials of daily living, sometimes it's hard to keep in mind that God **really is** in control. How much more do we need to be reminded of that truth when under pressures such as the Church faced then?

Chapter 13 is the site of much contention over the years and part of the reason for that is, it's a difficult chapter. Dogmatism is never a pleasant thing, but it is especially out of place here. Still, despite the difficulties connected with it — it is explainable. Keep your Bible and your mind open and let's go at it.

Chapter 12 states church was persecuted but not in what way it was persecuted.

Chp 13 will show the instruments of persecution. They are the two henchmen of the Dragon. They will persecute the church w/a great tribulation.

Describes earth beast & sea beast

p 206

Comments on Chapter 13

VERSES 1-10. And he stood upon the sand of the sea - Accepting the ASV text, it is the dragon who stands on the seashore. It's as if he has just called for help. If the KJV is correct (and there are grounds for the reading), it is John who has the ringside seat to what is about to happen.

And I saw a beast coming up out of the sea - What a book! Can't you visualize this? It's like something out of a science-fiction movie. A man may say what he likes about the book, but if he says it's dull, then the words have lost their meaning. **Who or what is this beast?** There are numerous views. **Milligan** holds the beast stands for world-persecuting power! Not any power in particular — just civil power as it manifests itself against God. **Hendriksen** holds the same view!

Walvoord and **Lindsey** (as all the premillennialists do) hold it to be the revived Roman empire under the Antichrist. **Max King** has written it is the Roman empire under Nero. King said: These were the four world dominions that exercised a rule over God's people, beginning with Nebuchadnezzar of Babylon, and **closing with Nero of Rome.** The period of these four beasts constituted the "times of the Gentiles," which ended with the destruction of Jerusalem...(emphasis mine). One would have thought if it closed with Nero of Rome that the "times of the Gentiles" would have ended over 2 years before the destruction of Jerusalem since that's when Nero moved off!

What's the truth? I think we have to say the beast is Rome! In the following presentation we'll be calling on Revelation 17 quite a bit, so be sure to have it there in front of you.

The beast comes up out of the sea. This is straightforward enough. The sea stands for the nations in their restless movements and unsettled state. Isaiah 57:20 speaks in that very fashion. Revelation 17:15 interprets "waters" as nations and peoples. Isaiah 17:12,13 speaks in the same way. The same prophet uses the waters of the Euphrates to speak of the people of Assyria (8:7,8). In Daniel 7:2ff we hear of the 4 world empires as coming up out of the sea. Later in the chapter we are told they arise on earth (17) so we are talking about human kingdoms and the sea speaks of the instability of the nations.

What John sees here is a "beast." This stresses its ferocious nature — its brute force. This is Rome from its standpoint as a civil persecuting power.

Having ten horns and seven heads - This is how the dragon was described in chapter 12:3. That's because it is the manifestation of the dragon at the time of John's writing. Of course, it would speak of power too, and completeness of equipment to do the job to be done (whatever be that job). The power behind this whole evil show is the dragon, but the manifestation of his malignancy takes the form of the civil-persecuting Rome. Let me take the seven heads first.

As we meet it here, it is described as having only seven, but as we'll see later — it really has eight. But what of these seven heads? We are not left in doubt as to what they are. See 17:9,10. The heads have a twofold significance: They stand for seven hills and they stand for seven kings! Everyone acknowledges that the seven hills are the seven hills on which Rome sits. (Wallace teaches this in his comments on 13:1, and strangely forgets it — or changes his mind — in his comments on 17:9,10). **What are the seven heads?** They are the seven hills of Rome! And what else? They are seven kings! Who are these seven kings? Let me plainly tell you what I think. Augustus, Tiberius, Caligula (Gaius), Claudius, Nero, Vespasian, and Titus.

Five of the seven (17:10) are fallen. Augustus, Tiberius, Caligula, Claudius, and Nero. One, we are told (17:10) is — that would be Vespasian. And another is not yet come — that would be Titus. And when he cometh, he must continue a little while. Titus ruled two years.

The whole picture is essentially taken from Daniel. In apocalyptic speech heads or horns may be used to stand for kings. In fact, in Revelation 17:9-12, we have that very thing happening. In Daniel, we have the same thing (2:38; 7:6; 8:8; etc.). With this in mind, let me share with you a comparison of these three pieces of scripture — Daniel 7, Revelation 13 and 17. (I suggest you take a look at my comments on Daniel 7 in the "Looking Into The Bible" book.) I believe Daniel uses horns in reference to the fourth beast where John uses heads. Read the text of Daniel 7, especially from verses 7 and onward. Daniel speaks of the fourth beast as having ten horns and then another horn which uproots three of the former horns (verses 7,8,19-25). Here's how it would look as presented by Daniel (if the view I'm now giving you is correct):

1. Augustus
2. Tiberius
3. Caligula
4. Claudius
5. Nero
6. Galba*
7. Otho*
8. Vitellius*
9. Vespasian
10. Titus
11. Domitian

> The eleventh horn according to Daniel is the chief personality. He is to get all our attention and so to him is credited the uprooting of three of the horns. This means the beast now has eight and the little horn is number 8. I'll talk to you soon about the significance of the number "8."

As presented by John, heads represent kings (17:10) as in Daniel, horns represented kings (7:24). In Daniel, three of the kings are **uprooted** by the eleventh king now become the eighth (7:24) and in Revelation, three are **ignored** and we are left with eight. John takes the vision from Daniel as he finds it — with three missing. But does John speak of eight heads? **Yes! In chapter 17:11.** Here's what we'd have then:

In Daniel	**In Revelation**	
1. Augustus (1)	1. Augustus	
2. Tiberius (2)	2. Tiberius	These would be the five that are fallen, 17:10.
3. Caligula (3)	3. Caligula	
4. Claudius (4)	4. Claudius	
5. Nero (5)	5. Nero	
6. Galba*		
7. Otho*		
8. Vitellius*		
9. Vespasian (6)	6. Vespasian	Vespasian would be the one that "is," 17:10. Titus, the other to come and abide a little while, 17:10.
10. Titus (7)	7. Titus	
11. Domitian (8)	8. Domitian	

* The three uprooted **and** the three John ignored.

Who is the fourth beast in Daniel? Everyone agrees it is Rome. If our parallel be correct, so is the beast of Revelation 13. We are encouraged in this view by the fact that the beast of Revelation 13 is a composite creature, made up of the elements which composed Babylon, Medo-Persia, and Greece. In Daniel, the order is lion, bear, and leopard (but then he's looking into the future), and in Revelation (13:2) it is leopard, bear, and lion, for John is looking backward. But what has this to do with identifying the beast of chapter 13? Daniel 7:12 makes the cryptical remark: And as for the rest of the beasts, their dominion was taken away: yet their lives were prolonged for a season and a time.

The "rest of the beasts" means the previous three beasts. They lost their dominion, but they didn't lose their lives — their lives are prolonged for a while. How's that? In the fourth kingdom, of course. The fourth beast embodied all their wickedness, and so is described as being made up of them. Just as in Daniel 2 the whole image remained until the fourth kingdom was smitten, so the three beasts lived on until the fourth beast was smitten.

Now let's return to the kings again and see if our hypothesis continues to make sense.

Why would John ignore these three? First of all, because three were uprooted in Daniel. And these three, although they were recognized as emperors, were so quickly removed due to horrible civil war that they made no contribution to the Empire. All three of them passed away within the space of parts of two years.

The picture suggested here would mean the book was written in the days of Vespasian, since he would be the one who "is" (17:10). That's true. And this accords with a lot of what is indicated in the book itself. You'll note that the persecution of which John speaks is going to come on the saints (11:7; 17:8). You **must note** that John says **twice** (17:8,11) that the beast **"is not."** What do you make of that? Reckon with it — what do you make of that?

Bear in mind now that John says that, in spite of the fact that he says "one is" (17:10). What does that tell you? There is a king ruling while John is writing but **he still says** "the beast...is not." That says to me (and I'll develop it in a little while), that Rome was not persecuting the saints at the time John was writing. In 11:7, we read of the beast "coming up out of the abyss" to persecute the saints. In 17:8 we read that the beast "is about to come up out of the abyss." Why does the beast come up out of the abyss? To persecute the saints, of course (11:7). The empire persecution is not yet going on while John is writing. Do you hear me? John said **"the beast...is not."**

But John was being persecuted even as he was writing, you say. That's true, but as J.W. Roberts and others have well observed, this doesn't mean there was an empire policy in operation. Local leaders often did those kinds of things. John still says, **the beast is not!** It's usual to date the book about 95 A.D., but surely John could hardly say, at that date, "the beast...is not." Domitian died the next year. His tyranny was over by that date. Wouldn't that be a little strange?

Furthermore, I've read all kinds of debate as to what Irenaeus really did mean by his statement concerning (?) the date of the book. Milton Terry in his book on "Hermeneutics" is very definite about it that Irenaeus may have said **John** was seen near the end of the reign of Domitian, and not **the vision.** At least, he says, it is an open issue. Milligan says anyone making such a claim as Terry doesn't know Greek. Terry knew Greek. So there. In any case, suppose Irenaeus said the Revelation was seen toward the end of the reign of Domitian. What if Irenaeus said it — does that make it infallibly correct?

But Roberts, it seems to me, has the best solution of all. He thinks it very possible that John was exiled toward the close of the rule of Vespasian — saw the Revelation— and that it was not released until he got back to the mainland. Following Vespasian, Titus reigned only two years. John could easily have spent that time on Patmos. The Revelation might well have begun to circulate early in the reign of Domitian and thus the tradition grew up that it was seen in Domitian's reign.

Back to the kings again. Should we not begin the list of kings from Julius Caesar? Why should we? Everyone knows that Julius was a self-appointed dictator and that he died 17 years before the Republic became an empire. Nor was he the first to grab the reigns of the Roman state. Marius and Sulla did some of that. Read Suetonius for yourself. Read almost anyone on who was the first Roman emperor.

In the 17th chapter (10ff) we have "5 fallen." This would mean Augustus, Tiberius, Caligula, Claudius, and Nero. The one who "is" would be Vespasian, who brought the empire back to stability. "The other is not yet come." Swete holds the Greek here suggests the idea of imminence — "when the accession of Titus was already in sight" (page 220). Titus ruled "2 years, 2 months, and 20 days" (Suetonius). That would deal with seven of the heads and if chapter 17 hadn't mentioned an "eighth" we'd have been through. **The eighth is Domitian!** He is said to be "of the seven" (17:11). Not "of the seventh" as Lindsey would have. John doesn't say he is of the "7th" but of the "7." Now Lindsey knows the difference between these two statements. He **needs** that of the "7th" business, so he takes it though he doesn't get it from the Word of God. Who is of the seven? The beast that "is himself also an eighth" (17:11). The beast is viewed by John as existing in the past ("was"), not existing now ("is not") and coming again into existence ("is about to come up out of the abyss"). Here indeed is a travesty of the resurrection of Jesus. He said of himself: I was alive — I became dead — and behold, I am alive forever more (1:18).

The beast is viewed as "is not" even though there is a king ruling in Rome. The beast died (13:12) and "was not" while John was writing, but was going to "come up out of the abyss" in a mock resurrection. With Nero, we have the beginning of the bloodletting of the Christians. I have here before me Tertullian's "Apology" and he says (chapter 5): Consult your annals, and there you will find Nero, the first emperor who dyed his sword in Christian blood, when our religion was but just arising at Rome.

With Nero, the persecution of the saints by the Empire ceased. That persecution began again with Domitian. Eusebius in his "Ecclesiastical History," (Bk. 3, Paragraph 17) says: He (Domitian) finally showed himself the successor of Nero's campaign of hostilty to God. He was the second to promote persecution against us, though his father, Vespasian, had planned no evil against us. With this agrees Tertullian, who said (in the place we quoted); A long time after, Domitian, a limb of the bloody Nero, makes some like attempts against the Christians...

Here is the "resurrection" of the beast. It arises out of the infernal regions — the abyss. The place where the Devil (the fallen star of 9:1) has the rule. The resurrection of the beast is Devilish in origin. Galba, Otho, and Vitellius were too busy staying alive (or trying to), to persecute the saints. Vespasian, as we've read, had no evil planned against the saints. The same is true of Titus. With "number 8" it began again. It is true that Domitian was not as vile as Nero and later emperors in the persecution respect, yet he did persue it. But there was the terrible tension promoted by him which affected the provinces. Hear Swete on this:

> In the foregoing chapters of this introduction, an attempt has been made to show that in the later years of Domitian's reign, the Caesar-worship in Asia was a danger which threatened the Church with imminent destruction. If that view is correct, there is no need to take into account the shortness of "the local reign of terror" at Rome under Domitian or the comparative length and severity of Nero's persecution...In Asia at the moment, there seems to have been good reason to expect a recrudescence of the policy of Nero, and something worse, if there were no recent martyrdoms, yet persecution was ready to break out upon the least excuse, and but for the death of Domitian, there would probably have been a general uprising of the pagan population against the Church (cv-cvi).

With Domitian, the scene is set for the outbursts of persecution of unparalleled fury and viciousness, which lasted until the year 311. The beast had shown itself in Nero — died. Resurrected again in Domitian, and in Domitian God judged it! In this number "8," we have the "Resurected" beast. The number "8" is the number of "resurrection, new beginning." It was Cyprian who called Sunday, the first day and the eighth! The day our Lord arose was the "8th" day and the first. In the Sibylline Oracles (i, 328), Jesus is spoken of under the number of 888. The 8th day is the beginning of a new week after seven full days. It was the day (8th and 1st) that the creation made its beginning. It was the day the leper was permitted to begin again as a reinstated member of the Jewish community (Leviticus 14:1-20, esp. verse 10). It was the number of the year of Jubilee. The fiftieth year, following 7 sabbatical years. That was to the years what the 8th day was to the days of the week. The Jubilee year was when everyone got a fresh start — they could begin again (Leviticus 25:8ff). The number 8 was the day in which boys were circumcised that they might enter in a new and renewed way into covenant relationship with God (Genesis 17:8).

The " eighth" we have been talking about is said to be "of the seven." John is being told: Look back at the seven and you'll find him there. We've already seen that Tertullian called Domitian a limb of the bloody Nero, and Eusebius called him Nero's successor. It's interesting too that around this time there was talk about Nero not really being dead. There was talk about him having risen from the dead. Others said he hadn't been dead, but had fled to the Parthians and was coming back. Some Christians may not have been sure but that Domitian wasn't the reincarnation of Nero. At least he was, policy-wise. Tacitus in his "Histories," page 22, speaks of "a charlatan masquerading as Nero." In any case, Suetonius and others mention this sort of talk. Some Jews thought it possible and hoped that in this "return" of Nero, Rome would be punished for her ungodliness. So this "return" of Nero may have provided the background (at least part of it) to the "resurrection" story.

Now we're back in chapter 13:1, and we've been talking about the seven heads (eight, really). The seven heads are seven hills — Rome. And they are seven kings: Augustus, Tiberius, Caligula, Claudius, Nero, Vaspasian, and Titus. The eighth — Domitian.

Having ten horns - Now what about these? These are the client kings of Rome. They are kings who have submitted themselves to Rome and therefore have Rome's approval to rule. Turn again to chapter 17:12ff. We are told there that these horns are "ten kings who have received no kingdom as yet; but they receive authority as kings, with the beast for one hour." Note then that they have no independent authority — they are sub-rulers, ruling for Rome. We hear in verse 17 that God put it into the heart of these kings to give their power unto the beast and yet are part of the beast by covenant, treaty, agreement (all guided by God, of course). This accords exactly with the picture as painted by Daniel. Here in Revelation 17, the beast (Rome, as a civil power) and the horns (the provinces of Rome etc.) bring about the destruction of the Harlot. (We'll talk about the Harlot shortly). We've already given enough material to show that the beast is indeed Rome and we have here the express declaration that these horns are people given the authority by Rome to rule. The text says (17:17): For God did put into their hearts to do his mind, and to come to one mind, and to give **their kingdom** unto the beast, until the words of God should be accomplished. So there is no doubt that these kings are those who by treaty (agreement) became part of the beast while yet being seen as (in some sense) independent of the beast.

This all was worked by God that his purposes might be fulfilled. God wanted to use Rome, and when he was through with her he would destroy her. The destruction of Rome by God, was in part due to the seething nature of her provinces. The Harlot (Rome, from her commercial and seductive standpoint) is supported by the civil might of the beast, but it is by that military might in combination with the provincial influence that the Harlot is finally destroyed.

And whereas you saw the feet and toes, part of potters' clay, and part of iron, it shall be a divided kingdom; but there shall be in it of the strength of the iron, forasmuch as you sawest the iron mixed with miry clay. And as the toes of the feet were part of iron, and part of clay, so the kingdom shall be partly strong, and partly broken. And where as you sawest the iron mixed with miry clay, they shall mingle themselves with the seed of men; but they shall not cleave one to another, even as iron doth not mingle with clay.
(Daniel 2:41-43)

And the king shall do according to his will; and he shall exalt himself, and magnify himself above every god, and shall speak marvelous things against the God of gods; and he shall prosper till the indignation be accomplished; for that which is determined shall be done. Neither shall he regard the gods of his fathers, nor the desire of women, nor regard any god; for he shall magnify himself above all. But in his place shall he honor whom his fathers knew not shall he honor with gold...and he shall deal with the strongest fortress by the help of a foreign god;

> whosoever acknowledgeth him, he will increase with glory; and he shall cause them to rule over many, and shall divide the land for a price. (Daniel 11:36-39)

The quote from chapter 2 permits no reasonable debate as to its reference to Rome. The point I want you to notice is the weakness and strength of the "divided" kingdom. The weakness is not due to it having toes. It is due to it being made of part iron and clay. This mixture speaks of the covenants made with the seed of men. As God would have it, this was a necessary thing in the making of Rome. The farther she spread her authority, the more help she needed, and consequently the more alliances she made. While this was the road to survival for a while, it was her weakness (the Bible says so!) and it led to her downfall. There never was the inner unity needed to keep such a huge kingdom alive. Read the text again and note that this is explicity stated: But they shall not cleave one to another, even as iron doth not mingle with clay.

I'll have to suggest you see my comments on chapter 11 in the little commentary on "Daniel." Let me here assert that the "king of the north" was the king who ruled north of the holy land even as the "king of the south" ruled (in Egypt) in the south of Palestine. When Pompey stalked into Syria in 64 B.C., he brought an end to the Seleucid (Syrian) kingdom which (as Daniel 11 clearly shows) had been the "king of the north." She doesn't rule any more. Rome now has the dominion north of Palestine — she is "king of the north." Our quote from chapter 11 speaks of Rome. And how well it describes her. The point we're particularly after here, is her "dividing the land for a price" and the fact that she gives dominion to "whosoever acknowledgeth" her. She makes use of foreign gods (and armies that go with it, of course) when she needs them. See the comments on the client kings of Rome and their necessity, in the Daniel commentary. What we are seeing here is the Roman alliances with foreigners — the same thought as is stressed in chapter 2 of Daniel.

Now we're back at Revelation 13 and 17. The horns stand for the alliances Rome was obliged to make with the foreigners. These alliances finally destroyed her. Read any good survey of the Decline and Fall of the Roman Empire. When we get to commenting on chapter 17, I'll relate the material we've just covered to the fall of the Harlot.

It's time for a summary. So far, we've said the beast represents Rome from its civil power standpoint. Its rise from the sea speaks of its rise from the midst of the restless nations (a quick glance at the rise of Rome on the Italian mainland, alone, would well illustrate this principle). Its seven heads and ten horns appearance agrees with the description of the dragon in 12:3, because she is the manifestation of Satanic activity at this time. Her seven heads and ten horns speak of the completeness of power which such a kingdom can possess (and still be under God's control). But more specifically — the seven heads stand for 1) The seven hills of Rome, and 2) seven kings of Rome. The eighth head is not mentioned in chapter 13, but it is involved in a "resurrection" as is taught by chapter 17. The ten horns stand for the kings with whom Rome was required to make alliances. These alliances, as the text goes on to show, will be involved in the downfall of Rome. This too was set forth clearly in Daniel 2 and is in line with the teaching of Daniel 11.

VERSE 1. And upon his heads names of blasphemy - This is mentioned again in chapter 17:3. It is almost certainly an allusion to the fact that on the statues of the "deified" they named the individual as gods. There are coins with the deified Augustus, Vespasian and others on them. These were deified by the senate after their death and it would be so stated on the coins and statues. This would of course be blasphemous indeed. Domitian didn't wait until he was dead — he wanted his deification while he lived and ordered that he be so addressed: Our Lord God Domitian!

VERSE 2. And the dragon gave him his power - As to his composite appearance, see the previous comments. It is spelled out clearly concerning the source of this beast's power and authority. It is to be understood that GOD IS IN CONTROL and that the Devil is only **permitted** to give power to the beast. It's not clear if we are to understand whether the dragon gave the beast "his" power (i.e. the dragon's power) or if the "his" refers simply to the beast's power (i.e. the power he ends up exercising). The result is the same.

VERSE 3,4. One of its heads as though it had been smitten unto death - That is, one of the seven heads. The "as though" clause is **not** suggesting the head **only appeared** to be smitten unto death. The head **is indeed** smitten unto death. The "as though" simply says "this is how it was portrayed." The beast was portrayed as having a head smitten unto death.

In chapter 5:6, John is shown the Lamb "as though it had been slain." This is not suggesting that the slaying was only in appearance. In the vision, the slaying was actually presented. In this case, it is the same. The cause for wonder in the world was that the beast had been slain and lived again. It was not merely a **near lethal** wound. It was slaughtered **unto death**. In the vision, a death had taken place. The obvious parody is that of the resurrection of Jesus. We have the two stars; the two women; the two cities; the name of the Father and the mark of the beast; the Lord, who was alive, became dead and is alive for evermore, and the beast who was, is not, and is about to come up out of the abyss.

The smitten head is Nero. With him the beast lived, and in his death the beast died. The bestial aspect of the creature is especially seen in its reference to the people of God — it is a persecutor. Seeing as it is one kingdom, it all comes under the heading of the "beast," even though all the emperors did not persecute the saints. Read again the comments on the beast's condition of "is not." While John is writing, the beast "is not." This makes it very clear that the persecuting of the saints is especially in view under the heading of "beast." With the death of Nero, the persecution ceased — the beast "died." But there is to be a resurrectioin. Head number "8" will arrive. His number tells of his resuming of the activity of the "beast." Nero, whose death was regarded by Christians as God's judgment on him, is (as it were) to live again (for the 8th is "of the seven"). In the 8th, the beast lives again! But are we told the **beast** died? Lindsey has protested: The beast is not said to have been slain, only one of its heads. What does the text say? "And he maketh the earth and them that dwell therein to worship the first beast, whose death-stroke was healed" (13:12, see verse 14).

Nor is it unworthy of notice that when Nero, the persecutor died, the whole Roman empire erupted. It seemed as if the "very fabric of civilization" was being torn apart. Here is punishment indeed on an empire which had dared to turn on the people of God. Not only had Nero himself been punished, but it seemed, the whole empire had gone under. The beast was dead!!!

And the death stroke was healed - This is not a near-lethal wound (as Lindsey must have), but it was a "death-stroke" which was healed. A death-stroke is not near-lethal — it **is** lethal. The Greek in verse 3 says the head was **"slain unto death."** You'd get the impression that was a death-bringing wound — right? But the beast lives again. It "was" and in this scene "is not" and "is about to come up out of the abyss." Number "8" (chapter 17:11), the "resurrection number" beast, brings it all to life again.

VERSE 4. And they worshiped the dragon...he gave his authority

V18 Here is wisdom. Let him who has understanding calculate the number of the beast, for the number is that of a man and his number is 666.

unto the beast - Isn't this the way it has been from the beginning? Demonstrations by the devotees of the foreign gods seem to prove their point: Our god, is indeed the god! Didn't the Assyrian make this argument before the walls of Jerusalem (see Isaiah 10:8-14; 36:13-20)? Sure he did. And at that time it must have happened to the Assyrian — 185,000 negatives to his affirmative, and that was only the first night of the debate. The Assyrian closed out the debate after the first night!

Who is like unto the beast? - What a demonstration. Didn't it prove that even the judgment of God couldn't stop the beast? No doubt there must have been many extremely disappointed Christians who just **knew** that this was the end of the line for the insolent, blasphemous, and persecuting beast. God would handle it. But could God handle it? At the "resurrection" there went up the cry: Who is like unto the beast? Isn't that phrase familiar? "Who is like unto?" It's the name of Michael, isn't it? "Who is like unto Jehovah?" And when Jehovah and the beast came into conflict — the world screamed "Who is like unto the beast?" Here the saints are being mocked. Back in the days of Moses, the dragon (Egypt with Satan at her back) oppressed the Lord and he wasted her. Up went the cry from Moses and his company "Who is like unto the thee, O Jehovah, among the gods?" (Exodus 15:11). And hadn't the beast, by his resurrection, proved his godhead? And, they asked, who can make war (successfully) with him? Jehovah, the God of the Christians? The resurrection of the beast makes it clear Jehovah can't handle the problem.

VERSES 5-8,18. A mouth speaking great things, and blasphemies -The first phrase speaks of boasting, arrogance, and the second of evil-speaking against the Lord and his Church. It's not strange when we turn to history, we hear that Domitian was both noted for his arrogance (Suetonius, 354,355) and his claims to deity. Here was arrogance indeed. Here was blasphemy indeed, and with a vengeance. I've heard it said again and again, but I've read nothing to indicate that Nero made any real effort to assert his godhead. In fact, the contrary has been suggested (Barclay). Nero was so self-centered, it is said, that he would not let any touch of divinity take away the credit for his own inherent talent. That people spoke of his divinity, there is no ground to dispute, but then they spoke of the deity of Claudius, who thought such a thing was ludicrous.

Given to him authority to continue 42 months - You'd expect after the build-up that he'd last forever. Thank God for the "42 months" expression. That cuts them down to size. See the prior comments on the significance of 42 months (on 11:1-3).

Once saved always saved
See last paragraph.
Indwelling of God

VERSE 6. To blaspheme his name and his tabernacle - The beast would blaspheme the name of God (that is, God himself, since the name stands for the person or thing). He'd also blaspheme God's tabernacle, that is, "those that dwell in the heaven." Here is how the Church of God is designated. We've said something about this already. The idea of God dwelling in his people and his people in him is alluded to all over the scriptures. Jesus discussed it in John 17. In his first epistle, John speaks of this over and over again (1:2,3; 2:24,27; 3:6,24 et al). See John 14:23; Ephesians 2:20ff; 1 Corinthians 3:16; 6:19. See comments on chapter 12:12.

VERSE 7. There was given to him authority - The authority he exercises is great, but it is "given to him." Whether by Satan or by God, it is ultimately by God. Nebuchadnezzar was told this, but wasn't sure he wanted to believe it. When God was through with him, he was a believer. The Most High ruleth in the kingdom of men and giveth it to whomsoever he will!

VERSE 8. And all that dwell on the earth shall worship him - All that "dwell on the earth" are unbelievers, as those "That dwell in the heaven" are the believers. We've commented on this already (see 12:12). In this passage, we have additional material on which to base the view already expressed.

Everyone whose name hath not been written - The saints are known as those who names are written in the Lamb's book of life. It's just that simple. It is the list of the saved (see 3:5; 20:15). Lindsey and Walvoord have trouble with this book. So do all Calvinists. The name can be blotted out of the book if the person doesn't continue faithful — that's the clear threat/promise of 3:5. Lindsey and Walvoord hold the "book of life" means the book which contains all who were ever (or ever will be) born. What sense would this then make here or in 3:5? That the names were written from the foundation of the world is no problem. Either it is a simple case of foreknowledge, or it is the result of God's working on the individual (no coercion involved) and bringing him to salvation.

Did God know from eternity who would become Christians? Well, of course! Did God foreordain people to salvation? Of course. (Ephesians 1:3-14).Did God violate anyone's free will? Of course not. Did he violate Jesus' free will? Read for yourself John 10:17, 18 and Acts 2:23. Did he violate Jeremiah's free will? Of course not. Read for yourself Jeremiah 1:4ff; 20:7ff. But if God foreordained people to salvation, how can they possibly be lost? Ask the Lord to work it out for you — he plainly says it. Do Christians need to be lost? Will saints probably be lost? The answers to these are "NO!". There is security in Christ. But if you can read the book of Hebrews and the book of Galatians and still tell me that one in Christ cannot ever possibly be lost — I can't help you.

VERSE 18. Let him count the number of the beast - The "him" who is to count the number of the beast is the one who has "understanding." The one who will follow the "wise" course. John is not here talking about an intellectual giant, he has the spiritual man in mind. The wisdom extolled in the Bible relates to the spiritual things. The "mark" of the beast (verse 17) is the same as the "name" of the beast, or the "number" of the beast. The "name" of the beast stands for the nature of the beast. This is true all the way through the Bible. If nature is not in mind, then status is in view, and at times these are not distinguished. "Jacob" spoke of the nature and status of the wearer. "Israel" spoke of a new status and a new man. The change of names throughout the Biblical record indicates that names had inner significance. Abram becomes Abraham; Sarai becomes Sarah; Forsaken and Desolate become Hephzibah and Beulah; Simon becomes Peter.

The prophet said of Jesus (Isaiah 9:6): His name shall be called...He was not telling us what Jesus would be called, but what he'd BE. This expression is an idiom meaning "he shall have the nature — he shall "be." The angel told Mary (Luke 1:35): The holy thing...shall be called the Son of God. He wasn't giving her a name for the child as we do — he was speaking of the child's nature. To do something in the name of Jesus is to do it in his authority **remembering** who and what he is and stands for.

In chapter 19:12-16, we hear of Jesus having a name "which no one knoweth but he himself." And yet we are immediately told of that name — The Word of God. Later the name (in such cases we never read of a plural — names) is King of kings and Lord of lords. But how can it be said no one knows the name but he himself when we are told what that name is? That's because the name stands for the nature and status of Jesus. There is no other like Jesus! Therefore no one "knows" his name. The same is true concerning the "new name" the believer receives (2:17, see comments there). Only he knows the name, for the experience and relationship he has with God belong to no other — it is peculiarly his!

To have the name of the beast placed on one was to acknowledge the beast as one's lord, even as to have the name of Jesus, his Father, and the New Jerusalem, was to acknowledge Jesus as Lord. The saints are told they can know the **number** of the beast's name. Letters in the Greek and Hebrew alphabets (and others) had a numerical significance, and numbers, as you know, are often highly charged symbols. And what is the number of the beast's name? **666**. And what does God say of the name?

It is the number of a man — There is no indefinite article in the Greek, as you know. This phrase might just as easily have been rendered: It is man's number. As it stands it carries the same thought, but as it stands, it more easily leaves the impression a certain individual is in mind. That's not the point. He doesn't mean: It is the number of a certain individual. He means: It is the number which rightly designates man! This is clearly seen in 21:17 and Deuteronomy 3:11. There we are told of the "cubit of a man." This doesn't mean some specific individual — it means a "man's cubit." In Galatians 3:15, Paul says: "Though it be but a man's covenant, yet when it hath been confirmed, no one maketh it void..." He doesn't mean: Though it be but the covenant of, say John Doe. He means: Though it be a human covenant, one made by man (as distinct from God's covenants)...You'll find this illustrated all over the Bible, if you just take a concordance and look.

Now what have we said? The beast's name stands for his nature and status. The name that best describes him has a numerical value. **The name is "MAN' and the numerical value is 666.** The number "7" stood for perfection, the fulness of power or virtues, etc. It was a favorite number of God when speaking of things related to his Son or his Church. You remember! Seven churches, seven Spirits, seven horns on the Lamb. It's also the number associated with God's work in judgment. Seven trumpets and seven bowls. Seven is the number of perfection and fulness. Six (6) spoke to the Jew of "falling short." Milligan offers:

> The number six itself awakened a feeling of dread in the breast of the Jew who felt the significance of numbers. It fell below the sacred number seven just as much as eight went beyond it...the number six was held to signify inability to reach the sacred point and hopelessly falling short of it. To the Jew, there was a doom upon the number six, even when it stood alone. Triple it...and we have represented a potency of evil than which there can be none greater, a direfulness of fate than which there can be none worse.

Six fell just short of the divine rest. It was the day on which man, who fell, was made. And of man Paul said: "For all have sinned and come short of the glory of God. Such a use of numbers is well known outside the Bible as well as in it, and Deissmann (2nd edition, p. 276) tells us of an example of graffiti on the wall of Pompeii. Someone wrote: I love her whose number is 545.

Now, what are the saints being told? Two things they must

16 And he causes all the small and the great and
the rich and the poor and the free men & the
slaves to be given a mark on their right
hand or on their forehead
17 And he provides that no one shld be able to buy or
sell 206 except the one who has the mark 13:9,10
either the name of the beast or the number of
his name.

36 cont'd

Suffering
& faith

Suffering
suits the
purpose of
God

really get a hold on — 1) Your opponent is evil! 2) Your opponent is human! He is evil so have nothing to do with serving him — remain faithful to me. He is not divine (see the comments on the miracles performed by the 2nd beast) and so don't be afraid of him!

VERSES 9,10. If any man is for captivity, into captivity he goeth — This is not the utterance of defeatism. It is not resigning to Lady Luck or mindless Destiny. It is the "patience and the faith of the saints." This sentence is how the saints are to view matters. God is in control of the whole affair. The sufferer is under his hands, as is the persecutor. The suffering has its place in the wisdom of God, for it suits his purposes. Herein lies the endurance of the saints. The road isn't always easy, but because they have committed themselves to God's care, they must patiently bear what he decides to lay on them. Nevertheless, the persecutor will get what's coming to him (for I hold here he who kills with the sword is the persecutor, rather than he who would defend himself). In this epistle, we read of an enemy wanting blood and God giving it to her (16:6). Here we have the enemy with the fondness for a sword — a sword then shall they get. So what is the destiny of the enemy? Destruction. This is the faith of the saints.

Now you know my view of this first beast — what about the alternatives? Milligan, Hendriksen, and Lindsey are in essential agreement in large areas of the beast. Then Lindsey goes his own little way. The beast, claims Milligan, represents worldly, persecuting power. None in particular. Though it may manifest itself in Assyria, Egypt, Babylon, Medo-Persia, Greece (five are fallen). Hendriksen makes 2 Babylons (ancient and new) rather than use Assyria. Lindsey stays with Milligan. All three come up with Rome as the kingdom that "is."

That takes care of five heads. There are two left to handle. Milligan is not at all clear on this matter. He does however state that the 7th head equals the "kings" who will gather up the pieces after Rome has fallen. I'm not sure what he holds about the 8th head, even though I've read him numerous times. Check him for yourself (pp. 901,902). Hendriksen is clear on the matter, even though he is not sure of his position. The first six heads finish with Rome. The 7th — of it Hendriksen asks: Is this seventh head the collective title for all anti-christian governments between the fall of Rome and the final empire of Antichrist that is going to oppress the church in the days just preceding Christ's second coming? (pages 204,205) Hendriksen never answers his own question. So the implied position of the man is never supported by any argument or exegesis.

Lindsey has the same problem, namely, how to deal with the two other heads. He accepts the fact that the sixth is historical Rome which was in John's day (page 236). He holds the seventh to be the coming revival of the Roman empire (as is being manifested in the European Economic Community). What does he do with the 8th? He claims that: John says...it briefly sprouts another, an eighth head, but this head is really only an outgrowth of the seventh (the revived Roman Empire) and is quickly destroyed. It's sort of like a **wart** that grows out of the seventh head of the beast and is cut off. ("New World Coming," pp. 237,238) From this we see the shambles which is developing. You can read the text for yourself and see if:

1. There is anything in there about the 8th head being sprouted "briefly."
2. There is any warrant at all for saying the 8th head sprouts out of the 7th head.
3. There is anything "wartish" about this fierce 8th head.

Lindsey goes on to tell us that this insignificant "wart" is the Antichrist himself! That's not the story he's been telling us about this world dictator, this brilliant orator and shrewd world politician. But the "wart" is more — it is the "extension of the Revived Roman Empire" and it comes into existence at the beginning of the 7-year period (Daniel's 70th week) immediately after the Rapture. This phase of the "wart" (the Antichrist and his kingdom) is not the real bad phase because in the **middle** of the 7-year period, the Devil indwells the Wart and then the heat is really on. Isn't this sad?

What is even worse. WHAT IS EVEN WORSE, is that Lindsey didn't take this view in his "Late Great Planet Earth." He either changed his view and said nothing about it to his readers, or he forgot what he had said in the former book. In the "Late Great Planet Earth" (page 105) he says: If you return to Revelation 13 and look again at verse 1 you will understand that the "ten horns" refer to this ten-nation confederacy, and the "seven heads" are the seven leaders who form a coalition with the Antichrist.

As I've already indicated to you, Lindsey in his "New World Coming" (page 236) has taken the position that the seven heads are seven kingdoms. He says: The first kingdom was Assyria...The second was Egypt...The third was the neo-Babylonian empire of Daniel's day...The fourth was Medo-Persia...The fifth was the Greek empire...(the sixth)...Rome...This was the sixth kingdom of John's vision.

Somewhere in Europe, now living, thinks Lindsey (New World, p. 183), is the Antichrist, nurturing devilish dreams. In the first quote above, there are seven heads of state who make a coalition with this now-living Antichrist. In the second quote, from the same man, six of those heads are long-buried kingdoms! Now, **this doesn't encourage our acceptance of his view of the seven-headed beast!**

There are additional difficulties in the man's view. In the 13th chapter we are told that one of the (seven) heads is smitten to death. There is no mention at all of the 8th head in chapter 13. It is one of the seven that is smitten. Read it for yourself and see. But Lindsey, who, as we've seen, equates the 8th head with the Antichrist, claims that it is the Antichrist who is so smitten. (N.W.C., p.189) Now how are we supposed to take Lindsey?

Are the heads modern statesmen who make a coalition with the Antichrist? Or are they long-buried ancient kingdoms? Lindsey versus Lindsey. Is the smitten head a smitten kingdom or a smitten modern statesman? Lindsey versus Lindsey. Is the Smitten one the Antichrist or one of his colleagues or one of the long-gone empires? Lindsey versus Lindsey versus the Bible!

It's time for another review! We've just covered the "sea beast." Who is he? He is Rome, the civil, persecuting power! Where does he rise from? From among the restless nations of the world. What are his seven heads? They are seven kings — Augustus, Tiberius, Caligula, Claudius, Nero, Vespasian, and Titus. Has he another head? Yes, he has an eighth. Who is that? It is Domitian. Who or what are the ten horns? They are the client kings and the provincial rulers which submitted to Rome. Why is the beast a composite? Because he embodies the characteristics of the three previous kingdoms (see Daniel 7). What is the significance of the "death-wound" to one of the seven heads? The death of Nero. What is the significance of the implied resurrection? The return of the beast in Domitian. What is the significance of the "number" of the beast's name? The name of the beast is "MAN" and the number 666 speaks of his humanity and evil nature. What is the destiny of the beast? Whatever God decides, but as a persecutor who kills with the sword he will die by the sword. Why is the dragon manifested as 7-headed and 10-horned? Because that's the appearance of his current manifestation in the Roman empire.

Now — **The beast from the earth.**

VERSES 11-17. I saw another beast coming up out of the earth —

King claims that "earth" in apocalyptic speech stands for "Palestine." Milligan "explains" the "earth" so as to deliver from it "religion." That is, he thinks the rise from earth proves its religious nature. Neither of these will do for all the beasts of Daniel 7, including the "sea beast" we've just talked about, are said to arise from the "earth" (7:17). What is in view in its rise from the "earth"? **Its human origin!** It doesn't descend from the sky or come on clouds. It rises out of the earth. It is not divine in origin.

Now we subsequently learn it is a religious beast, but we learn that from things other than its earthly origin. Since Babylon, Medo-Persia, and Greece are said to rise "out of the earth," we'll hardly be encouraged to adopt King's (or Wallace's) view of "earth = Palestine." We learn the beast is a religious-slanted beast both by its work and its name. It is twice called the "False Prophet" (16:13 and 19:20) and, for us, that should end the matter.

He had two horns like unto a lamb - Here we have the innocent look. Here's the hypocrisy. The Master spoke of wolves in sheep's clothing. Here we have the innocent "lamb" speaking with the voice of a dragon. Doesn't that get your attention? Woman's hair and lion's teeth; lamb with a dragon's voice. What a book! You can just hear the wheedle in the voice of this Roman representative: Come on now, just a little pinch of incense and then you can go on your way. Just the quick word: Caesar is Lord, and you are all right until next year!

VERSE 12. He exerciseth all the authority of the first beast - It is not said here that the sea beast "gives" this beast its authority. It simply says this beast exercises the sea beast's power, in the sight of the sea beast. Whoever this beast is — it has the authority of Rome in it!

He maketh the earth...to worship the first beast - Ah, now we know who it is. It is Rome with its religious clothes on! The first beast was Rome, the military-civil power. This beast is Rome, the religious pervert. The first was Rome-Egypt. This is Rome-Jerusalem. See on 11:8. Consult Sir William Ramsay's "Letters to the Seven Churches" for the full details on the religious councils which promoted both empire and Caesar worship. There were shrines all over the place. There were state priests, the Concilia, who rode the circuit promoting their garbage. The pagans by the thousands submitted (what difference does it make?) and some Christians were in two minds about the matter. Consult Swete's helpful survey of this whole thing. Especially under Domitian did the push come to worship the emperor. He took a great delight, says Suetonius, in being greeted as God when he entered the

13 and he performs great signs so that he even makes fire come down out of heaven to the earth in the presence of men.

amphitheatre. The provincial governors were given orders that he was to be addressed as a divine one. People approached his "divine couch."

48 **VERSE 13. And he doeth great signs** - I don't think we are required to understand this beast to be actually able to perform miracles. This may well be only the brush-strokes of the vision, saying, in some way or another, this beast cons people into accepting the first beast as divine. Look again at the comments on 11:5,6. Still, at best these works here are false miracles. They are lying wonders. They have the nature of the signs Simon (Acts 8) showed the people when he was able to convince them he was somebody special.

The record left about these Romish priests makes it clear they were professional con-men. They could perform all kinds of tricks and were experts at ventriloquism. This Caesar worship was a State function at which the high-ranking officers would make their appearance. The pagan priests would perform their little bag of tricks with the chief magistrates in as assistants. We don't need to accept any real miracles here any more than we accept the resurrection of the first beast.

VERSE 14. Saying...that they should make an image to the beast -This is not just a question of building a big image and bowing down before it, as say, in Daniel 3. Busts and statues were made and dedicated to the emperors and the chief magistrates. Suetonius mentions Tiberius rewarding some troops in Syria for "they alone had consecrated no image to Sejanus; (page 148). It was usual at these state functions to bring out busts of the emperors and acclaim them as divine. This was all part of the thrust to popularize the Caesar cult. So we're talking here, not about a single image, but the dedicating of images to the Caesars. Suetonius also (page 174) speaks of the Parthians paying homage "to the Roman eagles and standards and to the statues of the Caesars." Pliny tells us when the Christians were later tested, they were faced with the busts of the Caesars and asked to make the confession: Caesar is Lord!

VERSE 15. To give breath to it...that the image of the beast should speak - As I've already said, we are not bound to accept that any real miracles were wrought. We don't even have to accept that con-men were at work. We may well be expected to see the whole picture as simply saying: They really made people believe that Rome was worthy of worship. However it does look like the magicians really did the job. In Moses' day, the magicians did something. I don't think they worked miracles, and their observation on the third plague seems clearly to say that. See Exodus 8:18,19. Miracles were claimed for some of the emperors, of course, and

14 And he deceives those who dwell on the earth because of the signs which it was given him to perform in the presence of the beast telling those who dwell on the earth to make an image to the beast who had the wound of the sword & has come to life.

Vespasian was supposed to have been able to raise a man from the dead. So with all the con-men, the fire-eaters, the magicians, the ventriloquists, and the love of the magical, the abounding superstition put together, we have a good picture of what was going on. You'll recall the manifestation of the love of magic which existed at Ephesus (see Acts 19:18,19).

VERSE 16. A mark on their right hand or on their forehead - Here's the evil counterpart of the name of the Lord being placed on his disciples (see 2:12; 14:1). As no literal mark was involved in the first, so no literal mark is here involved. It is part of the vision. Furthermore, we have here more conflict because, as you recall, in chapter 7, the elect were sealed against harm — identified by the seal as belonging to God. Here we have the mark of the beast given to the beast's people, while the unmarked Christians are committed to death.

Leviticus 7:22ff speaks of the right ear, hand, and foot of Aaron being anointed when he was being inaugurated into office. The "right" side being (usually) the strongest, we have the individual's strength devoted to the Lord. The Jews wore phylacteries on their arms and scriptures on their foreheads. All in all, we have here a declaration as to who is on the beast's side and who is on the Lord's.

The economic pressure on the Christians when they came in conflict with the pagan guilds is well known. The deaths and threats of death were commonplace. See Ramsay in his discussion of the Thyatiran church.

Summary

Dragon
Rome - Egypt
Rome = Jerusalem

In chapter 12 we saw the two main figures behind the scenes. The Lord and the Dragon. In this chapter, we have seen the terrible trio at work. The sea beast is Rome in her priestly garb. The cunning and the power of Rome are here set forth. The saints are up against a mean opponent. There is the definite tone of suffering coming through in this chapter. The noise of the sea is in the air as we picture the sea-beast like an ugly Godzilla lashing its way out of the ocean at the bidding of a horrifying dragon. There is the quietness of a hillside, where a lamb is standing — a picture of innocence. And then the stillness is broken by the dragon-like roar from the lamb. Here's a lamb and the Christians have committed their souls to a Lamb. Can their Lamb match this one?

The pressure is on. Some will die, and "If any man is for captivity, into captivity he goeth." There will be economic pressure

during which God expects the saint to stay faithful. There is the threat to life and the temptation for the Christian to be deceived by the second lamb — what's a pinch of incense? This chapter fairly bristles with troubles and threats and creates the need for further comfort!

p 214

Chapter 14
1 And I looked and behold the Lamb was
standing on Mt. Zion and w/Him 144,000 having
His name and the name of His Father written
on their forehead
2 And I heard a voice from heaven, like the
sound of many waters and like the sound of
loud thunder and the voice which I heard
was like the sound of harpists playing on
their harps.
3 And they sang a new song before the throne &
before the 4 living creatures and the elders;
and no one could learn the song except
the 144,000 who had been purchased from the earth
4 These are the ones who have not been
defiled w/women, for they are celibates.
These are the ones who follow the Lamb
wherever He goes. These have been purchased
from among men as first fruits of God & to
the Lamb.
5 And no lie was found in their mouth;
they are blameless.
6 And I ~~was~~ saw another ~~angel~~ eagle flying in midheaven,
having an ~~other~~ eternal gospel to preach to those who
live on the earth and to every nation and tribe
and tongue and people;
7 and he said w/a loud voice "Fear God & give
Him glory because the hour of His judgment
has come; and worship Him who made
the heaven & the earth & the sea & springs of water.
8 And another angel, a second one followed
saying "Fallen, fallen is Babylon the great,
she who has made all the nations drink
of the wine of the passion of her immorality.
9 And another angel, a third one followed them
saying w/a loud voice "If anyone worships the
beast and his image and receives a mark on his
forehead or upon his hand,

10 he also will drink of the wine of the wrath of God which is mixed in full strength in the cup of His anger; and he will be tormented w/ fire & brimstone in the presence of the holy angels & in the presence of the Lamb.

Questions on Chapter 14

on Mt Zion the church

1. What's the first thing seen in chapter 14? The Lamb OF GOD Standing strong
2. Why do you think this is? for encouragement after chp 13 ends w/ false lamb of Rome
3. That are the 144,000 wearing and what's the point being stressed? name of Jesus & Father written on forehead and showing to whom they belong
4. Who sings the "new song"? the church, the 144,000
5. What's the significance of a "new" song? it points to newness deliverance etc from Egypt from calamities from slavery a new creature
6. What prophet talks a lot about "new" things? Isaiah
7. Why couldn't the song be learned by others than the select group? only those who have been delivered from slavery & have deep convictions & persevere when Satan attacks & stand strong Eph 6:10
8. Why are the 144,000 described in detail? to spur us on to right living
9. What happens when people look at the statue of Apollo in the British Museum? they stand taller -- are encouraged to be all they can be
10. What's the gospel the angel in mid-heaven is telling? devil & Rome defeated God triumphant
11. What's the judgment of verse 7? against all those who have sided w/ Satan.
12. What does this call for? a decision to follow God and worship Him
13. Who is "Babylon"? Rome
14. Why is she **not** said to be "falling"? because she has already fallen
15. Are verses 10,11 speaking of "hell"? NO! eternal punishment does not take place in heaven
16. Where is the fire located? in heaven evil dealt with where this present vision is taking place - its a heavenly vision
17. To what does the reaping of verses 14-16 refer?
18. What's the point of the gathering of verses 17-20?
19. The winepress was trodden outside what city? no specific city
20. How long is the river of blood to be? 200 miles
21. How deep? up to horse's bridle
22. What's the point in all this? God is serious, His wrath is no joke
23. What does Walvoord say of this river of blood? splattering of blood
24. How does Lindsey approach it? literalizes it

Counterpart of following of sea beast w/ dragon & land beast

to encourage us to live pure upright lives

protection for the righteous they shld feel secure (17–18)

11 And the smoke of their torment goes up forever & ever and they have no rest day & night, those who worship the beast and his image, & whoever receives the mark of his name.
12 Here is the perseverance of the saints who keep the commandments of God & their faith in Jesus
13 And I heard a voice from heaven saying, "Write Blessed are the dead who die in the Lord from now on!" & "Yes" says the Spirit, "that they may rest from their labors for their deeds follow w/ them.
14 And I looked and behold a white cloud and sitting on the cloud was one like a son of man having a golden crown on His head and a sharp sickle in His hand.
15 And another angel came out of the temple crying out w/ a loud voice to Him who sat on the cloud "Put in your sickle and reap because the hour to reap has come because the harvest of the earth is ripe.

16 And He who sat on the cloud swung His sickle over the earth and the earth was reaped.
17 And another angel came out of the temple which is in heaven and he also had a sharp sickle.

Analysis of Chapter 14

I. The vision of the 144,000: 1-5
- A. Their place: verse 1
- B. Their name: verse 1
- C. Their song: verses 2,3
- D. Their description: verses 4,5

II. The six great proclamations: 6-20
- A. Eternal good news: verses 6,7
- B. The fall of Babylon: verse 8
- C. The judgment of the beast worshipers: verses 9-12
- D. The blessedness of the righteous dead: verse 13
- E. The wheat harvest: verses 14-16
- F. The vintage harvest: verses 17-20

An Introduction to Chapter 14

You've just finished (I hope) going through the text of chapter 13. If you've read it rightly, you have felt the pressure which must have mounted in the minds of the saints. A gargantuan Dragon, frustrated and furious; a horrific sea monster lumbering out of the breakers in answer to the Dragon's command; a death and resurrection taking place, "proving" that the beast can't be killed, and demonstrating the colossal power of the Dragon; a lamb-like beast coming up out of the very ground and shattering the stillness with the nerve-shattering roar of a dragon's voice; the tremendous power of this "lamb," its "miracles" and threats; and last but not least, the spell which has been cast over the whole world as they all become zombie-like devotees of the sea beast.

What would you want to hear if you'd been a Christian back then? After that lot, what would you want to hear? You'd like to hear chapter 14! As the analysis will show, there are essentially two parts to the chapter and they are all good news — they are encouragement! They are assurance.

As newspapers usually head-up the story with a headline, so God here (following Summers) heralds what is to happen. Each of the proclamations is developed in later chapters. See the analysis and comments.

Comments on Chapter 14

VERSES 1-5. I saw...the Lamb standing on the mount Zion - What a super way to begin the next section following the horror of chapter 13. They'd just seen a lamb-like creature that spoke of fear, intimidation, and death. Now they are shown THE LAMB who spoke peace, comfort, and the answer to death! This Lamb cannot be afraid of death — this is the Lamb that "became" (Greek on 1:18) dead; that deliberately accomplished his death, and then walked-off with the gates of the city of Death!

He saw the Lamb "standing." Not "lying" slain. And where was he standing? On "Mount Zion." That Zion out of which salvation comes (Psalm 14:7). That Zion out of which the Savior comes (Isaiah 59:20 and Romans 11:26). That same Zion of which God spoke when he said: "Yet have I set my king upon my holy hill of Zion (Psalm 2:6). The passage is applied by Paul (Acts 13:32-37) to the resurrection and subsequent glorification of Jesus. **This** is the Lamb that is standing, and **this** is the place of his power.

And with him 144,000 having his name - And what a name! What a privilege. Wearing **his** name. It was said that a Greek soldier called Alexander was insolent, dirty, and lazy. He was brought before the Macedonian lord, Alexander the Great. The great one told him: Change either your way or your name! Is there no lesson here for us?

We've discussed the identity of these 144,000 back in chapter 7. I suggest you go there for the proofs that these are the Church of God. These wear the name of the Lamb and his Father (see 3:12), even as the worshipers of the beast wear his mark. They wear no ordinary name. They wear a name **that is enduring!** They wear a name **that carries power** with it (Acts 4:12). They wear a name that everyone **will one day bow to** (Philippians 2:9-11). They wear a name so select that men use it **for both cursing and praising.** About whose name do they write the hymns that stir the souls of millions in each generation? And whose name does the drunk or the profane slur and slander? (If something is to be profaned, profane something special).

And what is his name? Well now, that depends on which prophet and which passage you have in mind. Isaiah 9:6 says his name is Wonderful; it is Counsellor; it is MIGHTY GOD; it is EVERLASTING FATHER; it is Prince of Peace. These are the attributes of the Lamb. This is his name (not names) — **this** is his name, his character, nature, and status. Is he a match for the enemies of chapter 13? The song heard in the background answers the question.

VERSE 2. And I heard a voice from heaven - This verse is parenthetical. Verse 3 carries on the thought from verse 1. The voice seems almost like an intrusion into the thought, but we are being led to understand that heaven is here voicing its approval of what it sees. When we read of a voice from heaven without that voice being identified, it speaks the will of heaven. Heaven doesn't make a tiny sound (it is too grand in apocalyptic speech for that), but in this case, it makes a harmonious sound. Power is there, but so is the harmony. The deep power of rushing water (the sort of sound John would be hearing on his rocky, island-prison) is brought together into harmony.

VERSE 3. And they sing as it were a new song - That is, the 144,000 sing a new song. Swete is wrong here. The angels are not doing the singing. He holds the voice from heaven to be the angels who are singing the song. It is not "it" but "they" that sing a new song. Verse 3 takes up from verse 1 where the 144,000 are the subject — they sing, as it were, a new song.

A new song. The prophets and the psalmists knew a lot about "new songs." Isaiah knows a lot about a lot of "new" things. He talks of "new things" and "new names." He talks of a "new song" and a "new heaven and earth." In ancient times when God would do something great for Israel, they'd write a song and sing about it. See Exodus 15 for an example. But God promised other great things to Israel, so he tells the people: "Remember ye not the former things, neither consider the things of old. Behold I will do a new thing; now shall it spring forth; shall ye not know it? I will even make a way in the wilderness, and rivers in the desert...(Isaiah 43:18,19). Here the allusion is to the delivery from Egypt. He had at that time brought them out in a wonderful deliverance, but he brought them through a terrible desert. This time, he says, I will deliver you in even a more remarkable way — I will transform the desert. (Fulfilled in the return from Babylon and then in Jesus. Not literally fulfilled, of course.)

Then in 42:9,10 he said: Behold the former things are come to pass, and new things do I declare; before they spring forth I tell you of them. Sing unto Jehovah a new song, and his praises from the end of the earth. In this text, we have a new song because of a new manifestation of God's goodness. They sang songs of a wonderful deliverance from Egypt — he would give them occasion to sing a "new song" of a greater deliverance than that. Check a concordance.

And no man could learn the song save the 144,000 - The point clearly is that only those who've experienced the salvation of God can really sing of it. See the comments on the "new name" that only the individual could know who received the name (2:17). Pilate said to Jesus: "Art thou a king then?" This wasn't really a question — it was more of a probing statement. Jesus replied: "Sayest thou this of thyself or did another tell thee?" There's so much instruction here for us. How often do we sing and pray things which are not really our convictions? Or, if they are our convictions, we don't feel them as deeply as the song or the prayer indicates. "Sayest thou this because the songwriter told thee?" "Sayest thou this thyself or did the preacher (father, mother, friend) tell thee?"

These 144,000 are not merely the martyrs (J.W. Roberts) of the Church. They are the Church. They are the "purchased out of the earth." But can the 24 elders represent the Church and be sung before the 144,000 which is the Church? Of course. Each figure has its own point. Can the Church be both a woman and a city? The married wife and the "engaged" girl?

VERSES 4,5. These are they that were not defiled with women -We've already discussed these characteristics under chapter seven. See there. The section is written to inspire the saints to heroic living. Here is their ideal. This they ought to reach for. There is set before them what they can, in Christ, be or become. This is worth noting because I think our sermons could use this tactic more than they do. I think we need times to unambiguously, clearly, "skin" the brethren (but yet gently). I believe, more often than not we need to set before them the ideal and urge them to it.

We can just hear one of the saints murmur when this section is read out: Is that really me? It's certainly what God would have us to be. They tell of a boy who grew up looking at a carving of a face on Stone Face mountain. People swore that as the boy grew, he became more and more like the face on the mountain. Do you believe that? Probably not, but I'll tell you what I know to be true. In the British Museum in London they have a statue of Apollo. Apollo is a magnificent specimen of manhood. They've watched people who go in there and look at that statue. This is on record! Men will go in there slumped and slouching and walk away more upright than when they entered. Maybe if we are constantly brought face-to-face with what we ought to be, then we'll go away more upright than before.

VERSES 6-20. Another angel flying in mid-heaven - This makes him, like the eagle of 8:13, conspicuous. It gains the attention. Remember the book addresses the imagination, as well as the mind. He has "eternal good tidings." (This is not the Mormon gospel).

His story is that righteousness will be vindicated! The beast is not unbeatable. The Dragon has his limitations. God alone is worthy of worship, and the coming events will prove that clearly. Now this good news, is good news indeed. It doesn't matter in what age the Devil is manifesting himself — he is USING the nations. He "deceives" them and "blinds" them. His defeat is good news!

VERSE 7. The hour of his judgment is come - The judgment is the judgment on Rome and all who stand with her. It has two phases. The murder of Domitian is a clear and gripping judgment of the "resurrected" beast who called himself "Master" and "God." In this judgment on Domitian, God has declared his judgment on the kingdom for which Domitian stood. The god of that kingdom lay dead at the feet of God. He who was feared lies now with his life's blood ebbing away. What now of the bragging? What now of the blasphemy? The second phase of the judgment is the laying of the whole empire into the tomb. There are those who don't think the judgment on Domitian was of great importance — maybe if they'd lived in Domitian's day, they'd have thought otherwise. It's remarkable that God judged Judaism (then apostate) to death in 70 A.D., but that it still continues. Equally remarkable, that after this final judgment on an apostate system, it rose up in bloody fervor and challenged Rome again about 136 A.D.

Worship him that made...heaven...sea...fountains - And how will the apocalypse set this truth forth? God has already laid judgments on each of these — he will do more, shortly. He has whipped Satan in heaven and on earth. And the sea cannot bring forth what He won't permit. Comfort, comfort, and more comfort. But all of this calls for a decision! We've got to side with God. Shakespeare has Julius Caesar saying: "Who among you is so base that he would not be a Roman? Speak! For him have I offended!" And this challange rings forth to us also. Who among us is so base that he would not be a Christian? Speak, for him has God offended!

VERSE 8. Fallen, fallen is Babylon the great - Babylon is Rome viewed as a Harlot. It is Rome looked at from her seductive standpoint. All the nations wanted alliances with Rome. She was attractive. The reason for her attractiveness to other nations is that she was supported by such staggering civil power. We'll discuss her identity fully in comments on chapter 17.

Note that she is not 'falling" but seen as "fallen." It is the same God who said to Abraham: A father of many nations **have** I made thee. The same God I say who said Babylon is "fallen" has said "I **have** made thee the father of many nations." Paul will argue from that verb tense that this speaks of certainty of fulfillment (Romans 4:17). Think of the encouragement this type of speech must generate in the hearts of the believers.

VERSES 9-12. A third followed...saying...If any man worship the beast - What? He will be well-rewarded by the beast? He will be assured of a happy future? See how the saints lean over and turn the ear to catch this. "He will drink of the wine..." Yes, but what wine? The wine of "the wrath of God." There it is. The fearful phrase. Dreadful sentence! Filled with the woes of a million eternities. Filled with the echoes of hopelessness. Filled with the blackness of forever! The wine in "unmixed." Pure, unadulterated wrath! Warnings have been given and ignored. Delay has been used, but all to no avail. Here is "payday."

And he shall be tormented with fire and brimstone - Remember you are reading figures! We've been looking at pictures all along and asking ourselves, what do the pictures mean. Let's not start now and take the pictures literally. God in ancient times literally destroyed Sodom and Gomorrah with fire and brimstone and this historical judgment became a model for others which followed. In Isaiah 34:8-17, we have the same kind of use of the Sodom judgment. It is used as a model to speak of Edom's judgment. Read it for yourself. Go ahead. Notice that at one and the same time, the land is endlessly burning, night and day, and yet the wild animals live there. In the one passage, we have judgment spoken of in two different figures. One of endless burning and smoking, and the other of utter desolation. The figure of undying fire is used by Isaiah in 66:24, where the model is changed.

In that passage there is an allusion to the valley of Hinnom, which was so popular in the days of Ahaz for the burning of children to Molech. Later it became a rubbish dump where fires were kept burning. There we have the combining of the evil and the burning. They'd throw animals into the ravine at times, but sometimes the animal didn't get all the way to the bottom and flies would lay their eggs on it. Worms would breed and they would feed until the flesh was gone, and then they would die. The whole thing was taken to stand for the punishment of transgressors against God (Jesus so used it — Matthew 10:28 et al), but it was not intended to be taken literally. Well, read it for yourself.

Here in our present text is the fate of the wicked spelled out. Many of the saints had writhed in the fires started by Rome, but they only lasted until the body was overcome — then there was rest. For the wicked, our vision says there will be no rest, just endless writhing. I'd have you notice that this torment takes place: In the presence of the holy angels, and in the presence of the Lamb. Hell, the final end of all the unforgiven, **is not here under discussion.** The everlasting punishment of the unforgiven does not take place in heaven! It does not take place in the presence of the holy angels of the Lamb. Paul says: Who shall suffer punishment, even eternal destruction from the face of the Lord and from the glory of his might (2 Thessalonians 1:9).

VERSE 12. Here is the patience of the saints - This helps the saints to endure. There is no vindictiveness taught here. There is relief. Can't you hear the oohs and ahhs in the assembly when that piece is read? Don't you know relief flooded the church that the Lamb was **with** them?

VERSE 13. Blessed are the dead who die in the Lord - Ah, what a passage! Jesus never looks better than he does at a deathbed. With the philosophy of Russell, words like these are useless. With a view like O'Hair's, the passage is flat. These doctrines rob people of so much. I've heard of atheists who recanted on their deathbeds, but I've never heard of a Christian who rued his service to Jesus.

The "blessed" dead. Who could have said such a thing without a revelation? Here, Swete nicely says, is a new beatitude which needed a voice from heaven to bring it to us. But who, looking at the pale and fixed look of the dead, can speak of "blessed"? The weeping loved ones, the silent march to the tomb, the yawning earth, the leaving of the loved-one behind — lonely, solitary. What makes the dead "blessed"? Because they are "in the Lord." There's what makes the difference. There are only two places to die. In the Lord or out of Him. The second doesn't bear speaking of.

There's debate as to how the passage ought to be rendered. Should it be "Blessed are the dead who die in the Lord from henceforth..."? Or should it be "Blessed are the dead who die in the Lord, from henceforth...they shall rest"? Most versions follow the ASV (the first rendering). The NEB takes the second. The ASV rendering suggests "From this moment on, the dead are to be viewed as blessed." The NEB seems to suggest, "Those who die in the Lord are from that moment on, blessed." This latter rendering is plain enough. The first one provokes the question "Why should they be said to be blessed from this moment onward? Was it not true before?" The answer would be, of course it was always true, but since this is a critical hour, producing martyrs, it needs to be plainly said concering **them**.

That they may rest from their labors - On the whole the NEB rendering seems smoothest as to sense. What labors? Don't people who have died serve the Lord? Yes, but they're not subject to the

18 and another angel, the one who has power over fire came out from the altar and he called w/a loud voice to him who had the sharp sickle saying, "Put in your sharp sickle and gather the clusters from the vine of the earth because her grapes are ripe.

14:13-18 221

strife they've been under. There is no **toil** in their service anymore. This is not just rest, it is rest from labors. It is the reward of service. That's what the saints need to hear. There is a big difference between the reward of the saints and the reward of those following the beast. Right?

VERSES 14-16. Behold a white cloud; and...one like unto a son of man - Deity sits or rides on clouds. Only deity rides on the clouds. Others have ordinary chariots, but the Lord rides the clouds. See Psalm 18:9ff; Isaiah 19:1 and Psalm 104:3. The cloud here is "white," indicative of purity and majesty and victory. The one sitting on it is Jesus. He is **the** Overcomer and wears his golden crown. In his hand he has a sharp sickle with which to reap the harvest.

VERSE 15. Send forth your sickle and reap: for the hour to reap is come - The reaping here has to do with the wheat. The Greek says the "harvest of the earth **is dry.**" The term is used (LXX) of the grain in Joel 1:17, except that there it is dry too long. Here it is timed just right.

The protecting of the righteous is often set forth in the Bible as the gathering in of the wheat into the garner. See Matthew 3:12; 13:30. Check a concordance. Amos speaks of the preservation of the righteous as wheat going through a sieve that none of it be lost amidst the chaff (9:9,10). **Verse 16** shows this being done and so, in vision, we are told the security of the righteous is secure.

VERSES 17-20. And another angel came out from the temple -Knowing what is coming, this sounds ominous. The angel comes out from the place where God himself dwells (the Church is not in view here, only the dwelling of God in the O.T.), as if with a special commission. Certainly this is a very holy angel on an errand of justice for his Lord. He has a sharp sickle too, but what a difference in intention.

VERSE 18. Another angel...he hath power over fire - As the one with the sickle leaves, the second one, a judging angel (thus with power over fire), calls in a commanding tone that he get on with it. The second angel is associated with the altar of burnt offering (brazen altar) at which all the sacrifices are burned. God is about to sacrifice something...or someone. Judging angels often stood by the brazen altar, signifying a sacrifice about to take place (Ezekiel 9:1,2; and see Revelation 8:5).

VERSE 19. And gathered the vintage of the earth - The classic Biblical figure for the judgment on the wicked. Grapes for the "winepress of the wrath of God." The redness of the grape, so like blood. The trampling fierceness of God as he presses upon the ungodly. Above we heard of the ungodly being made to drink the wine of the wrath of God. The figure has now changed and they become the grapes trodden under his terrible feet. Sinner, this isn't written for nothing! God takes sin seriously.

It's worth noticing that the press is called a "wine" press. What came directly from the press was "wine." Direct from the winepress, it was not intoxicating. So "wine" doesn't always mean an intoxicating drink. By the time you read this (if the Lord tarries, etc.), you will be able to examine a tract I have written on the "Bible Wine" issue.

VERSE 20. The winepress was trodden without the city - There has been a lot of discussion as to what city is here alluded to. Perhaps there should be. Some have said it is Rome, for that is one of the two great cities in the book. Lindsey says it can't be anything else but Jerusalem. Perhaps not, but what does he offer in proof of his position? Nothing but his word!

But I'm not sure that any particular city is in mind. Saints are to suffer with Christ (the Hebrews were told — 13:12,13) outside the camp or the city, but who's to say that there is anything of this thought here? Vineyards and winepresses were usually outside the villages. Whole villages would leave their homes and live in booths at vintage time (I.S.B.E.). To this agree Smith's Bible Dictionary and Hasting's Bible Dictionary. In Isaiah 63, God is represented as coming back to the city after having been to the winepress. It's true that he was treading Edom, but still, he was treading outside the city. Perhaps then, we are not to look for "which city"?

Blood...even unto the bridles of the horses - This says the carnage will be incredible. Walvoord, a literalist, admits this isn't possible and settles for "a literal spattering of blood." Can you beat that? The bold Lindsey literalizes. But he does more. He measured it all out.

The bridles of the horses, as far as 1600 furlongs - Now get this. Here is a river of blood, 200 miles long and as deep as a horse's chest! Lindsey measured from the Valley of Armageddon all the way to the Gulf of Aqabah, "approximately" 200 miles. So he literalizes, measures, and approximates! The whole valley of the Jordan, including the Dead Sea area (how could he get that to be horse-bridle deep?) and south, is to be filled with "war materials...and blood." Now the Bible says blood — where did these war materials come from? There is not enough blood in the whole world to make that kind of river. Work it out for yourself. What utter nonsense it all is. Walvoord does little better with his "liberal spattering of blood." Are we to suppose the blood "splatters" 200 miles? I'm sure we are expected to take this seriously, but in all candor, it's very difficult.

The whole expression is intended to say that when God begins to execute his judgment on the enemy, the result will be frightening indeed. We've heard of rivers of blood being shed. This is a figure of speech which every nation is acquainted with. Swete quotes "Enoch," c. 1,3: "In those days the fathers together with their sons will be smitten in one place...until it streams with their blood like a river...and the horses will walk up to the breast in the blood of sinners, and the chariots will be submerged to its height." This apocryphal book was written about 100-50 B.C.

Summary

The chapter comes as an encouraging response to chapter 13. In it we have the picture of triumphant saints (martyrs and non-martyrs). They already sing a "new" song concerning the new deliverance. The saints are pictured as loyal, pure, obedient, and courageous followers of the Lamb. Six proclamations are made which stir the hearts of the godly! The enemy is going to pay and you are blessed even if you die! The wheat is gathered and the grapes are trampled!

Chapter 15
1 And I saw another sign in heaven, great & marvelous
seven angels who had seven plagues, which are
the last because in them the wrath of God is finished.
2 And I saw as it were, a sea of glass mixed w/fire
and those who had come off victorious from
the beast and from his image and from the
number of his name standing on the sea of
glass holding harps of God.
3 And they sang the song of Moses the bond-
servant of God and the song of the lamb
saying Great and marvelous are Thy works
O Lord God, the Almighty
Righteous and true are Thy ways
Thou King of the nations
4 Who will not fear, O Lord & glorify Thy name?
For Thou alone art holy;
For all the nations will come & worship before Thee
For Thy righteous acts have been revealed.
5 After these things I looked and the temple of the
tabernacle of testimony in heaven was opened
6 and the 7 angels who had the 7 plagues
came out of the temple clothed in linen
clean and bright and girded around their
breasts w/golden girdles.
7 And one of the 4 living creatures gave to the
7 angels 7 golden bowls full of the wrath
of God who lives forever & ever.
8 And the temple was filled w/smoke from
the glory of God and from His power and
noone was able to enter the temple
until the 7 plagues of the 7 angels were
finished.

Questions on Chapter 15

1. In what way does chapter 15 accord with the pattern of the book so far?
2. What is the wrath of God that "is finished" in 15:1?
3. What do you make of the sea of glass "mingled with fire"?
4. To what Old Testament scripture would the song of Moses point?
5. What reason do they have to sing as if the job were already over?
6. Do you think the "victors" are limited to the martyrs?
7. What is the "testimony"?
8. What is the "tabernacle of the testimony"?
9. What is the "temple of the tabernacle of the testimony"?
10. Why is the scene set there?
11. How does the dress of the angels suggest the kind of work they're doing?
12. If the angels were wearing jewels, what might be the point?
13. Who or what are the "living creatures"?
14. What's the significance of the temple being filled with smoke?

An Analysis of Chapter 15

I. The angels with the seven plagues: 1

II. The victors over the beast: 2-4
   A. Where they were: verse 2
   B. What they were: verse 2
   C. What they sang: verses 3,4

III. The seven angels appear: 5-8
   A. Where they were: verses 5,6
   B. How they were dressed: verse 6
   C. What they were given: verse 7

IV. The smoking temple: 8

Introduction to Chapters 15 and 16

Before the seals were opened in chapter 6, we have a vision of heaven (chapters 4,5) assuring the brotherhood that the throne of the universe was not in Italy, but in heaven. God and the Lamb were in control and were working out below, their plans. Then the seals were ripped off.

Before the trumpets were blown in chapters 8,9 we were shown a silent period in heaven and the angels offering up the prayers of the saints with incense — the symbol of acceptable prayer. It was then we were informed that what was about to happen on earth was the work of God in heaven in answer to the prayers of the saints for justice — in answer to God's own demands made in holiness. Then the trumpet blasts came.

And here again we have a scene in heaven before the bowls are poured out. The victors over the beast are there to see it. We are told of the angels of the plagues. They are in the inner sanctuary where God alone dwells. He is (as it were) giving them final instructions. They are given the bowls of wrath by the Cherubim who ever hover around the throne of God and speak of his holiness. We are being told before the bowls are poured out that this is the work of God. There's nothing accidental here. This is no Fate or Luck. Here is deliberate and holy judgment poured out on the kingdom of Rome — the current manifestation of the Devil's moral and spritual lunacy. The warnings are over — they are ignored. The bowls speak of the full wrath of God. Please note further the introduction to chapters 17-19.

Comments on Chapter 15

VERSE 1. Seven angels having seven plagues - The assembly at which this was first read must have been on the edge of their seats by this time. Here in the 20th century, the urgency is not felt. The demand for relief is not there (for most of us). Today in some area of the world this book is read with great feeling. One brother recently rehearsed to us a visit he had made behind the Iron Curtain. The brothers and sisters had gotten together to study and the police came in and disrupted and threatened. Later as they again assembled, they read together from the epistle, and the comfort was visible. One can almost see the faces of the worshipers as the epistle is being read. How they would look at one another with eyes reflecting confidence and the "well-here-it-comes-at-last" look.

The same feeling must have been felt among many Jews on the night when Moses said to Pharaoh: One more plague and then you'll let us go! This will be the last plague. The Jews had seen others, and had heard the moans of a stricken Egyptian nation. They'd even seen some Egyptians turn to Jehovah because of it all, but now there is one more crushing plague to fall. And what made it all so much the more impressive — the plagues were all declared prior to their fulfillment.

For in them is finished the wrath of God - The word "for" points us back to the statement that these plagues are "the last." This is not to suggest that God is exhausted, but that these are all he needs to finish the job. He warned the Jews in Ezekiel (7:2,6): "An end: the end is come upon the four corners of the land...An end is come, the end is come..." You'll notice here it is not just "an" end but "the" end. He will strike and need to do so no more.

The wrath of God in this book is his wrath against Rome. I need hardly tell you that the principles which are taught in the book apply to God's dealings with all nations at all times and so it is just as relevant today as it ever was.

VERSES 2-4. A sea of glass mingled with fire - This is the same sea of glass as in 4:6. See the comments there. The sea of glass is the approach to God. It is modeled after the laver (Solomon's "brazen sea"). The priest had to go through the laver in order to enter into the sanctuary to serve God. Therefore the sea of glass speaks of the holiness of God — his unapproachableness. It is here said to be mingled with fire.

A number of the versions render the last part of verse 2 to say that the victors "stand on" the sea of glass rather than "stand beside" it. Goodspeed, Wuest, C.B. Williams and the NAS so understand it. This may be pertinent to our understanding of the "fire" in the sea of glass. If we understand they have moved up closer to the throne. And this is a very probable view, for it is through trials and suffering that one enters more deeply into that fellowship with Jesus that Paul seemed to be speaking of in Philippians 3:10ff. He certainly does set forth the advantages of trial in Philippians 1:27-30. Peter and James both tell of the benefits which come through suffering. It is even taught that the Master himself was "perfected" and learned obedience through the things he suffered.

If the victors are standing "by" the sea, then clearly we have the Red Sea in view. This sea, standing as it did in ancient times between the saints and God, the saints and freedom, would be here viewed as crossed. It was in that sea that God manifested his holiness. Twice Moses in Exodus 15 alludes to the holiness of God and here in verse 4, we hear of God's righteous acts being manifested.

If they stand "by" the sea of glass, they have moved closer to God and their enemies have been judged. The fire would certainly speak of the righteous acts of God, whether they relate to the purification of his people or the judgment of their enemies...or both! Perhaps we are not to choose either, but take both.

Them that come off victorious - Are these simply martyrs as Roberts and others suggest? Why don't you read again the comments I made earlier (2:7) about "overcomers." I'm just sure we're not supposed to hold the victors to be restricted to martyrs. The comfort in John's book is not simply for the dead people, or the members of the dead one's family. Those who live on have also overcome the beast. Living or dying, the faithful one is a victor. "They overcame him..." Only the dead ones? Surely not!

VERSE 3. They sing the song of Moses...and...the Lamb - In Exodus 15 we have a song recorded there. The dragon (Egypt) has now been slain. The bodies of the soldiers in the sea would be mute testimony of the power and holiness of God. But they would be more than that — they'd be mute but graphic proof that God is finally, as always, the Victor, and the God of gods! Moses and his company sang: "I will sing unto Jehovah, for he hath triumphed gloriously: the horse and his rider hath he thrown into the sea."

In Psalm 77:10ff, the Psalmist muses on the ways of God in olden times when he delivered Israel from Egypt at the Red Sea. He says of God that his way "is in the sanctuary" (i.e. marked by holiness). In verse 4 of this chapter, it is affirmed of God that he alone is holy. Over and over again, we are having the holiness of

God brought out. The saints are to know that the battle is not just between them and Rome, but between God and the Dragon — between God and Satan — between holiness and unholiness!

But the delivery in the days of Moses, marvelous though it was, is overshadowed by the deliverance of both body and soul under the present distress. A greater deliverer makes for a greater deliverance. And though the body goes down into the grave, **this** Redeemer has said: "Blessed are the dead." For a dead Israelite, Moses could do nothing. The Lamb knows no such limitations.

VERSE 4. Who shall not fear, O Lord, and glorify thy name? -There is no promise here of worldwide conversion. The nations will know, but they will not accept the Lord as Lord. This is seen over and over again in the lives of Bible characters. See the conduct of Nebuchadnezzar, Darius, and Belshazzar. The peoples of Canaan, Moses said, were frightened half to death, but look what happened when Israel arrived there (see Exodus 15:14ff). One thing is sure — all would be forced to acknowledge the Lord (see Philippians 2:9ff).

VERSES 5-8. I saw the temple of the tabernacle of the testimony -The "testimony" was the "10 commandments." The ark of the testimony was the ark which held the ten commandments. The tabernacle of the testimony was the tabernacle wherein was the ark which held the testimony. The "temple" was the inner sanctuary of the tabernacle wherein the ark was that held the testimony.

In that inner sanctuary God dwelt. Alone and solitary. It stressed his holiness. No one but the High Priest was ever permitted to enter that awful place. And he, only on one day of the year. And when he did go there, he had to enter with the blood of an innocent victim. He carried into that place a censer of incense. It billowed sweet-smelling smoke all around him in that sacred and awful place. This ensured that he did not "see" God. It was said by ancient Hebrew writers that when the High Priest entered there, the whole nation stood with bated breath until he returned. And when he did, they say, the breathing again of the people was like the wind passing over the wheat field.

VERSE 6. And there came out...the seventh angel - Where had they been? In there where the awesome Jehovah dwelled in all his terrible seclusion. At a time of crisis, when the president calls in his cabinet, how everyone eyes them as they come walking out of the cabinet room. What will they say? What is to happen? (What a book!) Even though we may know already what is to happen, what **has** to happen, just to hear it from them has an effect all its own.

Arrayed with precious stone...and golden girdles - The ASV reading is rejected by all the other major versions which render the passage "clothed in fine linen." This is less awkward. The dress is priestly, of course, as the golden girdles make clear (see on 1:13). If the angels are wearing fine linen, they are wearing what the High Priest would wear on the day that he entered the holy of holies (see Leviticus 16:2ff,23). If the angels were wearing a jewel as a robe (see Ezekiel 28:13; Isaiah 61:10, etc., for jewels in clothing), we might well be reminded of the fact that the High Priest wore twelve precious stones on a breastplate. In this he was designated as the representative of the whole nation before the Lord. Take your pick.

VERSE 7. One of the four living creatures gave...seven golden bowls - The living creatures are the Cherubim. They are the chariot of God — 1 Chronicles 28:18; Psalm 104:3 with 18:9,10. They are those whose business it is to see that the holiness of God is recognized. They demand the punishment of the transgressors. See the comments on 4:6-8, and also the comments in Ezekiel, chapter 1. These are delivering the bowls unto the duly-commissioned representatives of both God and the people.

These are acting in a priestly fashion. This must not be forgotten. This is not a war of politics. This is not dealing with a cultural or social upheaval. It is dealing with rebellion against high Heaven! David, when approaching Goliath, never viewed the conflict as anything other than an insult against God, and the necessary defending of God's honor.

VERSE 8. The temple was filled with smoke - This just emphasizes the solemnity of the occasion. See the Old Testament record for a number of occasions when this happened. Exodus 40:34ff; 1 Kings 8:10,11; 2 Chronicles 5:13,14 and others. On these occasions, we have the dedication of the temple or tabernacle to the Lord, and to impress them with his holiness and majesty, he came down on the dwelling place. We are told expressly (twice) that this made the priests unable to work in there. Something like this occurred also in Numbers 16:31-50, when God became exceedingly angry with the nation and plagued them. He's about to plague the enemy here and so the house fills with smoke. In Leviticus 16:2,17, no one was allowed in the tabernacle limits. The solemnity warranted this.

Summary

We're getting ready for the final outpouring of God's wrath. The victors are poised to see the development. They are singing as if the whole thing were already accomplished. They have reason to, because Babylon is not "falling," but has "fallen." When the song of victory is ended, the tabernacle is the center of the stage. Out of the inner sanctuary of that tabernacle come seven angels involved in priestly activity. They have been in to commune with God on behalf of his people and now they are given the plagues with which to bury Rome! The word is now "GO!"

Chapter 16
1 And I heard a loud voice from the temple,
saying to the 7 angels "Go and pour out the
7 bowls of the wrath of God into the earth."
2 and the first angel went and poured out
his bowl into the earth and it became a
loathsome and malignant sore upon the men
who had the mark of the beast and who
worshiped his image.
4 And the ~~second~~ third angel poured out his bowl
into the rivers and the springs of water and
they became blood.
3 And the second angel poured out his bowl
into the sea and it became blood like
that of a dead man and every living thing
in the sea died.
5 And I heard the angel of the waters saying
"Righteous art thou, who art and who wast
O Holy One because thou didst judge these
things.
6 "for they poured out the blood of saints &
prophets and thou hast given them blood to
drink. They deserve it."
7 And I heard the altar saying, "Yes, O Lord God
the Almighty, true and righteous are thy
judgments."
8 And the fourth angel poured out his bowl upon
the sun and it was given to it to scorch men
w/ fire.
9 And men were scorched w/ fierce heat and they
blasphemed the name of God who has the power
over these plagues and they did not repent so
as to give Him glory.
10 and the 5th angel poured out his bowl upon the
throne of the beast; and his kingdom became
darkened; and they gnawed their tongues
because of pain
11 and they blasphemed the God of heaven
because of their pains and their sores
& they did not repent of their deeds.
12 And the 6th angel poured out his bowl upon the
great river, the Euphrates; and its water was
dried up, that the way might be prepared
for the kings from the east.

13 And I saw coming out of the mouth of the dragon and out of the mouth of the beast and out of the mouth of the false prophet three unclean spirits like frogs.

10 God's trumpets to bring repentance & bowls bring just wrath

Questions on Chapter 16

1. Why are we constantly told that what is about to happen is the wrath of God? God is serious — rebellion against God who is a holy God.
2. What are the "bowls" signifying? punishment from God — told & complete
3. What Egyptian plague is in view under the first bowl? 6th — boils
4. What does the second remind you of? smiting Nile River
5. Can this be literally true and the rest of the book literally true? No p236
6. What is the premillennial difficulty here? There could be no human existence period & yet they claim after that there will be nuclear war (see p 236–237)
7. What plague comes to your mind under the third bowl? drinking water
8. Does this ease the premillennial position any? NO p237
9. In what way does the 4th bowl differ from the 4th trumpet? less light during 4 trumpets — light intense during bowls, scorching heat — blamed God
10. What's the significance? greater intensity w/ bowl — heat greater God powerful
11. What does "darkness" suggest relative to the throne and kingdom of the beast? totally incapable of leadership ruling & governing (moral darkness)
12. What's the significance of the "Euphrates"? dried up river shows military defeat & Red Sea
13. Who are the kings from the east? Army of God coming from rising sun
14. What makes you think so? They come from the rising sun
15. Why is it incredible that it should be a 200-million-strong Chinese army? can't take this literal — 20 million lived in London in 1985
16. What do you know about a frog? P242 v13 the commentary on has no mention of a frog. (lying demon spirit that urge kings to war against God)
17. In what chapter will the battle of Armageddon be fought? see p242 Ch. 19
18. What's the significance of the battle of Armageddon? enemies of God drawn into battle w/ God — shear punishment & judgment
19. Why is the seventh poured out of the air? the air the place of Satan's power (Satan rules the air — it defeats Satan's power)
20. Could "such as was not since there were men on the earth" be proverbial? Yes it is proverbial because it has already occurred
21. What would it indicate? this expression has been used in other instances where there was severe punishment
22. Do you have any Biblical illustrations to sustain your point? like pp 243–244 (see pp 243–244) Israel rebelled & went into captivity
23. What's the point of Babylon being divided into three parts? (utter destruction)
24. What's the point about islands fleeing away, etc.? P244 God shook up their world.
25. What does the hail bring to mind? Egypt

14 for they are spirits of demons performing signs which go out to the kings of the whole world to gather them together for the war of the great day of God the Almighty

15 Behold I am coming like a thief. Blessed is the one who stays awake and keeps his garments lest he walk about naked & men see his shame.

16 And they gathered them together to the place which in Hebrew is called Har-Magedon.

Analysis of Chapter 16

I. The great commission: 1

II. The first bowl poured out: 2

III. The second bowl poured out: 3

IV. The third bowl poured out: 4-7

- A. Drinking water turned to blood: verse 4
- B. The irony and righteousness of the judgment: verses 5-7

V. The fourth bowl poured out: 8,9

- A. The sun's heat intensified: verse 8
- B. The blasphemy and impenitence: verse 9

VI. The fifth bowl poured out: 10,11

- A. The beast's kingdom darkened: verse 10
- B. The blasphemy and impenitence: verse 11

VII. The sixth bowl poured out: 12-16

- A. The river Euphrates hit: verse 12
- B. The kings of the east prepare to march: verse 12
- C. The enemies gather together for The War: verses 13-15
- D. The arena: verse 16

VIII. The seventh bowl poured out: verses 17-21

- A. The air is smitten: verse 17
- B. The earthquake and its results: verses 18-20
- C. The great hail and the blasphemy: verse 21

Comments on Chapter 16

VERSE 1. And I heard a great voice out of the temple - Undoubtedly the voice of God himself, since it comes from the inner sanctuary and since there is now no one (15:8) in the sanctuary. A lot of blasphemous nonsense had poured out of Rome. A lot of silly boasting came out of Rome. Here we have a short, terrifying sentence: Go ye, and pour out the seven bowls of the wrath of God into the earth. The expression "wrath of God" occurs over and over again. This is the fifth time it has occurred since we saw the two beasts in chapter 13. We are being informed over and over again that what is about to happen is no accident! Moffatt usually renders the word "wrath" as "fury." That word alone speaks volumes, doesn't it. In quick succession, we'll see the bowls being outpoured.

VERSE 2. The first went and poured out his bowl - Angels, the good ones, are wiser than humans. When God says "go" they just get up and go. You think there's a lesson here for us? The bowls parallel the trumpets. The trumpets were to warn, but the bowls are to recompense. The time for warning is over. The trumpets are partial, but the bowls are total and complete.

It became a noisome and grievous sore - Loathesome and painful, foul, and malignant (NEB). These were "a foul and pernicious suppurated sore" (Wuest). The Egyptian plagues are brought to mind — the sixth plague. In this we are explicitly told that the boils were also on the priests, the representatives of Pharaoh. They protested, but Pharaoh wouldn't listen.

On them that had the mark of the beast - The boils didn't have any trouble in finding who to attach themselves to — just look for the fool with the beastly mark. Lindsey talks of tattoos — literally tattooed with the beast's mark. All before about 1988. There quickly follows the next plague.

VERSE 3. And the second poured out his bowl into the sea - The sea was attacked in the trumpets and one-third of it became blood. In this, the whole oceans are attacked and they become (not fresh) blood, but the blood as of a dead man. The smiting of the Nile is brought to mind. In that judgment, a lot of the river animals died. In this ALL living things died. That is, the living things in the sea. Now are we supposed to take this literally? The literalists are, of course, committed to that position. The only trouble with these people is that they never stay consistent for more than a verse or two at a time. At the end of the study, I'll list for you the cases where Lindsey and Walvoord have figurized, so that you can see for yourself all this talk about a millennial kingdom, because we must interpret scripture literally, is so much patter.

Is God intimating here that he will literally turn all the oceans to a dead man's blood, thus slaying every living thing in the oceans? Of course not. The prophet Zephaniah wrote about 625 B.C. (or approximately between 640-609). His message was one of doom for Judah, because of her wickedness. This is how God spoke of their coming doom:

> I will utterly consume all things from off the face of the ground, saith Jehovah. I will consume man and beast; I will consume the birds of the heavens, and the fish of the sea...and I will cut off man from off the face of the ground, saith Jehovah. And I will stretch out my hand upon Judah, and upon all the inhabitants of Jerusalem.
>
> (1:2-4)

Jeremiah (4:23ff), speaking of the judgment brought on Judah by Nebuchadnezzar, said it this way:

> I beheld the earth, and, lo, it was waste and void; and the heavens, and they had no light. I beheld the mountains, and lo, they trembled, and all the hills moved to and fro. And I beheld, and, lo, there was no man, and all the birds of the heavens were fled...the fruitful field was a wilderness, and all the cities thereof were broken down at the presence of Jehovah...

Now Jeremiah said he saw the earth like it was before the Lord got to working on it to put man and the animals on it. What is happening here? If he doesn't mean it literally, why does he say it this way? That's his business. He's promoting horror! They are emotional descriptions. This is an apocalyptic book! Read of the fall of Babylon is Isaiah's writings. See Isaiah 13. In verse 17 we are told Babylon would fall to the Medes. Didn't it? It surely did. The Medo-Persian armies under Cyrus brought the Babylonian kingdom to an end and it hasn't come back up. God said this would happen. But have you read the description of the fall in the language of the prophet? I think it's time you did. Read Isaiah 13:10-13, 17-22. None of this literally happened at the fall of Babylon. Well, go ahead and read it. Research its past and present history for yourself. Did you know that Babylon fell with hardly a shot being fired? Did you know that the gates were opened by the priests to let Cyrus' troops in after some had sneaked in by a river bed and had slain Belshazzar? And are you aware that the city of Babylon was not destroyed by the Medes? It wasn't even destroyed by the Greeks. Alexander the Great made it his headquarters and died there. But Isaiah says it would fall to the Medes as Sodom fell.

He said it would never be dwelt in from that time forth forever. He said no one would pass through it from generation to generation. Do you know that none of this was literally fulfilled? Do you know that they are dwelling there this very day?

Did Babylon fall forever? Well, of course it did. Will it rise again? Of course, it won't. Did it fall literally as described? Indeed not. How can anyone possibly believe that Edom was overthrown as Isaiah described it in chapter 34? And there's no possibility for it to rise again. And even if it did, it couldn't go out again as Isaiah described it (literally) for, on millennial terms, the old earth is to be annihilated. This would mean the land of Edom could not burn forever nor could the porcupines dwell there forever.

I want you to bear this in mind — the millennialists believe that after the bowls are poured out, the nations of the world still get together to wage nuclear war! Keep this in mind as you're reading these bowls.

What does the second bowl say? That commerce is utterly wasted! The naval power, or any other which depended on the sea, would be blasted. In Zechariah 9:4 he swears he will so waste the Tyrians (proverbial as sailors) that he: Will smite her power in the sea. I'll say more on this in chapter 18.

VERSE 4-7. And the third poured out his bowl into the rivers - To hit the sea was to hit commerce. To hit the river in Egypt was both to hit commerce (some) and the drinking supply. Here the drinking water is destroyed. All the drinking water is turned to blood. And do millennialists still (inconsistently) hang-on to their literalism? Listen to Lindsey:

> As if the bloodied sea wasn't enough, the third angel poured out his bowl of judgment into the rivers and springs of waters, and they became blood also. It gets pretty grim when there is no fresh water to drink anywhere on earth. There's going to be a big run on Coca-Cola, but even this will give out after a while!

I guess he's serious about the Coca-Cola. I know he's serious about the drinking water being destroyed. Now, what I'd like to know is this: Are we to believe that in these states, or conditions, that the nations of the world are still marching on each other? That 200 million Chinese are going to march on Israel to meet the Antichrist in battle, and there hasn't been a drop to drink for over seven months? (I'll talk later about the seven months here. These are Lindsey's figures.)

What are we to learn from this bowl? It is just another strike against the gods of the Roman world and the Roman world itself.

The bowls are all to be put together and we are to see Jehovah judging the Roman from every angle. He's attacking the Roman world just as he attacked the Egyptian world. He is here symbolically setting forth that attack!

VERSE 5. Righteous art thou...because thou thus judged - The sarcasm is thick here. The emphasis should be placed on the word "thus" judged, as the next words show. They wanted blood; they seemed to enjoy it, for they shed enough of it! Blood they wanted and blood you gave them! The punishment suited the crime. In the vision, there would be blood everywhere. The seashore waved it, the rivers flowed it, the springs gurgled it. The ships would be red with it and the oceans would stink to high heavens because of all the billions of animals in there that have died. The rivers would smell of the stench of decaying flesh as well as blood! blood!

VERSE 7. And I heard the altar saying, Yea, O Lord - Yes, the altar. The altar from which they took the fire and cast it on the earth. It played its part, too. The altar around which the slain had gathered, asking (without vindictiveness) for justice. We hadn't heard from them, so the altar cries out for them! Let this ring out: JUSTICE WILL BE DONE. For all the ungodliness done on earth, a day of reckoning will come. For all the tears of lonely little boys and girls sitting by themselves in the corner of an orphanage wondering what's gone wrong; for all the hard-working wives who lie senseless beneath the pounding feet and hands of drunken bums; for all the tortured youths who live under the slavery of the drug traffic; for all the exploited and intimidated young girls whose lives are full of shame and disgrace; for all the poor who live under the grinding power of the loan sharks; for all the victims of the Mafia; for all the slandered souls; for all those children who were born in the straw and nurtured in infamy — for these, there will come a day! Justice will be meted out. The criminals will pay. If there's a God, there's got to be a judgment day. And in that day, the altar will cry out, YES, Lord! And those Roman thieving generals who stole the modesty of sweet young ladies; for those Roman soldiers who raped and plundered; for those howling mobs who watched our brethren and sisters writhing in torture; for that Nero, for Domitian, for Diocletian, Decius and Galerius, and the rest of their tribe — their day came in histroy, but a greater day is yet to come when all the robbed, cheated, raped and ravaged, intimidated and hounded — that day when all the "victims" watch while the cutthroats and villains are placed on trial — THAT DAY IS YET TO COME! Such has been the scandalous treatment of the Family of

Jesus Christ, that were there no judgment day, the rocks would cry out — the altar would continue to cry out!

VERSES 8,9. And the fourth poured out his bowl - The sun is hit. The last time God hit it, it was turned-off for four hours of the day. The light was lessened. This time the heat is intensified. A terrible burning and scorching. The Romans have been good with fire. They had a lot of practice since the days of Nero when he lit up his gardens with burning Christians. Fire they had and fire he'd give them!

And what of the saints? What were they promised? What did they have even in the face of fiery trials? The Lamb, we were told, would guide them by fountains of water of life (the Roman world would drink blood) and the sun wouldn't strike them with any scorching heat (chapter 7:15-17). The whole wide universe is under the control of the God of these Christians. The Roman world is under assault by Jehovah. You remember he warned the worshipers of the beast that they ought to worship Jehovah who made the heavens (sun included), the earth, and the sea. The proof that he did indeed do this, is in his use of all these things.

VERSE 9. And they blasphemed the name of God...they repented not - In reading these texts, one might wonder how people under the judgment of God would not repent. Those who know the scriptures can (at least in the Bible) see that these events are the judgments of God, but it is not that plain to the ungodly. So sometimes impenitence is due to lack of conviction. But there are times when the heart is just so hard. Take a look at Pharaoh in the days of Moses. Are you not staggered by his impenitence? Look at the career of the Israelites on their way to freedom and marvel at the stubborness of the human heart.

VERSES 10,11. And the fifth poured out his bowl - In quick succession, John sees blow after blow fall on the oppressor. This angel attacked the throne of the beast's kingdom. Darkness set in. Plague nine on Egypt was darkness, so that they couldn't see to move for three days, the Israelites had light in their dwellings.

In this plague, the upper echelon is hit. And when the head is bruised, the body suffers. The leaders are confused and become the more brutal as they continue in moral darkness. God has often punished nations by giving them (as it were) children to rule them. In Isaiah 3:2-4, the Lord threatens to:

> Take away from Jerusalem and from Judah stay and staff, the whole stay of bread and the whole stay of water; the mighty man, and the man of war; the judge and the prophet, and the diviner, and the elder; the captain of fifty,

> and the honorable man, and the counselor...And I will give children to be their princes, and babes shall rule over them.

This is a terrible thing when men of state are inept. Foolish and incapable of making decisions which involve the lives of millions. Ecclesiastes 10:16 says: Woe to thee, O land, when thy king is a child, and thy princes eat in the morning. The wisdom is taken from the Roman leaders. We are not short of illustrations in Roman history of this kind of thing.

And they gnawed their tongues for pain - You see, this is no ordinary darkness. It is obviously like the Egyptian darkness which the text says was "darkness which may be felt" (Exodus 10:21). Still, the next phrase may be an adequate explanation of this tongue-gnawing, for we are told:

VERSE 11. They blasphemed...God...because of their pains...and sores - The effects of the other plagues are not to be construed as having passed. This is just an added burden. Now comes with the pain and the suppurating ulcers, this heavy darkness, this suffocating darkness, this oppressive blackness. The populace is hurting and the hierarchy is going wild in their brutality and in their stupidity. Natural disasters, economic slumps, inept leadership and all such things in the hands of God become terrible swords. And still...They repent not!

VERSE 12-16. And the sixth poured out his bowl upon the great river - That is, the river Euphrates. We've said already that the Euphrates stood for militarism — for nations at war and the power manifested in that. It was from the Euphrates that Assyria came, and the terrible Babylon.

And the water thereof was dried up - In the advance of armies, the river is said to flow or rush (Isaiah 8:7,8; 17:12; etc.). They are not said to be dried up. If this does stand for armed, military might (and the remarks on 9:14 with the scriptures just given establish that), then the drying up of the waters is not the movement of armies, but of the defeat of armies. It's the removing of the power. The waters cannot then overflow — cannot surge. But is the drying up of waters a Bible phenomenon? You know it is. Who speaks to waters and dries them up? Who rebuked the Red Sea that it opened up and left dry land so that Israel could cross? Who alone in the Bible ever crossed water on dry land?

> And Moses stretched out his hand over the sea; and Jehovah caused the sea to go back by a strong east wind all the night, and made the sea dry land, and the waters were

> divided. And the children of Israel went into the midst of the sea upon dry ground. (Exodus 14:21,22)

And when Moses was gone, and Joshua took over? Who needed a sign for the people's benefit, that they might know that God was with him, even as he had been with Moses? Joshua did. And as they had been "baptized unto Moses" (1 Corinthians 10:1,2) by entering into the Red Sea (thus accepting his leadership), so would they accept Joshua as their new God-given leader then:

> They that bare the ark were come unto the Jordan, and the feet of the priests that bare the ark were dipped in the brink of the water...that the waters which came down from above stood, and rose up in one heap, a great way off at Adam...and those that went down toward the sea of the Arabah, even the Salt Sea, were wholly cut off: and the people passed over right against Jericho...and all Israel passed over on dry ground. (Joshua 3:15-17)

Sometime later we read of Elijah and Elisha taking a walk together. Elijah is soon to leave and he is going to pass on the task to Elisha. What happened then?

> They two stood by the Jordan. And Elijah took his mantle, and wrapped it together and smote the waters, and they were divided hither and thither, so that they two went over on dry ground...He took up also the mantle of Elijah that fell from him, and went back, and stood by the bank of Jordan. And he took the mantle of Elijah...and smote the waters, and said, Where is Jehovah, the God of Elijah? And when he also had smitten the waters, they were divided hither and thither: and Elisha went over. (2 Kings 2:7-14)

And many years later when God through Isaiah (11:1-16) told of glorious deliverance for the believer, how did he describe it? Among other things, he said:

> And Jehovah will utterly destroy the tongue of the Egyptian sea; and with his scorching wind will he wave his hand over the River, and will smite it into seven streams, and cause men to march over dryshod. And there shall be a highway for the remnant of his people, that shall remain from Assyria; like as there was for Israel in the days that he

came up out of the land of Egypt (Isaiah 11:15,16).

Check with a concordance and see for yourself how often this is alluded to in scripture. See, for example, Isaiah 51:10; Psalm 106:9; Zechariah 10:10-12. (If the literalist will be consistent, he is going to have another drying up of the Red Sea and the drying up of the Euphrates that the Israelites might cross. That makes it difficult for Lindsey and the rest, when we consider the plan they have laid out for the future developments.)

What have we said then about the drying up of the River? That this is the work of God. That it speaks of the putting down of military might. But for what purpose?

That the way might be made ready for the kings...from the east - These kings are on their way to the battle of Armageddon to face the foes on the beast's side. The battle is briefly described in chapter 19:11-21. On the one side is the Dragon, the sea beast, and the earth beast with their supporters. Who is on the other side? Jesus and his loyal allies, the redeemed. That accords very well with the preview we are given here. The three beasts on one side and the kings from the "sunrising" on the other. This one truth alone dismantles the whole scheme set forth by Lindsey and company.

VERSES 13,14. Out of the mouth of the dragon...beast..false prophet - The terrible trio! They open their mouths and out come lying spirits. "Demons" they are called. Old fashioned doctrine, someone says — maybe, but Bible, we say. They are called "unclean spirits" and for the benefit of those who don't believe in spirit beings, it must be said, here is the documentation.

And what is their place in this narrative? They are to be permitted to urge the nations into a war against God. They've got to be unclean to do that. They've got to be short on sense, too. The mode for this is not hard to find. Back in the days of Micaiah, Ahab wanted to go to battle against Ramoth-Gilead. He urges Jehoshaphat to join him. Jehoshaphat wants to hear from Micaiah. The false prophets have already given their story in behalf of the desires of Ahab. Finally Micaiah speaks. He tells of lying spirits which receive permission from God to go deceive Ahab into war (1 Kings 22:19-23). So it is the world against God and his people.

VERSES 15,16. Behold, I come as a thief. Blessed is he that watcheth - The coming here mentioned is the coming of 1:7. See the comments there. Christ will never (and never has) come as a thief in regard to those who watch. Conflict is in the air. Better choose your side well. And once you've chosen, he says, hang-on in there. The location of the battle is "Har-Magedon." It is not the "valley" of

Megiddo, but either the "mount" or "city" of Megiddo. Still the general location seems clear enough. Megiddo! Where Israel thrashed Jabin into oblivion — where Sisera was blistered and stars in their courses fought against God's enemies! See Judges 4,5. Megiddo! Where even an Egyptian could win if he was doing the will of God. That's what happened when Necho slew Josiah. See 2 Chronicles 35:20-27. Necho assured the Judean he was on an errand for Jehovah. The Bible writer says he was indeed. Josiah would have none of it and he died.

Megiddo! A huge battlefield where Napoleon is said to have remarked "All the armies of the world could make battle here." But then Napoleon didn't live in a nuclear age. The idea that the Orient would march into the valley of Megiddo with 200 million to battle an army with (presumably) many millions is just too silly to talk about. Nevertheless, a great natural battleground for armies of the nature of ancient times, and you must remember the whole book not only involved those ancient times, but was written in the terms of ancient times. So here is a good battleground to set the scene for the final battle of God and Rome. You will remember, won't you, that this all comes under the heading of a bowl. The nations are being drawn into war with God and that's got to be a judgment!

VERSES 17-21. And the seventh poured out his bowl upon the air -The place of the Devil's power. See Ephesians 2:1ff and the comments on chapter 9:2ff. The whole ungodly world has been smitten. Evil has been searched-out and thoroughly punished. The power behind it all, the "god of this world," must be smitten also. As the book develops, we'll see the fall of Babylon dealt with, though it was already declared back in 14. We'll see the battle of Armageddon dealt with, though it is already mentioned here. And, in chapter 20, we'll learn of the defeat of the god of this world.

It is done: and there were lightnings... - More apocalyptic tokens of the fact that God has just wrought or, is about to work, judgment. We have the usual heavenly voices with thunder and lightning. We read of a "great earthquake," the like of which there's never been. This too is a well-known phrase in the Bible. It is used in Ezekiel 5:8,9, to speak of what God did to Judah at the hand of Nebuchadnezzar. Read it for yourself and see. Make sure you grab a hold on the context, for that's very important. If the context will show that the phrase refers to something that's already happened, it will prove that the phrase is a proverbial expression. Look, Ezekiel says:

Therefore, thus saith the Lord Jehovah: Behold, I, even I,

> am against thee: and I will execute judgments in the midst of thee in the sight of the nations. And I will do in thee that which I have not done, and whereunto I will not do anymore the like, because of all thine abominations.

If that be literally true, then there never has been a judgment on Israel any worse than that delivered by Nebuchadnezzar. Jeremiah thought the judgment was without comparison (Lamentations 1:12; 2:13). If Ezekiel is literally true, then Jesus couldn't have been speaking literally in Matthew 24:21, for he spoke of the 70 A.D. affair in the same terms Ezekiel spoke of the 586 B.C. affair. What does the phrase indicate? **The epitome of horror!**

VERSE 19. And the great city was divided into three parts - There's no doubt but that the "great city" is Rome. See the comments on chapters 17 and 18. Its being divided into three by an earthquake stresses the utterness of its destruction. God in Ezekiel 5 speaks of the utter destruction of the people and divided them into three units. When wishing to thoroughly examine the person enthroned on the Cherubim in Ezekiel 1:27, the prophet divides him into two. From the loins and upward, he was fire. From the loins and downward, he was fire. Why didn't he just say he was all fire? Thoroughness of description is obtained when the unit is divided. The city is utterly destroyed being divided into three.

The cities of the nations fell - These are the allies of Rome. The call was made to choose-up sides. The nations went with Rome and lost the game!

VERSE 20. Every island fled away, and the mountains were not found - That's because God shook them. This is speech characteristic of the prophets. Check a concordance. See Micah 1:2-4; Nahum 1:5; Psalm 97:4,5. And see Psalm 18:7-15. On millennial terms, it would be hard for Jesus to step on a mountain at his coming, if this be literally true.

VERSE 21. And great hail, every stone about the weight of a talent - That's about 100 pounds. No water in the oceans; no water in the rivers or the fountains; no mountains or islands; boils all over them; the sun burning their brains out; and now 100-pound hail stones! That'd get you discouraged, wouldn't it? I'd yell uncle, but these? They blaspheme.

Here's another plague out of the Egyptian history. It's written that they had never seen hail like they saw in Moses' day, but we're sure they'd agree that this was just a shade worse. Do you really believe this is to be literally fulfilled? Do you think the millennialists **really** believe this to be literally fulfilled? It was the hail that destroyed all of the crops in Egypt and even broke down their

Battle of Armageddon previewed here but developed in Chp 19.
Chp 14 - Babylon is fallen - Rome fell here in Chp 16 but described in detail in Chp 17-18

Satan defeated here & developed in 20

trees. The Bible says there was no hail on the children of God.

Summary

The word is "It is done!" God has buried Rome and her allies. Some of the elements of the bowls have yet to be developed, but they are all covered in the record of the bowls. The city fell under the seventh, but the fall will be described in chapters 17,18. The battle of Armageddon is previewed here, but will be developed in
17 chapter 19. The Devil has been defeated "in the air" but his defeat p249
will be developed in chapter 20.

17 And the 7th angel poured out his bowl upon the air and a loud voice came out of the temple from the throne saying "It is done."
18 And there were flashes of lightning and sounds and peals of thunder and there was a great earthquake such as there had not been since man came to be upon the earth so great an earthquake was it and so mighty.
19 And the great city was split into 3 parts and the cities of the nations fell. And Babylon the great was remembered before God to give her the cup of the wine of His fierce wrath.
20 And every island fled away and the mtns were not found.
21 And huge hailstones about 100 lbs each came down from heaven upon men and men blasphemed God because of the plague of the hail because its plague was extremely severe.

Chapter 17 Same beast in Chp 13

1 And one of the 7 angels who had the 7 bowls
came and spoke w/me, saying, "Come here, I
shall show you the judgment of the great
harlot who sits on many waters;
2 w/whom the kings of the earth committed
acts of immorality and those who dwell on
the earth were made drunk w/the wine
of her immorality.
3 And he carried me away in the Spirit
into a wilderness and I saw a woman
sitting on a scarlet beast, full of
blasphemous names, having 7 heads
and 10 horns.
4 And the woman was clothed in purple
and scarlet and adorned w/gold &
precious stones and pearls having in
her hand a gold cup full of abominations
and of the unclean things of her immorality.
5 and upon her forehead a name was
written a mystery, "Babylon the Great,
The Mother of Harlots and of the Abominations
of the Earth."
6 And I saw the woman drunk w/the blood of the
Saints and w/the blood of the witnesses of
Jesus. And when I saw her I wondered greatly.
7 And the angel said to me "Why do you wonder?"
I shall tell you the mystery of the woman and
of the beast that carries her which has the 7
heads and the 10 horns. see p139 Word 12-abyss
8 The beast that you saw was & is not and is
about to come out of the abyss and to go to
destruction. And those who dwell on the
earth will wonder whose name has not
been written in the book of life from the
foundation of the world when they see the
beast that he was and is not & will come.
9 Here is the mind which has wisdom. The 7
heads are 7 mtns on which the woman sits,
10 and they are 7 kings; 5 have fallen, one is,
the other has not yet come and when he
comes he must remain a little while.
11 And the beast which was & is not, is himself
also an 8th and is one of the 7 & he goes to
destruction
12 And the 10 horns which you saw are 10 kings
who have not yet received a kingdom
but they receive authority as kings
w/the beast for one hour.

13 These have one purpose and they give their power and authority to the beast.
14 These will wage war against the Lamb and the Lamb will overcome them because He is Lord of Lords and King of Kings and those who are w/ Him are the called and chosen and faithful.

Questions on Chapter 17

1. What does Milligan make of the Harlot? apostate church ... religion battle between good & evil
2. What does Hendriksen make of the Harlot? personification of worldlin[ess]
3. What do millennialists make of the Harlot? enormous false religious system
4. What do Wallace and King make of the Harlot? Jerusalem, a nation
5. What does this book make of the Harlot? Roman Empire
6. What did Alexander Campbell make of the Harlot? Roman Catholic Church
7. Why doesn't the angel go quickly into the judgment on the Harlot? Lets her boast & show her power beauty success and then let everyone see her fall from great heights
8. Can you list the six reasons this book gives for the position it takes? Yes p251
9. What do you make of the seven hills the Harlot sat on? 7 hills are Rome.
10. What does Luke 2:1 establish? God & Bible speak in universal terms when whole universe not included
11. Can you state a reason why "earth" in Revelation doesn't always mean Palestine? universal language not to be taken literally (See p 253 top)
12. Does Daniel 7 have any bearing on this issue? If so, what bearing? kings of earth ruled by Rome
13. How does 17:18 embarrass the millennial position? If the city is Jerusalem that has Jews reigning & ruling over earth
14. What is the major characteristic of the Harlot which leaps at you out of verse 18?! Its a city that reigns over kings of earth in John's Day
15. Does whoredom, or fornication, in the O.T. always imply religious apostasy? No
16. Can you cite a scripture on that? Isaiah, Nahum, Ez. p255
17. Is the Harlot ever called an "adulteress"? No! but a fornicator
18. How does verse 8 really blow the theory of Hendriksen? Shows Rome is in power at writing of John's Rev. (See p 257 bottom)
19. In what way does it blow Lindsey's theory? See p 258
20. How does King try to get around it? See p 258
21. What does Lindsey make of the seven heads in his LGPE? modern statesmen
22. What does he make of the seven heads in his TNWC? 7 kingdoms against God
23. Can you say in what way the beast "was"? Nero
24. Can you say in what way the beast "is not"? Nero & persecutions stop
25. Can you say what is meant by "and is about to come up"? persecutions begin again w/ Domitian
26. Of what does the "ten horns" speak? 10 client kings who ruled but subservient to Rome
27. What famous historian cites inner strife as a chief cause of Rome's fall? Gibbon
28. What chapter in Daniel speaks of inner division as Rome's weakness? Daniel Chap 2
29. What does verse 17 make clear to us? GOD is moving & controlling all of these
30. Does verse 18 teach the Harlot was ruling over the earth in John's day? Yes!

31. If it were teaching she **once** ruled over the earth - would we know it? *Yes, but it says "she reigns"*

32. If it taught she **would** rule over it someday - would we know it from there?
33. Is verse 18 the vision or the explanation of the vision?

vision*

Fall of Rome Chp 16 —— explained in detail here!

An Analysis of Chapter 17

I. The Harlot: 1-6
   - A. The Harlot as the object of coming judgment: 1,2
   - B. The Harlot and her description: verses 3-6a *blasphemy, rich in abominations + uncleanness + immorality*

II. The explanation concerning the beast the Harlot rides on: 7-14
   - A. The threefold aspect of the beast: verse 8 *was, is not, is about 2 come...*
   - B. The seven heads and their meaning: verses 9-11
   - C. The ten horns and their meaning: verses 12-14

III. The fate and identity of the Harlot: 15-18
   - A. The meaning of the waters she sits on: verse 15
   - B. The fate of the Harlot: verse 16,17 *eaten alive from within + without*
   - C. The Architect of her fate: verse 17
   - D. The identity of the Harlot: verse 18

Introduction to Chapters 17 and 18

The bowls have been poured out. The judgment is completed. Rome has been destroyed. But the details have not been given yet. In these two chapters we will have the obituary of Babylon. She was said to have "fallen" in chapter 14. In 16:19 we saw her completely destroyed, but without any real detail. In these two chapters she will be described in all her ugliness and cruelty. Her arrogance will be set before us, and her well-earned doom.

The question we will need to answer is: Who is she? People like Milligan, holding as they do the philosophy of history approach to the book (ie. that this is the battle between good and evil in picture form — that and no more), believe the Harlot stands for the Apostate Church — apostate religion. Milligan fervently denies this applies to the Roman Catholic Chruch.

Hendriksen sees the Harlot (Babylon) as the personification of worldliness. As the personification of all the elements which would seduce people to stay away or fall away from God.

Lindsey and his cohorts hold Babylon to be "an enormous false religious system." It would be a false religion embracing all the wicked practices you can name from witchcraft, sensuality, demon communication, black magic, and the rest. This "lady" will be the dominant leader in the world around 1981-1984 and will convert into her flock the bulk of the world from the Buddhist to the atheist, from the Hindu to the Unitarian. (See pp. 230-235 of TNWC.) This runs in the same general direction with Milligan and a little of Hendriksen.

Foy Wallace and Max King, for different reasons, come to the conclusion that Babylon is Jerusalem.

I've already told you what I think. I believe this is Rome viewed from her commercial power and worldly success angle.

Still others hold, as did Alexander Campbell, that the Harlot speaks of the Roman Catholic Church. On this issue, you will have to make up your mind, because it is an issue which looms large in understanding the book as a whole. But as you can see, there are plenty of choices. I'm not able to handle all the points in the arguments, and even if I could, I have neither the time nor the space. If I pass over something you think is crucial, it was due either to ignorance or forgetfulness. It hasn't been intentional.

The trouble involved in trying to be fair to everyone's view is that some of them are so general that a lot of what is said will be truth, or part truth, or potentially truthful. This criticism applies mainly to the conclusions of Hendriksen, Milligan, and Lindsey.

For example, this Harlot is involved in witchcraft, immorality, slavery, and other such things. Can you name a major power throughout the ages which didn't involve itself in these to one degree or another? It's hard to discuss the overall view of a nation without bringing something in about religion, especially if that nation is in opposition to God. Milligan finds reason to believe the Harlot is religious in nature, but is this really surprising? Remember now, neither Lindsey, nor Milligan, nor Hendriksen believe the Harlot is a nation. They hold it to be the personification of a system. King and Wallace, at least, hold it to be a nation with certain characteristics, but nevertheless, a nation. This is more concrete and is therefore more susceptible to testing for truth or error.

Comments on Chapter 17

VERSES 1-6. I will show thee the judgment of the great harlot - One would suppose he'd have gone right on in to show her wasted, but he doesn't. He first shows her power, "beauty," and success. Why is this? Because this is part of her judgment that she falls from such a height! As we'll see, she is arrogant and proud. Her beauty is a world-wide topic. All the nations consort with her.

Why did God, for example, permit Goliath 40 long days of bragging before he completed his contract on him? It works to the glory of God to have the enemy reach to his highest. In a wrestling match, it's often true that the loser reaches his highest point just before his opponent smashes him to the canvas. The more the braggart boasts, the greater the fall is assessed by all who heard the boasting. Read chapter 18 and see this principle well illustrated.

Who is the Harlot? I believe the Harlot is Rome! And why is that? There are several reasons:

1. She sits on seven hills: 17:9
2. She rules the earth in John's day: 17:18
3. She is a terrible persecutor of the saints: 17:6; 18:20,24
4. She is the leading commercial power on earth: 18:3, 11ff,15-19
5. She is supported by the military might of Rome: 17:3,7
6. She is destroyed by her own military power, etc.: 17:16,17

On the first four, you need no more than read the texts cited to see that they are accurate descriptions of the Harlot. If these be true, then many of the views are already seen to be untenable.

If she sits on "seven mountains," we have a well-known description of Rome. A host of writers of old have spoken of Rome in this way. Ovid, Vergil, Martial, and Horace, to name but four. Wallace in his comments on chapter 13:1, says this very thing, but then repudiates it in his comments on 17:9. King says absolutely nothing about the seven mountains. One would have thought he'd have a word to say about this since it is so obviously opposed to his position. Hendriksen acknowledged that the "seven mountains" made the passage speak of Rome. He then proceeds to make Rome symbolize something else. That may not be an objectionable thing, but it does make it very convenient for Hendriksen. (You do recall that he has the difficulty of making the seventh head stand for all the governments from Rome to just before the final coming of Jesus.) Milligan also acknowledges that the seven hills probably speak of Rome, but proceeds to make Rome symbolize something else.

Concerning point 2: The woman is explicitly said to be the world ruler in John's day. Who ruled John's world? Rome and no other but Rome. I'd have thought that this should end the matter but there are at least three objections we need to notice. Before we do, however, I'd like you to tell yourself what the words of the text (17:18) would say to you.

Objection 1, from Milligan, says that Rome never did have this great dominion and that she didn't literally rule every acre of the world. The declaration is true, but the objection is futile. It is customary in the Bible (despite what the millennialists say) for God to use accommodative speech. At times, universals are used when they are not intended to be taken literally. Here are just a few examples.

Luke 2:1 tells us Augustus gave a decree that the "whole inhabited earth" be subjected to a census. The passage closes us up to one of three conclusions: Regard the decree as one of utter lunacy, for this was utterly beyond the imagination of a sane man; regard Luke as having misinformed us, or accept the fact that such universal speech is not intended to be pushed to its limits.

Daniel 2:38, in speaking of the dominion of Nebuchadnezzar, said: "And wheresoever the children of men dwell, the beasts of the field and the birds of the heavens hath he given into thy hand, and hath made thee to rule over them all." This passage creates the same difficulty as Luke 2:1. Either Daniel was right out of his head, or such universals speak simply of far-reaching dominion.

Objection 2. This one would come from King and Wallace. Wallace very clearly says what he thinks about the "kings of the earth" in his text. He says it means kings of Judah. The "earth" in Revelation, he claims, has reference to Palestine. King in his book (page 330) is also very explicit. He says the kings of the earth are Jews and the "earth" is Palestine. King would then say that 17:18 speaks of Jerusalem as being the capital city of the Jews (the kings of the earth). Wallace says almost exactly this on page 375.

I don't think this is an acceptable position. In **Revelation 1:5,** we hear of Jesus as "the ruler of the kings of the earth." For Wallace, the new kingdom came around 33 A.D., and so there was no Judaic kingdom. If the "kings of the earth" are Judean kings, what does this passage mean? King feels the pressure of this passage too, and so he claims, Jesus is the ruler of the kings of (the new) earth, ie. the Church. Well, that's all right if you **must have** it, but it looks suspiciously convenient.

Another difficulty with this position is that a concordance will show that the "earth" doesn't always mean Palestine at all. Look at 5:10; 12:16; 16:14; 20:11 and so many others.

A reading of chapter 18 makes it clear that Babylon and the "kings of the earth" and the "merchants of the earth" are not the same. The kings of the earth and the merchants of the earth survive the fall of Babylon and are lamenting that they are left without someone to make them rich.

Furthermore, Rome, as well as the three kingdoms which preceded her, are said to have arisen "out of the earth" (Daniel 7:17). King sees this problem and claims that the problem lies "in faulty translation" (p. 317). He claims the LXX text has "which shall be destroyed from the earth." King's problem has been that he reads too much from the Pulpit Commentary and doesn't do his own research. The LXX says no such thing. It agrees with the Massoretic text, as is reflected in the major versions. The Pulpit doesn't accept, but reflects, the Chigi manuscripts. These are known as notoriously defective. But even if King were right, it wouldn't be a problem of "faulty translation," but a difference in textual authority. So he doesn't have a case on Daniel 7:17. But after all that, he still loses his case on 7:23, where Palestine can't possibly be the meaning of "earth." King gets himself in further trouble, because he forgets to be consistent. He talks of the Devil being defeated in "heaven" (ie. in regard to Judaism) and is cast out into "Roman territory" (pp. 312,313). What King forgot to remember was, that the Devil was cast unto the "earth" (Revelation 12:9).

Objection 3. This would come from the millennialists. They'd claim that the Harlot is not the ruler of the kings of the earth in John's day, but is spoken of simply in vision as if she were. They would claim she will be the ruler of the kings of the earth in our day.

I don't see how we can accept that. It not only runs contrary to the explicit statements of the book (1:1,3; 22:6,10) that the book was unfolding in John's day, but it runs contrary to this section.

Verse 18 is not a part of the vision - it is the interpretation of the vision. The Harlot is being explained to John, not shown to him. He's already seen her. Now he is having her explained. He is not told: She will reign over the kings of the earth. He's told: She rules over the kings of the earth (NIV and the rest).

Wallace so interprets this as to make it say: She used to rule over the kings of the earth. But that's not what the text says. The Harlot is, at the time of John, the world ruler, and sitting on seven hills over nations and people (17:15).

It's easy, of course, to give it a double application. This double application thing has been the savior of many a faulty view. The millennialists do this regularly. King does it incessantly. He says Babylon in the O.T. was a type of Jerusalem. What Babylon was to the world politically, Jerusalem was religiously.

Concerning point 3. That Rome was a terrible persecutor of the saints, no one disputes. So here is a natural point of indentification when taken with the other points.

Concerning point 4. I honestly can't read chapter 18 and get anything out of there but the fact that the Harlot was a corrupt and ruthless commercial power. It's written all over the chapter. Well, go ahead and read it.

I wouldn't know how to get a religious system out of there if I had to. Can you really see this as a description of Jerusalem? Or the apostate Church? Or worldliness? That she is involved in wickedness, no sane man will doubt. That there is evil being promoted by her, cannot be questioned, but this is true of any nation that ever was or IS. This doesn't justify us making the Harlot a religious system or abstract worldliness.

Concerning points 5 and 6. What made the woman so attractive for the nations to "fornicate" with, was what she had supporting her. That's why people made alliances with other nations — it was to their profit to deal with the more powerful. What city of the earth in John's day — and which had anything to do with the Church of God — had devastating military might as her support? We'll say more about this later.

Concerning her fall due to that same militaristic power, I've said something already in the comments on chapter 13. See there. You'll pay special attention to the passages from Daniel 2 and 11, which fall into line with what we read here in chapter 17. What woman, known in John's day, ended up being devoured by the very forces which made her supreme? Rome, of course! Every schoolboy knows that.

VERSE 1. That sitteth upon many waters - The many waters are interpeted for us in verse 15. They stand for nations upon which the woman sits. She is indeed the city that rules the world.

VERSE 2. With whom the kings of the earth committed fornication - "Fornication" is something of which the Old Testament speaks a lot. It speaks of alliances. Now those alliances often involved idolatry, but they didn't always do so. "Whoredom" (which is the word usually employed under these circumstances) does often speak of going after gods other than Jehovah (if Israel be under discussion). However, it would be very wrong to think that this is heart of the thought each time we read of harlotry, whoredom or fornication.

Milligan and others stress the point of **religious** apostasy in this whole matter. In a sense, they have a point, because most of the whoredom practiced in the O.T. and mentioned, deals with Israel. She had the true God and any moves in any direction which would suggest he was inadequate, were classed as whoredom. Since Israel was a peculiar nation — a theocracy — religion was at the heart of her constitution. Thus when we hear of Israel's fornication, it is closely associated with religious apostasy. But I do think we need to bear in mind that other nations are said to have practiced whoredom, and the idea of religious apostasy in them, is absent from the context.

Tyre, says Isaiah 23:13-18, would play the harlot. She had no national relationship to God. The prophet had in mind what Tyre had been doing most of her national existence. She went in and out among the nations making alliances with every one of them — thus committing fornication with them. We don't have the time or space to discuss what exactly Isaiah was speaking of at this time, but that is not needed in order to see this point. Tyre was a harlot! She wasn't apostatizing from God; she was making alliances with the nations around her.

Nahum (3:4) speaks of Nineveh, capital of the Assyrian empire, as one "well-favored harlot." She was no apostate from God — that is, in her whoring, the idolatry is not the central issue. She was not leaving the truth to run after other gods. People would come running to Assyria for help and she would make alliances with them. Whether or not these people worshiped the gods of Assyria was of no consequence. Whether foreigners worshiped the gods of the Tyrians or vice versa, was also of no consequences. The alliance was the thing.

The real crime of Israel was believing that God was not adequate. When they called on Egypt against the Assyrian and the Babylonian (Isaiah 30,31; Ezekiel 17) the real problem was not that they worshiped their gods, but that they rejected Jehovah!

Israel is called an "adulteress" because she had God as her "husband" but this Harlot is not called an "adulteress." Nor are the other nations, such as Egypt, Babylonia, Assyria or Tyre. Their husband is never talked about. Israel's is — often.

Now we're back at Revelation 17:2. In what way did the kings of the earth commit fornication with the Harlot? They made alliances with her. That's what made them rich. See 18:3,11ff, 15-17,19. Now I'm not saying that there was not mutual exchange of gods going on. I know that there are indications that various nations became involved in the worship with each other as a token of mutual respect. I know, for example, that Rome offered peace offerings at the Jerusalem temple. (There was never an offering made at the Jerusalem temple TO any Roman or anyone else among the nations.) Now what made these other nations rich? Was it worshiping a Roman god or was it the alliance they made with Rome? Rome didn't require that other nations worship their gods. In fact, this is one of the remarkable things about her treatment of the Church. She was most lenient about religion (see the Introductory remarks) early on and when she came into conflict with the Church, it was because the Church spoke of universal dominion and was evangelical. These and other things led to the rift between Rome and the Church.

VERSE 3. Into a wilderness: and I saw a woman - John had seen another woman, and she had fled into a wilderness. There was quite a difference between the two. This one is supported by the seven-headed beast, but the other was sustained by the Lord God. The one woman was the city of the Living God and the other was the "Eternal City" (as Rome is called over and over again).

Sitting upon a scarlet-colored beast - This is Rome, the civil power. For a full discussion of this, see the comments on chapter 13.

VERSE 4. And the woman was arrayed in purple and scarlet - She is rich enough, but her soul is wasted. She is royal enough, but inside she is disgusting. She is a well-dressed tramp — a gaudy whore!

Having in her hand a golden cup - Here's what she offered the nations. Join in my success, she seems to be saying. Drink with me the cup of my success and let me show you the way to riches. Of Babylon, God said (Jeremiah 51:7), "Babylon hath been a golden cup in Jehovah's hand, that made all the earth drunken: the nations have drunk of her wine; therefore the nations are mad." The nations looked at Babylon and saw her success and wanted in on it. The success Babylon had was given her by God (Daniel 2:38), and it was given her (among other things) that God might have occasion against the other ungodly nations to hurry them to their doom. So it was with Rome. She succeeded only because God would have it so. The nations saw her success and wanted to be successful also. They got together; they "committed fornication." Whatsoever Rome would do for success, they'd do it too.

VERSE 5. Mystery Babylon the Great, the Mother of the Harlots -The Queen of Vanity Fair. The "Godmother" of the Harlots. The

Great Harlot, teaching all the little harlots how to be good little harlots. What a distinction — what a title to hold. "And in this corner — the world's greatest Harlot!" She arrogantly displays her name. Wears it where the High Priest wore "Holiness unto Jehovah." Wears it where the saints wore "Father...Jesus Christ." They paraded the love of their lives and she paraded her shame! And do you think this spirit is dead? Haven't you heard how some drunkards boast? Haven't you heard the libertines rehearsing their "conquests"? Haven't you heard the man or woman extolling their own virtues because they were able to "cut down to size" some unsuspecting sister or brother?

VERSE 6. And I saw the woman drunken - And what a disgusting sight it is to see a man drunk. Somehow, sad to say, it seems even more revolting to see a woman drunk! What a disgusting industry the liquor business is too. What a cheap way to make a living. Thriving on the blood and tears of fellow humans, while the rot-gut is being poured out by the millions of gallons. Armies of psychologists are hired by this industry to find out more ways to encourage more people to drink more often! The only thing this industry doesn't want is a dead drunk! But it has produced over 9 million alcoholics in the U.S. And I'm sure you've noticed in recent months how civic-minded the industry has become. They want to conserve our materials by recycling our cans! Our **beer** cans. THEIR beer cans. I think that's sweet of them.

Here in our text is a pathetic, ungodly creature, rolling drunk...but not on rot-gut. On the blood of our brothers and sisters! And John is staggered by her decadence. Amazed at her cruelty. Wondering at her blasphemy. "Is this someone I know?" you can hear him thinking.

VERSES 7-14. The beast...was, and is not; and is about to come up - This eighth verse is a real problem to millennialists. It hurts King and Hendriksen also. It's not easy to say what it does to Wallace, since it isn't always easy to put Foy's points together.

Hendriksen, who has gone on record saying the beast represented ungodly civil power aimed against the people of God, has difficulty here. The beast "was" he says, suggests the destruction of those kingdoms in which it was manifested, namely, Babylon, Egypt, Neo-Babylonia, Medo-Persia, and Greece. Since these are gone, the "beast is not." That's simple enough. The only problem is, he has forgotten Rome! We couldn't say of Rome when John was writing that it was "is not" (pardon the grammar). Hendriksen himself has confessed that the sixth head of the beast is the Rome of John's day. If that be true (it's what he says) then the beast had not disappeared — it was right there with John! He then goes on to show that the beast will one day show itself again just before Jesus comes. But you can see his problem — right?!

King is in trouble too. He sees the problem before he says anything about it. Then he enters the issue with a question. Now watch how he words the question, and then read the text again. Here it is: But what is meant by the beast that was, and is not, and yet is? You noticed it right away, didn't you? That's not what the text says. His problem in the book is that he has seven consecutive years hanging around his neck — the 70th week of Daniel. The first 3½ years are the years Nero persecuted the Christians (?). That's the time when the beast "was." At that point he ceases to persecute the saints — that's how the beast "is not." But at that same time it is persecuting the Jews and that's how the beast "is not." Let me say again, King is shackled by a literal 7-year period in the book of Revelation. He claims that the 70th week of Daniel was an exact and literal seven-year period which ended with the destruction of Jerusalem in August 70 A.D. That would mean, if 3½ years (he gets this from the 42 months, etc.) were devoted by Nero to the persecution of Christians and then 3½ more to the attack on the Jews, the whole seven-year period would have had to begin on August 63 A.D. This is contrary to the clear testimony of history which tells us Nero set fire to Rome in July 64 and from that point began to persecute the saints. That'd really blow the whole theory. And, by the way, Nero died in June 68 A.D.

In any case, the phrase doesn't say, the beast was, is not, and yet is. It says the beast was, is not, and is about to come up out of the abyss. Wallace has the book written in the days of Nero, but I'm not sure exactly what he says here.

And the millennialists are in trouble. Lindsey is discussing the seven heads which he thinks represent seven kingdoms which went against the people of God. (Unless you read his LGPE in which he thinks the seven heads are seven modern statesmen). John, he tells us, has just finished looking at the first six heads and now looks at the seventh. He then says:

> Looking from this perspective, he says the beast **was,** and **is not,** and then **will exist again** and be destroyed. He must be referring to the fact that Rome existed in his day, but that day was coming when it would no longer exist. Then it would rise again and be destroyed (TNWC, p. 237).

You can see his difficulty of course. He too believes the sixth head the one that "is" (17:10) is the Rome of John's day. So he can't have John saying the beast "is not." So he's got to get John out of his own time slot so that the Rome phase of the beast becomes the "was" phase. Neat — right?! Between the historic Rome and the "revived Rome" of premillennial doctrine is an "is not" phase. Reading the text you'd get the impression that the "is not" phase is in John's time, wouldn't you?! And when Hal is dealing with the "one is" (17:10) he has no trouble seeing that "this **has** to be the Rome of John's day" (p. 236). Now here is a remarkable thing. The expression "one is" means it **has** to be in John's day, but the phrase 'is not" doesn't refer to John's day.

See the comments on chapter 13 concerning this phase of the beast. I think we've suggested a reasonable view of the matter which will face the text as it stands, rather than what it might have been. In Nero, the beast persecuted the people of God. The beast "was." Nero died and the persecution ceased. The beast "is not" (it was during this time that John wrote the book). The beast begins its work again when Domitian comes on the scene and resumes persecution. Thus the beast "is about to come up out of the abyss." See this discussed in the remarks on chapter 13.

Whose name hath not been written in the book of life - See the comments on 13:8 for a brief discussion of this passage.

VERSES 9-11. Here is the mind that hath wisdom - For a full discussion of these verses, see the comments on 13:1ff. The seven mountains speak of the seven hills on which Rome stands. The seven kings mentioned are Augustus, Tiberius, Gaius (Caligula), Claudius, Nero, Vespasian, Titus. The first five had fallen when John wrote the epistle, Vespasian was the ruler. Titus was yet to come and when he came, he ruled just two years. The eighth head was Domitian in whom the policy of persecution was resurrected. Domitian was the second to persecute the Christians (Tertullian and Eusebius) and is viewed as the resurrected Nero (thus, "of the seven"). Between Nero and Domitian, the state did not persecute the saints so that the "beast is not." See the full discussion of these things in the discussion of chapter 13:1ff.

VERSES 12-14. And the ten horns - These we've discussed fully at chapter 13:1ff. See there for comments. They are the provinces of Rome and the client kings system. Merrill Unger (following Perowne) said this of the client king system:

> But Herod's client-kingship in Judea was no new institution in Rome's expanding government. It had already existed for two centuries, and client kingdoms at this period were found in Armenia, Cappadocia, Galatia and Commagene, in each case Rome making even kings the instruments of servitude. Herod might be the means to rule

the difficult-to-manage Jews of Palestine, but it was really Rome that ruled, and always the client king held his kingdom on the basis of imperial favor. If this was offended he could be dethroned at will.
("Archaeology and the New Testament," pp. 53,54)

Edward Gibbon, the famous agnostic and historian who wrote of the Decline and Fall of the Roman Empire, listed four reasons for its fall. Three of them were external invasion; inner decadence; and inner strife. He said:

> The story of its ruin is simple and obvious; and instead of inquiring **why** the Roman empire was destroyed, we should rather be surprised that it had subsisted so long. The victorious legions, who, in distant wars, acquired the vices of strangers and mercenaries, first oppressed the freedom of the republic, and afterwards violated the majesty of the purple...
> The decay of Rome has been frequently ascribed to the translation of the seat of the empire; but this history has already shown that the powers of government were **divided,** rather then **removed.** The throne of Constantinople was erected in the East; while the West was still possessed by a series of emperors who held their residence in Italy, and claimed their equal inheritance of the legions and provinces. This dangerous novelty impaired the strength and fomented the vices of a double reign:
> ("Decline and Fall," Vol. 2, pp. 661,662)

See in this edition (Washington Square Press, 3 Volumes, August, 1973), Volume 3, pp. 113ff for his discussion of the four causes of the decline. But, what is more important — see the passages in Daniel 2 about Rome's inner weakness! It has been noted by more than one writer on the history of Rome that it was from the Grachii brothers that Roman leaders realized: There is no power without the army. Marius and Sulla were the first two to really capitalize on this. From that moment onward, generals courted their armies, and the armies began to dictate terms as to who would or who would not become emperor. See Gibbon's discussion of Augustus in this regard. Revelation 17 teaches Rome fell (partly) from within!
VERSE 14. And the Lamb shall overcome them, for he is Lord of lords - King refuses to believe that the Lordship was an established fact before this book was written. He doesn't believe the Lordship of Jesus was an established fact until the events the book deals with

(Jerusalem's destruction, etc.) were completed. This passage buries that notion (so do a number of other clear passages), because this victory doesn't constitute him Lord of lords. The victory is sure because he IS (already) Lord of lords.

Lindsey has explicitly denied the already-established Lordship of Jesus. He believes that Jesus will be Lord of lords after the victory at the battle of Armageddon. See the comments on 1:5 and the quote there from Lindsey.

And they also shall overcome that are with him - These are not just martyrs. It wasn't only martyrs that "fought with" Jesus in the battle pictured in this book. It was every man, woman, boy and girl who refused to buckle under to this ungodly nation. Whether they lived or died was of no consequence! The Church of God whipped Rome. Those with Jesus are said to called "chosen and faithful." That "chosen" means "choice." As David had his chosen men (see 2 Samuel 23) so does Jesus. But all who are with Jesus are "choice" or chosen men!

One army of the Living God
Before one throne we bow,
Part of the host has crossed the Flood,
And the rest are crossing now!

VERSES 15-18. And the waters which thou sawest - The explanation is sufficient. This justifies our speaking of the sea as sometimes referring to nations as in Isaiah 57:20 and other places. The Woman has the rule over these. She is the ruler (here and verse 18), the persecutor of Christians (17:6), and the world's leading commercial power (18:3, 9ff, 15ff). She is Rome!

VERSE 16. And shall eat her flesh - See the remarks above on the inner strife of Rome, leading to this. The picture of flesh being eaten is a common one in apocalyptic speech. In chapter 19:18, we have the beasts called to do just that. In Ezekiel 38 and 39 we have pictured the battle of Gog and Magog. In chapter 39:17ff, God calls all the birds and beasts to a big feast he is giving. Since the literalists are bound to literalism, this will be quite a situation. Remember there hasn't been any water in the oceans for some time. There's been no drinking water and thus the bulk of the grass and trees are gone (a third went in one trumpet). But still the beasts and birds are doing all right.

VERSE 17. For God did put into their hearts to do his mind - Whatever goes on, we're being told, God is in control of it all. We are not to suppose that the nations knew what they were doing was God's will (has that ever been the case?), but it was nevertheless. See Isaiah 10:5ff.

Summary

We've seen that the Harlot is Rome viewed form her commercial and seductive standpoint. We've seen that she is brutal and vicious. We've seen that her success is due to her military support and that her demise was (in part) to be due to the same principle. It's been made clear that all of this is the result of the will of God. We are now ready for the description of the fall in chapter 18.

Further details of the fall of Rome. 26a

Questions on Chapter 18

1. Why do we have an angelic announcement before the chapter really opens?
2. Why is the fall not dealt with more swiftly?
3. When Babylon fell (historic Babylon), did the fall take place as literally described?
4. Do nations, as well as individuals, have responsibilities to other nations?
5. Who are the merchants of the earth?
6. Why the need to tell the saints to come out of "Babylon"?
7. Why do the merchants of the earth weep over Babylon?
8. What does this tell you about Babylon?
9. How long did Nero's fire burn in Rome?
10. What's this "voice of a mill"?
11. Why were Babylon's "merchants" princes of the earth?
12. What was found in the Harlot?
13. What did we say about the composite nature of the beast in the comments on 13:2?

An Analysis of Chapter 18

I. The angelic herald of the fall of Babylon: 1-3
- A. The herald: verse 1
- B. The fall and its certainty: verse 2
- C. The fall and its reason: verse 3

II The appeal to the people of God: 4-5
- A. The appeal: verse 4
- B. The reason for the appeal: verse 5

III. The Harlot's judgment and the nature of it: 6-23
- A. The judgment to be doubled to her: verse 6
- B. The judgment due to arrogance: verse 7-8
- C. The judgment to be thorough and complete: verses 9-19
- D. The judgment a cause for righteous rejoicing: verse 20
- E. The judgment to be final: verses 21-23

IV. The Harlot's judgment and reason for it: 23-24
- A. She caused other nations to be deceived: verse 23b
- B. She murdered the righteous: verse 24

Chapter 18
1 After these things I saw another angel coming down from
heaven having great authority and the earth was
illuminated w/ his glory.
2 And he cried out w/ a mighty voice saying "Fallen
fallen is Babylon the great. And she has become
a dwelling place of demons and a prison of
every unclean spirit and a prison of every hateful
bird.
3 For all the nations have drunk of the wine of the
passion of her immorality, and the kings of the
earth have committed acts of immorality w/ her
and the merchants of the earth have become
rich by the wealth of her sensuality.
4 And I heard another voice from heaven saying "Come
out of her, my people, that you may not participate
in her sins and that you may not receive
of her plagues
5 for her sins have piled up as high as heaven
and God has remembered her iniquities.
6 Pay her back even as she has paid, and give
back to her double according to her deeds;
in the cup which she has mixed, mix twice
as much for her.
7 To the degree that she glorified herself and lived
sensuously to the same degree give her torment
and mourning for she says in her heart, "I
sit as a queen and I am not a widow and
will never see mourning.
8 For this reason in one day her plagues will
come, pestilence and mourning and famine
and she will be burned up w/ fire for the
Lord God who judge her is strong.
9 And the kings of the earth who committed acts
of immorality and lived sensuously w/ her
will weep and lament over her when they see
the smoke of her burning,
10 standing at a distance because of the fear of
her torment saying, "Woe, woe, the great city.
Babylon the strong city. For in one hour your
judgment has come.
11 And the merchants of the earth weep &
mourn over her, because no one buys their
cargoes any more;
12 cargoes of gold and silver & precious stones
and pearls and fine linen and purple & silk
and scarlet and every kind of citron wood
and every article of ivory and every article
made from very costly wood & bronze & iron
and marble,

Comments on Chapter 18

VERSES 1-3. Another angel coming down out of heaven having great authority - Here again we are being told that the work about to be done is begun in heaven! The Lord never tires to tell his people in this book that heaven is completely in control of things. It's a lesson never too soon learned. How much more at peace we'd be if only we had this as our deep and abiding conviction. Peace would then really guard our hearts and lives.

VERSE 2. He cried with a mighty voice...Fallen is Babylon - By this time, we wonder if the city is going to fall at all. We might feel like asking (as Kiddle suggested) with Daniel: How long shall it be to the end of these wonders? But the lead-up is long-drawn-out, because the issue must be indeliby marked in the mind. The fall must be remembered. It must be wanted, longed for. They must (almost) be impatient for it, so that when it finally comes, it will be relished and absorbed.

And is become a habitation of demons - Of the historical Babylon is said something like this in Isaiah 13:17-22. There's no doubt about the judgment there being a past historical judgment, for it was to be accomplished by the Medes. Now take a moment to read that text now. You'll find it worth it. Have you read it? I want you to note that the description wasn't literally fulfilled when the Medes buried Babylon. The city and the land remained as beautiful as ever, and as I mentioned already, Alexander the Great, 200 years later, made the city his home away from home. In fact, that's where he died. The description you read of the fall of Babylon was God's word against the Babylonian kingdom. Babylon did fall and that kingdom will never live again. That's what he's saying. Here was a glorious and proud world empire, bragging about her glory. God said: I will desolate you so that you will never rise again. And he describes it in physical terms as if the land would be a sort of spooky graveyard. The same speech is here in Revelation 18.

VERSE 3. For by the wine...of her fornication all the nations are fallen - She was responsible (in part) for other nations falling into pernicious and ungodly ways. She encourged others in wickedness; therefore, God would bury her. He said this very thing of Nineveh in Nahum 3:4. Listen:

> Because of the multitude of the whoredoms of the well-favored harlot, the mistress of witchcrafts, that selleth nations through her whoredoms, and families through her witchcrafts.

How did she do this? She made great claims and professed her gods, or her ways, accomplished her goals. The proof seemed to be there in a demonstration. Wasn't she getting her way? This is what the Assyrian said in Isaiah 10:12-14, when he said (in essence): I raped the earth and no one could stop me. I was like a man raiding a nest for eggs, and no one opened the mouth to chirp against me. And how did I do it? By my gods and my ruthlessness. (Isaiah 36:4-20), but especially by power and ruthlessness. And again, their actions seemed to be proving her words. Haven't you noticed how this happens even in this very day? You noticed how, after one sky-jack was successful, we had a rash of them. It was "shown" that this area was the way to get our way, so everyone went after it. For encouraging nations in her own ungodly ways, Babylon would fall. Nations too have responsibilities.

And the merchants of the earth waxed rich by the power of her wantonness - It seems clear from this that we're discussing a commercial power and that the "merchants of the earth" involve all the nations which would have trade agreements with Rome. She became stronger and went farther and this meant she opened up more markets. Those who were "friends" of Rome would be introduced to those new areas and everyone would benefit.

VERSES 4,5. Come forth my people out of her - This was the cry God sent out to the Jews in Babylon. See Jeremiah 50:8, 51:6,9,45 and Isaiah 52:11. There were those when taken to Babylon, began to put down their roots there. They were beginning to partake of the ways of the heathen and God urges them out in order that they too might not die. Maybe principles were slipping. Worldiness was setting in. People were just wanting to live and let live. They were urged out in Jeremiah's day and here in John's, they were given the same message. The pile of her guilt is also given in Jeremiah for their leaving. It is mentioned here in verse 5. We can't fail to see how all of this is modeled in the Old Testament record. Principles don't change much, so the same language will suit numerous different occasions.

VERSES 6-23. Render unto her even as she has rendered - Here's why it is bad to be ungodly, for in one way or another, one reaps what he sows. That is, he reaps what he sows as to quality, but very often, he reaps more than he sows as to quantity. The voice from heaven wants her to get a double dose. There is no vindictiveness in heaven, so we can't claim it is spite here. This "lady" deserves all she can hold.

VERSE 7. How much...she glorified herself.,...so much give her of torment - O what a punishment. The more strut, the more hurt. The more swagger, the more pain. The more she preened, the more she'd moan. For she said in her heart:

I sit a queen and am no widow, and shall in no wise see mourning - The proverb says: Keep your words few and sweet because you might have to eat them. Wasn't that good advice?! These words are taken from Isaiah 47:8ff; Zephaniah 2:15. Assyria and Tyre thought they were big stuff and Babylon thought there was no one like her. But the tombs hold a lot of nations. Isaiah's picture of the Babylonian king going into the underworld to be greeted by all the other fallen nations, makes sober reading (see Isaiah 14:3-23).

VERSE 8. Therefore in one day - Because of all that arrogance, her destruction will be utter and complete. One moment glory, and the next, stench! Pride and haughtiness do go before destruction. This applies equally to individuals as to nations.

VERSE 9-10. The kings of the earth...shall weep and wail over her - There is no love here. These who lived well because of her have just watched the Queen of Whores perish. In such an utter fashion too! See Jeremiah 51:9.

VERSE 11. And the merchants of the earth weep - The kings of the earth and the merchants of the earth survive her destruction (which would deal with the Wallace and King views). The merchants aren't in love with Babylon — they're crying because they've just lost their meal ticket. "Because" we're told "no man buyeth their merchandise anymore." This Babylon is Jerusalem? Judaism? This Babylon is a false religious system? This Babylon is the personification of worldliness? It seems to be coming right out of the text that whatever she is, she is the leading market of the world.

VERSES 12-14. Merchandise of gold and silver - It must be admitted that this section must be a difficulty to all who do not regard Babylon as Rome. She is sitting on nations, ruling the kings of the earth in John's day, persecuting the Christians, and trades in this remarkable manner in the things listed here — surely this must be Rome! She is told in verse 14 that her days as a commercial world power are over!

VERSES 15-20. The merchants...made rich by her, shall stand afar off - This whole section reminds us of Ezekiel 27 and 28. Take the time to read it sometime. One could just as easily get a religious **emphasis** out of those two chapters as get it out of here. Read this over and over again and see if you don't get commerce out of it. This is why the Harlot was so popular — she made everyone rich. Alliances with her was money in the bank. The Harlot is Rome as a commercial world leader. With whom to commit fornication was a promise of prosperity.

VERSE 19. In one hour is she made desolate - We've already

19 And they threw dust on their heads and were crying out weeping and mourning saying Woe, woe the great city in which all who had ships at sea became rich by her wealth for in one hour she has been laid waste.

spoken on the significance of an "hour" in John's wrtitings. See
the comments on 8:1. Here the thought of utterness and
9 thoroughness is stressed. Burned to the gound in one hour. Nero set
fire to Rome and the fire raged for one week without destroying all
the city, but then that was a man-made fire. God's fires burn
quickly and completely.

VERSE 20. Rejoice over her thou heaven, and ye saints - Her judgment is seen as a real cause for rejoicing. Heaven can't but rejoice at the death of such a monster. Apostles have every reason to. Prophets (Daniel or John) will have reason to smile. Their word has come true and their fellow servants are now having rest from the ungodly Harlot.

God hath judged your judgment on her - The saints wanted her dead. Not for spite, but because she earned it. Because she was the world's oppressor as well as theirs. They counted her worthy of death. Back in 11:18, we read about the time having come to judge the dead. In this passage, we have a manifestation of that judgment. The picture will be completed in chapter 20.

VERSES 21-23. As it were a great millstone and cast it into the sea -See Jeremiah 51:63. A great millstone. Used in grinding the grain. The I.S.B.E. mentions some millstones up to five feet in diameter. I'd say that would sink well enough to make the angel's point. We have finality being taught here. There will be no revived Roman empire. There may be a European Economic Community, but there will be no revived Rome — God forbids it! It's worth saying for those who hold Babylon to be Judaism, that Judaism was no more dead after 70 A.D. (in the eyes of God) than it was before it, when Jesus died on the Cross.

10 **VERSE 22. And the voice of a mill shall be no more heard at all in thee** - This would be an interesting point to explain on the "religious system" view. They say that the noise of a mill, to ears which are unaccustomed to it, is not at all pleasing. But they also say that those who are used to it will be helped to go to sleep by it. Jeremiah 25:10 lists the absence of the sound of millstones as one of the punishments.

VERSES 23,24. For thy merchants were the princes of the earth
11 -Her great success would determine her punishment. The measure
of her success would measure her shame. Her merchants, because
she was so powerful, were regarded as princes in the earth. Her
success and philosophy made her representatives important people
and it also urged the world to follow in her ways.

And in her was found the blood of prophets - It was her cruel
12 way that led to bloody wars. Talmadge has said that there were

20 Rejoice over her O heaven and you saints &
apostles and prophets because God has pronounced
judgment for you against her.

more than 160 million people who died in the wars of Rome. She promoted war with a fervor when she needed to. But she didn't just kill anyone; she slew the saints and God's messengers. The other was bad enough, but when she touched God's people, she was hurting the "apple of God's eye." For her wicked warring ways (see Daniel 11:36ff) she must die! "Whoso killeth with the sword, by the sword shall be be killed." For abusing the people of God, she must die!

Summary

We've seen a bloody Whore described in her death throes. We've been told that heaven is responsible for it. The reasons have been given and the extent and nature of the punishment have been made clear. She stands as a burning warning to all nations and at all times! LEAVE MY PEOPLE ALONE OR SUFFER THE CONSEQUENCES! p 273

21 And a strong angel took up a stone like
a great millstone and threw it into the
sea saying Thus will Babylon, the great
city be thrown down w/ violence and
will not be found any longer:
22 And the sound of harpists & musicians &
flute players and trumpeters will not be
heard in you any longer and no craftsman
of any craft will be found in you any longer
and the sound of a mill will not be heard
in you any longer;
23 and the ~~last~~ light of a lamp will not shine
in you any longer; & the voice of the
bridegroom & bride will not be heard
in you any longer; for your merchants
were the great men of the earth,
because all the nations were deceived
by your sorcery.
24 And in her was found the blood of
prophets and of saints & of all who have
been slain on the earth.

Chapter 19
1 After these things I heard as it were a loud voice of a
great multitude in heaven saying
2 Hallelujah, Salvation & glory & power belong to our God
because His judgments are true & righteous for He has
judged the great harlot who was corrupting the
earth w/ her immorality and He has avenged
the blood of His bond-servants on her.
3 And a second time they said Hallelujah! Her smoke
rises up forever & ever.
4 And the 24 elders & the 4 living creatures fell down
and worshiped God who sits on the throne saying
Amen. Hallelujah.
5 And a voice came from the throne saying Give
praise to our God all you His bond-servants you
who fear Him the small & the great.
6 And I heard as it were the voice of a great
multitude and as the sound of many waters &
as the sound of mighty peals of thunder saying
Hallelujah For the Lord our God the Almighty
reigns
7 Let us rejoice & be glad & give the glory to Him for
the marriage of the Lamb has come & His bride
has made herself ready.
8 And it was given to her to cloth herself in
fine linen bright & clean for the fine linen is the righteous acts
of the saints
9 And he said to me "Write, "Blessed are those
who are invited to the marriage supper of the wedding
Lamb" and he said to me, "These are true
words of God."
10 And I fell at his feet to worship him. And
he said to me, "Do not do that; I am a
fellow-servant of yours & your brethren
who hold the testimony of Jesus worship
God. For the testimony of Jesus is the
spirit of prophecy.
11 And I saw heaven opened and behold a white horse,
and He who sat on it called Faithful & True;
and in righteousness He judges and wages war.
12 And His eyes are a flame of fire and upon His
head are many diadems and He has a name
written upon Him which no one knows except
Himself.
13 And He is clothed w/a robe dipped in blood;
and His name is called The Word of God.
14 And the armies which are in heaven, clothed
in fine linen, white & clean were following
Him on white horses.

15 And from His mouth comes a sharp sword so that with it He may smite the nations; and He will rule them w/ a rod of iron and He treads the wine press of the fierce wrath of God, the almighty.

Questions on Chapter 19

very Important See p 133 Read this first

1. The figure of an endlessly burning city is used to teach what truth? God's judgment utter defeat + complete
2. What prophet uses a burning land in the same way? Isaiah
3. Can you say why the endlessly burning land cannot be taken literally? Sodom would still have to be burning today
4. What other figure does that prophet use concerning the same land? Wild animals survive & vegetation grows
5. What's the solution to the "conflict" in both figures? both describe utter defeat of Rome by God
6. Has there ever been a time when God was not reigning? NO
7. What makes you say that? the word aorist and speaks of something already done – Reigns
8. How can you explain the point of 19:6 taking into account the tense on "reigneth"? aorist meaning its continuous
9. What's the point of bringing in a marriage feast here? happy occasion to celebrate
10. Does the N.T. ever use the figure of the Church being **married** to the Lord? Eph 5:22-23 church married to Jesus
11. Are marriage feasts, etc., ever brought into scripture to teach differing truths? Yes
12. Is **a betrothed** wife "one flesh" with her partner — is her body his and his hers? NO
13. Who teaches the Whore of Revelation 17 was the wife of the Lord? millennialists + Max King
14. Who teaches the Lord was married to the Whore and at the same time had the Church as an espoused wife? sames as #13
15. What may be the intent of the record that John tried to worship the angel? teaching Saints only God gets glory
16. What do you make of "the testimony of Jesus is the spirit of prophecy"? Could be Jesus always did will of God & that glorified. Could be heart of prophesy is Jesus + the spirit of Jesus
17. How many white horses in the book are singled out as individuals? one
18. What's the point of an "unknowable" name that is made known to us? Unknowable name is the true nature & status of Jesus & only deity knows that yet reveals it in Word of God which is stated in verse 13 (verse 12)
19. What Psalm helps us explain verse 14? Ps 110:1-7
20. Where is the speech of verses 17,18 borrowed from?
21. What does the "lake of fire" signify? See p 219

~~total separation from God both physically &~~ spiritually to live ~~tormented~~ & still be alive and this is in the presence of the Lamb & the church so it can't be the final judgment

We know only thru Word of God the truth about Jesus. We cant know it on our own; we must be taught by God who reveals all truth.

Analysis of Chapter 19

I. The first hallelujah: 1-2

II. The second and third hallelujahs: 3-4

III. The call for and the fourth hallelujah: 5-8
- A. The call from the throne: verse 5
- B. The mighty response: verses 6-8
  1. The thunderous response
  2. The reason of the response
  3. The wedding feast

IV. The angel and John: 9-10
- A. The angel's instruction: verse 9
- B. John's response and the angel's warning: verse 10

V. The battle of Armageddon fought: 11-21
- A. The army of Right: verses 11-16
  1. The white-horsed leader
  2. The white-robed army
  3. The position and power of the Leader
- B. The great supper of God : verses 17-18
  1. The angelic invitation
  2. The guests and the food
- C. The army of Evil and its defeat: verses 19-21
  1. The allies
  2. The fate of the two beasts
  3. The fate of their allies

Introduction to Chapter 19

Although Babylon has fallen, we know it only from the witnesses of her fall. This is something to sing about and so this chapter speaks of four hallelujahs and an invitation to a wedding feast. The Lamb's wife has not only survived Babylon's demise — she has surpassed. It is fitting that she should be rejoicing and that joy is set forth under the figure of a wedding feast.

The Harlot is gone! The reason for her success has been her military might and the promotion of her ungodly religion. The battle of Armageddon which was previewed in chapter 16 will now be fought. Here, as in chapter 16, we have two armies: The Lamb and his holy army and the terrible trio and their allies. The battle results in victory, of course, for the Lord. Rome, with all her fearfulness and in all her facets, has gone down in fire and blood and smoke.

The beasts are cast into the lake of fire but the Dragon (as we'll see) is only imprisoned. The reason for this will be brought out in the comments on chapter 20.

It only remains here to urge us, those of us who have been following this whole narrative understanding it to be figurative, to remain consistent. Remember we've been looking and saying: This is the picture, what is the truth it is intending to convey?

Comments on Chapter 19

VERSES 1,2. A great voice of a great multitude in heaven - Perhaps this is the great multitude of chapter 7. Whoever it is, they are pleased at the fall of Babylon. This is one song which comes from heaven: Let righteousness triumph and iniquity be destroyed.

Hallelujah; salvation, and glory, and power, belong to our God - Praise to Jah! Who can save but "our" God? Who then should have the glory? Who has the power which alone can save? OUR God. Not theirs. Ours! Our God is a tried stone, a precious corner stone.

VERSE 2. For true and righteous are his judgments - The greatness of our God, they are saying, rests not only on his great power, but on the righteousness of his character. A little power corrupts a little — absolute power corrupts absolutely. Isn't that what they say? Of **men**, Yes. One of the proofs that he judges righteously is what he has done to the great prostitute. She is a graphic example of the way God righteously judges. God had avenged his servants of the great Whore. The servants are not to take vengeance into their own hands (Romans 12:19) for it is such a temptation to develop spite. God is capable of rendering vengeance since he is not bothered by irrational emotionalism.

VERSES 3,4. And a second time they say, Hallelujah - This is repeated for emphasis. To let us know of their deep feeling in the matter. The "they" must surely speak of all the Church of God, for it wouldn't only be martyrs who would be rejoicing in God that the Harlot is brought down. They see in the harlot a prime example of the defeat of all their enemies and God's faithfulness.

And her smoke goeth up for ever and ever - She is a burning city. Set on fire of God. No Nero started this fire and no mere mortal can put it out. The city is here viewed as burning perpetually. The burning never ceases. This must be borne in mind. Of Sodom, Jude said (7): "Set forth as an example, suffering the punishment of eternal fire." Clearly Jude is not saying the fire of Sodom was still burning (though it had eternal consequences). Nor is John here affirming that the fire which devours Rome will endlessly burn. She is pictured in the vision as endlessly burning before the eyes of all as an example of judgment by God. This same route is taken by Isaiah (34:8ff). Listen:

> For Jehovah hath a day of vengeance, a year of recompense for the cause of Zion. And the streams of Edom shall be turned into brimstone, and the land thereof shall become burning pitch, and the dust thereof into

> brimstone, and the land thereof shall become burning pitch. It shall not be quenched night nor day; smoke thereof shall go up for ever; from generation to generation it shall lie waste; none shall pass through it for ever and ever. But the pelican and the porcupine shall possess it; and the owl and the raven shall dwell therein...And thorns shall come up in its palaces, nettles and thistles in the fortresses thereof; and it shall be a habitation of jackals, a court for ostriches...no one of these shall be missing, none shall want her mate; for my mouth it has commanded, and his Spirit it hath gathered them. And he hath cast the lot for them, and his hand hath divided it unto them by line: they shall possess it for ever; from generation to generation shall they dwell therein.

Notice the two strands of different thought in this one text. If you'll read the verses preceding these, you'll hear him mention Edom as the specific object of his judgments on the nation. He talked there of dismantling her world. Now here he discusses her judgment from two different standpoints. He speaks of her as a never-ending lake of fire. The whole land becomes burning pitch. This is another Sodom, only worse. But clearly, Sodom is the model. Notice carefully what he says about Edom — it will burn forever and will not be put out. Yet he immediately goes on to say that nettles and thistles will grow there in their palaces. What can this mean? The two presentations cannot be literally true. But both are true! He speaks here of ending the kingdom existence of Edom. She is to be judged by God and brought into oblivion. How does he present it? He presents her as being judged as was Sodom — only worse. Her fire never dies. Can this be literal? If so, the earth must endure forever and Edom must burn perpetually. It is her **land** that burns endlessly. Then he talks of her as a place that's been utterly desolated, where only wild animals will dwell. He says these wild animals will inherit the land of Edom forever. Is this literal? Can the animals dwell in a lake of fire? Can nettles and thistles grow in a fire? Will the animals be running around Edom in eternity?

You'll notice that these two descriptions are given of Babylon. In chapter 18, she burns and in 18:2, she is like a haunted graveyard. Which is true? Both are true. Utter desolation is the point and two different figures are used to convey that truth. In Isaiah 66:24, the utter defeat of the enemy is described by their unburied bodies lying there being eaten-on by undying worms in the midst of an undying fire. These are figures.

Perhaps you feel that God made it very difficult to understand the Bible. Well, I'd be the last to say all the Bible is easy to understand, but I also would be among the first to say that it can be understood, if we put a bit of work into it. It's amazing how more knowledge produces a realization of an existing ignorance. The more you get to know, the more you realize you need to know. But you shouldn't let yourself be discouraged. Don't get mad at God. Ask him to help you be a good student and then get to work.

Back to this ever-burning city. What is the picture? There's a picture of a city in flames and smoke. What's the lesson? Rome is an everlasting illustration of defeat at the hands of God! **That's the lesson!**

VERSE 4. And the 24 elders...the 4 living creatures...say...Amen, Hallelujah - The whole of heaven agrees with the song they heard. The cherubim Amen the notion of God's righteousness and offer to him the praise.

VERSES 5-8. And a voice...saying, Give praise to our God all ye his servants - Praise, said the Psalmist, is comely in the saints. The angel is winding them up for one huge acclamation. At the amphitheaters, the multitude would hail the emperor or his representative. Here the only one worthy of praise is hailed by all the servants of God, dead or living. The huge host speaks forth its praise in a voice like the thundering of the sea — like the booming of the thunder in a terrible electric storm.

The Lord our God, the Almighty, reigneth - The "Lord" speaks of his Mastery! The "Almighty" speaks just of that — his illimitable power. The Greek says "Pantokrator." The thought is of awe-inspiring power. Barclay speaks of it as implying an "almighty grip" on things. Rome was the "iron" army. It stomped across the world crushing everything under its feet. Its legions were irresistible and kingdom after kingdom fell — king after king submitted. There was one king, however, who stopped them in their tracks — the Pantokrator!

"Reigneth" is "Probably ingressive prophetic aorist" (Robertson). He renders it "God became king." The word is aorist and speaks of something done! C.B. Williams gets close to it when he renders it: For the Lord, our Almighty God, has now begun to reign. The NEB says "has entered on his reign." Wuest says: The Omnipotent has assumed his Royal authority. Goodspeed says: The Almighty now reigns. Fenton renders it: The Lord God Almighty has reigned.

Now get a hold on this, for it can't be overstressed. God Almighty has never been doing anything else but reigning! It isn't possible for God not to reign! His Kingship is based on his

Creatorhood, and since he cannot cease to be Creator, he can't stop reigning. Jehovah, said Moses, shall reign forever. The Psalmist (29:10) said: Jehovah reigned as King at the flood. Jehovah shall rule for ever. He mentions the flood as a specific manifestation of God's sovereignty. There is no suggestion in that passage that he didn't rule as King before the flood. It is even so in this passage. **There is absolutely no thought whatever that God wasn't reigning prior to the fall of the Harlot.** Perish the thought. We are here being told that God manifested in a special way his Kingship. Here is a demonstration in the world of men that God really was always in control. **That manifestation** of that ruling power is called "taking thy great power and ruling" (11:15 — see the comments there).

VERSE 7. Let us rejoice...for the marriage of the Lamb is come - The victory of the Lamb and his Church is an occasion of rejoicing, and so we have pictured a wedding feast. This figure gives the Lamb and his Church the opportunity to rejoice in one another. This is the sole purpose of the figure! Rejoicing is the truth to be expressed, and so a marriage feast is called on. In chapter 7, it was a Feast of Tabernacles — here it is a marriage feast.

It's not out of place here to say a word or two about using figures to build doctrines on. If the doctrine is not clearly taught in other plain sections of scripture, it's a foolish man indeed who founds a school on a figure! Haven't we seen enough of this in the world? We've had men fill us with their types, double applications and allegories.

The wedding feast or a marriage is a common figure in the New and Old Testaments. Sometimes one part of the whole process is called on to teach one thing and another part of it (ie. the Jewish marriage process) is called on to teach something else. In Matthew 25:1ff, for example, the disciples are being taught watchfulness. That, and that alone, is the point! In John 3:28-30, the wedding scene is used again, but for entirely different reasons. John the Dipper is wishing to show that Jesus merits all the praise and the glory he was then receiving, and so he tells them: I'm just like the best man at a wedding. The best man is not the central figure. The Bridegroom is. That's how it should be.

In Matthew 22:1-14, the marriage feast again is called on to illustrate several things. The ungodliness of the Jew in respect to Jesus and the mission entrusted to him by his Father; the rejection of those Jews and the making of the offer to all and sundry; the necessity of a reverent obedience to the wishes of the Lord of the feast. These things are taught in the course of the parable.

In Luke 12:35-40, the wedding feast is brought in again, but this time it is subservient in the text. Watchfulness is being enjoined and the disciples are urged to be like servants waiting for their master to return **after** the wedding feast.

In the passage we're now considering, rejoicing is the issue to be expressed, and what better figure to express rejoicing between the Lamb and his wife, than a wedding feast. There is no doctrinal overtone here about the saints not yet being married to Jesus until that point. That view won't bear looking at.

In Ephesians 5:22-33, Paul discusses marriage in light of the relationship between Christ and Church. (No, it's **not** the other way around). In the course of his discussion, he makes it clear that the Church is the body of Jesus — it is "one flesh" with the Lord. That is clearly and explicitly **said** in the text. Now in the Jewish marriage process, there was a betrothal stage at which time the woman could be called the **wife** of the man she would later marry. See the case of Joseph and Mary, "his betrothed wife." However, they were not regarded as **one flesh** during the betrothal stage! Listen, they **were not one flesh**, one body, during the betrothal stage. That stage didn't exist until after the marriage. The state that Paul speaks of in Ephesians 5 was not betrothal — it was a married wife stage he had in mind. He says that, doesn't he?!

Now the same writer tells the Corinthians (2.11:2) that he had betrothed them to Jesus. Here the figure is the earlier part of the marriage process. Now what are we to do here? What do the millennialists and Max King do? They deny Ephesians 5 is speaking of a married wife. This is an important point in their doctrinal development, so tie it down well.

King has affirmed in his "Spirit of Prophecy" that Babylon (Jerusalem-Judaism) was the wife of the Lord until 70 A.D. On page 230, he said:

> Whatever this Babylon was, its fall opened the way for the marriage of the Lamb. This identifies her as a wife of the Lord by a previous relationship, which must first be entirely dissolved in order for the second marriage to take place.

He goes on to assure us that the only people this could apply to was Israel. What happened then was, the gospel was preached and two Israels emerged. One was (as you can see above) the faithless wife of the Lord. The other became espoused to the Lord, but couldn't marry Him until the first marriage was entirely dissolved. As you can see, this puts the Lord in the position of having one woman espoused to him while the other has not been divorced from him. Quite a neat little arrangement. And quite foreign to scripture, as you can plainly see. King has specifically claimed that this Whore, the wife of the Lord (he says) had the right of "primogeniture" until 70 A.D. See also page 30 of his book. See the McGuiggan-King debate for this whole issue.

We've said enough about this. The marriage feast here has its place because the ecstacy of the Lamb and the saints needs expression, and so the feast is called in. Ephesians 5:22-33 and Romans 7:1ff are enough for most thinking people to convince them the church was "married" to the Lord before 70 A.D. Later in chapter 21, we'll read again about this type of thing when a different point will be stressed.

VERSE 8. She should array herself in fine linen, bright and pure - This fine linen stands for the righteous deeds of the saints. This is a good place to say again that while symbols are not used arbitrarily, they don't always say the same thing. There is consistency, but there isn't always uniformity. White garments here speaks of righteous acts, but that's not always the case. See 3:4ff; 7:9. "Stars" sometimes speaks of individuals, but this isn't always the case. "Heaven" is used in different ways as can be seen by an examination of the numerous texts in which it occurs. Of course, the context almost always makes clear how we are to approach the symbol. Here is a loyal bride pictured — she is pure! Thus, her white garments.

VERSES 9,10. Write, Blessed are they that are bidden to the marriage supper - A rare privilege indeed. Those bidden to the feast here are those who have the love of the Lamb at their heart. This in itself is a great blessing indeed. But being a friend of the Lamb is such a privileged position.

The angel assures the prophet that what he has been revealing (see 1:1) throughout the book is true! The good and the bad.

VERSE 10. And I fell down before his feet to worship him - The rebuke (or maybe "rebuke" is too strong) certainly suggests that the "worship" John was about to deliver was improper. We'll do well to consider that this occurs in the vision. We are not here hearing about a real-life action by John. What we may have here is God's way of telling the brotherhood that no one, not any one, is to be praised for their deliverance. In verse 5, we heard "Give praise to our God." In 14:7, everyone is told to "Fear God and give him the glory." It would seem strange for John in actual experience to fall and worship (in an improper way) a created being. So perhaps we are to see this (in the vision) experience as another way of God to tell the saints to praise only him. See 22:8.

I am a fellow-servant with thee and with thy brethren - Would to God that everyone was so modest and aware of their station in life. Here is some exalted angelic being who admits to being only another servant. Man, we are told, was made a little lower than the angels, but the difference in kind! We've got to think of ourselves no more highly than we ought to think (Romans 12:3ff). If we're not careful, the modest people will go the way of the buffalo.

The testimony of Jesus is the spirit of prophecy - It's not easy to confidently say what this means. The testimony of Jesus may be the testimony that Jesus bore or bears (see 1:1). The point then might well be that as Jesus did only what the Father would have him do, thus glorifying the Father, he set an example of giving glory to the right One. Therefore: Worship God, even as Jesus glorified Him by bearing the testimony he bore.

But in the same place the angel spoke of being a fellow-servant with those who "hold the testimony of Jesus." That would make it the "testimony concerning Jesus." This sounds so much better to me. The point would then be that the heart and aim of prophecy was Jesus. 1 Corinthians 12:1-3 speaks to this point. The result of all prophecy results in the glorifying of Jesus and not angels, however exalted they be.

VERSES 11-21. A white horse, and he that sat thereon called Faithful - There was another white horse in chapter 6:1ff. That was Jesus too, under the figure of a Parthian warrior. This is the only other singled-out white horse in the book. Later in this chapter (19,21) Jesus is designated as he that sits on "**the** white horse." In 16:12, the saints may well come under the figure of Parthians.

There had been those who undoubtedly were not there when the saints needed them. There were those liars who bore false witness against the saints, but here was their leader. Reliable and True. "True" in the sense of "genuine, substantial, and fully manifested." See Trench's "Synonyms" on "true." This warrior makes war — so did Rome. But this warrior makes war in righteousness.

His eyes see all, miss nothing. They pierce into the very soul. He wears many diadems, because he IS King of kings and Lord of lords. On his unknown name, see comments on 2:17 and 13:18.

VERSE 13. He is arrayed in a garment sprinkled with blood -Whose blood? The blood of enemies? Indicating that he is experienced in war? His own blood? Bringing to rememberance that he has already given his all for his followers and will not be persuaded to let them go now. Both of these thoughts are nice.

VERSE 14. And the armies which are in heaven followed him -Makes you feel almost proud to be a part of that family as they follow the Lamb whithersoever he goeth. In here we have a reflection on passages such as Psalm 110:1-7. In that passage, we hear Jesus urged to rule in the midst of his enemies. Isn't that what we have here? In that passage we hear of his people offering "themselves willingly in the day of thy power, in holy array...the Lord at thy right hand will strike through kings in the day of his wrath." That is exactly what we have in this passage. The garments of the army that follow the Lamb are called by the Psalmist "holy array." Here we have the priestly touch. This accords well with what we said in chapter 16:12. Here are the holy members of the holy family led by their holy Leader moving against the disgusting manifestation of Satanic power.

He shall rule them with a rod of iron - Here we have Psalm 2 again, and what an inspiring passage that is. A king having the heathen for his inheritance and the uttermost parts of the earth (and heaven) for his possession. The army is not made up simply of martyrs. John holds **all** the saints to be victors and followers of the Lamb.

VERSES 17,18. An angel standing in the sun...saying to all the birds - Here he is (at noon) standing right in the center of the sky where all can see him. He gets the attention of all the predators and urges them to join at the table prepared by the Lord. They would eat of the flesh of kings. The great supper speech is reflected already in Ezekiel 39:17-20. We'll have something more to say about that passage later in chapter 20. The angel has no doubt about the outcome of the battle anymore than the Lamb who has written on his garment and thigh: KING OF KINGS AND LORD OF LORDS.

VERSES 19-21. I saw the beast and the kings of the earth, and their armies - This is the alliance we read of in chapter 16 when the three frogs went on their round-up.

VERSE 20. And the beast was taken, and with him the false prophet - The Harlot has been dealt with. The sea beast and the earth beast (see chapter 13) are both taken and cast alive into the lake of fire. I've already told you that I believe the lake of fire stands for the utter defeat of the enemy. See comments on 14:10,11; 19:3,4. In Revelation, as in Isaiah, this is the picture which says, "Utter defeat and judgment by God." Be sure to read the comments on the passages just cited. Note that these two are cast alive into the fire — they are not slain.

VERSE 21. And the rest were killed with the sword - The sword belongs to the rider on the white horse. Notice that the army of him on the white horse is not pictured as doing anything. Of course, with a leader such as this, they need to do nothing. Right?! And the

17 And I saw an angel standing in the sun; and
he cried out w/a loud voice, saying to all the
birds which fly in midheaven, "Come, assemble
for the great supper of God;

birds eat the flesh of the allies of the beasts.

Summary

The fall of Babylon has occasioned a series of "Hallelujahs." The fall of that Lady has long been desired. The scene is one of delirious joy and is described in the terms of a wedding feast.

The battle which is the basis of the fall of Babylon is described as involving the Lamb and his holy-arrayed followers. The outcome is so sure that an angel puts out an invitation to all the birds of the heavens. The two beasts are cast alive into the lake which burns with fire (which some might think, would mean they weren't judged) and the smoke of their torment goes up forever because they stand as an example to utter defeat! The allies of the beasts are seen as killed by the sword and then eaten by the birds. They are not cast into the fire, yet.

p 287

18 in order that you may eat the flesh of kings 18
19 of the earth and their armies assembled to make
war against Him who sat upon the horse and
against His army.
19 And I saw the beast and the kings 19
18 and the flesh of commanders and the flesh of
mighty men and the flesh of horses and of
those who sit on them and the flesh of all
men both free men & slaves and small & great."
20 And the beast was seized and w/him the
false prophet who performed the signs in
his presence by which he deceived those
who had received the mark of the beast &
those who worshiped his image; these
2 were thrown alive into the lake of fire
which burns w/ brimstone.
21 And the rest were killed w/ the sword
which came from the mouth of Him
who sat upon the horse and all the
birds were filled w/ their flesh.

3. any battle any time where Satan manifests himself against christians and the church

Questions on Chapter 20

Satan had key to abyss + totally defeated so angel now has key + chain + binds Satan for 1,000 yrs. Throws him into abyss

1. Why does another angel now have the key to the abyss?
2. What's the significance of the 1,000-year binding? *In regard to Rome Satan thoroughly*
3. What's the significance of the "little time" of loosing? *see above* *stopped + Saints thoroughly victorious*
4. In what way would the binding prevent Satan from deceiving the nations? *total defeat + no tempting, deceiving, lying to Saints 1000 yrs bound means in the pit + the pit closed*
 Nature see thru fraud of Rome
5. Who sat on the thrones? *The triumphant over Rome Saints living + dead*
6. What's the judgment which was given unto them?
7. Did John see martyred saints resurrected bodily?
8. What's the significance of the 1,000-years' end? *the ungodly die + dead until end 1,000 yrs since they can't be present at victory*
9. Who are the "rest of the dead"?
10. Why don't they live until the 1,000-years' end?
The martyrs share in the victory along w/ living Saints + reign in victory.
11. What's the significance of the "first resurrection? *only dead saints come back to life*
12. Why the "first" resurrection? *and saints only go thru 1 resurrection which is to victorious life*
13. Is the "first resurrection" the rising to life in Jesus at baptism?
14. What is the "second death"? *this only for those who oppose God separation for eternity from God*
15. How does Gog and Magog fit into this picture? *anyone who comes against God + church*
16. What prophet in the Old Testament talks about Gog?
17. How does the Old Testament prophet use Gog?
18. What's the significance of the "lake of fire"?
19. What prophet has a judgment scene just like this chapter?
20. With whom did that judgment scene deal?
21. With whom does this judgment scene deal?
22. Why do millennialists have trouble with the phrase, "the **first** resurrection"?

resurrections of the church— beginning of 7 yr period + at end*
23. What's the significance of death and Hades being cast into the fire? *they totally defeated in regard to Rome of 7- yr period*

see p. 299–230

Analysis of Chapter 20

I. The binding of Satan: 1-3
- A. The binding: verses 1-2 *binds Satan w/ chain & throws him*

 into abyss & covers the abyss

- B. The duration of the binding: verses 2-3 *1000 yrs - no chance to*

so people can see
- C. The purpose of the binding: verse 3 *any power over Christians*

his deceptive *and/or church especially*

ways & what a fraud he is *B loosening* *to lie & deceive*

1000 yrs *I'll protect you ever*

II. The reign of the righteous: 4-6 *all living & resurrected martyrs*

- A. The enthroned ones: verse 4
- B. The resurrected and reigning ones: verse 4
- C. The 1000-year death: verse 5 *ungodly stay dead*

 while above reign w/ Christ

- D. The blessedness of the first resurrection: verses 5-6 *reign*

 w/ Christ & never go

 thru second death &

 second resurrection

III. The loosing of Satan: 7-10
- A. Satan's loosing: verse 7 *have another go against church.*

that's god mogog
- B. Satan's work of deception: verse 8 *has large army against*

but one again *God*

God totally defeats
- C. Satan's invasion and utter defeat: verses 9-10 *despite this*

 totally beaten

 Deals w/ ungodly *Saints totally*

only

IV. The judgment of the great white throne: 11-15
- A. The throne and the passing of heaven and earth: verse 11 *Rome dismantled completely removed*

ungodly *found no more*

name not
- B. The books, the resurrection, and the judgment: verses 12,13,15
- C. Death and Hades cast into the lake of fire: verse 14

DEATH: no,

LIFE - judge *shows graphically what*

guilty - punishment *has always been true*

wrath of God - utter *since Jesus & Cross*

apocalyptic - adjective, of or like apocalypse; affording a revelation or prophecy pertaining to the Apocalypse or book of Revelation predicting or presaging imminent disaster and total or universal destruction; the apocalyptic vision of some contemporary writers.

Apocalypse a prophetic revelation especially concerning a cataclysm in which the forces of good permanently triumph over forces of evil

Introduction to Chapter 20

Rome, in all its apocalyptic manifestations, has been downed. The Devil, therefore, because Rome is his "incarnation" in the book, is utterly and totally defeated. In regard to Rome, the Devil is not slowed up, but thoroughly stopped! In regard to Rome, the brotherhood is perfectly triumphant. They have not merely won over Rome — they have annihilated her. These two concepts are set forth in the 1,000-year period.

But the Devil will manifest himself again, sometime, somewhere, before the Church is removed from this world to a better place. This truth, is set forth under the figure of a little season of loosing. When the 1,000 years have expired, the Devil is let loose to have another go at Christ and the Church. This is God's way of speaking of any other manifestation of Satan. In that case, he will get, not Rome, for she's gone, but "Gog and Magog." "Gog and Magog" stands for anyone, anytime, who would be Satan's tool against the Church.

The state of those who belong to Christ is set forth in a reigning picture. The state of those who have died for Jesus is set forth in a resurrection and reigning picture. But what of the dead which died in the service of Rome? How does their condition compare with that of Christ's people? Their state is set forth in a 1,000-year death and a resurrection to a lake of fire.

Now, it is crucial for us to bear in mind we are looking at pictures. Up to this point, we've been looking at the picture of a red Dragon, recognizing it to be a figure and saying: Now, what is the truth conveyed under this figure? We've seen an "earth beast" and said: That's the figure, now what's the truth conveyed under it? We've seen a "sea beast" and said: That's the figure, now what's the truth conveyed under it? When we saw the eternally-burning city, we said: That's the picture, now what's the truth being conveyed? When we get to the binding of Satan, we'll say: That's the picture, now what's the truth being conveyed? When we see the resurrection of the righteous, we'll say: That's the picture, now what's the truth being taught under that picture? When we see the Devil loosed and getting the huge army, we'll say: That's the picture, but what's the truth taught under it? When we get to the resurrection at the end of chapter 20, we'll say...what? What do we usually say? We usually say, "That's no picture, that's the truth literally told." This just won't do. We've had a binding and a loosing of Satan and called it a figure for some truth. We've had a resurrection of saints and called it a figure for some truth. We've had a 1,000-year period of reigning while the "rest of the dead" stayed dead, and we called it a figure for some truth and **then** we get to a resurrection involving the wicked and we drop the figurizing and make it literal.

Then in chapter 21, we read of a new heaven and a new earth, and we immediately begin to figurize again! We don't want that "new earth" business (that's premillennial and Jehovah Witness doctrine, isn't it?). We get down to where there's no death or tears and we literalize again. Is it really surprising that these people are upset with us? Let's attempt to be consistent. **It looks just as good on us as on them!**

It won't hurt us to list some of the main images and phrases occurring in this chapter. There is:

1. A 1,000-year binding
2. A 1,000-year reigning
3. A first resurrection
4. A 1,000-year death
5. A little season of Satanic freedom
6. A Gog-Magog host
7. An invasion of a holy city
8. A second resurrection
9. A second death
10. A judgment scene
11. A lake of fire

Now the question which faces you and me: Since all of these present truths, which of them is a figurative presentation and which is literal?

> Simply told, the pictures of this chapter say this: An angel comes down out of heaven and binds the Serpent and locks him away for 1,000 years, so that he can't deceive the nations for that period.
>
> At the point when the Serpent is being bound, those who were martyred for Jesus are resurrected. This resurrection is said to be the "first" resurrection. From the moment of their resurrection, they reign with Jesus for 1,000 years while the dead who died in the service of the beast remain dead for that 1,000 years during which the resurrected saints ruled.
>
> When the 1,000 years are finished (ie. the 1,000 years during which the saints ruled and Satan was bound), Satan was turned loose for a little while. He calls together a great host called "Gog and Magog" and they attack a holy

city together. Fire comes out of heaven and devours them and the Devil is thrown into the lake of fire.

A judgment scene follows at which time the "rest of the dead" are resurrected and judged. Those whose names are not found written in one of the books (ie. the book of life) are thrown into the lake of fire, which is the equivalent of dying a second time.

Two things are especially interesting to me. They are:

1. There is a first resurrection mentioned and a second death — these imply (to me) a second resurrection and a first death.
2. There is a resurrection which is followed by a 1,000 years of life and there is a 1,000 years of death followed by a resurrection resulting in a second death.

Chapter 20 see p 139
word 12 abyss, p. 60
1 And I saw an angel coming down from heaven
having the key of the abyss and a great chain in
his hand.
2 And he laid hold of the dragon, the serpent
of old who is the devil and Satan and bound
him for a thousand years,
3 and threw him into the abyss and shut it &
sealed it over him so that he should not deceive
the nations any longer until the thousand years
were completed; after these things he must be
released for a short time.
4 And I saw thrones and they sat upon them
and judgment was given to them. And I saw
the souls of those who had been beheaded
because of the testimony of Jesus and because of
the word of God and those who had not
worshiped the beast or his image, and had
not received the mark upon their forehead
and upon their hand and they came to life
and reigned w/ Christ for a thousand years. of beast
5 [And the rest of the dead (those who died in sin ~~not martyred~~) not saints
did not come to life until the thousand years
were completed.] This is the first resurrection
6 Blessed and holy is the one who has a part
in the first resurrection; over these the
second death has no power but they will be
priests of God and of Christ and will reign
w/ Him for a thousand years.
7 And when the thousand years are completed
Satan will be released from his prison,
8 and will come out to deceive the nations which
are in the 4 corners of the earth, Gog & Magog,
to gather them together for the war; the
number of them is like the sand of the seashore.
9 And they came up on the broad plain of the
earth and surrounded the camp of the saints
and the beloved city and fire came down from
heaven and devoured them.
10 And the devil who deceived them was thrown
into the lake of fire & brimstone, where the
beast and the false prophet are also, and
they will be tormented day & night forever &
ever.

Comments on Chapter 20

VERSES 1-3. An angel coming down out of heaven having the key of the abyss - Satan, who had the key of the abyss in chapter 9:1ff, is now a defeated foe. This angel "comes down out of heaven." This seems clearly to imply the scene has an earthly viewpoint, ie. John is on earth when he sees it.

VERSE 2. And he laid hold on the dragon...and bound him for 1,000 years - He uses the chain of verse 1 to bind the serpent. As we'll see, he throws him into the pit; shuts it up; and seals it closed for 1,000 years. Whatever we have here, it speaks of a perfect binding. Despite Lindsey, I think we should hold this all to be a picture. It is a picture with a truth to tell. What is that truth? Here it is: The Devil is totally, perfectly, and flawlessly defeated and bound. (This is, of course, with reference to his working through Rome against the Church.)

Not only will the chain, the throwing into the pit, and the sealing of it closed, tell of this perfect binding, but the duration of the binding tells us of it too. The "duration" is 1,000 years. Numbers are the symbols for ideas (Hazelip) and the idea here, is the perfection of the job of binding.

At this point (having stated my own view), let's examine three views which are to be reluctantly rejected. **There is the view that the 1,000 years means the whole of time — the Christian dispensation.**

This has the difficulty of having a period of time **after** the Christian dispensation (if the 1,000 years = the Christian dispensation) since the text speaks of "after the 1,000 years are finished" there will be a "little season" when the Devil will be loosed to deceive the nations.

It might be answered that the "little season" is a figure. This would provoke the rebuttal: 1) If the thousand years speak of time, it looks as if consistency would require the "little season" to speak of time, so we'd have a period of earth history after the Christian era. 2) Even if the "little season" is a figure, it would mean **something** and that something clearly involves earth history **after** (on this view) the Christian era. That's objectionable.

Hendriksen holds that **the 1,000 years speaks of all time until just before the 2nd coming of Jesus.** We've got to reject this too, for at least two reasons: 1) It spoils the perfectness suggested in the symbol of 1,000. (And Hendriksen holds it to be a symbolic number.) 2) It runs foul of the reign, life, and priesthood of the martyrs. They are said to live and reign with Christ for 1,000 years, and that they are to be priests during that 1,000 years. The difficulty is obvious. If the 1,000 years reaches only until "just before" the 2nd coming, we'd have no alternative but to say the living, reigning, and priestly status lasts only that long. The Christians would only be priests then, and reigning, for less than the whole Christian era.

Roberts holds that **the 1,000 years speaks of the period of time following the destruction of Rome when the Gospel triumphed.** I think we should reject this too for at least 3 reasons. 1) It too spoils the perfectness in the symbol of 1,000 and makes it refer to an indefinite "period of time." 2) It has the difficulty of explaining the "little season" following the 1,000 years. If I understand Roberts correctly, he applies the "little season" to a revival of Satan's work just prior to the end of the world (p. 175). This means the 1,000 years is separated from the little season by something like 1900 years. I realize this isn't conclusive, but don't you get the feeling that John is suggesting, in the vision, the little season follows on immediately after the finish of the 1,000 years? With Roberts' view, John moves from a period of time following the destruction of Rome, when the gospel flourished, to a period of time just prior to the end of the world. Thus spanning about 1900 years and saying nothing about the terrible years of pressure and testing in between. 3) It has a real difficulty in handling "and the rest of the dead lived not until the 1,000 years should be finished."

The phrase clearly suggests that the "rest of the dead" lived again when the 1,000 years ended. (We'll mention Wallace's objections to this later.) The RSV rightly renders the phrase in question, "The rest of the dead did not come life again until the thousand years were ended." Roberts holds that the resurrection involving the rest of the dead is the general resurrection at the end of time. If what I'm saying about the phrase teaches "the rest of the dead" rise at the end of the 1,000 years, then we'd have (on Roberts' view) a resurrection just after this period of Gospel prosperity following on the destruction of Rome. What do you think?

I've asserted my view already, so let's examine it for reasonableness. I believe with Wallace, Milligan, and others that the "1,000 years" does not speak of a period of time at all. It speaks of a state of affairs, a condition of things. When it applies to the binding of Satan, it means he is perfectly and altogether bound. When it applies to the saints, it speaks of their perfect and total victory and triumph.

The use of the number "1,000" is fairly common. You remember how often we have read of thousands and ten times ten thousand, etc. This is to convey the idea of bigness, exhaustiveness,

That's how many angels do service for the Lord, Daniel tells us. Twice ten thousand times ten thousand is the "number" of the fearful army of chapter 9 in Revelation. "Thousand" speaks of bigness, completeness, totality.

God owns the cattle on "a thousand" hills (Psalm 50:10). His ownership is total and complete. Why do you think he used "a thousand" when he meant total ownership? If we never know, we can still be sure of what he meant by it — right?!

In Deuteronomy 7:9, we are told that God keeps "covenant and lovingkindness with them that love him and keep his commandments to a thousand generations." (See the NEB and others for the sense here). How long does God's faithfulness last? What of generation 1,001? He needn't worry — God's faithfulness knows no bounds or limits. See too Exodus 20:6, the footnote of the ASV and the text of other versions.

1 Chronicles 16:15 and Psalm 105:8 both speak of God's word, which he "commanded to a thousand generations." How many did God command his word to? To all (the generations of the Jews, in these passages). Totality is the thought. In none of these cases is 1,000 intended to be understood literally and strictly. This doesn't mean we **automatically** rule it out as literal in Revelation, but it does show that to understand it other than literal, is not unreasonable exegesis.

What have we said then about verse 2? We've said that the Devil is completely defeated in his use of Rome. That he's been stopped dead! That this is no limitation under discussion, but an utter defeat! One writer recognizes that the 1,000 years does not speak of a literal period of history, and furthermore, he sees that it speaks of the "thoroughness of the restraint." But even more, he holds that "1,000 should be taken as the ultimate symbol of perfection" and then goes on to talk of the 1,000 years as being a "limitation" of Satan's power. It looks to me as if he had a touchdown right there and then fumbled. The binding relates to his operation in Rome — it was a catastrophic defeat and no limitation. **That's the truth John wants to convey.**

VERSE 3. Cast him into the abyss...shut it...and sealed it over him - The millennialists protest when people make this a mere limitation. I think they have a genuine grievance. It looks all the world to me like a complete stoppage! Of course, the millennialist has his problems too. How he can get a world to multiply in wickedness for a thousand years without a Devil, is a question needing an answer. Still, if he can convert 144,000 and an innumerable host, without the Holy Spirit, this problem ought to be simple.

he should deceive the nations no more, until the 1,000 ...l) — The defeat of Satan relative to Rome was a work of God, that the nations might see through the old Fraud. Those who wished to see, could see that the God of the Christians has whipped Satan and was truly the King. That they didn't see through him wasn't God's fault. The fall of Rome was a big enough advertisement.

After this, he must be loosed for a little time — He has another service to render God in this apocalyptic unfolding. This is why he wasn't cast into the lake of fire immediately after the battle of Armageddon.

The little time loosed gives Satan the opportunity to raise another army and try again. This little time is no time period. It is one of the elements which makes up the apocalyptic picture. A time figure has already been used and so the book consistently stays with the time figure.

What God wants made clear is: Just as surely as I've protected you right now, I will protect you in the future. Just as I have made you victorious through this present crisis, I will make you victorious in the future. As surely as I've defeated Rome for you, I can and will do it with anyone, and at anytime.

This so well accords with how he approached the Jews in the days of Ezekiel. In chapters 1-24, the prophet says only one thing: Jerusalem must fall. In 25-32, he says only one thing: Foreign nations must fall. In chapter 33, we hear: The city (Jerusalem) is smitten. In 34-48, the prophet says only one thing: Jerusalem must be comforted. So he begins to speak to the dejected Jews in terms which meant something to them. To the now-kingless Jews, he offers a restoration of the kingdom under "David." To the countryless Jews, he offers a restoration to their "country." To the Jew without hope of ever regaining his national dignity, he offers just that, and he offers it as really **one** nation under one king, "David."

This would mean, of course, defeating their present enemy, Babylon. Still, God had promised he would do it. It's at this point, we can imagine a down-at-the-mouth pessimist saying: Oh, we had all that before. Someone else will come along and take it all from us. We had David, and a piece of property, and we even had one nation, but look at what happened. Egyptians, Philistines, Assyrians, and then Babylonians. **What guarantee do we have for the future?** It's at that point, chapters 38 and 39 tell their truth. To assure the Jews of the future under their Messiah (Jesus — "David"), the Lord calls an army so huge, no one has ever seen the like of it or ever will. (See my commentary on "Ezekiel" for a discussion of this.) This army he calls from the four points of the compass relative to Jerusalem, brings it against Jerusalem, and destroys it without Israel having to "fire a shot."

This is the place of the Gog and Magog battle in this "little time" in Revelation 20. The thousand-year binding and reigning speaks of the utter defeat of the present oppressor. The "little time" and the Gog-Magog host assure the Church for the future. See further discussion on this below.

VERSES 4-6. And I saw thrones, and they sat upon them — And who are these? These to whom "judgment was given?" They are the saints! They are no one else! They are on "thrones." They have lived faithfully through the crisis and have been given the kingdom. Jesus promised the overcomers they would share with him in the ruling over the nations (2:26f; 3:21).

This is what Daniel had prophesied so many years before. Go there and read chapter 7 all the way through. Then go back again and read from verse 17 to the end. Daniel is told of four kingdoms which would rise up but "the saints shall possess the kingdom," he was told. In verses 21,22, we hear of the little horn making war with them (see the comments on 13:1,2 and the commentary on "Daniel"). He prevails until the Ancient of days came and "judgment was given to the saints of the Most High, and the time came that the saints possessed the kingdom."

That's exactly what you've read here. Whoever these are that are sitting on thrones (thus having the kingdom), they are those to whom "judgment was given." What judgment is this? The judgment on the Whore. God said in 18:20: God hath judged your judgment on her. Back in 11:15-18 (see the comments there) we hear of God, having come in judgment on the great city, taking his great power and beginning to reign. At that time, we're told he judged the enemy and gave "their" reward to the saints.

Notice how all this fits together. In chapter 2:26ff; 3:21, Jesus promises the overcomer a share in the kingdom. In chapter 11:15, the "kingdom of the world becomes the kingdom of our God and of his Christ." This (see the comments relative to the time of that judgment) results in the saints getting "their" (the world's kingdom) reward with Jesus.

The same discussion is going on in Daniel 7. In verses 21,22, the saints get the kingdom at the destruction of the beast. In verses 26,27 we hear "But the judgment shall be set, and they shall take away his dominion, to consume and to destroy it unto the end. And the kingdom and the dominion and the greatness of the kingdoms under the whole heaven, shall be given to the people of the saints of the most high; his kingdom is an everlasting kingdom."

And when Rome went down in blood and fire and smoke, who received the kingdom? God, Christ, and the saints. You'll notice in the Daniel quote above, how, having said the kingdom would be given to the saints, he goes on to say and "His" kingdom is an everlasting kingdom?! While Rome was burning (in a figure) whose judgment was being wrought on her? While the Whore burned, who were sharing the dominion with the Lord? Who were enthroned while the fire raged around the Harlot? **Don't tell me the saints don't rule the world!!!** Name the foe they didn't meet and fracture. Name the foe their Lord can't handle. And when the last day comes, we'll hear then just how much the prayers of the saints have wrought in the earth!

These are the living! But what of those who went down under the Whore's wrath? There's no comfort for those. So, says the critic, don't tell me of "perfect victory."

And I saw the souls of them that had been beheaded for — For what? For whom? — is a better question. What difference does it make? The dead are all dead. It's one and the same. Ah, but this is forgetting that the Lord God said "write!" He said: "Write blessed are the dead who die in the Lord..." These died for "the testimony of Jesus." And how did John see them? Weeping? Moaning in despair and full of remorse that they had given their lives in the service of Jesus? Search for that man or woman if you will, but take a lunch, for you'll be a long time in search. Search in the sea and the sea will say: Not in me. Then go to the forests and they'll say: Not in us. Go to the stars and the stars will shine: Not here. Ask the wind and the wind will blow: Not with me. Go to the very depths of hell and it'll moan: No! Not in me. Then ascend to heaven and ask: Is there anyone here that rues their service to Jesus? Then listen for the laughter at such foolishness. Wait for the multitudes to come to you and tell you of how glad they are that they endured the fire and the sword, the rape and the arson, the shame and the deprivation.There is no defeat in death for the saint.

And such as worshiped not the beast, neither his image — Some have held that these are a different group from the martyrs. Maybe. It's hard to say. But since we're covering all the saints in two groups, the living and the dead, perhaps it's best to view this phrase as simply descriptive of the martyrs who died because they would not worship the beast.

And they lived and reigned with Christ a thousand years — Here we have another aorist for "lived." It undoubtedly ought to have been rendered "came to life." The RSV has "came to life again." The NAS has "they came to life." The NEB has "came to life again." The NAS has "they came to life." Goodspeed has "they were restored to life." The NIV has "they came to life." Barclay, Vincent, and a number of others agree with the above. Robertson admits the possibility of the above, but comes down firmly on no side.

The rendering as it stands in the ASV and others does not conflict with the above — it simply doesn't decide the issue. They "lived" after they were dead, clearly implies they "lived again." This is in keeping with what John is told: This is the first **resurrection.** Now whatever view one takes of the "resurrection" it **has** to be true that there can be no resurrection without the coming to life of that which was formerly "dead." That's "living **again**."

John doesn't see "souls" resurrected. He sees people resurrected. "I saw the souls of **them**...and **they** lived (again) and reigned with Christ a 1,000 years...this is the first resurrection." Wallace is right about the passage **not** teaching the resurrection of the soul (spirit) since the soul (spirit) doesn't die. Nevertheless, John does see "them" rising from the dead. I'm not saying the resurrection is not a symbol — I'm saying John does see, in a vision, a bodily resurrection. But what that resurrection is intended to mean must be determined. To deny that John **sees** a bodily resurrection is to deny what seems plainly to be **said** by the text. We gain nothing by saying **too** much about the text, but we also lose by saying too little.

It doesn't make any difference what text is in view, if there is a resurrection seen — something which was dead must come to life again. Otherwise there is no resurrection. If the passage in question (say, Ezekiel 37) speaks of a national restoration from captivity under the figure of a resurrection, what is the nature of the vision? A nation comes out of its graves. That's exactly what we **see** in Ezekiel 37. The meaning of that resurrection is made very clear — it's the nation restored, but this doesn't alter the fact that in the vision we have bodies coming out of tombs. The **form** of the vision is an actual bodily resurrection.

If the passage be Isaiah 26:11-21, where the resurrection of Israel is in mind (Wallace is absolutely correct in his exegesis of this passage!), we find that the form of the vision is a bodily resurrection.

In our present text, we are reading of the resurrection of people who have given their lives for Jesus. In the vision, "they" come to life again. Not their "souls" but "them," "they." Now, whatever the truth be about the resurrection's significance, we've got to admit with John, that a "resurrection" took place. There can be no "resurrection" of **anything** (nation, cause, or individual) unless there first be the death (real or only in the vision) of the entity "resurrected." There can be no "resurrection" envisioned of individuals without the rising of a body. John **saw**, in the vision, a bodily resurrection of the martyred Christians.

Picture if you will, a battleground with slain scattered all over it. Some of them have the name of Jesus written on them and the others have the mark of the beast on them. Imagine John surveying that battle scene and then seeing the souls of the righteous entering into the bodies — he thus **sees** them (those saints) live again. He **sees** them resurrected. They then take their places on thrones along with the other living saints. This, John is told, is the "first resurrection."

VERSE 5. The rest of the dead lived not until the 1,000 years (are) finished. - The first part of this verse is parenthetical. To get the sequence between verse four and this, one should skip the phrase quoted above and read the end part of verse 5 immediately after verse 4. We'd get this: I saw the souls of them that had been beheaded for the testimony of Jesus...and they lived (again) and reigned with Christ a 1,000 years...this is the first resurrection.

Who are the "rest of the dead"? They are the dead who died in the service of the beast. See the last verses of chapter 19. They are not inclusive of the faithful to Christ (as Roberts holds). There are two groups of faithful to Christ — the martyrs and the still-living. The martyrs have just been dealt with and there is no other class but the living saints. So the "rest of the dead" does not address itself to saints. Living or dead.

We are told of them, ie. the "rest of the dead," that they "lived not **again**" until the 1,000 years were finished. We have the same aorist and the same general unanimity among the versions and the scholars that "living again" is the acceptable rendering. These ungodly dead (who served the beast) do not live again until the 1,000 years are finished. Is it implied that they live again at the end of the 1,000 years? **Of course!**

Why don't they live again until the 1,000 years is finished? Because of what that 1,000 years stands for. It speaks of triumph in Christ. It is the experience only of saints. They have neither part nor lot in a victory. They were living losers. They are dead losers and they will live again only to be losers!

This is the first resurrection - What is the "first resurrection"? The resurrection of the martyrs for Jesus! Why is it the "first"? Because John is about to see a "second" resurrection. He has seen a "first" death (as it were). He will see a "second death." Saints and sinners alike die under the first death (some in service of the beast and some serving Jesus), but the saints are in the "first resurrection," so the second death holds no fear for them. That "first" resurrection is to life and reigning, but the "second" resurrection will be to a "second death."

But what does the "first resurrection" mean? If we weren't in a book such as Revelation (and with other plain scriptural teaching on the general resurrection), such a question would be foolish (or at least **seem** foolish). What does the vision of a resurrected group of martyrs speak of?

Was Augustine (followed by many others) right when he said that was the sinner rising to life in Jesus? (As, for example, Romans 6:3ff). When the question is asked in that fashion, its clear to see that Augustine was wrong. Those who experience the "first resurrection" are already saints. In fact, so faithful and stedfast in Christ have they been, that they were murdered for refusing to leave him. Augustine's "resurrection" would have the people involved leaving the Devil and going to Christ. These already belong to Jesus and have sealed their faith by their death. They **then** are seen as resurrected.

What then? Is it the vindication of the cause of the martyrs? Well...yes! But not in the sense that people now flock to their cause. (I'm not even sure if that happened after the fall of Rome. Farrar speaks of the Church being invaded by the world after the fall of Rome). What then? It's the vindication of the martyrs (and thus their cause is vindicated). We are being told truths about what we cannot see. The assemblies of the saints after Rome was buried were visible proof that the saints whipped Rome and their judgment was judged on her. What of the dead? This visionary resurrection tells us that the dead in Christ share in the victory just as surely as do the living! **That's the message.**

The fact that this is called a "first" resurrection gives the premillennial school trouble. You see, they wish to stay with a literal interpretation viewpoint (even though they can't live with it), and this is hard when their scheme of things requires a resurrection of the whole Church (and a translation of the living Church members) 7 years before the "first" resurrection. The millennialists say, at the Rapture, Jesus is coming for his Church. At that time, the sum total of all Church members will be taken from the world (along with the Holy Spirit). The living ones will be transformed and the dead ones will be raised incorruptible. They use 1 Thessalonians 4:13ff for their Rapture theory. The Rapture begins the 7-year period (the 70th week of Daniel) of the Great Tribulation. This 7 years is divided into two 3½-year periods. The latter is the worse, and strictly speaking, is the period of the Great Tribulation. At the end of the 7 years, Jesus comes and finally establishes his millennial kingdom. It's at this point — the beginning of the millennium — that this "first" resurrection takes place. It includes not only the martyrs of the Tribulation era, but all the righteous of all the ages. This means, on their terms, that the **first** resurrection takes place 7 years after the resurrection of the Church.

What are they to do with this? Acknowledge that they have missed the boat? No. They make **this** resurrection **part of** the first resurrection which began with (at the least) the resurrection of dead Church members. So that the expression "the first resurrection" includes the resurrection of Jesus, the Church, and what we have in this text. That's convenient enough.

Let's sum up what I've said so far — all right?! We've said that the thousand-year binding and the thousand-year reigning speak of the same thing from two different angles. The first, from Satan's angle, speaks of utter and absolute defeat in using Rome against the Lord and his people. The second, from the standpoint of the saints, speaks of total victory and triumph in the battle against Rome!

We've said the living saints are viewed as enthroned, having been given the kingdom of the world. They are joined in that rule by the martyred saints who are viewed as having been raised to sit on thrones with their brothers. These martyrs are viewed as having been raised from among the dead and the rest of the dead (those who've died in the service of the beast) don't live again until the 1,000 years have finished. **They have to endure a 1,000-year death while the martyrs enjoy a 1,000-year life, and rule with Jesus.** (The idea that the rule of Jesus lasts only 1,000 years is absolutely foreign to the text — in anybody's exegesis).

The first death (which is implied — so it seems to me — by the phrase the "second death") is experienced by both saints and beast-servants. The first resurrection is experienced only by those who died for Jesus. The reason the wicked don't experience this is because it is a resurrection to life and rule, to triumph and vindication. It is the experience only of martyred saints.

The "little season" is used to stay consistent with the time figure (1,000 years) already adopted. The 1,000 years doesn't speak of a period of history, nor does the "little time." It is needed to set forth the truth that although the Devil has been utterly broken in the destruction of Rome, the Church will hear from him again. However (see comments below), that's only half the story, for involved in the "little season" of rebellion is the record of Satan's utter overthrow. This is to assure the saints of their future triumph **whatever** comes to pass. See the comments below and on verse 3 above.

VERSE 6. Blessed and holy is he that hath part in the first ressurection - He is blessed because he is one who has died "in the Lord." Since only those dying for Jesus experience the first resurrection, they are those who've "died in the Lord." We have already been told: Blessed are those who die in the Lord!

He is also holy. The first resurrection implies a second resurrection. The first ressurection only involves the holy and blessed, and the second resurrection involves only the unholy. There is no blessedness without holiness! "Follow after holiness without which no man shall see God."

There is a beauty in holiness (real holiness) which all right-thinking people desire. Holiness has two aspects — the objective and initial holiness of which all saints are partakers. They all belong to Jesus (1 Peter 1:2), equally. They all have been called out of the world and belong to the Lord (which is the basic idea of holiness). In this respect, no Christian is more holy than another. There is another side of holiness — it is the subjective and progressive holiness. It speaks of the personal worth and character of each individual. In this respect, one may be more holy than another. Everyone knows there are people more dedicated than themselves. (This raises an interesting issue which we can't discuss here — namely, the prerequisites to discipleship as reflected in such passages as Luke 14:25-35).

All the saints I know by personal acquaintance wish to be more holy. They want to follow after holiness. Most of them feel an utter inadequacy to deal with temptation. They often despair of further growth and are frustrated with their weaknesses. Do you know what I think? I think I've discovered in my own life that I excused myself too much for weakness. But do you know what basically was the cause of this? I was ignorant. I was ignorant of what Jesus actually accomplished at the cross. I knew about redemption (thank God!) and the victory reflected there, but I'd not really grasped the victory Jesus won (for me) over the powers of darkness.

I'd missed the real power of Colossians 2:15; 1 John 3:8; Hebrews 2:14 and others. These with 1 Corinthians 10:13 have really helped me grow. I thought (not always consciously or with deliberation) that Jesus had weakened the evil powers, but I now believe that he did more than weaken them — he utterly defeated them, and I should not feel the need of heeding their call **at all**. I will refuse to credit to them **any** power against me and believe with a deep conviction that my sinning is a totally voluntary act of submission to them. I don't have to think their way! I don't have to feel they've beaten me to submission. They don't have that power — Jesus utterly defeated them **for me**! That's why James says if we resist the Devil, he **will** (not might, or will probably) **flee**. That's why God had been saying to me: I will not let you be tempted above what you are able to bear. Do you know (say what you like about this), that I'm a stronger man — dramatically stronger — since beginning to insist on that truth? Think about it. Maybe it will help you too. And then again, do you know what has really helped me to be more righteous? (I'm not bragging, honestly. I've such a long way to go, but I'm pleased with what God is working in me by these truths, I want to share my joy with you). I've thought of the example of Christ at the cross. For 33½ years, the Devil was working on him and he refused at any time or in any place to make peace with Satan. The cross speaks of the last defiant act of Jesus in his great refusal to come to peace with sin and Satan. That has made me proud of Jesus and more than ever, desirous of following him. At the cross, Jesus said: WHATEVER the cost, I won't bow to sin! I like his nobility. I adore his person. I want (and so do you) to share in his victory over a disgusting, loathsome, and **defeated** enemy.

Over these the second death hath no power - The reason for this is, the resurrection of the righteous is to life and victory and the second death is a symbol of utter defeat. You see, the resurrections in this section tell truths about the things that cannot be seen — one way or another. In the whole section, the resurrections deal only with those who have "died." There are two kinds of death — One is "in the Lord" and the other is "out of" the Lord. But who can tell the difference? Who can say whether the dead Christian has it over the dead servant of the beast? The Lord can. We can see the living saints, that they have survived the death of Rome! The Church then is indeed the eternal City. But what of the dead?

The dead Christians are equally victors with their live brothers. The dead servants of the Devil are losers. How is that truth told here? It is told in a vision. The righteous live again and rule a 1,000 years. That's the way their victory is depicted. The unrighteous dead are losers. How is their condition depicted? They endure death for a 1,000 years and then are raised to die again! This is the second death. How is that "second death" portrayed? By a lake of fire!

You'll notice that it is called a "second" death. But that's only in reference to those who are contrasted with the saints in a resurrection. The proof of this is that the beasts are cast into the lake of fire. See 19:20. The Devil himself is cast into the lake of fire without dying (first or second time). So the same symbol is used in two different ways, but with ultimately the same point in view. The saints rise to enjoy triumph and to be tokens of victory against the Dragon. The wicked rise to be eternal tokens of utter defeat against Christ.

In both of these resurrections, we have a figurative representation of truths. Neither of the resurrections is to be understood literally. Nor are the sequences which follow each resurrection to be taken literally. We are not to conceive of the martyrs literally ruling on thrones for a literal 1,000 years. Nor are we to conceive of the "rest of the dead" as being thrown into a literal lake of fire. Now that that's what is pictured for us in the text before us, we're not in the position (nor do we desire) to doubt. However, we're not committed to a literal view of Revelation 20. See the McGuiggan-Jordan slide presentation on "An Examination of Millennialism," where we discuss the philosophy of literal interpretation as set forth by the premillennialists and the consequences of such.

They shall be priests of God...and shall reign...a 1,000 years -As we've already said, the duration of the reign of Christ is not even hinted at in this text, whether one literalizes or not. The reign spoken of here is the reign of the martyrs and the other saints. It is a "with" reign. A number of kings in the Old Testament ruled "with" their fathers. To say how long they ruled "with" their fathers does not at all even hinge on how long was the reign of the father.

Ahaz was co-regent with Jotham for about 12 years. Manasseh was co-regent with Hezekiah for 8 to 9 years. See Thiele's "Mysterious Numbers of the Hebrew Kings," and R.K. Harrison's "Introduction to the Old Testament" (p. 187). Now suppose we read in scripture: And Ahaz ruled with his father, Jotham, for 12 years. Supposing we read that, we'd realize two things: 1) The reign of Jotham is not the real issue. 2) There is absolutely nothing said about the duration of Jotham's reign. (It is implied, of course, that Jotham's reign was at least 12 years long).

That's how it is in this text. The discussion is not how long Jesus rules, but how long the saints rule. This being true, to put a length of time on "the millennial reign" of Jesus is wholly without support, even supposing there was to be a millennial reign of Christ.

We learn from this text that these saints are not disappointed in God. The proof of this is that they are "priests" to God and Christ for a 1,000 years (assuming they are priests as long as they reign). It is worth noticing too that what they had before they died (priesthood) is continued after they've died for him. So, live or die, it is victory. Live or die — its in service to God.

VERSES 7-10. When the 1,000 years are finished, Satan shall be loosed - He is not loosed during the 1,000 years, for that would disrupt the truth in the number of years. These must be permitted to expire and thus have their full symbolic force. It is for the same reason that the "rest of the dead" do not live again until the 1,000 years are expired.

The loosing is "for a little time." This not only stays with the time figure already introduced (ie. remains consistent with the overall picture), but it enables the Lord to show us the Devil is not through when he is whipped in Rome. He'll have another go, sometime, somewhere.

The loosing is for "a little time" and this undoubtedly stands in contrast with the thought of a "thousand years." The "little time" is a period of loosing, reminding us in a very real way that the Devil is under control. He is permitted to do what he is now doing. The little time would indicate the weakness of the Devil. He is not able to continue for long. We are reminded, though thay are not exegetically connected, of the declaration that he "hath but a short time" (12:12).

VERSE 8. And shall...deceive the nations - The reason he was bound for a thousand years was so the nations could see through him. His defeat in Rome exposed him so the the world could see he was useless and a "con-man." But who, or how many, have learned from history? Did Pharaoh? Did Nebuchadnezzar? Do we?

Which are in the four corners of the earth, Gog and Magog - Who are Gog and Magog? They are anybody and yet no one in particular. They were used in Ezekiel in the same way they are being used here (there's a difference in the use of the titles). Ezekiel has presented the glory the Jews would experience under the Messiah, and he has presented it by terms which would speak clearly to them (see comments on verse 3 and the "little time"). To make it clear to them that under the Messiah their glory was secure he presented the defeat of any possible enemy under the terms of a "Gog of the land of Magog" battle. See the comments on this in the "Ezekiel" commentary.

In that place, as in this, the army is called from the four points of the compass with "Gog" as the leader. In that place, as in this, the defeat of Gog and his hosts was decisive and total. In that place, as in this, Gog made his appearance after the vindication and glorification of God's people. In that place, as in this, the size of the host is staggering (see Ezekiel 39:12,13). In that, as in this, the defeat takes place without the people of God having to lift a finger.

As already stated, this affair is used in the apocalypse to say to God's people: I have already defended and vindicated you in this present crisis, and I will do so again, when the need arises. Anywhere and at any time. The army is said to be "as the sand of the sea." Here, bigness is stressed. In Ezekiel 39:12,13, we are told twice, that the whole house of Israel would be involved in the burial detail. It takes them 210 days (7 months) to get the job done. Counting only 2 million for the whole house of Israel and giving only 1 corpse per day per person (surely an awfully small number), the number of corpses would be 420 million. In Ezekiel's day (as in ours), that kind of an army not only was never seen, but would never have been dreamed of. (Yes, I've heard the Chinese could now put 200 million into the battlefield). On the basis of burying only 2 per 24 hours per person (and surely with the stench, etc., this couldn't be a large estimate since they'd want them buried quickly), the number of the corpses would be 840 million.

Why does he choose such huge numbers? To stress the inability of the enemy to overcome the people of God. If ever they would be beaten, an army such as Gog's would do it. And what is the result? Gog loses, and utterly.

VERSE 9. They...compassed the camp of the saints...the beloved city - What do the premillennialists make of Gog and Magog? Here are a few difficulties indeed. These people insist that "Gog" means Russia (ie. when they're exegeting Ezekiel 38,39). In that Ezekiel battle, Gog is utterly devastated — so no more Gog. Who then is Gog here? Lindsey thinks Gog here, are the decendants of the Gog enemies of Israel. But if Gog was utterly devastated, how could he have left decendants? Perhaps a lot of Gog's people didn't come to the battle and thus were not slain. But how did they get into the millennial knigdom which (the millennialists are very definite about this) is only for the born-again ones? Perhaps some of Gog's people were born again and they got into the millennium. If the world was so wicked during the Great Tribulation, how did these Gog people escape the purge? But in any case, if they did enter the millennium, how could they have turned against Jesus, since (both Lindsey and Walvoord are Calvinists) they were born-again and coudn't apostatize? Perhaps some of the children they had during the millennium didn't obey Christ and they are the armies that Satan mustered.

You can readily see the extremes to which these people are going to hang on to their views. Listen! During the Tribulation, there is no Holy Spirit at work restraining sin (so say Lindsey and Walvoord, explicitly!), and yet 144,000 Jews are converted within 7 years — over 20,000 per year. These in turn, without the Holy Spirit restraining sin, convert an innumerable host. This is remarkable. Now we have something, surely equally remarkable. This 1,000 years begins with no one but saved people, who can't fall away. Everything is perfect as to environment and government. THE DEVIL IS **COMPLETELY** INOPERATIVE; Jesus is promptly putting down in death those who oppose him (how's that possible with the Devil totally inoperative?). All of these things are allegedly true, yet the Devil is able to round up at the end of the millennium, this staggeringly huge host. Can you beat that? Bet you can't!

Walvoord doesn't go the "descendants of Gog" route. He figurizes and makes this whole battle the Devil's "Waterloo." So that Gog is not a person, or people — it is a figure of speech. But why bother doing this? Why not just say that this is the battle of Ezekiel 38,39? They can't, for the two battles (on their terms) are fought about a 1,000 years apart. One at the beginning of (or just prior to) the millennium and the other after the millennium. See this mentioned again under "The Chronology of the Millennial View" later in this book.

VERSE 9. They...compassed the camp of the saints...the beloved city - The city in the vision is Jerusalem. The truth is, it's the Church of God. The fire out of heaven ends the contribution of Gog to this apocalyptic story. Since this army and invasion stand for any and all of the Devil's assaults against the Church (after the Roman offensive), it's failure signals the end of Satan's career as an opponent, So:

VERSE 10. The devil...was cast into the lake of fire and brimstone - Lindsey is fond of making "fire and brimstone" into a "nuclear war" in this book. It's wonderful that he didn't do that here.

I've said several times already that the lake of fire is a symbol, in this book, of total and irrevocable defeat, were it not for the fact that he would be permitted to try again with others. This last effort summerizes all the later attempts (though none in particular), so that we now have utter defeat, not only in one specific attempt, but in all his attempts. The lake of fire says he is altogether and forever defeated. No one comes out of the lake of fire to do anything.

Wallace is postively right. These passages were not written as a dissertation on eternal punishment. We have a book full of pictures teaching truths dealing with the distress of the Church in the early days of its life. Those **pictures** set forth truths which lie behind the pictures . See the comments on 14:10ff.

VERSES 11-15. I saw a great white throne...and...the earth and heaven fled - Verses 4-10 have been dealing with the victory of the saints. Their present triumph (over Rome) and the assurance of their future stability. That's how the saints came out in the battle of Armageddon. How did the other side come out? Verses 11-15 tell us. We've been hearing about the saints **judging** and receiving the kingdom. We've been hearing about the martyrs, their resurrection to life and vindication. We'll now hear about the "rest of the dead" and their resurrection. We'll hear about them **being** judged and of the "second death."

The judgment scene in 20:4 wasn't literal, neither is this one. The judgment scene in 20:4 was not the general judgment, neither is this one. The picture of God sitting in judgment is a common one. Just pick up a concordance and look for yourself. Psalm 9:4-7 is especially helpful. But the one which helps us most is the one in Daniel 7:9-12. Here's what it says:

> I beheld till thrones were placed, and one that was ancient of days did sit: his raiment was white as snow, and the hair of his head like pure wool; his throne was fiery flames, and the wheels thereof burning fire. And a fiery stream issued and came forth from before him: thousands of thousands ministered unto him, and ten thousand times ten thousand stood before him: the judgment was set, and the books were opened. I beheld at that time because of the voice of the great words which the horn spake; I beheld even till the beast was slain, and its body destroyed, and it was given to be burned with fire. And as for the rest of the beasts, their dominion was taken away: yet their lives were prolonged for a season and a time.

See comments in my "Daniel" on the section. Let me assert here what you can easily check for yourself. This judgment here is the judgment on the fourth beast, which (everyone agrees) is Rome. There are so many points of agreement between the two judgments. In both we have a throne occupant! In both we have the books mentioned! In both we have the fire element (after the judgment)! In both we have (exegetically) the Roman element! In both (it seems to me) the point is the total defeat of the opponents of God's people — Rome and/or her allies.

On the fleeing away of the heaven and earth, see below the

discussion of the "new heaven and earth." Whatever it is that passes away, there is no place found for them. This is what is said of the giant image in Daniel 2. The meaning is not that it is just impaired, but that it is completely removed. In Daniel 2 we know what the discussion is; for what this means, see below.

VERSE 12. I saw the dead, the great and the small...judged out of ...the books - Here we have the second resurrection. When John spoke of the "first" resurrection, he was contrasting it with this one. Those who participated in the first resurrection were blessed and holy. They were holy and they were blessed because they were raised to live and reign, to share the victory of the Lamb. These are the unholy. They died too, and now they are (in a figure) raised, but only to die a second time. What they received, they fully deserved, for they were judged according to their works.

VERSE 13. And the sea gave up the dead...death and Hades gave up the dead - Everything which God has shown himself Lord over in the book gives up the dead. He has smitten everything and is thus its Lord. It delivers to him when he demands. Death and Hades are, of course, personified in this book (see 6:8). The statement that "death gives up the dead that were in it" makes the personification (is that the right word?) stand out. There are no righteous in this resurrection — they were partakers of the first resurrection (see the notes there). We are dealing here with all those who died in the service of the beast. ALL of them, we're being assured, are subject to the verdict we're about to hear.

VERSE 14. And death and Hades were cast into the lake of fire -These two are viewed as enemies of God even though he makes use of them. Christ had long ago defeated them, but they are being treated in reference to **this** crisis just past. The dragon had been utterly defeated by Jesus at the cross and resurrection, but he is dealt with too in reference to the present issue. The martyrs had overcome death and Hades in reference to Rome, but the sending of them into the lake of fire speaks of their defeat (as it spoke of Satan's) as for all time and anywhere. Note once more, that the lake of fire is only a "second" death with reference to those who died in the Roman conflict on Rome's side. The beasts are thrown in alive — so are the Devil and death and Hades.

VERSE 15. If any man was not found written in the book of life -This is not implying that any of the ones being judged would be found so written. It is simply declaring that there's another side of this going-into-the-lake-of-fire issue. It's true that they are being judged according to their works, but it's also true that they are

12 And I saw the dead, the great & the small
standing before the throne and the books were
opened and another book was opened which is
the book of life and the dead were judged from
the things which were written in
the books according to their deeds.

defeated because they don't belong to Jesus. Milligan says it well:

> ...it harmonizes with this that the book of life is not opened in order to secure deliverance for those whose names are inscribed in it, but only to justify the sentence passed on any who are cast into the lake of fire.

Summary

Why is the Devil said to be bound a "thousand years"? To indicate he is perfectly and totally defeated in reference to his use of Rome against the Lord and his Church. Why is he loosed a "little time?" Because after Rome, there will be others to oppose the Church and that "little time" is the way the future efforts of Satan are covered. To whom was judgment given? To those who sat on the thrones and who represented the saints who lived to see Rome go under. What of those who died in faith to Jesus? They are presented as experiencing a resurrection to thrones along with their brothers. Why is the reign said to be a "thousand years"? To portray its perfectness and completeness. Why is their resurrection designated as the "first"? To differentiate it from the next one he sees — the "second." Who are the "rest of the dead"? Those who didn't die for Jesus, but in the service of the beast. Why don't they live again during the "thousand years"? Because that's an experience only for the triumphant saints — victors over Satan and Rome. What do they endure? They endure a thousand years of death while the saints reign and then they're resurrected to die a second time. What does the second death symbolize? Utter, irrevocable defeat. p 313

13 And the sea gave up the dead which were
in it and death & Hades gave up the dead
which were in them and they were judged
every one of them according to their deeds.
14 And the dead and Hades were thrown into
the lake of fire. This is the second death,
the lake of fire.
15 And if anyone's name was not found
written in the book of life he was
thrown into the lake of fire.

Chapter 21
1 And I saw a new heaven and a new earth; for
the first heaven & the first earth passed away
and there is no longer any sea.
2. And I saw the holy city, a new Jerusalem,
coming down out of heaven from God, made
ready as a bride adorned for her husband.
3 And I heard a loud voice from the throne
saying, "Behold, the tabernacle of God is
among men, and He shall dwell among
them and they shall be His people and God
Himself shall be among them.
4 and He shall wipe away every tear from their
eyes and there shall no longer be any death
there shall no longer be any mourning or
crying or pain the first things have passed away.
5 And He who sat on the throne said, "Behold
I am making all things new." And He said
"Write, for these words are faithful & true."
6 And He said to me "It is done. I am the Alpha
and the Omega, the beginning and the end.
I will give to the one who thirsts from the
spring of water of life without cost.
7 He who overcomes shall inherit these things
and I will be His God & he will be My son.
8 But for the cowardly & unbelieving &
abominable & murderers & immoral people
and sorcerers & idolaters and all liars,
their part will be in the lake that burns
w/ fire & brimstone, which is the second death.
9 And one of the seven angels who had the 7 bowls
full of the 7 last plagues came & spoke w/ me
saying Come here I shall show you the bride
the wife of the Lamb.
10 And he carried me away in the Spirit to a
great and high mtn & showed me the holy
city, Jerusalem, coming down out of heaven
from God,
11 having the glory of God. Her brillance was
like a very costly stone, as a stone of crystal-
clear jasper.
12 It had a great & high wall w/ 12 gates & at
the gates 12 angels & names were written
on them which are those of the 12 tribes
of the sons of Israel.

13 There were 3 gates on the east & 3 gates on the north & 3 gates on the south & 3 gates on the west.

14 And the wall of the city had 12 foundation stones and on them were the 12 names of the 12 apostles of the Lamb.

Questions on Chapter 21

1. What was meant by the passing away of the heaven and earth in 20:11? His judgment of Rome shook its foundation & crumbled it to pieces so it totally dissintegrated. The ungodly perish wrath
2. What does a "new heaven and earth" stand for? oppression no longer exist — a state of blessing
3. What is the characteristic language of the prophets regarding judgment? God dismantles whole world judged brings it down – annihilates it
4. What is the characteristic language of the prophets regarding blessing? everything flourishes like Garden of Eden
5. How much of the universe did Nebuchadnezzar rule? Babylonian world
6. What is meant by: "The first things are passed away"? oppression gone & future secure
7. What's the thrust of 5b-7? A call to decision pp 322-323
8. Is the Lamb's wife a literal city? NO, it's the people
9. Since the number "12" is constantly associated with the city, what do we know?
10. Since the 12 apostles are the foundation, what is the city? the church of God
11. What's the two-fold point of measuring in this chapter? holiness & glory
12. Why is the city four-square? bc it is the holy of holies
13. Why is it **12 thousand** furlongs wide, long, and high?
14. Is a jeweled city a new thing to prophecy?
15. Does verse 23 say there is no sun or moon?
16. On whom do the nations depend for light?
17. The fact that we have nations, and they depend on Jerusalem for light, what does that say about the setting of chapter 21?
18. What prophet talks about the nations bringing their glory into Jerusalem?
19. In what way is that prophecy fulfilled?
20. What is the thrust of verse 27?

15 And the one who spoke w/ me had a gold measuring rod to measure the city & its gates & its wall.

16 And the city is laid out as a square & its length is as great as the width; & he measured the city w/ the rod, 1500 miles; its length & width & height are equal.

17 And he measured its wall 72 yards according to human measurements, which are also angelic measurements.

18 And the material of the wall was jasper and the city was pure gold, like clear glass

19 The foundation stones of the city wall were adorned w/ every kind of precious stone. The first foundation stone was jasper; the second sapphire, the third chalcedony, the 4th emerald;

Analysis of Chapter 21

GOD DWELLS –

I. The panorama of the "new": 1-5a
   A. The new heavens and earth: verse 1 — new environ
   B. The new Jerusalem: verses 2,3 — beauty – a bride — speaks of her purity innocence joy she has been true to her Beloved
   C. The new circumstances: verses 4,5

II. The call to decision: 5b-8
   A. The rewards offered: verses 5b-7
   B. The threat stated: verse 8

III. The church as a glorious city: 9-27
   A. The invitation: verse 9
   B. The vision of the city: verses 10-27
      1. Her divine origin - 10 — precious in site of God
      2. Her light-glory - 11 — Jesus reflected God's glory, so does church (beauty)
      3. Her wall and gates - 12,13 — stable, holy, glory (strong)
      4. Her foundations - 14 — built on teachings of Jesus
      5. Her shape and size - 15-17 — holy, set apart stable, glory
      6. Her preciousness - 18-21 — walls, etc made of precious stones
      7. Her temple - 22 — He dwells in me & I in Him
      8. Her light - 23 — Lord shining on Her.
      9. Her testimony - 24 — shivering back to the wall little flock is now light set on a hill
      10. Her security and honor - 25-26
      11. Her holiness - 27

no fear of being taken gates secure

She spiritually illuminates the world nation must walk by its light

20 the 5th sardonyx, the 6th sardius, the 7th
chrysolite; the 8th beryl; the 9th topaz, the 10th
chrysoprase, the 11th jacinth the 12th amethyst.
21 And the 12 gates were 12 pearls, each one of
the gates was a single pearl. And the street
of the city was pure gold like transparent glass.
22 And I saw no temple in it, for the Lord
God, the Almighty & the Lamb are its temple.
23 And the city has no need of the sun or the
moon to shine upon it, for the glory of
God has illumined it, and its lamp is the
Lamb.
24 And the nations shall walk by its light & the
kings of the earth shall bring their glory into
it.
25 And in the daytime (for there shall be no night
there) its gates shall never be closed.

Introduction of Chapters 21 and 22

The Church has come through a major crisis. She had defeated her enemy (thanks to her Lord), and there follows in these two chapters a description of the triumphant and vindicated Family of God. He will talk about her "newness." He will speak about the "newness" of her environment. He will talk of her beauty and purity. He will speak of her stability and strength. He will speak of her importance and her testimony. He will speak of her holiness.

And each of these things he will set forth in different figures. For example, her new environment will be spoken of as a "new heaven and earth." He will speak of her beauty in the terms of an unbelievably precious city with golden streets and jeweled walls. He will speak of her purity and dedication to him under the figure of a bride. He will talk of her stability and strength under the figure of her "four-squaredness" and her incredible walls of height and thickness. He will speak of her importance and testimony in terms of the light she, as a city, gives to the nations around. Each of these will have their place.

Is this a description of the Church in eternity? I don't think so, although if the Church were described as being in eternity, a lot of the figures used here would be absolutely right for that description. See as we go through if you don't agree that there are some things said in these chapters which would militate against the "in eternity" view.

Comments on Chapter 21

VERSES 1-5a. I saw a new heaven and a new earth: for the first...passed away - In chapter 20:11, we read of the heaven and earth fleeing away from God, so that no place was found for them. We're in an apocalyptic book and right in the middle of a highly symbolic section. We need to remember this.

The passing of the heavens and earth is not a new figure at all. If you'll spend some time with a concordance and the prophets, it will become very clear that this figure is used over and over again. And being a figure, it wasn't intended to be taken literally.

In speaking of the judgment on Babylon **by the Medes**, God spoke of the dismantling of her world (Isaiah 13:6-22). He talks of disruption in the constellations, sun, and moon. He talks of "punishing **the world**" for its iniquity. He speaks of shaking the earth right out of its place. And yet he says it would be done by the Medes and when they were through, the animals would inherit Babylon. You know history well enough to know none of this literally occurred. It wasn't intended to literally occur. This was the apocalyptic description of God's attack on the world of the Babylonian.

When Daniel told Nebuchadnezzar God made him king, he speaks as if Nebuchadnezzar were absolute sovereign of the whole globe. Read it:

> Thou, O king, art king of kings, unto whom the God of heaven hath given the kingdom, the power, and the strength, and the glory; and wheresoever the children of men dwell, the beasts of the field and the birds of the heavens hath he given into your hand, and hath made thee to rule over them all:

That's Daniel 2:37,38, and that was Nebuchadnezzar he was talking to. Now you know, I know, and everyone else knows that Nebuchadnezzar had no such power. These are universals which are not intended to be pressed into universal use. But, the area over which Nebuchadnezzar ruled was Babylon's world. They dominated it — said who lived or died or moved. It was their world. The passages in Isaiah 13 speak of an attack on the world of the Babylonian — **his world**, was coming to an end.

In the case of the flood in Noah's day — Peter speaks of it as a flood in which "the world of the ungodly perished" (2.2:5). Why did he call it the world of the ungodly? Because they ran the show. With the flood **their** world came to an end. It perished (2 Peter 3:6).

In Isaiah 34:1-17, we read of God judging the nations and Edom in particular (vv. 5ff). He describes the judgment as a dismantling of the universe:

> And all the host of heaven shall be dissolved, and the heavens shall be rolled together as a scroll; and all their host shall fade away, as the leaf fades from off the vine, and as a fading leaf from the fig tree. For my sword hath drunk its fill in heaven: behold it shall come down upon Edom, and upon the people of my curse, to judgment... And the streams of Edom shall be turned to pitch, and the dust thereof into brimstone, and the land thereof shall become burning pitch. It shall not be quenched night nor day; the smoke thereof shall go up for ever; from generation to generation it shall lie waste; none shall pass through it for ever and ever. But the pelican and the porcupine shall possess it; and the owl and the raven shall dwell therein... and thorns shall come up in its palaces, a habitation of jackals, a court for ostriches. And the wild beasts of the desert shall meet with the wolves, and the wild goat shall cry to his fellow...

And on it goes (vv. 4ff) in the same fashion. Now an intelligent reader has to do something with this text. What to do? Throw up the hands in frustration? That's no good. Understand all of it literally? That's not possible. Well, read it again and see how there could be any Edom when the world has been literally dismantled. How could Edom burn forever, while animals all live there? **What do we have here?** We have the prophet's way of describing the end for Edom. He first says **her** world is brought to an end. Then he changes his figure to an unending fire. Then he changes that figure for one of wild desolation. **He says the same thing three different ways.**

You think this is unusual? It's not. When God is spoken of as bringing justice upon the ungodly, he is said to attack their world, their land, their skies. His coming in judgment on Nineveh is given in the most graphic speech by Nahum:

> The burden of Nineveh...Jehovah is a jealous God and avengeth; Jehovah avengeth and is full of wrath: Jehovah taketh vengeance on his adversaries, and he reserveth wrath for his enemies...Jehovah hath his way in the whirlwind and in the storm, and the clouds are dust of his feet. He rebuketh the sea and maketh it dry, and drieth up all the rivers...the mountains quake at him, and the hills melt: and the earth is upheaved at his presence, yea the whole

> world, and all that dwell therein.(1:1-5)

Here are allusions to past events — quaking mountains, dried-up rivers and seas, and burning pasture land. These describe the God who's about to judge Nineveh, but he doesn't do these things in destroying her. The prophet Micah makes use of the same speech here and claims God will do it to Judah:

> For, behold Jehovah cometh forth out of his place, and will come down and tread upon the high places of the earth. And the mountains shall be melted under him, and the valleys shall be cleft as wax before the fire, as waters that are poured down a steep place. For the transgression of Jacob is all this, and for the sins of the house of Israel. What is the transgression of Jacob? Is it not Samaria? And what are the high places of Judah? Are they not Jerusalem? Therefore I will make Samaria as a heap of the field, and as places for planting vineyards; and I will pour down the stones thereof into the valley, and I will uncover the foundations thereof.(1:3-6)

In what you've just read, we have the description of what God did to Jerusalem and Samaria, the capital of the northern kingdom. None of this literally happened. In Zephaniah, we have God's threat to judge Judah for her ungodliness and his intention to destroy from them the idolatry of Chemarim and Baal. He's going to attack the world of Judah and here's what he says:

> I will utterly consume all things from off the face of the ground, saith Jehovah. I will consume man and beast; I will consume the birds of the heavens, and the fishes of the sea, and the stumblingblocks with the wicked; and I will cut off man from the face of the ground, saith Jehovah.(1:2f).

This was never fulfilled (since you are here to read this), as you very well know. Here is an attack on Judah's world in the terms of the flood in Noah's day. Judah's world is under attack by God.

Now let me bring this into perspective with a quote from my little scope of Isaiah (p.23):

> When God is said to visit the iniquity of the ungodly upon them: He is said to turn their whole universe upside down! He destroys the heavens under which they live; He melts the stars of their sky; causes their forests and grazing land to wither; deprives them of the light from their sun and moon; dissolves their whole heaven; makes their moun-

tains to melt like wax and their whole earth to be without form, and void.

So, what did John see in Revelation 20:11? He saw the destruction of the world of the ungodly. Rome's world came to an end as did Babylon's, Edom's, and Judah's (see Jeremiah 4:23ff). Now, sometimes God did literally cause mountains to shake and fires to burn; sometimes he literally dried-up the waters and rivers. And it is the very fact that he did these things that enabled the prophets to borrow the language when speaking of judgments. WHAT THEN IS THE LANGUAGE OF JUDGMENT? God's dismantling of the ungodly man's world! **And what is the language of blessing?**

The opposite! Rivers break out in deserts and they blossom like roses. Animals become once more as they were in the days of the garden of Eden. Soil brings forth superabundantly. Men live much longer, and each one has his own piece of property. Infant deaths are banished; dead seas produce fish of every kind; hills and mountains drop milk and sweet wine. **God makes for his people a new heaven and earth!** If the language of judgment on the ungodly and oppressor is the destruction of their heaven and earth, what is the language of blessing? **The opposite!** Think about it a little. A new heaven and new earth for his people to live in.

What is the "new heaven" and "new earth"? It is a new environment, a new state of affairs. In that new heaven and earth, the oppressor doesn't exist. He's been dealt with, and his world has been destroyed. It's a new beginning for the people of the Lord. It deals specifically with the removal of a specific oppressor or a radical change of circumstancs.

Isaiah 65:1-end, tells us about just such a change in circumstances and environment. The earth part of the chapter tells about the ungodly and their ways. The Lord says he will destroy them and leave their name for a curse (to be used in taking oaths, since their judgment will be so horrifying) to the saints. The righteous are viewed as having undergone great pressures (15b), but the Lord says they will come through it all trusting in Jehovah "because the former troubles are forgotten, and because they are hid from mine eyes" (verse 16).

He goes on to tell them he is creating "new heavens and a new earth and the former things shall not be remembered, nor come into mind." In the 16th verse, he talked about the "former troubles" having passed away. In this verse, he speaks of "former things" having passed away. He has just said he creates "new heavens and a new earth" and now he urges them (v. 18), "But be ye glad in that which I create; for, behold, I create Jerusalem a rejoicing and her people a joy.

These two things explain each other: I create a new heaven and a new earth! I create Jerusalem a rejoicing and her people joy!

You'll notice he doesn't say he creates "Jerusalem." He says he creates Jerusalem **a rejoicing** and (he creates) her people **a joy**. The new heaven and earth is not Jerusalem. It's a state of affairs concerning Jerusalem. It's a condition surrounding Jerusalem. John saw the new Jerusalem **coming down out of** the new heaven — she is not the new heaven or earth. She dwells in the new heaven and earth.

Peter (2.3:13) says the Church ("we") looks for a new heaven and earth. This makes it very clear that the new heaven and earth is not the Church, but that which the Church looks for. If it be replied that Peter is saying: We are looking for the glorified state of the Church (if that is argued), I'd find nothing objectionable about it. It's not exactly the point, but it does make it clear that it's not the Church itself in view, but a state of, or condition of, the Church.

Let me sum up what I've been saying: I've been saying that when the oppressor is raging against the saints, or the ungodly is dominating the world, the world is said to belong to the oppressor or the ungodly. When God moves in judgment against the ungodly, he attacks **their** world (we've seen that in the trumpets and in the bowls, here in Revelation and in the plagues on Egypt). This is characteristic of the speech of the prophets. Since this is the language of judgment, we need to ask ourselves, what is the language of blessing? Logic says, the opposite. The scriptures bear out this conjecture, speaking of superabundant land, docile predators, remarkable longevity, and a new heaven and earth.

I've said, in light of Revelation 21:1f and 2 Peter 3:13, that the new heaven and earth is not the Church because according to John, he saw the Church coming down out of the new heaven. And Peter claims the Church was still looking for a new heaven and earth.

We've looked at Isaiah 65 and noted that two phrases are used relative to what God creates: I create a new heaven and earth!

I create Jerusalem a rejoicing and her people joy! The conclusion in light of all this is that the passing away of the old heaven and earth in Revelation 20 is the destruction and removal of the Roman world and the bringing in of a new environment, a state of blessing as indicated by the coming of a new heaven and earth.

VERSE 1. And the sea is no more — The sea here is not the glassy sea, for however holy men become, there will always be the awful holiness of God separating his creation and himself. This is not denying close (and closer) communion in eternity. It's simply affirming an unalterable truth about the transcendent holiness of God.

And furthermore, the context better suggests the sea from which the oppressor arose. Out of the earth came the lamb-like horror with the dragon's voice. Out of the sea came the gargantuan sea beast. These are gone, never to rise again. The whole Roman world is gone!

VERSE 2. I saw the holy city, new Jerusalem - This is no literal city, for we're told that it is "the bride, the wife of the Lamb" (9ff). Why is it called "new" Jerusalem? Because it is in contrast with the "old" Jerusalem? That's very likely the truth. True or not, this doesn't say the "old" Jerusalem has only now passed away. New Hampshire, New England, New York — these names have been around a long time. The "new" part doesn't necessitate a recent origin. The "new Jerusalem" was around a long time before Revelation was written.

Coming down out of heaven - The arrival of the new Jerusalem is seen from an earthly viewpoint. The city obviously comes down to earth. Why is that? What's being stressed? Its divine nature and origin. The two beasts came up out of the sea and earth. There is their human origin (see the comments on 13:1ff). This happens too in Daniel 7. While the beasts are said to rise out of the sea and the earth, the Messianic kingdom (embodied in the Son of Man) rides in the heavens. Here we have divine nature and origin contrasted to human and evil origin.

As a bride adorned for her husband - See the comments on 19:7ff concerning the marriage with the Lamb issue. Here we see the wife of Jesus. How does she look? Bloodstained, smoke-covered, and red-eyed? Indeed not. She has come through her great trial unsullied and looking the better for it. There is a purity connected with it all. She has been true to her Beloved and her dress speaks of her innocence, fidelity, and joy.

VERSE 3. The tabernacle of God is with men - The Church is spoken of as the dwelling place of God in numerous places. 1 Corinthians 3:16; Ephesians 2:20ff; 1 Peter 2:5 and others. Here is the condescension of God and the uplifting of man. That God would dwell in people is a remarkable privilege indeed. It's also a very great responsibility for him or her who is the temple. But it's more — it is a great boon to the world that the Church is the "house" of God **and here on earth!** We are being told in this passage that God isn't ashamed of his people. He is willing to be called their God. No, not willing, but pleased.

VERSE 4. And he shall wipe away every tear from their eyes - This has reference to the past troubles, of course. This is promised by Isaiah, to Israel, again and again. In 14:3, speaking of the pressures from Babylon, he says God will give you rest from your sorrow. In 65:19, he says that (under Jesus) there would be no weeping in Jerusalem, because the former troubles would have passed away. In verse 14, he contrasts the condition of the saints with the ungodly and says: My servants will sing for joy of heart, but ye shall cry for sorrow of heart. In 30:19, when he is discussing their troubles with Assyria, he rebukes them for running to Egypt for help instead of coming to him. However, he does assure them that he will take care of the Assyrian problem and that they will: Weep no more! He means of course in reference to the Assyrian problem. In 35:9, he is speaking of the glory the Jew would enjoy under Jesus (if they'd only accept him) and part of it is: They shall obtain gladness and joy, and sorrow and sighing shall flee away.

In 25:8, we have a prophecy of God's going to punish Israel's enemies who have had the power of life and death over her (and usually gave her death). In the process of presenting it, he said: He hath swallowed up death for ever; and the Lord Jehovah will wipe away tears from off all faces; and the reproach of his people will he take away from off all the earth. That the Holy Spirit has two things in mind in this passage, I'm not willing to dispute, but that he's talking about removing Israel's enemies and taking away her reproach off the earth, I think, is clear. These and others help us to see that the joys expressed in Revelation are connected with the immediate problem they faced. (I don't mean by that, those O.T. passages speak of immediate problems — the language is similar to that in Revelation 20 — therefore, Revelation 20 speaks of an immediate problem. That would be poor argumentation altogether). If you've been given no contextual reasons for believeing that Revelation 20 is dealing with an immediate problem, you've been given nothing worthwhile.

And death shall be no more...the first things are passed away - Death has been personified in this book. It is an enemy of the people. It was used by Rome against God's people, but God defeated her. **Rome would martyr no more!** What we said about the Devil **not** being cast into the fire immediately after the defeat of Rome is true also of death and Hades.

It's interesting that in Isaiah 65:20ff, the blessings to be found in Christ are expressed in remarkable longevity. Infants, **if** they die, die at one hundred years of age. Men live as long as trees. Here is the direction our Revelation passage may be going. Isaiah pictures his blessings by the virtual abolition of death, and John by the abolition of death. (Bear in mind the vision of the resurrection to 1,000 years of life in 20:4).

But I think the prominent thought in all of this is found in passages like Isaiah 28:14-18. There we find that the Judean leaders had made a "covenant with death" and they had an "agreement with Sheol." The point? They had bribed Assyria (who had the power of death) to leave her alone. Assyria, the oppressing power, is called "death" in this passage. Does that startle you? Sound strange? Don't close your mind now. Read the passage for yourself.

Ahaz paid tribute to Assyria to destroy Pekah, king of Israel, and Rezin, the Syrian king. The prophet Isaiah was telling the king he didn't need Assyria, and in any case, she was not to be trusted — she would turn on him. The reaction of the Judeans was that they had an agreement with "Sheol" and a "covenant with death." God assures them in 28:16 that the only thing which would save Jerusalem and the people, was himself. He was the only foundation upon which Jerusalem's future was secure. He was a **tried stone**. To prove his point, he says he will "annul" their "covenant with death" (v. 18), and he would see to it that their "agreement with Sheol" would not stand.

He did just that! Assyria finally came against Judea and blitzed all the fortified cities, leaving only Jerusalem to be taken. Sennacherib and his army surrounded the city, but God stopped him in just one night (see chapters 29,36,37). Now why was Assyria called "death and Sheol?" Because at that time, she had the power of death — she could destroy nations. **But God brought her to naught!** See again Isaiah 26:14-21. Read it carefully. Under Babylonian oppression and captivity the Jews were viewed, apocalyptically, as in their graves (Ezekiel 37:12ff).

In defeating these nations, God defeated "death." In defeating Rome (or anyone else like her), death is defeated. **This is the point in Revelation 21:4.**

The first things are passed away...I make all things new - This, it seems to me, accords with what we've been saying. The oppressor's gone and the future is secure, come what may!

VERSES 5b-8. These words are true, Write - This was not just talk! This Jesus to whom the revelation was given to give to the servants, wore that very name, "Faithful and True." He told no lies, and what is more, he spoke the full truth. But this is being said to lead up to the decision which he must call them to make. He has declared what is about to begin transpiring, but the telling of it is over; they must make up their minds what they are going to do.

VERSE 6. They are come to pass - That is, the "things" are come to pass of which he has been speaking. There we have the certainty of their fulfillment. It is not: They will surely be done. That would do, but it is not as dramatic or as mind-catching. Statements like these are pondered more, and thus gain their end.

I am the Alpha and the Omega, the beginning and the end -This is more than a marker of time. It speaks of purpose and goal. It began because there was a reason for its beginning, and that purpose will be accomplished. It will end only when God has seen that his purposes are fulfilled. He is the beginning and the end; **therefore,** he is in a position to know of the certainty of fulfillment. So when he says "they are come to pass," we can be sure of it!

I will give unto him that is athirst...freely - Here all the blessings God has to offer are summed up in the "water of life" figure. This can be seen by the next statement: He that overcometh shall inherit **these things.** That is, the things mentioned in verses 3ff. They will be given freely. God will be pleased to call him his "son" and He is God. (Here's another indication that the overcomer is sometimes promised **the continuation** of things he already enjoys.

VERSE 8. But for the fearful, and unbelieveing - Here's the call to decision he's been working up to. A choice must be made. The joys offered are free, but there must be a commitment to God by the one to enjoy them. He that is so afraid that he will not commit himself to the Lord, will have to perish with the rest of the ungodly crew. It is either living water or endless fire. Both of these are figures. It's a wild abuse of this scripture, to teach that because someone now and then, due to embarrassment or fear, doesn't speak about Jesus when they could have, are heading for the lake of fire. If there is repentance, there is utter forgiveness!

VERSES 9-27. I will show thee the Bride, the Wife of the Lamb - We've said enough about the Church's relationship to the Lord as a "wife." See Ephesians 5:22-33. We'll do well to keep this invitation in view, for what he is about to show him is the Church — **not heaven!!**

VERSE 10. And he carried me away...to a mountain - Ezekiel had a similar experience in chapter 40:2-4. Both prophets have a similar (in general) vision. Both saw the glory of the Temple of God (City of God) and the blessings associated with it. John sees the new Jerusalem coming down out of heaven. We have here her divine origin.

VERSE 11. Having the glory of God - She is no earthly city, and so she glows with a heavenly glory. The very glory of God himself. As Jesus her master came down from heaven and reflected the glory of his Father (John 1:14), so now does the Wife of the Lamb.

VERSE 12,13. Having a wall, great and high; having twelve gates -The gates are what we are specially called to see here. They are twelve in number — the number of the people of God because she is the "city" or "people" of God. When the tabernacle was raised in days of old, it took the central place and the twelve tribes encamped around it — three on each side — north, south, east, and west. See Ezekiel 48:31-35. On the gates are the names of the twelve tribes. Everything about this city marks it out as the city of God's people, BUT IT IS NOT A LITERAL CITY. We've been told, it is the Lamb's wife — the people! We'll hear more about the gates and walls soon.

VERSE 14. Twelve foundations...on them...names of the 12 apostles - One more time we are assured that we are here seeing an image of the Church of God. In Ephesians 2:20, we hear of the "foundation of the apostles and prophets." This doesn't mean the apostles themselves are part of the foundation — the Church is built on what they taught. (The Mormons are fond of telling us we must have living apostles or else we have the wrong foundation. It's interesting that they don't have living prophets (plural), which is what the passage demands. I guess they have the wrong foundation too — huh?

VERSES 15-17. A golden reed to measure the city - Ezekiel had the same experience. Everything he saw, he measured (see chapters 40-43). What's the point of the measuring? It's twofold — 1) To stress its holiness. 2) To stress its glory.

In Ekekiel 42:20, we are told this very thing was true of his measuring. We'll find that when John measures, he learns it is foursquare, just like a huge "holy of holies." It's a cube. As long and broad as it is high. How long is it? It is twelve (there's that number again) thousand (there's that number again) furlongs. This is the city of GOD'S PEOPLE. How high? How broad? Its whole measurement says again and again: This is the city of GOD'S PEOPLE! How **thick** are the walls? 12 by 12 cubits. Everything about its measurements say: This is the city of GOD's PEOPLE.

But this has a responsibility with it. This isn't Babylon in which iniquity dwells. This is the Church wherein GOD dwells. This constant reiteration (by measurement) that it is the city OF GOD demands holiness. Listen to how God summed up the measuring of Ezekiel (see 43:10-12):

> Thou, son of man, show the house to the house of Israel, that they may be ashamed of their iniquities; and let them measure the pattern. And if they be ashamed of all that

> they have done, make known unto them the form of the house...that they may keep the whole form thereof, and all the ordinances thereof, and do them. This is the law of the house: upon the top of the mountain the whole limit thereof round about shall be most holy. Behold, this is the law of the house.

You'll observe that measurements were to be given to Israel to make them ashamed! The measurements spoke of holiness! If they acknowledged, by being rebuked into repentance by the mere measurements, they were then to be told about the form of the house that they "might keep" it.

But the measuring also spoke of its glory and security. It was 1500 miles wide, long, and high. Now get this — about 250 times higher then Everest in the Himalayas. Walvoord observed that this is "somewhat **higher than** the skyscrapers we know." I'd say so — wouldn't you? Walvoord and Lindsey hold this to be a literal city, and these, literal measurements. John's point is clear — its squareness would speak not only of holiness, but of stability. No one could climb its walls. No one could crash the gates with 12 angels there. No one could batter down the walls (on an 18-inch cubit, they are 216 feet thick). There is then, no fear of being taken. Such a massive city would be the talk of the world. From Egypt (the border) to the Euphrates was only (about) 490 miles. What do you think these measurements would do to the eyes of a person in that part of the world? Oh, that's a silly question — what would it do to anyone's eyes, from any part of the world?

VERSES 18-21. The wall thereof was jasper and the city was pure gold - There follows a staggering description of preciousness. It makes Solomon's temple seem like a shanty. The description, however, is not new to John. Isaiah 54:11ff has already introduced us to the thought of a city of jewels. Yes, John's city is more grand, but it is on the same lines. Now the millennial principle of interpretation is this: If you read something in prophecy which has not been literally fulfilled, look for it in the future. That's **exactly** how they apply it! Now, I'm wondering, since the city has never been built as Isaiah 54:11ff describes it, if they are expecting it in the future to be built. John's city has a pearl for each gate. Isaiah's has a carbuncle for each gate. Who is going to build the Isaian city?

VERSE 22. And I saw no temple therein - That would have spoken of separation between God and his people, and this is not the point being stressed here. In the Old Testament, there was a tabernacle with an especially holy place, into which none could go but the High Priest, and he on only one day of the year. That awful "room" was not only to keep the people out, but to keep God in.

In our idealized picture here, of a city, there is no inner, exclusive sanctuary. They dwell in God and he in them (see the comments on verse 3), as 1 John 2:24 and other passages make clear. This in no way negates the fact that God is awfully holy!

VERSE 23. And the city hath no need of the sun - Isaiah had long ago said this of Jerusalem (60:19ff). In the picture given to us in Isaiah 60:1-end, we have Israel going through some very trying times — she is drifting through darkness. But her dawn comes. Her dawn, however, is not the coming up of the physical sun, but of her Lord shining on her and giving her a new "day." While others may stumble in darkness, Jerusalem will be well lighted. For this cause the nations will come to her that they might walk in her light. Need I say, the point is spritual illumination? So it is here.

VERSE 24. And all the nations shall walk amid the light thereof -We are led to this from the previous verse. This looks to me to be a real difficulty for anyone who would place the point of these visions, chronologically after the final judgment and in eternity. If this be in eternity, where do these "nations" come from? Were not all the unsaved cast into the lake of fire after the final judgment and the end of the world?

Some have tried to get around this by saying these "nations" are Christians, but this will hardly do, for the word is not so used in the book. And furthermore, if they were Christians, they would BE part of the city. Remember, what we are reading about is not a literal city, but the people of God. **If these nations are the people of God, they ARE the city.**

It creates a difficulty for the premillennialists for the same reason. He insists the "new Jerusalem" is a literal city and so avoids the criticism which would insist that saved nations would be a part of the "city." However, he is open to the criticism that nowhere in the book of Revelation, does the phrase "kings of the earth" speak of believers. And how anyone can insist that this is a literal city is beyond me. Lindsey even feels the city might be suspended in the sky all the while the millenium is going on.

And the kings of the earth shall bring their glory into it - Isaiah had spoken of this too (60:10ff). Read the text for yourself. This was God's way of saying that Jerusalem would be vindicated. Isaiah sees her hurt and in captivity, but she would not always be. One day she'd constitute the Church and all the nations would flow into her and bring with them their talents, strength, and help. Isaiah did not say **all** the nations would be converted. He simply said that the day would come when Jerusalem would not be under the heel of the world anymore. In Jesus Christ, the believing Jew was glorified. We go to them for a Savior (a Jew) and for Jewish apostles and prophets and for a Bible — written by Jews (Luke got his material from Jews). Salvation is of the Jews (said Jesus). This was Isaiah's point. In the Revelation, Jewishness is lost, but the Church is yet the light-bearer. Earlier in the book, the Church was under the whip, but now she has been vindicated! In her alone lies the hope of the nations. If they walk in light, they walk in her light! The Church which they despised and beat is now the city set on a hill. The shivering and huddled little flock whose "only crime was Christ" was now astride the nations!

VERSE 25. The gates...shall in no wise be shut by day - Isaiah 60:20 speaks like this. We are told there would be no night for Jerusalem because "the days of thy mourning shall be ended." Read the text in Isaiah. Night and darkness in Revelation as you know, speak often of the gloomy side of things — the evil side of things. Since the Lord will act as their sun, they will have no night.

You've got to bear in mind now, that the light of the Lord is only shining in the city of Jerusalem. This is clearly seen by the fact that the nations have to walk in her light. They themselves are without it, making it clear once more that the millennial view (and others), which places this whole series in eternity, is incorrect, for we have here unsaved nations and kings of the earth.

VERSE 27. (There won't) **enter into it anything unclean** - Chapter 22:15 seems to say there are the ungodly outside the city, but they won't be permitted to enter because it is a city of holiness. Because there are angel guards.

Perhaps as well as holiness, we are hearing about security. Isaiah 52:1,2 says this:

> Awake, awake, put on thy strength O Zion; put on your beautiful garments, O Jerusalem, the holy city; for henceforth there shall no more come into thee the uncircumcised and the unclean. Shake thyself from the dust; Arise, sit on thy throne O Jerusalem: Loose thyself from the bonds of thy neck, O captive daughter of Zion.

Whether this is true or not, the emphasis is on the complete holiness of the city. The only people permitted to enter the city are saved ones.

Summary

Chapter 21 is the triumphant Church. **But it is the triumphant Church in history.** It has not moved into heaven. It still shines among the nations and brings light to those that walk in darkness.

The figures used to show its triumph and glory could just as easily be used of her eternal abode in heaven, but that is not what John uses them for. Most of his language comes from the prophets (especially Isaiah) as **this** context shows. It is used in the same fashion as the language of the prophets.

The prophets spoke of this present age under Jesus and their language paints the ideal picture. I suggest you just sit down and read Isaiah (without delving into it), just to acquaint yourself with the form of his language. Chapter 20 saw the wrap-up of all that was connected with Rome. But then it went on to speak to us of the assurance for the future. No enemy, however large or strong, would dent a wall of Jerusalem. This is the perspective of chapter 21.

The **picture** in chapter 21 is of a new universe and a huge jeweled city coming down out of heaven and resting on the earth. The people who live in that city are smiling and happy — they have no fear of any invasion and death. It is a huge city having twelve gates and twelve foundations and it is 12,000 furlongs broad, long, and high. It is a city full of supernatural light and it is in this light that the nations of the earth walk. The city is honored and foreigners bring their glory into it.

1 And he showed me a river of the water of life clear as crystal coming from the throne of God & of the Lamb,
2

Questions on Chapter 22

1. What does the water of life stand for? blessings from God and the Christians [illegible]
2. What prophet uses the same type of figures? Ezikeel
3. Why twelve fruits and twelve yields? to provide for God's children
4. What were the leaves of the tree for? for healing for the nations
5. What do you make of "no more curse"? Like the Eden curse for eating from the [illegible]
6. What's meant by "they shall see his face"? closeness & communion
7. What are we told about the things the angel showed? They are about to happen
8. Why do we read again that John bowed to the angel? to show only God is to be worshipped
9. Who was told to seal up his book? Daniel
10. Who was told not to? John
11. Specifically now, why was he told not to? be. what he was told would soon happen.
12. What do you make of that? truth
13. What's the thrust of 11-15? See analysis p 330 v. Warning & challenge
14. Specifically now, what plagues will be added to the one who tampers with the book? the plagues in this book
15. What does that let you know about the plagues? anytime plagues in this book will hit you if you tamper.
16. Could a tamperer who lived in the 5th century be plagued with the plagues written in the book? Yes
17. Could tamperers in the 10th century have been plagued with a nuclear war and oceans turned into blood? No
18. What does this tell you of the millennial view? not truthful
19. What could be taken from a tamperer? the life from tree of life
20. Do non-Christians have a share in the tree of life or the new Jerusalem? No
21. What does that prove to you? Do not tamper w/ God's Word, period!

2 in the middle of its street. And on either side of the river was the tree of life, bearing 12 kinds of fruit yielding its fruit every month and the leaves of the tree were for healing of the nations.
3 And there shall no longer be any curse and the throne of God & of the Lamb shall be in it & His bond-servant shall serve Him.
4 and they shall see His face and His name shall be on their foreheads
5 And there shall no longer be any night and they shall not have need of the light of a lamp nor the light of the sun because the Lord God shall illumine them & they shall reign forever & ever.

6 And he said to me "These words are faithful + true
+ the Lord the God of the spirits of the prophets sent
His angel to show to His bond-servant the things
which must shortly take place.
7 And behold I am coming quickly. Blessed is he who
heeds the words of the prophecy of this book.

Analysis of Chapter 22

I. The river and the trees of life: 1-3 , of God + the Lamb

river as it gets deeper heals more.

river of life

A. The river from the throne: verse 1

B. The trees on each side of the river: verse 2 blessings from God

C. The curse removed; verse 3 The Garden of Eden

II. The close communion: 3-5 Closeness like the Garden of Eden

A. The communicants: verse 3

B. The closeness of the communion: verses 4-5 See God face to face like Moses - need maturity

The saints reign now + forever.

C. The duration of the communion: verse 5

III. The assurance and the encouragement: 6-7

A. The certain truth of the visions; verse 6 An Angel came and told John the truth, that was about to happen.

Blessed are those who heed the words of this prophecy.

B. Blessing associated with obedience: verse 7

IV. John and the angel: 8-9

A. John's attempt to worship the angel: verse 8 Shows that only God can be worshipped

Angel made it clear to John + to us that only God is to be worshipped.

B. The rebuke and instruction: verse 9

V. Warning and challenge: 10-15

A. The explicit instruction: verse 10 do not seal up the book for the time is near.

B. The call to endurance and incentive given: verses 11-15

VI. More assurance, invitation, and warning: 16-20

everyone invited by the Son to come to Him.

A. Assurance and invitation: verses 16-17

B. Warning: verses 18-19 once saved not always saved the right can be taken from you.

C. More assurance: verse 20

VII. Closing salutation: 21

8 And I John am the one who heard and saw these
things. And when I heard and saw, I fell down
to worship at the feet of the angel who showed
me these things.
9 And he said to me, "Do not do that. I am a
fellow-servant of yours and of your brethren
the prophets and of those who heed the words
of this book; worship God."

Comments on Chapter 22

VERSES 1-3. He showed me a river of water of life — As I write this, I'm thirsty and this crystal clear water is exciting my thirst. What a book! Jesus spoke of "living water" to the woman of Samaria, so the figure isn't fresh with John. Water is such an important thing — such a blessing. To us who (normally) have it at our disposal in such quantities, the figure isn't quite as gripping as it would be to a Jew from Palestine or any native of that area. Men in many areas of the world still fight and die for water.

But this isn't ordinary water. (Lindsey thinks it will be a "tangible" manifestation of the Holy Spirit — there he goes figurizing again when he doesn't need to.) In John 4, Jesus uses it (the figure) to speak, I think, of all the blessings which flow from being his child. In John 7:37-39, he used it of the Holy Spirit. This may mean we're supposed to see, from both passages, that the water stands for the blessings of God brought to us through the medium of the Holy Spirit.

Whatever the water is intended to mean, specifically, it is part of an overall picture of the provisions of God for his people. In 7:16,17, we are told that the Lamb would provide just what they have here. The notion that one doesn't get to drink of the waters of life until eternity, is not countenanced here (21:17), nor in John 4 where Jesus offers it to the woman at the well (verse 10).

Ezekiel in 47:1-12 offers us a similar picture (differing in some things — as usual). Zechariah (14:1,8) speaks, not of one, but of two rivers which flow in opposite directions. Joel (3:18) also gves us the picture of a river flowing from the house of Jehovah. Ezekiel's picture is fuller, and it associates the trees of life with the river as does John.This picture of a river flowing and trees of life send us back, of course, to the garden of Eden. You must read Ezekiel's picture. He speaks four times of the healing produced by the river and the trees. Listen to him:

> An he brought me back unto the door of the house; and behold, waters issued out from under the threshold of the house eastward...Then he...led me round by the way without unto the outer gate, by the way of the gate that looketh toward the east; and, behold, there ran out waters on the right side. When the man went forth eastward with the line in his hand, he measured a thousand cubits, and he caused me to pass through the waters, waters that were to the ankles. Again he measured, and caused me to pass through the waters, waters that were to the knees,

> Again...waters that were to the loins. Afterward he measured a thousand; and it was a river that I could not pass through..behold, upon the bank of the river were very many trees on the one side and on the other...These waters issue forth toward the eastern region, and shall go down into the Arabah; and they shall to toward the sea: into the sea shall the waters go...and the waters shall be healed...and the water of the sea shall be healed, and everything shall live whithersoever the river cometh...But the miry places thereof, and the marshes thereof, shall not be healed; but shall be given up to salt. And by the river upon the bank thereof, on this side and on that side, shall grow every tree for food, whose leaf shall not wither, neither shall the fruit thereof fail; it shall bring forth new fruit every month, because the waters thereof issue out of the sanctuary; and the fruit thereof shall be for food, and the leaf thereof for healing.

The whole picture is one of the blessedness of the people of God. The provisions God has made for them. Here is a river which flows from the sanctuary (which is, in Ezekiel, God's throne, 43:6,7), but without tributaries. The farther it flows, the deeper it gets, and the more healing it does. Are we wrong in concluding that this speaks of the blessings of God, provided for the righteous, and that these blessings flow from God through the righteous into the barren and dead places of the world?

Proceeding out of the throne of God, and of the Lamb — (The distinction between the throne of God and the throne of David is not countenanced by scripture.) In this phrase we have the mercy and the authority of God combined. God's mercy and his authority are not in competition one with another. People, there has to be authority, somewhere in someone, or else there can be no order or blessing. Anarchy cannot bring blessing. The only real hope for the future is to let God rule in our lives. That will enable him to best provide for us. God deliver us from a future in which man is going to be the savior! We've had enough of man's working it out for us. Isidor Isaac Rabi (the 1965) Chairman of the general advisory committee to the Atomic Energy Commission, and Nobel Prize winner for physics (1944) claimed: Somehow the scientific education diminishes the ambition for power and worldly influence. He went on to suggest we can depend on science to do the best for our world, because he (the scientist) has "a feeling for the possibilities of development or evolution in a current situation" and "a certain sense of rightness and equity, sometimes naive but rarely on the wrong track'' (quoted by Rushdoony in ''The Mythology of Science,'' page 21). I'd say Rabi must be a staggering good physicist, but is really out of touch with the heart of man. Jeremiah could have taught him a thing or two about that (17:9).

Does the fact that the throne is said to be ''and of the Lamb'' suggest that we're still considering the delegated authority which Jesus is exercising now? If that were true, then we'd have another reason to conclude that this secton has no ''after-judgment-in-eternity'' chronology attached to it. When the present scene winds up, Jesus surrenders the kingdom unto the Father and then takes his place as Ruler, no longer with a delegated authority, but sovereignty by virtue of his own deity. See 1 Corinthians 15:24f.

VERSE 2. The tree of life, bearing twelve manner of fruits — There's that number 12 again. The tree of life figure is borrowed from the literal tree in the garden of Eden. We just read in Ezekiel that his vision was built partly on that Eden scene also. This fruit is provided for the people of God even as the first tree of life was provided for God's children.

Yielding its fruit every month — Not only does this tree provide twelve different kinds of fruit, it provides them twelve times a year. Over and over again, we are being told that these blessings belong to the people of God. The whole scene takes place inside the city and for its inhabitants.

The leaves of the tree were for the healing of the nations — There we have those nations again. They are clearly distinguished from the city! (Remember the city is not a literal city, but is a figure for the people of God!) The blessings of the city, while partaken of only by the populace of that city, are yet to be made a blessing to others. Others are offered the opportunity to drink of the water of life freely (22:17). In this passage we are told the leaves are for the healing of the nations.

Can this really be set in eternity? Where would the ''nations'' come from? (Check the rest of the book and see if the ''nations'' speak of the people of God.'' And in what respect would they need healing? Is this physical healing? On anyone's view, this can't be right — right?! It would have to speak of spiritual healing. But in eternity, will there be a need of spiritual healing?

Walvoord and Lindsey are hit with this problem, so they both assert that the word ''healing'' should be rendered ''health.'' This word and its cognates occur 48 times in the New Testament. NOT ONCE is it rendered ''health.'' None of the Greek scholars I have at my disposal even hint that this might be its meaning. The versions all militate against this claim.

Moffatt: The leaves served to heal the nations.
RSV: The leaves of the tree were for the healing of the nations.
KJV: The leaves of the tree were for the healing of the nations.
NIV: And the leaves of the tree are for the healing of the nations.
NAS: And the leaves of the tree were for the healing of the nations.
NEB: The leaves of the tree were for the healing of the nations.
Williams (C.B.): And its leaves contained the remedy to cure the nations.
20th Century: And the leaves of the tree are for the healing of the nations.
Goodspeed: And its leaves were a cure for the heathen.
Douay Version: And the leaves of the tree were for the healing of the nations.
Authentic N.T.: The leaves of the tree were for the healing of the nations.
American Bible Union: The leaves of the tree are for the healing of the nations.
NLB: The leaves were used for medicine to heal the nations.
Young's Literal: And the leaves of the tree are for the service of the nations.
Basic English: And the leaves of the tree give life to the nations.
Wuest: And the leaves of the tree were for the health of the nations.

As you can see from the survey of all these, only one takes the position held by Lindsey and Walvoord. He's a fellow-premillenarian, and if you've read his works, you know that he is deeply committed to it. He, with Lindsey and Walvoord, saw the problem and knew that he couldn't have "healing" going on in heaven and so gives us "health." And how did Wuest render Luke 9:11 where the same word and the same form of that word occurs? "Healing!"

The Basic English doesn't even look like a translation, for no one would ever get "life" out of "therapeia." Young gives the word one of its possible renderings. The root word carried with it the idea of "service." Check an Englishman's Greek Concordance or examine the valuable "Greek-English Concordance" by J.B. Smith (Herald Press).

What is the testimony then of the Greek scholars and the versions? That "health" is not the meaning of the word here! "Healing" is how it should be rendered. If that is true, it would be beyond doubt that John is not seeing a presentation of things as they are in the after-life, in eternity.

Our passage, then, is telling us that there are nations who are in need of healing and that the blessings which the Church of God has at its disposal are capable of answering the needs of the nations. The city gives light to those nations and the leaves of the tree offer healing to those nations. The river offers them water to drink and the tree has fruit for them to eat of.

VERSE 3. And there shall be no more curse — Zechariah 8:13 speaks of Israel as having been at one time, a curse among the nations. They would beat her and submit her to shame and slander. God there promised he would bless her and that she would no more be a curse but "a blessing." Perhaps this is what John has in mind. On the other hand, we are calling on things from the garden of Eden, and we may well be hearing here an allusion to the curse which came on the ground for man's sake (Genesis 3:17ff). In this park-like scene, we are seeing a river bank producing food and healing elements — this is no cursed land. Zechariah (14:9-11) also knows this use of the expression, for he will speak of the property of Jerusalem being "made like the Arabah." He goes on to say: And men shall dwell therein, and there shall be no more curse: but Jerusalem shall dwell safely.

As we can gather from the comparison of Zechariah and Ezekiel (see the passage above), the Arabah had two aspects to it. The Arabah was/is the great ravine beginning between the Lebanons and the Ante-Lebanons (mountain ranges) and runs all the way down into central Africa. It takes in the whole Jordan valley which is luxuriant and tropical, but it also includes the section of the Dead Sea and southward, which is barren and desolate. Zechariah was alluding to the luxuriant section and Ezekiel to the barren. So "no more curse" may well be calling once more on the garden of Eden for its point (as does Isaiah 11:6ff).

VERSES 3-5. The throne of God and of the Lamb shall be therein — But this is nothing new, for the Lord has always been viewed as ruling from the Church, his dwelling place. The "therein" speaks of "in the city." See Ezekiel 43:6,7 and Isaiah 24:23 with Psalm 2:6. Lindsey and Walvoord hold that the Lord will have his throne on the earth, in the new Jerusalem, for all eternity.

And they shall see his face...his name shall be on their foreheads — This speaks of closeness of communion. To see one "face to face" is to see with real clearness. Job, speaking of God, said he had heard of him with the hearing of the ear but now: Mine eye seeth thee (42:5). Deuteronomy 34:10 speaks of God having known Moses "face to face." This is what he meant when he said in Numbers 12:8 that he would speak to Moses "mouth to mouth, even manifestly." Read that whole section (1-8). The Psalmists spoke of the righteous seeing the face of the Lord (11:7; 17:15) and dwelling in his presence (140:13). Paul spoke of a stage of immaturity in which, lacking love, the Corinthians were gaining no real conception of God. True they had spiritual gifts (miraculous in nature too), but they were not grasping the real nature of God through these because they were loveless. They saw through a glass darkly. Once perfection (maturity, due to love) came, they'd see "face to face." See 1 Corinthians 13:8-end.

John spoke here of a closeness of communion between the Lord and his people. He wasn't indicating they didn't have close communion before, only that it would continue and deepen. Since they had become his children, they had his name on their foreheads (the High Priest carried a kind of medallion on his forehead saying "Holiness to the Lord"), so what we are being told here is nothing new. The joys and privileges they possessed would always be theirs. That's the message!

VERSE 5. There shall be night no more — Since the city depends on the Lord for her light, and he ever shines, there is a nightless city! What a beautiful picture. Now there is nothing wrong with night, but it is often used as an equivalent to darkness and that speaks, in apocalyptic literature, of gloom and evil.

They shall reign for ever and ever — Here's more of the same. We are told in 5:10 that this kingdom of priests "reign on the earth." We have been told in 20:4 that the martyrs "reigned." So live or die, the saints reign. Now and for always, the saints reign. They reign because **He** reigns.

VERSE 6,7. These words are faithful and true — The book of Revelation was only a book (yes, it was God's book, but it was only a book), and the people might forget the truths here told when the hard times came. They have been told already, several times, and will be told again several times, that what is written is true! Depend on it!

The things which must shortly come to pass — He who doesn't take this expression into account has not been fair to the book. See the comments on it in 1:1. Lindsey doesn't even touch the phrase! The events of John's book had to begin right there in his days or we can know absolutely nothing about them. If we can't understand that expression, how dare we say we understand the rest?!

VERSE 7. And, behold, I come quickly — The word "taku" occurs 7 times in the book. In 2:5,16; 3:11; 11:14; 22:7,12,20. Its cognate "takos" occurs twice — 1:1; 22:6. Thayer defines "taku" as: Quickly, speedily (without delay) — p. 616. He speaks of "takos" in the New Testament as meaning, quickly, shortly, speedily, soon (Ibid.). What do you think?

Blessed is he that keepeth the words of the prophecy — Here again we are seeing the saints being strengthened by warning for the trials they are going to face. The Christian is about to face a war which would be long and drawn out. He needs encouragement and he needs to be warned!

VERSES 8-9. And I John am he that heard and saw these things — These churches knew John. He is adding his name here, once more, to confirm to the brethren the authoritativeness of this book.

I fell down to worship before the feet of the angel — I cannot but believe that this is written because it is a part of the vision God gave him, rather than his own personal response. It has already happened and he's been rebuked for it. If the first had been in non-visionary life, I'd be surprised. If the second was in non-visionary life, we should be utterly amazed. What then might be the point? It is what we have already suggested. This is one sure way to get the brethren to see their hope lies in God, and in no other! Further, if holy angels cannot be worshiped, much less can some blasphemous emperor or emperor's representative! Only God can deliver; therefore, only God should be worshiped.

VERSE 10-15. Seal not up the words of the prophecy of this book The opposite command given to Daniel. And why was the opposite command given? For the opposite reason. Look: **Daniel 8:26**

> But shut thou up the vision; for it belongeth to many days to come.

> Seal not up the words of the prophecy of this book; for the time is at hand.

What do you think of a whole school of interpretation which builds its case on the book of Revelation and which says: Nothing in the book of Revelation from chapter 4-22 has ever been fulfilled. It is all still future.

John F. Walvoord is the present president of the Dallas Theological Seminary in Dallas. He's been president since 1952. Wilbur Smith holds him to be the leading exponent of millennialism in America. He taught Hal Lindsey, who has done more to popularize this theory (in this day) than anyone in the country. It was Walvoord who said:

"The book of Revelation is, of course, the classic passage on premillennialism. Revelation...if taken in its plain intent, yields a simple outline of premillennial truth...the only method of interpretation of Revelation which has ever yielded a consistent answer to the question of its meaning is that which interprets the book...as having its general revelation plain, one to be fulfilled literally, and therefore subject to future fulfillment" ("The Millennial Kingdom," p. 118)

This makes it clear how important to their whole system is their view of the book of Revelation. Now look again at the two statements from Daniel and Revelation. **What strikes you about these?** Are you not told by these that one vision relates to a long time in the future and the other speaks of one just about to unfold?

Are you aware that the prophecy in Daniel was fulfilled within 400 years? Read the two phrases again and ask yourself: In light of these two verses (both uttered by God to men) —

1. Is Daniel's vision said to be at some distance in his future?
2. Is John's vision said to be at some time distant in his future?
3. Is John's vision said to be at some time close to his day?
4. Does not the putting of John's vision to over 1900 years in his future reflect badly on the author of his book who said "the time is at hand" and "this concerns things which must shortly come to pass"?

Do you wonder why Lindsey said ABSOLUTELY NOTHING about this text (or the other 3)? See the comments on 1:1,3.

VERSES 11-12. He that is unrighteous, let him do unrighteousness — These verses reflect Daniel 12:10 and Isaiah 32:5-8. The Lord is not encouraging the wicked in their wickedness. He's stating their character in general. Daniel (in the place cited) is concerned because he has just heard his people are going to go through the mill. He is told not to worry because the righteous will be blessed in their doing and the evil will be punished for theirs. There is a broad line drawn between the wicked and the righteous. God recognizes the various types of men, but puts them into only two categories. He speaks the conclusion that experience knows, that (apart from notable exceptions) people get into their ruts and continue that way.

But more, in Isaiah 32, we hear of the coming day of the righteous, when the evil men will be recognized for what they are. The righteous will see through them and will not be fooled by them. The "fool shall be no more called noble, nor the churl bountiful..." God's people will recognize the difference between wickedness and righteousness. When the saints, says John, see wickedness, they'll know what it is (reference to emperor worship, etc.), and they'll know what righteousness is, and will get on with it.

VERSE 12. To render to each man according as his work is - one earns God's favor, but there is no one who is in favor with God who makes a practice of evil. 1 John 3:5-7 speaks clearly to this point.

VERSES 13-15. I am the Alpha and the Omega — We've already commented that this stresses more than eternality, but speaks of the ground or basis for living. With his will, life begins and ends — the whole creation was made "unto" him as well as "by" him (Colossians 1:16).

Blessed are they that wash their robes — Here we have an allusion to 3:4 and 7:14. There is in this remark the idea of the individual's commitment and the ability of Jesus. Here the point stressed is the person's going to Jesus rather than what Jesus can do for him. In this whole section the stress is on the human participation in the divine work. See 19:8.

That they may have the right...to the tree of life — The tree of life is in the city and only the faithful live there. The "right" is a privilege granted to those who belong to Jesus, but that right can be taken from the saint. 22:19 says that God will "take away his part from the tree of life" who meddles with the book. This clearly proves (it seems to me) two things: 1) We are not here discussing conditions in eternity; 2) The notion of "once saved, always saved" is not a Bible doctrine.

VERSE 15. Without are the dogs, and the sorcerers — Outside the city this is the society. Get a concordance and go through the New Testament on "dogs." In our part of the world a "dog" speaks of a lot of nice things. We think of a boy and his dog; a man and his dog; a shepherd and his dog. Dogs in the east, however, mostly ran in packs and were scurvy, mangy, and altogether unpleasant. See Philippians 3:2 and Psalm 22:16. John here associates their unmanageableness and uncleanness with people of a certain character.

VERSES 16-20. I Jesus have sent mine angel to testify unto you these things — Here is more assurance for John and for the Churches that this book is indeed a revelation from the Lord. We who have inherited the Bible after many centuries know beyond a shadow of a doubt that it is indeed God's word, but these churches needed assurance. And besides, this was no ordinary letter, like say, Philippians. That one spoke of joy and the finer things of life in Christ. This one spoke of fierce persecution and war!

I am the root and the offspring of David — He is the promised Redeemer. He is the fulfillment of prophecy; therefore, when he speaks of true prophecy (not always "fore-telling"), he knows what he's talking about. We have been talking in Old Testament terms (Jerusalem, etc.), and so the root of David is used here rather than some other title.

VERSE 17. And the Spirit and the bride say come — What bride? The bride we've just been reading about — the new Jerusalem with the river of life in it and the tree of life with healing in the leaves. Not only does the Spirit invite, but the bride is inviting. Inviting them to what? When does this inviting take place by this beautiful bride? Clearly not in eternity.

He that is athirst, let him come: he that will — Here the invitation is open to all to partake of the blessings offered in that great city. It is all there for the asking. Let him take "freely." That means "without price."

VERSES 18-19. If any man shall add unto them, God shall add unto him — Here is one interesting verse. The plain import of the passage is, that as man had better not tamper with the book, or else, God will punish him. What is especially interesting is that he will add unto him "the plagues which are written in this book." I would have thought this made it clear that in these plagues we don't have a series of specific plagues for a specific period of time. It surely looks like the plagues are the judgments of God painted in apocalyptic fashion. Plagues which hit the enemies of God back there and which **could** hit any man at any time.

Let me make this plainer. Suppose we take the premillennial route and accept the plagues of the book literally. How could they have been added to a man, say, in the 3rd or 4th century? According to the millennialists, the plagues involve an ocean of literal blood; 100-pound hailstones; utterly unique earthquakes; the world water supply literally turned into blood; 200-million-men armies invading; millions of mutant locusts and other such things.

Now how could God add these plagues to men who tampered with the book? It cannot be said he would do it in eternity, for these are plagues which involve the earth and its waters. The millennialists have it still to apply to the future, literally as described. In fact, Walvoord speaks of men who "have tampered with this book and other portions of scripture in arrogant self-confidence that they are equipped intellectually and spiritually to determine what is true and what is not true in the word of God" (page 338). And what happened when they so tampered? Did those plagues occur? It is of little avail to say John didn't mean **those** plagues would fall on them, for that's exactly what John **said**. And he said very plainly that the plagues were not just plagues in general, but "the plagues which are written in this book."

Will God resurrect such critics as those that have died in order for them to live when these plagues are going to fall? Is it an idle threat? Must we give up the literalizing — **again**?

Lindsey is even more specific. Listen to him:

> This book is admittedly difficult to understand in places and there are devout scholars who disagree on some points. But what is meant by "adding to" or "taking away" **is a warning not to change the message** of Christ's work as Savior, Lord, and Judge. To do so is to risk incurring all the plagues in the revelation and a loss of citizenship in the New Jerusalem. Believe me, that is a terrible risk! I personally feel that an individual who deliberately avoids studying or teaching this book is getting **very close** to the same things as "taking away" from it.
>
> (TNWC, p. 307)

I emphasized the first point and he emphasized the last one. Now get this, Lindsey is not only premillennial, he is Calvinistic. He believes the new Jerusalem is the city which comes down out of heaven **in eternity**. He says that anyone changing the message in the way he just stated is risking "loss of citizenship in the New Jerusalem." What can this mean? Not only does he blow his Calvinism by showing one falling away, he says people in the eternal city in eternity can be lost! What will he do? He either will have to stick with his guns and speak of lostness, even in eternity, or admit that his whole scheme of things in the Revelation development is out of whack!

Furthermore, he says plainly that anyone changing the message is liable to be hit with the plagues mentioned in Revelation. That can't be, on his terms, for they are plagues which are peculiar to the last days. You've got to grab hold on this — Revelation is a chronological plan of the events of the days just before the 2nd coming of Jesus (say the millennialists). The plagues in there are peculiar to that time. There is nuclear war in this book (say the millennialists). **How could a fifth century critic be subjected to a nuclear war?** What of the radical liberals of late last century or of today? How will those dead liberals be punished with the nuclear war threat? Will he be hailed on with 100-pound hailstones?

Obviously, none of this can happen. What shall these people do? Claim this passage doesn't mean **what it says?** They really critique us for the same thing. If they surrender the literal understanding here, what of the 1,000 years? The binding of Satan? The new heavens and earth? What of their interpretation of Old Testament prophecy? One more time and then I'll leave it alone. How can those who have tampered with the book from the day it was written be subjected to the plagues written in this book? There are only 3 alternatives:

1. All the dead tamperers will be resurrected so that they can live during the Tribulation period when the plagues of the book are to be fulfilled.
2. All the dead tamperers will suffer these very same plagues when they are in eternity (thus necessitating nuclear war on an earth; the resurrection of the Chinese Reds; a Euphrates river; mutant locusts; oceans and rivers to turn to blood; the resurreciton of the hosts of Gog, Russia, and others to go through the wars; hailstones 100 pounds in weight, etc., etc.)
3. The tamperers will not be plagued with the plagues written n this book. (This necessitates claiming either that the plagues are a figurative presentation of God's judgments on the wicked or the threat was an idle one.)

And if any man shall take away...God shall take away — This passage really hurts Walvoord and just to read his treatment of it, shows it. He says the passage "assumes that a child of God will not tamper with these scriptures" (p. 338). But the passage says that the tamperer can have something taken away from him. Now what that is, is very specifically spelled-out. "His part of the tree of life or the holy city." Walvoord claims the warning is to non-Christians. How can that be? Non-Christians have no part of the tree of life or the holy city. The word "part" in this version is the word "meros" and it means "share." It is used in 20:6, when we are told "blessed and holy is he that hath **part** in the first resurrection." In 21:8, it speaks of the ungodly who shall "have their **part** in the lake that burneth with fire and brimstone." You can see from these texts what it means, but you may check any lexicographer you wish. What does the text affirm? There is the possibility of someone with a share in the tree of life and the holy city, and the possibility of such a one so tampering with the book that he would lose that share! It's awfully plain.

Which are written in this book — No other holy city is in mind. No other tree of life is in mind but the one mentioned in this book. This helps us to pinpoint the plagues to which he was alluding in the verse above. Not just any old plague, but the ones mentioned in the book. Not just any tree of life or holy city.

VERSE 20. I come quickly: Amen: Come Lord Jesus — In judgment, Jesus paid Rome a visit, until he finally bombed her right out of existence. We have here more encouragement for the saints to hang in there. John likes the news and adds his "Amen" to it. "Lord Jesus" is such a good way to end a book, isn't it?!

VERSE 21. THE GRACE OF THE LORD JESUS BE WITH THE SAINTS. AMEN.

16 I, Jesus have sent My angel to testify to you
these things for the Churches. I am the
root & the offspring of David, the bright
morning star.
17 And the Spirit & the bride say "Come." And
let the one who hears say "Come." And let
the one who is thirsty come; let the one who
wishes take the water of life w/o cost.
18 I testify to everyone who hears the words
of the prophesy of this book; if anyone adds
to them God shall add to him the
plagues which are written in this book.
19 and if anyone takes away from the
words of the book of this prophesy, God
shall take away his part from the tree
of life and from the holy city which
are written in this book.
20 He who testifies to these things
says, "Yes, I am coming quickly"
Amen. Come Lord Jesus.
21 The grace of the Lord Jesus be
w/all Amen.

A Summary of the Book

We've reached the end of the road. Thank you for staying with me. What have we seen in this book? The central thrust of the book is comfort and assurance of ultimate triumph. In its unique way, the book told of a coming and terrible storm. The survey at the beginning (see pp. 16-19) will indicate how the book developed.

We saw that the heart of the universe is a heavenly throne! That God and the Lamb rule — not Italy.

We saw the seals reveal, the trumphets warn and the bowls punish in a full and complete way. We saw the saints sealed against the coming fury upon the ungodly; saw the world, piece by piece, attacked; her seas were bloodied as were her water supplies; her commerce was ruined and her armies defeated while their property was invaded; her gods were punished while her society ran riot in decadence.

We saw the Church under the heel of the oppressor and the Witnesses preach in sackcloth, with death awaiting them. But we saw the inner sanctuary hold and the Witnesses loyally preach and, after death, be vindicated in resurrection. We saw the people of God in a wilderness, but saw them nourished while the Devil is impotent on earth and in heaven.

We saw Rome go under in blood and fire and smoke. Rome in all her apocalyptic manifestations from the civil persecution sea beast to the religious pervert, the earth beast. And the God of all power broils the sea beast; and the seductive power of a commercially successful Rome (Harlot) is set on fire by no man's hand and burns like Nero's fire never did — eternally and thoroughly.

We saw the end of Rome pictured in the battle of Armageddon and heard the Serpent thresh as he was bound and salted away for a thousand years, while the saints, living and dead, sat enthroned with their Lord!

We saw the full story told of those who died in the service of the beast. They were raised to no thrones but to die one more time, finally, in a lake of fire. We hear from God, through the "little time" of loosing the Devil, that all attempts by the Devil are doomed to failure, anytime and anywhere.

And then we saw the picture of the Church of God. Consecrated in her service; glorious and honored in her reputation and appearance; unbeatable in her strength; intimate in her communion; a blessing to the world and beloved of her Lord. HER FUTURE SECURE AND HER TRIUMPHS ETERNAL!

(Appendix I)

The Chronology of the Millennial View

The following attempt to give you a chronological view of the millennial picture from here on is not "doomed" to **success**. This is, in part at least, because the millennial view is not clear. I'm using five books for my sources of information. Three of them are by John F. Walvoord and the other two by Hal Lindsey. The reason I've chosen these is because Walvoord is the leading millennialist scholar in America (so says Wilbur M. Smith) and Lindsey is, without doubt, the most popular millennialist in this country.

Walvoord's books are "Armageddon," which he co-authored with John E. Walvoord; "The Millennial Kingdom" and "The Revelation of Jesus Christ." The first is a Lindsey-style popularization of the events coming up soon. The second is a definitive work on Millennialism — what the theory is and why it is. The last is a commentary on the book of Revelation. Walvoord is the present president of the very influential Dallas Theological Seminary.

Lindsey's books are "The Late Great Planet Earth" and "There's a New World Coming." The first is a readable and popular treatment of the events about to happen, as Lindsey sees it. The second is another popular type treatment of the book of Revelation.

The two men don't always agree (which is not a very great criticism), and so at times I'll be giving what both of them have said. The books will be designated by the initials of the titles, thus A (is "Armageddon"), MK ("The Millennial Kingdom"), TRJC ("The Revelation of Jesus Christ"), LGPE ("The Late Great Planet Earth"), and TNWC ("There's a New World Coming").

Central to all modern millennialism is the prophecy concerning the 70 weeks in Daniel 9:24-27. This section of scripture and the philosophy of "all scripture, including the prophetic sections, must be literally interpeted" are of critical importance to the picture as painted by millennialists.

It is the "70th week" of Daniel's prophecy which is at the core of all the time-setting attempted by the millennialists. This, they tell us, is a 7-year period not yet fulfilled. It is the Tribulation period we hear of often. It is said to be divided into two equal sections, of 3½ years each. The latter half is specifically referred to as the "Great Tribulation." The following chart will give you some idea of how the millennialists teach it.

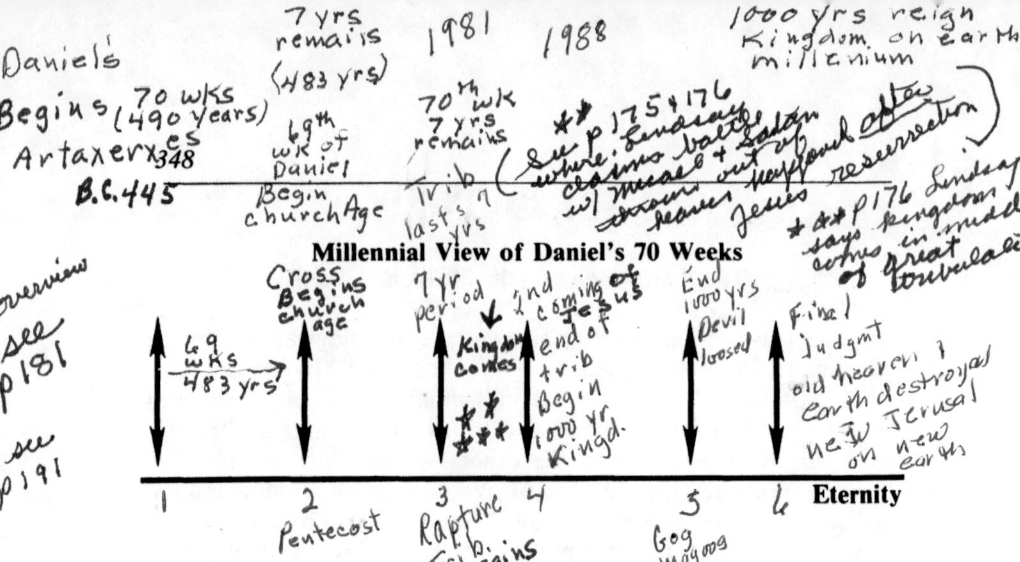

1. This stands for the decree of Artaxerxes I in 445 B.C., which is said to begin the 70 weeks (490 years) of Daniel. See TNWC, p. 100; A, pp. 139f.

2. This stands for the Cross of Christ and the terminating point of 69 weeks (483 years). It also begins the Church Age which was totally unknown to the Old Testament. See MK, pp. 231ff; TNWC, pp. 100f.

3. This stands for the Rapture and the point at which the 70th week of Daniel (7 years) begins. The Rapture is said to be the Lord's taking the Church off the earth at which time the Tribulation begins. The Tribulation lasts 7 years. The first 3½ years is relatively peaceful. The last 3½ are "the Great Tribulation." See TRJC, pp. 86ff; LGPE, pp. 135ff; MK, pp. 256ff.

4. This stands for the 2nd coming of Jesus and the end of the Great Tribulation. It is also the time for the 1,000-year kingdom to begin on earth with the restoration of the Levitical priesthood and sacrifices, etc. LGPE, pp. 168ff.

5. This stands for the end of the millennium and the point at which the Devil is loosed of a "little season" to get Gog and Magog together for their final assault against Jesus and Jerusalem. TRJC, pp. 300ff; TNWC, pp. 276ff.

6. This is where eternity begins with the final judgment having just taken place. The old heaven and earth are destroyed and a new heaven and earth brought in. It is from the new giant Jerusalem on the new earth that God will reign for all eternity. See LGPE, pp. 177ff; MK, pp. 324ff.

Chp 7 all righteous sealed before tribulation but not removed from earth in some type of rapture

Lindsey and the 70th week of Daniel:

1. He thinks the 2nd coming of Jesus will occur somewhere around 1988. The 2nd coming ends the 7-year period, so it must begin somewhere around 1981. See LGPE, pp. 53,54.

---

c. 1981

Conversion of 144,000 Jews...Rev. 7; TNWC, 120-123

Their work results in an innumberable host of Gentiles, etc., coming to Christ...Rev. 7; TNWC, 123-125; LGPE, 111.

Moses and Elijah (2 witnesses) preach for 3½ years...Rev. 11:3ff; TNWC, 161-165.

Jews build a temple under Antichrist's protection...Daniel 9:27; LGPE, 150-152; TNWC, 156-161.

3½ Years

Antichrist continues to grow in power...TNWC 238; Rev. 13; LGPE, 108.

Babylon (religious system of the earth at this time) has been growing in power in association with the Antichrist...Rev. 17; 18:2; LGPE, 133; TNWC, 228-239. She dominates him until he destroys her **about 1984, in the middle of the 7-year period**...Rev. 17; LGPE, 133; TNWC, 239.

Antichrist slays Moses and Elijah **at the end of 3½ years**...they are raptured 3½ days later... Antichrist at that time turns on Jews and claims he's God...Rev. 11:3-12; 2 Thess. 2:1-12 LGPE, 109, 110; TNWC, 162-165. **See below.**

This coincides with the time Satan invades heaven and is repulsed — **midway through the 7-year period**...TNWC, 175; Rev. 12:7-12. **See below.**

Midway

Midway	**Second seal......**	Russia invades Israel . . . Rev. 6; Ezekiel 38-39; LGPE, 59-71; TNWC, 104.
	Third seal........	Worldwide famine and depression... Rev. 6; TNWC, 105.
	Fourth Seal......	Death on massive scale...1 billion die... Rev. 6; TNWC, 105,106.
	Fifth Seal.........	Mass murder of believers...innumerable host...Rev. 6,7; TNWC, 108,123.
	Sixth seal.........	First nuclear war...World literally shaken apart...cobalt bombs..."fractional orbital bombs"...Rev. 6; TNWC,108-111.
	First trumpet....	One-third of earth's vegetation destroyed...Rev. 8; TNWC, 130.
	Second trumpet.	Third of oceans turned to blood...Rev. 8; TNWC, 131.
	Third trumpet...	Third of earth's drinking water polluted...Rev. 8; TNWC, 132.
	Fourth trumpet.	Third of light diminished...nuclear pollution...Rev. 8; TNWC, 133.
	Fifth trumpet....	Mutant locusts...demons...maybe helicopters...Rev. 9; TNWC, 136-138.
	Sixth trumpet...	200 million Red Chinese invade Israel... kill about 1 billion on way...Rev. 9; TNWC, 139-142; LGPE, 81-87.
	First bowl........	Worldwide epidemic of malignant sores...Rev. 16; TNWC, 217.
	Second bowl.....	Oceans completely turned to blood... Rev. 16; TNWC, 217,218.
	Third bowl.......	All drinking water totally destroyed... Rev. 16; TNWC, 218,219.
	Fourth bowl.....	Global heatwave without water...Rev. 16; TNWC, 219,220.
	Fifth bowl........	Thick darkness over Rome...Rev. 16; TNWC, 220.
	Sixth bowl.......	200 million Chinese prepare to cross Euphrates...Rev. 16; TNWC, 221-225. Demons urge western powers to aid Antichrist against 200 million...Ibid...
c. 1988	**Seventh bowl....**	Multiplied millions slaying each other...gigantic "earthquake" which levels all major cities...nuclear war...100-pound hailstones...Rev. 16; TNWC, 226,227.

Walvoord and the 70th week of Daniel:

Walvoord's picture of the 70th week (A, 154-156) agrees essentially with Lindsey's, except in a few really important points. Two of them are the Russian involvement in Israel, and the period of the ministry of the two witnesses of Revelation 11.

Walvoord holds to two Russian entries into Israel (A, 121-129, 181) and Lindsey holds to only one. Walvoord says the first (using Ezekiel 38,39) occurs during the first half of the 70th week and the second, some time late in the last 3½ years of the 70th week. Lindsey claims only one Russian entry and that is early in the second half of the "week."

Walvoord holds the two witnesses preach during the 2nd half of the 70th week. Lindsey holds they preach during the first half of that period. See Walvoord's TRJC, 178.

Concerning the Witnesses:

Walvoord very reasonably argues that the witnesses do not prophesy during a period of peace (which is how the first 3½ years are characterized), since they are clearly being persecuted. So much so, in fact, they have to resort to turning water into blood, causing drought, calling fire down to destroy their enemies, and smiting the earth with plagues. See Revelation 11:3ff.

While he has a good (millennial) case on this, he creates for himself another very real difficulty. The 70th week is supposed to close the "times of the Gentiles." It is supposed to close with the 2nd coming of Jesus (MK, 259,260,261; A, 181) and the beginning of the millennium.

Now, if the witnesses preach for the last half (1260 days) of the 70th week, their testimony should end at the 2nd coming of Jesus. Read the text. As you can see from the text, when the 70th week is ended, instead of Jesus coming, the witnesses are murdered and lie dead for 3½ days. That means the 2nd coming of Jesus occurs 3½ days after the 70th week has ended. **Christ's coming is 3½ days late!** Then after these 3½ days, the bowl-judgments have to be poured out, so we have even more delay. Daniel's prophecy is now in ruins.

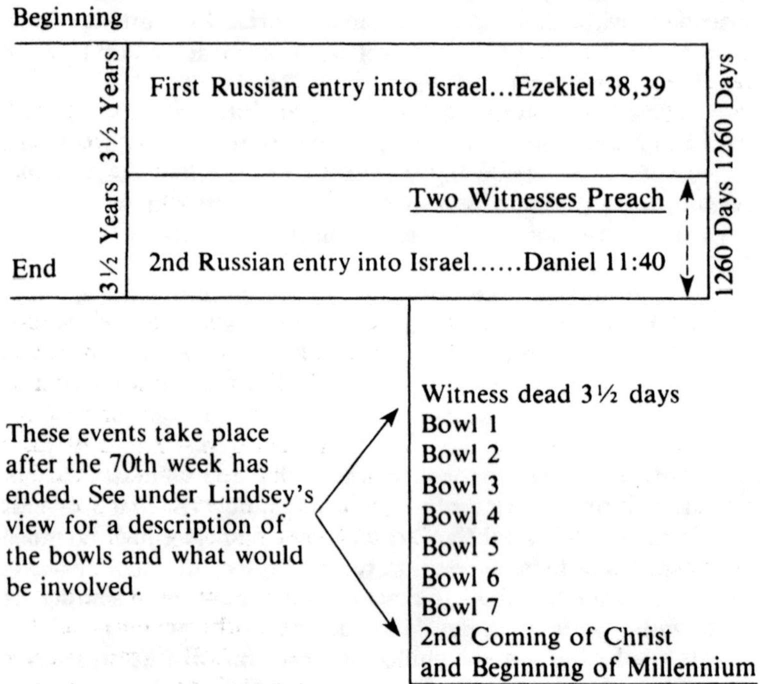

As you can easily see, the whole Daniel chronology is shot. The "times of the Gentiles" ran longer than Daniel said: the 2nd coming of Jesus is late and therefore the millennial kingdom is late.

Concerning the Russian involvement:

Walvoord argues for two because he **must have** two. The Ezekiel 38,39 invasion happens during the time Israel sits in peace and undefended (38:8,11). This can't be during the 2nd half of the "week" for those are certainly not the conditions of the 2nd half. The first half, millennialists agree, is one of peace under the Antichrist's treaty with Israel. This fractures Lindsey's view. Besides this, Daniel 11:40 (involving a Russian invasion), occurs only after the Antichrist is world boss and claiming diety. So the two periods are clearly involved.

The real problem with the theory of Walvoord is that it requires Russia to lose millions of men and still invade in force about 3 years later. See Ezekiel 39:12,13, and my comments on that piece in the "Ezekiel." So great is the Russian loss, that it takes a solid **seven months** with "all" Israel acting in the burial detail; it takes seven months to bury all the corpses. Now bear in mind, they not only sustain that loss, but beginning with the middle of the 70th week, famines, plagues, heatwaves, and other terrible judgments sweep the earth. In spite of all this, they are said to invade a second time in order to war against the Antichrist in Israel.

Points in common:

Both writers have much in common. Two things of especial interest. **One, both stress the nearness of the events.** Lindsey as I've already shown you, goes for about 1988 as the second coming (LGPE, 53,54), and thus, about 1981 for the beginning of the Tribulation. Walvoord gives no specific dates, but constantly uses expressions such as, the Antichrist should emerge "momentarily" (A, 116); the rapture is "excitingly near" (A, 199); the "prophetic play is about to begin" (A, 206); "Christ's coming for his own is very near" (A, 207).

But then they both vacillate and throw in a bushel of "maybes" or "it could well be" or some other equivalent. The "Armageddon" book was published after the LGPE really became a phenomenal seller. It has the same promise-of-much and delivery-of-nothing approach.

The **second** similarity is that **both writers paint the same absurd picture of the nations persisting in going against each other.** See the descriptions of the seals, trumpets, and bowls under Lindsey's view. These judgments leave the world without ocean water, marine life of any kind, drinking water of any kind (Lindsey has them drinking cokes!), vegetation and a full day's light; the judgments force them to endure world-wide famine, world-wide depression, world-wide epidemic of malignant ulcers, drought, demon-possessed locusts, or demon possession for 5 months, nuclear air pollution, world-wide earthquakes which flatten **all** the mountains, incredible heat waves, swarms of meteorites...ALL THAT and 200 million coke-drinking Red Chinese still want to fight at Armageddon. ALL THAT and the Antichrist is still able to get all the western nations to join him in war in Israel.

Read the description again of the seals, trumpets and bowls, and ask yourself who could muster an army of 200 million which slays 1 billion on the way to battle in Israel. What are they eating with world-wide famine, vegetation fires, bloody oceans? What are they drinking when there's no water? Even the Euphrates the Chinese are said to cross is blood and not water. We are asked to believe these people are demon-possessed for five months and in torment, ulcerated all over their bodies, without water to drink, afflicted by extraordinary heatwaves; suffocating with nuclear pollution, the bulk of the earth's surface now blood (not **like** blood, but blood — read the text), AND THEY'RE STILL SLAYING EACH OTHER IN MULTIPLIED MILLIONS IN PALESTINE. And, get this, while they're doing it, it is hailing 100-pound hailstones.

(Appendix II)

The "Literal Interpretation" Philosophy

The millennialists are forever calling us to adopt their literal interpretation policy. Perhaps we would, if the Bible example were not opposed to the universal use of that philosophy. And furthermore, perhaps we would if the millennialists could show us how to be consistent in the use of it. I've not read to any length any millennialist who was consistent in this matter.

"Clouds" in Revelation 1:7 are "saints" says Lindsey.

"Ten days" in Revelation 2:10 means "10 eras of persecution" says Lindsey. Walvoord isn't sure what is meant.

"Ten thousand times 10,000" in Revelation 5:11 is not literal, says Walvoord (TRJC, 166).

"Stars" in Revelation 6:13 may be meteors or "orbital bombs" says Lindsey.

"Locust" in Revelation 9:3ff may be "mutant locusts" or "helicopters," says Lindsey. Walvoord isn't sure, but they're bigger than ordinary locusts — that he knows.

"Fire and Brimstone" in 9:17f probably speaks of nuclear warfare, say both writers.

"Flood of water" in 12:15 is a flood of "pursuers" says Lindsey. Walvoord isn't sure, but perfers to figurize.

"Death-stroke" in 13:3,12,14 is undoubtedly not literal, say both writers.

"Blood" in 14:20 is not really a river of blood, but a "liberal spattering" of blood, thinks Walvoord. Lindsey measures and gives an approximation of blood, bodies and war materials.

These examples and many more make it clear these men figurize when they **don't** need to. The bows, arrows, spears, bucklers and horses of Ezekiel 38, 39 either indicate there will be a future disarmament (A, 125), or they stand for modern weapons. Can you beat that? They can't lose for winning.,

For the absurdities involved in their literalizing, read again the picture of the warring nations presented in the last appendix, the last paragraphs.

The millennialists have long insisted that "everlasting" means eternal, and that without exception. It is remarkable how soon they forget this when it comes into conflict with their position. They want "everlasting" to mean just that when it comes to the land promise (see Genesis 17:8 and MK, 174-182).

Walvoord and Lindsey both agree (TRJC, 326; TNWC, 293) that there will be no need for a temple in eternity, for the shadow system will be gone for ever. What then are we to do with passages which say the Aaronic priesthood is "everlasting"? What are we to say about Genesis 17:13, which said circumcision was an "everlasting" convenant? See Numbers 25:13 and Exodus 40:15.

If we are told the Jews would "dwell in the land I have given unto Jacob my servant, wherein your fathers dwelt; and they shall dwell therein, they and their children, and their children's children, for ever: and David my servant shall be their prince forever."? See Ezekiel 37:24,25.

How can they dwell "for ever" in the land their fathers dwelt in when this old earth is going to be destroyed and everyone will move to a new one on which their fathers never dwelled? How can David be their king for ever? See Ezekiel 37:22,24,25; Genesis 17:8.

How can both be literally true?	Leviticus 16:34 and Hebrews 10:17,18.
How can both be literally true?	Genesis 17:13 and Galatians 5:1-4.
How can both be literally true?	Isaiah 40:2-5 and Luke 3:3ff.
How can both be literally true?	Num. 25:13 and Heb. 7:11ff; Psalm 110:1,4.
How can both be literally true?	Isaiah 35:9 and Isaiah 11:6ff.
How can both be literally true?	Ezekiel 36:35b and Ezekiel 38:11.
How can both be literally true?	Malachi 4:5 and Matthew 17:10-13.
How can both be literally true?	Revelation 16:20 and Zechariah 14:4. (See TRJC, 241).

See the McGuiggan-Jordan slide presentation on "An Examination of Millennialism."

Everyone agrees that there are figurative scriptures and literal scriptures. The question is how to determine which are which. The millennialists have no monopoly on wisdom in this area. We all need to study this area. We all need consistency.

Bibliography

Balsdon, J.P.V.D., **Roman Civilization**, Pelican, 1969
Barclay ,W., **The Revelation of John**, 2 Vols., Westminster, 1962
Barrett, C.K., **The New Testament Background**, Harper, 1961
Barrow, R.H., **The Romans**, Pelican, 1970
Bruce, F.F., **New Testament History**, Doubleday, 1972
Campbell, A., **The Campbell-Owen Debate**, Nashville, 1957
Deissmann, A., **Light from the Ancient East**, Hodder & Stoughton, 1911
Dimont, M.I., **Jews, God, and History**, Signet Paperback, 15th prtg.
Edersheim, A., **The Temple**, James Clarke, London, 1959
Eusebius, **Ecclesiastical History**, 2 Vols., Harvard-Heinemann, London, 1975
Farrar, F.W., **History's Witness to Christ**, MacMillan, 1892
Fitchett, W.H., **The Beliefs of Unbelief**, Cassell, London, 1908
Gibbon, E., **The Decline and Fall of the Roman Empire**, 3 Vols., Washington Square Press, 1972
Glover, T,R., **The Ancient World**, Pelican, 1964
Graves, R., **The Greek Myths**, 2 Volumes, Pelican Original, 1969
Hastings, J., **Hastings Bible Dictionary**, 4 Vols., T & T Clark, 1903
Hazelip, H., **Restoration Quarterly**, Volume 18, Number 4, 1975
Hendriksen, W., **More Than Conquerors**, Baker, 1965
International Standard Bible Encyclopedia, 5 Vols., Eerdmans,
Josephus by Whiston, Wm.
Kiddle, M., **The Revelation of St. John**, Hodder & Stoughton, 1941
King, M.R., **The Spirit of Prophecy**, Warren, Ohio, 1971**
Lindsey, H., **The Late Great Planet Earth**, Zondervan, 1973**
Lindsey, H., **There's a New World Coming**, Vision House Publishers, Cal., 1973**
McGuiggan, J., **The Book of Daniel**, International Biblical Resources, 1978
McGuiggan, J., **The Book of Ezekiel**, International Biblical Resources, 1979
McGuiggan, J., **The Book of Isaiah**, International Biblical Resources, 1985
McGuiggan-King Debate, Warren, Ohio, 1975
MacKendrick, P., **The Roman Mind at Work**, Van Nostrand-Reinhold, New York, 1958
Milligan, W., **Revelation** in **The Expositor's Bible**, Vol. 6, Eerdman, 1956
Milligan, W., **The Revelation of John**, MacMillan, 1886

Milman, H.H., **History of the Jews**, 3 Vols., Murray, London, 1883

Moffatt, J., **Revelation** in **The Expositor's Greek Testament**, Vol. 5, H & S, 1897

Morris, L., **The Revelation of St. John**, Eerdmans, 1969

Peake, A.S., **The Revelation of John**, Holburn P.H., no date, London

Perowne, S., **Caesars and Saints**, Hodder & Stoughton, 1962

Perowne, S., **Life and Times of Herod the Great**, Hodder & Stoughton, 1963

Plumptre, E.H., **Revelation** in **The Pulpit Commentary**, Eerdmans, 1962

Ramsay, W., **The Letters to the Seven Churches**, Baker, 1963

Roberts, J.W., **The Revelation to John**, Sweet Publishing Co., Texas, 1974

Robertson, A.T., **Word Pictures in the N.T.**, Vol. 6, Broadman, 11th printing

Rushdoony, R.J., **The Mythology of Science**, Craig Press, N.J., 1967

Scullard, H.H., **From the Grachii to Nero**, Univerisity Press, London, 1972

Suetonius, **Lives of the Twelve Caesars**, Modern Library, N.Y., 1959

Smith, W., **Bible Dictionary**, 4 Vols., Murray, London, 1893

Summers, R., **Worthy is the Lamb**, Broadman, 10th printing

Swete, H.B., **The Apocalypse of St. John**, Eerdmans, no date

Tacitus, **The Histories**, Penguin, 1964

Tenney, M.C., **New Testament Times**, Zondervan, 1963

Tertullian, **Apology**, Ancient and Modern Library of Theological Lit., London, no date

Thayer, J.H., **Lexicon of the New Testament**, Zondervan, 1963

Unger, M., **Archaeology and the New Testament**, Zondervan, 1966

Versions of the Old and New Testaments

Vincent, M., **Word Studies in the New Testament**, Eerdmans, Vol. 2, 1965

Wallace, F.E., **The Book of Revelation**, Wallace Publications, Nashville, 1966

Walvoord, J.F. **Armageddon**, Zondervan, 1974**

Walvoord, J.F., **The Millennial Kingdom**, Zondervan, 1971**

Walvoord, J.F., **The Revelation of Jesus Christ**, Moody Press, 1966**

Wight, F.W., **Manners and Customs of Bible Lands**, Moody Press, 1966**

**Quoted by Permission.

Printed in the United States
118391LV00004B/85-228/A

9 780932 397102